After the New Criticism

FRANK LENTRICCHIA

After the New Criticism

The University of Chicago Press

The University of Chicago Press, Chicago 60637
The Athlone Press, London

84 83   5 4 3

Library of Congress Cataloging in Publication Data

Lentricchia, Frank.
    After the new criticism.

    Includes bibliographical references and index.
    1. Criticism—History—20th century.   2. Criticism—
United States—History—20th century.   I. Title.
PN94.L43   801'.95   79–23715
ISBN 0–226–47197–7

For Melissa

Contents

Antihistorical method is nothing but metaphysics.

Antonio Gramsci, *Prison Notebooks*

. . . in the case of almost every insoluble problem
we perceive that the search for a solution leads us
to history.

Georg Lukács, *History and Class Consciousness*

Acknowledgments

In an effort to provide me with fresh evidence for Harold Bloom's theory of the "anxiety of influence," my daughters, Amy and Rachel, aged eight and six respectively, asked me to credit them with writing this book. They will understand (maybe) that I can't put their names on the title page. But I can say it here: Amy and Rachel wrote this book. Hostile reviewers may blame their father for all failures.

It is a pleasure to acknowledge my more traditional debts. Homer Brown and Ralph Freedman read a late version of the manuscript and made several helpful suggestions; I am grateful for their commitment to the project. To my colleague and friend, John Carlos Rowe, I owe the sort of debt that cannot easily be calculated. He listened endlessly to my ideas and problems, and read every page of the manuscript with scrupulous care—many of them more than once. It will have to be sufficient for me to say that he has given me an education, and with the sort of diplomacy that he alone could have managed. Robert Boyers of *Salmagundi* and William Matchett of the *Modern Language Quarterly* kindly granted me permission to reprint pages that originally appeared, in different form, in their magazines. Portions of the manuscript were read at the University of Rochester, Williams, Skidmore,

Northwestern, Rice, and Berkeley; I thank my various hosts and audiences for their invitations, their attentiveness, and their questions.

I won't try to explain the dedication to Melissa Lentricchia. Those who know her, and her work, will understand immediately.

Preface

In the chapters that follow I have written an exposition and an evaluation of the course of critical theory in the United States for roughly
the past two decades—a period I take to be the richest and most confusing in our critical history. As exposition, this study is intended as
a historical account of what has happened here since the American
New Critics passed out of favor; as evaluation, it is intended as a
critique of various forces that have shaped contemporary thought
about literature and the criticism of literature. Which is to say that this
book has a point of view: some kinds of thinking I find more productive than others and I have tried to say why. Since my point of
view is worked up from a number of the thinkers I have examined, I
claim no originality for it. In fact, as I think will become clear in the
pages ahead, I believe that the desire for originality, in all of its senses
and variants, has seriously marred and enervated more than a few
of the most brilliant critics on our contemporary scene. My perspective is implicit throughout; my reader will encounter it most overtly,
however, in chapters 4 and 5. One of the lessons that I hope I've learned
from reading contemporary criticism and philosophy is that no one
is in a worse position to judge the blindnesses of a particular point of

view than the one who subscribes to it; I must leave to others, therefore, the task of specifying and evaluating my perspective.

What I wish to emphasize here is the historical focus of my study: the past two decades of critical theory in the United States. In the second part of this book I have selected for analysis four American theorists who, I believe, are exemplary: Murray Krieger, E. D. Hirsch, Paul de Man, and Harold Bloom have each in distinctive ways significantly shaped critical thought in this country. Their careers were initiated in the middle to late 1950s; through the 1960s and 1970s each developed an influential mode of thought and a number of significant texts. Though they are by no means the only important theorists writing in the United States today, it is my judgment that Krieger, Hirsch, de Man, and Bloom, because of the kinds of things that they do, the fullness and energy with which they do them, and the range of theoretical implication they have managed to achieve, have the strongest claim to being the major theorists in American criticism since about 1957. Some of the younger theorists who interest me most, and who have influenced my thinking (Fredric Jameson and Edward Said, to name two of them), are just now beginning to have impact on our critical thought, and that is why they are mentioned only in passing.

Reaching back far earlier than 1957, I have tried, in the first and longer part of my study, to establish theoretical contexts for my American theorists and to give a chronological exposition and critique of the major figures (most of them are Continental) from those earlier contexts. Northrop Frye, Wallace Stevens, Frank Kermode, Jean-Paul Sartre, Georges Poulet, Martin Heidegger, Ferdinand de Saussure, Claude Lévi-Strauss, Roland Barthes, Jacques Derrida, and Michel Foucault have largely set the terms and themes of recent critical controversies in this country. Theodor Adorno, Walter Benjamin, Georg Lukács, Antonio Gramsci, Louis Althusser, Lucien Goldmann, and others in their tradition have a great deal to say to American critics, but in the period I have chosen to study they have not been shaping influences. It would have been possible for me to have argued that the absence of these thinkers is a crucial part of the story. But that would have required yet another volume, which is for someone else to write.

The title of this book may unfortunately suggest to my reader, at the very outset, two misleading perspectives—one on the New Criticism, the other on the historical character or lineage of contemporary theory—which my text will not sustain. *The* New Criticism was in fact no monolith but an inconsistent and sometimes confused movement; the differences among variously identified New Critics and their progenitors—Kant and a number of writers of the nineteenth century —are real. Still, the most important scholarship done on the New Critics, Murray Krieger's definitive book of 1956, *The New Apologists for Poetry*, and Gerald Graff's *Poetic Statement and Critical Dogma* (1970), establish beyond much doubt a unifying effort which in Krieger's later books assumes the proportions of a crisis that contemporary theory ("after the New Criticism") has not resolved but deepened and extended. The crisis is generated—I can put this only in crude fashion here—by, on the one hand, a continuing urge to essentialize literary discourse by making it a unique kind of language —a vast, enclosed textual and semantic preserve—and, on the other hand, by an urge to make literary language "relevant" by locating it in larger contexts of discourse and history. If my title suggests, then, that the New Criticism is dead—in an official sense, of course, it is— I must stipulate that in my view it is dead in the way that an imposing and repressive father-figure is dead. I find many traces (perhaps "scars" is the word) of the New Criticism and of nineteenth-century thought in the fixed and identifiable positions we have come to know as contemporary theory. Such traces or scars produce, in turn, another effect, not easy to discern: an intertextual mingling among contemporary theorists. I am arguing not only that the ruptures separating nineteenth-century aesthetic traditions, the New Criticism, and contemporary theory are not absolute but also that the differences among contemporary theories are not clean discontinuities. In my opinion it is the very condition of contemporary critical historicity that there is no "after" or "before" the New Criticism: no absolute presence *in the present* means that the present is opened up to the "drift from the other ends of time."[1] The traces of the New Criticism are found in yet another way: in the repeated and often extremely subtle denial of history by a variety of contemporary theorists. The exploration and critique of this evasive antihistorical maneuver is one of my fundamental concerns. What I intend positively by the terms "history" and "historicism" is woven through my chapters in a kind of dialogue with the theorists I have examined.

The difficult term "history" necessarily, then, plays a decisive role in my argument. Since it is a heavily contested and abused term in recent critical thought, and since (as I think) its fate may determine the direction of critical theory in the years just ahead, I want to note here the metaphysical senses of history that I find controlling vast areas of contemporary criticism. History as the teleological unfolding of a promised end, whether in a secular or theological sense; history as continuity, or mere repetition, according to certain notions of "tradition"; history as discontinuity—a series of "ruptures" which mark "periods" of semantic saturation and plenitude: these are the ruling conventional senses of a conception that leans on a temporally and culturally uncontaminated ideal meaning situated at some primal origin, or at the end of things, or within temporality as its secret principle of coherence. These are conceptions of a "history" which would generate itself as a unity and a totality while resisting forces of heterogeneity, contradiction, fragmentation, and difference: a "history," in short, which would deny "histories." These are conceptions of history which go hand in hand with the antihistorical impulses of formalist theories of literary criticism. That odd connection, perhaps more than anything else, is the object of my polemical focus. Though I mean something different from what Hayden White means when he collapses the terms history and historicism, and says that methodology determines perspective (no innocent readings of the past) and that all writing of history is also philosophy of history, I essentially accept his premise.[2] If I have any message to deliver, it is that such acceptance need not imply radical relativism, or subjectivism and egoism, or an unconcern with the past; I have written this critical history under the guidance of an historiographical method which I do not believe descends into such irrelevancies.

Part One

A Critical Thematics, 1957-77

One

... we ... had to complete our argument by removing all external goals from literature, thus postulating a self-contained literary universe. Perhaps in doing so we merely restored the aesthetic view on a gigantic scale, substituting Poetry for a mass of poems, aesthetic mysticism for aesthetic empiricism.

Northrop Frye, *Anatomy of Criticism*

... the subject—the striving individual bent on furthering his egoistic purposes—can be thought of only as the enemy of art, never as its source.

Friedrich Nietzsche, *The Birth of Tragedy*

The Place of Northrop Frye's "Anatomy of Criticism"

Northrop Frye published his monumental book in 1957, one year after Murray Krieger in *The New Apologists for Poetry* had summed up the position associated with the New Criticism, explored its theoretical contradictions and dead ends, and predicted—correctly, it turns out—that the New Criticism had done all that it could do for American literary critics (and the teaching of literature in the United States) and that newer movements were waiting in the wings to take its place on center stage. As if in confirmation of Krieger's prognostication, 1957 also saw the publication of two crucial summary documents intimately related to the end of the New Criticism. One of these, Frank Kermode's *Romantic Image*, a cultural synthesis of immense reach, placed the New Criticism at the end of the line of neo-Coleridgean movements in poetics, all of which in one philosophical context or another had affirmed the autonomous and autotelic nature of the single, lonely poem. The other, the imposing history of criticism of W. K. Wimsatt and Cleanth Brooks—its historical acumen aside—has been taken since the time of its publication[1] and even more so now as a final statement of New-Critical poetic and as a type of Hegelian history-writing driven by the belief that the course of critical theory is shaped by philosophical and critical themes which come to fruition in such writers as John Crowe Ransom, Allen Tate, Brooks, Robert Penn Warren, and Wimsatt.

By about 1957 the moribund condition of the New Criticism and the literary needs it left unfulfilled placed us in a critical void. Even in the late 1940s, however, those triumphant times of the New Criticism, a theoretical opposition was already quietly gathering strength: Ernst Cassirer, the key twentieth-century philosopher of mythic consciousness, emigrated to the United States in 1941 and published his first English-language work (and a microcosm of his system), *An Essay on Man*, in 1944. Only two years earlier his student, Susanne K. Langer, had published *Philosophy in a New Key*. A number of translations of Cassirer were appearing, notably those by Langer (*Language and Myth*, 1946) and Ralph Manheim (*The Philosophy of Symbolic Forms*, 1952–57). In 1954 Philip Wheelwright published his Cassirer-dominated *The Burning Fountain*, and in 1955 a nativist tradition of critical and cultural inquiry in the mythic mode (Richard Chase's *Quest for Myth*, 1949, was an important earlier document) was brought to a culmination by the appearance of R. W. B. Lewis's *American Adam*. (Much earlier, across the Atlantic, several richly suggestive examples of anthropological scholarship had been offered in the works of Jane Harrison, F. M. Cornford, Sir James G. Frazer, Gilbert Murray, and Jessie Weston.)

From his long list of acknowledgments we learn that the *Anatomy* itself had been underway from the beginning of Frye's career; numerous sections of it had been published before. Moreover, readers of his study of Blake, *Fearful Symmetry* (1947), know that that book had forecast the whole of his literary theory as well as the furious rebirth of interest in a problematic writer. Its general critical claims aside, the *Anatomy* gave the Blake revivalists their proper poetics, the renewal of interest in Jung their proper psychology. So the emerging force of Frye's reputation, together with a series of theoretical events favorable to the partisans of myth and symbolic forms, made the time propitious for the appearance of a major theoretical treatise which would somehow move us beyond the New Criticism and its isolating habits of mind. (The last chapter of the Wimsatt-Brooks critical history, "Myth and Archetype," is an uneasy survey of those newer critics on the horizon who by absorbing the isolated text into large mythic structures appeared to be issuing a direct challenge to the old New Critics.) Nineteen-fifty-seven was the right time; Northrop Frye turned out to be the right man; *Anatomy of Criticism* the right book.

1

Frye's cutting allusion to the New Criticism (toward the end of the *Anatomy*) as "the aesthetic view"[2] is only the last in a series of anti–New Critical polemical remarks throughout the book. There is a strong tendency in Frye (but he is hardly alone in this) to link the New Criticism somewhat unfairly to art-for-art's-sake critical doctrines, then to label both as precious or "delicate learning" for the initiated and elite few, those of "mandarin caste" whose possession of special techniques enables them to engage in "vaguely sacramental" activity in which the "cryptic" comment and the "ritual masonic" gesture are expressions of a priestly understanding "too occult for syntax."[3] Geoffrey Hartman's view that Frye's essential thrust is "to democratize criticism and demystify the muse" is an accurate summary of Frye's primary educative intention with which Frye himself has registered agreement.[4] (It has been argued cogently that the New Criticism also democratized criticism, but Frye's charge of mystification cannot be brushed easily aside: too many generations of students came out of New-Critical classrooms convinced that their teachers possessed knowledge of the "hidden" meanings of texts to which there was no systematic and disciplined access.) But Frye's worry that he might be charged with gigantically pumping up the very poetic theory for which he had such contempt is testimony to the powerful pressure that the supposedly moribund older movement was capable of exerting, even on a critic as wittily independent and self-confident as this one. Key postulates and prejudices of the New Criticism and the cultural tradition it exemplified are summarized and criticized in Kermode's *Romantic Image*; Kermode helps us to see clearly how Frye's poetics is, from one perspective, contrary to the New Criticism, and, from another, yet one more (this time fantastical) document in the history of symbolist thought.

Kermode's synthetic intention in *Romantic Image* has the defect of deliberately subordinating and sometimes ignoring important philosophical differences in the critical tradition he traces from Blake and Coleridge to Arnold, Pater, the French symbolists, the English poets of the 1890s, Yeats, Pound, Eliot, and the New Critics—Kermode tends to revise the critical ideas of the English romantics from Poe-esque and Mallarmean perspectives. But his virtue in this book, as in most of his other books, is that he is able to perceive, before most, basic likenesses among the apparently disparate. With twenty more years of hindsight than he enjoyed, we can see how Kermode discovered that a fruitful dialectical opposition in romantic thought—between the poet as "representative man" (Emerson's phrase) of universal passions and the poet as different from others to the point of "isolate individuality,"[5] cut off and irredeemably alienated—quickly gets dissolved in the obsession with difference and uniqueness, an obsession which after Mallarmé becomes increasingly the way poets think about themselves. The reward for the poet who must become this pariah is that he is allowed, because he is closed off from normal interactions with social reality, to enjoy the visionary mode of contemplation—and to possess a power of perception which will allow him to create what Kermode calls the "Image," but which fidelity to the language of post-Kantian theoretical history would force us to call "symbol." "Poetry," Kermode writes, "by virtue of the image is; prose merely describes."[6] Elsewhere, and much to the same point, he quotes Yeats on a distinction we can find everywhere in romantic thought between symbol and allegory.[7]

The distinction that Kermode wants to make is the ontological one ("the image is") which Coleridge made when he wrote that symbol "partakes of the reality which it renders intelligible," while allegory is "unsubstantial," a "translation of abstract notions into a picture language." In so many words, symbol is ontologically full while allegory is thin at best, and at worst "unsubstantial" (the Latinate resonance in the philosophical term "substance" makes Coleridge's point), only an illusion of being. As a special unarbitrary mode of language, symbol not only permits us a vision of ultimate being—this is the epistemological implication of "translucence" in Coleridge's definition—but, because it "partakes" of being (Coleridge's response to Plato's banishment of the imitative tribe), symbol permits us, as well, to partake of being as it closes the distance between our consciousness and the ultimate origin of things. As a type of arbitrary and abstract discourse, allegory maintains ontological separation and the division of subject and object. From Coleridge to Mallarmé, and from Yeats to Cleanth Brooks, Philip Wheelwright, and Northrop Frye, a dualism very like that between symbol and allegory is carried through as a distinction between the poetic or literary and the scientific or ordinary kinds of discourses. Brooks told us that it was heretical to paraphrase; within the perspective afforded by romantic tradition we may come to feel that the urgency in his injunction is motivated by a long-standing romantic need to protect a quasi-religious, ontological sanctuary from all secularizing discourses that would situate literature in history.

The major effort of Kermode in *Romantic Image* is to show what astounding difficulties such views in poetics make for a modern poet (Yeats, in this instance) who inherits them from his most vital tradition and yet must in some sense free himself from them if he is to be responsive to the world beyond his "differentiated" ego. The troubles of a symbolist poetics do not fade after Yeats but continue to haunt the landscape of contemporary theory, and in more powerful ways than Kermode could have foreseen in 1957. The poet's difference as a human being, and the differences of his discourse (which is not, strictly speaking, discourse at all) quickly escalate into "privilege" (to use a word crucial, these days, to structuralist terminology but nevertheless, in this context, sharply descriptive). The poetic language of symbol is not merely different from ordinary language; it is clearly better, since it is the locus, so it is argued, of our most satisfying and valuable experiences as human beings. Given the option, would we choose (to cite the constricting but telltale alternatives which Yeats had trouble thinking beyond) to be money-changers, journalists, or visionaries? But the privileged "discourse" of the poets is problematically enclosed in an isolate vision; it is not, once we move beyond Shelley and Emerson, the possession of a "visionary company." More and more, as difference escalates to privilege, privilege, in a supreme irony, drives the seer and his expressive language into the silence of solipsistic revery. The humane bond that the mature writer wants to establish with an audience is broken, and "poetic value"—the term tends to be portentously intoned after Coleridge—whatever it might be, is inaccessibly shut off from others, even from that tiny community of fit readers.

In the last pages of *Romantic Image* Kermode makes a plea for the necessity of returning statement to poetry as a "correction to the symbolist theory of language."[8] When he says that words "are so used to being discursive that it is almost impossible to stop them from discoursing,"[9] he does not speak in the tones of tragic lamentation appropriate to a symbolist having such a perception. Kermode expresses a desire to return poetry to a more-than-poetic community, to merge symbolic language with ordinary language, and to integrate the poetic imagination with general human intellectual capacities. Art, he writes, "was always made *for* men who habitually move in space and time, whose language is propelled onward by verbs, who cannot always be asked to respect the new enclosure laws of poetry, or such forbidding notices as 'No road through to action.'"[10] The great hope for literary critics in 1957, when the hegemony of the New Criticism was breaking, was that the muse would be demystified and democratized and that younger critics would somehow link up poetry with the world again as, in Clive Bell's contemptuous formalist phrasing, they brought art down from the "superb peaks of aesthetic exaltation to the snug foothills of warm humanity"[11]—to the place where the forbidden subjects of history, intention, and cultural dynamics could be taken up once again. In some ways the *Anatomy of Criticism* would be the fulfillment of that hope; in other, more essential ways, it would frustrate the hope for demystification as it never had been frustrated before.

2

Frye's attack on the uniquely differentiated, isolate self who creates the isolate "romantic image" begins in a witty reflection on the copyright laws: "In our day the conventional element in literature is elaborately disguised by a law of copyright pretending that every work of art is an invention distinctive enough to be protected. . . . Demonstrating the debt of A to B is merely scholarship if A is dead, but a proof of moral delinquency if A is alive."[12] Then in a comment which looks at once back to the tradition summarized by Kermode and forward to Harold Bloom's poetics of anxiety, he makes the essential point: "The underestimating of convention appears to be a result of, may even be a part of, the tendency, marked from romantic times on, to think of the individual as ideally prior to his society."[13] But it is only the "inexperienced reader," he concludes, in a remark that should be read with some pain by Bloom, "who looks for a residual originality. . . ."[14] Though he has no interest in philosophizing on the nature of the self, Frye never hesitates to deploy a conception of it in his attack on romantic literary ideals of original genius. The self is not ideally prior to its society; the individual poem is not isolated from literary tradition: "The new baby *is* his own society appearing once again as a unit of individuality, and the new poem has a similar relation to its poetic society."[15] It is not that Frye wishes to deny the clearly undeniable, that at a certain level of existence a self may be distinctively differentiated from other selves; it is just that he believes that at the deepest and most authentic levels of existence—far below the conscious and willing surfaces of being—the self is a capacious and generous sort of medium peculiarly suited for the transmitting of those capacious literary structures called archetypal mythoi and images.

Frye's hope that literary critics may avoid the subjectivism and irresolvable disputes of taste, and thereby achieve objectivity of description, is based on his cornerstone assumption that all literary expression is controlled by a small number of abiding literary universals, "four narrative pregeneric" categories which are "logically prior" to the usual literary genres.[16] These pregeneric mythoi, these models of all models, these deepest of structures which are the inevitable constituents of a literary imagination, are not meant to be taken as the fictional projections of Frye's lively imagination: they are the fundamental object of the critical consciousness whose task is to receive those structures and communicate them to others. In a much-noticed passage Frye adopts the "hypothesis" that "just as there is an order of nature behind the natural sciences, so literature is not a piled aggregate of 'works,' but an order of words."[17] The misleadingly termed "hypothesis" is in reality not the critic's heuristic device but the unmanipulable iron law which guarantees the objective order of the literary universe. Frye's disclaimer in the final chapter of the *Anatomy*, that his "present book is not designed to suggest a new program for critics," is disingenuous.[18] Not only does he suggest a new program, but he claims for it the realist's highest honor as the only program which can produce objective—he uses the word "scientific"[19]—and comprehensive descriptions of the literary universe. He is confident that criticism can be systematic because he believes that "there is a quality in literature which enables it to be so."[20]

On the other hand, any critical position (like the New Criticism) which refuses his concept of the literary universe is forced into the subjectivism of the hand-to-mouth approach. Such an approach is unscientific, in Frye's terms, because, bereft of the guiding principle of the literary universe, it is left with a text that is fundamentally indeterminate. The "commentaries" produced by the hand-to-mouth critic are often "elegant," and in his "Tentative Conclusion" Frye adds the compliments of "brilliance" and "ingenuity."[21] But these compliments are not quite genuine. The New Criticism turns out to be but one more "futile" continuation of a tradition which likes to allegorize myth and in the process treats texts rather like inkblots that call forth the endless responses of "taste." Such responses can be interesting and bold, but never (by definition) accurate. With an understanding of the archetypal shape of literature as a whole, however, the critical situation presumably becomes more hopeful. Or such must be the essential claim for this critical scientist.

Frye's antiromantic contention that the self is not prior to its society is followed through, in his examinations of literary structure, only in that he places literature within a literary society, and the history of literary society, never within a broader social context; his contention has, apparently, no force whatsoever for the critical self. As he rises, unconstrained by cultural and historical determinates, carried on the wings of an unsituated critical discourse to a realm of transparent consciousness, our archetypal critic believes that he sees the text in its actual determinacy of form—that he can make letter-perfect mimetic reports on the structural foundations of literature. With his fear of indeterminacy, with his relegation of taste and subjectivity to the realm of irrelevance, and with his heavy reliance on a subject-object model drawn from nineteenth-century science and nineteenth-century theories of interpretation, Frye, like E. D. Hirsch a few years later, practices, or thinks he practices, a hermeneutics of the innocent eye.

While Frye's thought seems to put great distance between itself and a solipsist-courting poetics of isolation, another thrust in it appears to seek the very separations desired by Kermode's romantics. This isolationist tendency is somewhat obscured by the fact that it is not the individual poet who is given a privileged place by Frye but the society of all poets across history: "poets as a whole class," he tells us, "are entrusted" with a "total body of vision."[22] (Who or what does this entrusting we are never told.) What is it that most qualifies one as a poet? Like the critic who must free himself from his nuanced subjectivity in order to perceive the archetypal shape of literature, the poet must release himself from his particular existence. But the poet must go one mysterious step beyond the critic. He must merge his isolate being with the archetypal currents because—to put it in terms close to Frye's thought and almost perfectly prophetic of the structuralist critique of phenomenology—literary expression is not the exfoliation of a subject, an individuated consciousness anterior to all discourse and worldly determinates; it is the function of a system, a literary universe which is the source of all models of expression, and to which the self submits in order that it may be permitted to speak. (Heidegger's unnerving remark that it is language, not man, who speaks, has never been troublesome for structuralists and other critics familiar with Continental perspectives, and should present no difficulty, up to a certain point, for American readers who have assimilated Frye's poetics.) Structuralism reads the "system" (following Saussure's analysis of verbal discourse) as a semiotic monolith which refuses to permit the romantic ontological distinction between a discourse which is uniquely literary and one that is not. Frye, half-structuralist, half-aesthete, continues to press for the privileged place of the literary, especially in his distinction between the *centripetal* and *centrifugal*,[23] diametrically opposed movements of meaning in linguistic structure that are strongly reminiscent of Coleridge's master dualism of symbol and allegory. Like "symbol," the centripetal movement of meaning is "inward" to discourse itself, inward to a closed linguistic space where meaning and linguistic structure are wedded; whereas the centrifugal movement of meaning is toward a place discursively beyond the confines (the "prison-house") of a particular linguistic configuration, a semantic situation whereby a variety of largely synonymous expressions, to allude to one of E. D. Hirsch's recent formulations, may point to the "same" conception.

Frye's various accounts of the creative process all suggest an activity of deindividuation (a "process of un-selving,"[24] Nietzsche called it in *The Birth of Tragedy*) wherein the conscious and willing subject wills itself into a condition of will-lessness. Frye's fondness for saying that "literature shapes itself and is not shaped externally"[25] is not only an anticipation of structuralist attacks on the prelinguistic subject as the source of all shaping, but also a summary of a radical tendency within romanticism epitomized by moments in Shelley and Shopenhauer that, with the transcendental baggage thrown away, look decidedly pre-structuralist. The romantic habit, displayed by Frye's centripetal- centri-fugal division, of opposing literature (as something of the most urgent value) to everything else (mere refuse in comparison) is further evident in Frye's psychologically grounded distinction between literature and the "descriptive or assertive writing which derives from the active will and the conscious mind, and which is primarily concerned to 'say' something."[26] Or, less absolutely but yet firmly:

> poetry is the product, not only of a deliberate and voluntary act of consciousness, like discursive writing, but of processes which are subconscious or pre-conscious or half-conscious or unconscious as well. . . . It takes a great deal of will power to write poetry, but part of that will power must be employed in trying to relax the will, so making a large part of one's writing involuntary. . . . creation, whether of God, man, or nature, seems to be an activity whose only intention is to abolish intention, to eliminate final dependence on a relation to something else. . . .[27]

If the anti-intentionalism of those remarks appears to recall the New Criticism, then it probably ought to be noted that it is not W. K. Wimsatt's austere essay on intentionalism that is being evoked: "The true father or shaping spirit of the poem is the form of the poem itself, and this form is a manifestation of the universal spirit of poetry, the 'onlie begetter' of Shakespeare's sonnets who was not Shakespeare himself. . . ."[28] Though they wanted to protect the poem from a pre-poetic intention as the arbiter of meaning and value, the New Critics never denied the crucial role played by the poet's "conscious will" (Coleridge's term, echoed by Frye) in bringing a poem or any other piece of writing into existence. Coleridge redundantly insisted on the place of the conscious will in his discussion of secondary imagina-tion, balancing conscious and unconscious forces, human intentionality with organic spontaneity; Frye, in contrast, leans toward the uncon-scious and an unqualified organicism: "as long as the father of a poem is assumed to be the poet himself, we have once again failed to distinguish literature from discursive verbal structures."[29] Coleridge's redundancy functions most importantly, however, as an indication, in the face of the revolution on behalf of spontaneous feeling, of his concern (not felt by a number of his more zealous inheritors) that romanticism was tipping too far toward all-out irrationalism, that a place for rationality had to be saved in the poetic process. Compare, again, what in Frye a structuralist might understand as an attack on the concept of the author, but what in actuality is pure irrationalism: "The fact that revision is possible, that a poet can make changes in a poem not because he likes them better but because they are better, shows clearly that the poet has to give birth to the poem as it passes through his mind."[30] In fairness to the Shelleys (John Crowe Ransom once rhymed Shelley's name with lemon jelly) and in the interests of accuracy, probably Schelling's balanced and mature remarks on the relations of unconsciousness to consciousness in the creative process might be compared to Frye's preference for what Ernst Cassirer called the somnambulistic view[31]: "It was long ago perceived that, in art, not everything is performed with consciousness; that, with the conscious activity, an unconscious action must combine; and that it is of the perfect unity and mutual interpenetration of the two that the highest in art is born."[32]

The line is fairly direct from Schopenhauer and Shelley to Frye and the recent structuralist critique of the phenomenologist's obsession with the unique subject. Shelley's contempt for the particular willing self, with its Christian and Eastern tonality, is not less severe than Frye's or Lévi-Strauss's: "Poetry," Shelley tells us, "and the principle of self of which money is the visible incarnation, are the God and Mammon of the world."[33] Shelley's Neoplatonic One, Frye's literary universe, and the forces of *langue* for structuralism, though they do not share the same philosophical ground or content, all serve as determinative agents in relation to a subject whose individuated, distinctive voice is overpowered by the systemic voice that speaks through it. But that is a sentimental way of putting it: Frye and the structuralists do not recognize an individuated subject, anterior to all system, that is later "overpowered"; for them it is the system itself that permits individuation, even as the determining and embracing universals of the system are the basis of community. Shelley was prepared to take literally Milton's deference to convention that the muse dictated his "unpremeditated song." Again, however, we must not too quickly lord our sophistication over Shelley: Frye and the structuralists also habitually portray the process of writing as a passive activity, mere clay in the hands of Frye's archetypal mythoi or structuralism's semiotic systems. Frye and the structuralists are open to the common criticism that they

ignore Saussure's stipulation that *langue* and *parole* are related dialectically; that they cannot deal with particularities of texture and
nuance; that they cannot account for the power of a distinctively individuated text.

The movement of antihumanist perspectives on the subject from
Shelley to Frye to structuralism is a movement, then, which needs
to be distinguished from the irreducible humanist romanticism of
Coleridge and Wordsworth. Rather than locating the origin of expression in a large, all-inclusive system which "authorizes" the single
self, as mere passive medium, to speak poetic language, Coleridge and
Wordsworth instead preserve the active, conscious subject as the trig-
gering force in the poetic process (and, in Coleridge's case, as the
gentle guide *[laxis effertur habenis]* of the imaginative process). Thus
to Coleridge's insistence on the place of "conscious will" ought to be
added Wordsworth's carefully articulated account of his progress of
composition which begins in "long and deep" thought upon the self—
and he means his single, somewhat private feelings—*in order to* discover "what is really important to men."[34] By taking trouble to stress
the role of the active, personal self in the poetic process of achieving an
expressive discourse that would reflect more general human dimensions
of selfhood, Coleridge and Wordsworth try to account for variation,
for distinction in expression, which neither Shelley, Frye, nor Lévi-
Strauss can approach, or would want to approach.

Against Kermode's tradition of the romantic image which celebrated
the "unique" text authored and authorized by the isolate subject, Frye
brings his mythic conception of a largely unconscious self, a sort of
communal subject, as the origin and authority for a text whose identity
is not "different." To put it in a way that has become increasingly *de
rigueur* since Jacques Derrida's philosophizing, Frye dismantles (he
"deconstructs") the more naive versions of expressive theory which
value ("valorize") originality and locate it in the unique self. In place
of romantic ideals of originality—which we are helped to see, after
Derrida, as ideals of origin closely linked to the notion of a uniquely
individuated and "free" subject—Frye substitutes this view of origins:
"Originality returns to the origins of literature, as radicalism returns
to its roots. The remark of Mr. Eliot that a good poet is more likely to
steal than to imitate affords a more balanced view of convention, as it
indicates that the poem is specifically involved with other poems. . . .
The copyright law, and the mores attached to it, make it difficult for a
modern novelist to steal anything except his title from the rest of
literature. . . ."[35] And in a similar vein, Frye plays once again with the
etymology of "originality": "The possession of originality cannot make

an artist unconventional; it drives him further into convention, obeying the law of the art itself, which seeks constantly to reshape itself from its own depths. . . ."[36]

If originality means a return to origin, what then more precisely is the origin? Behind the conscious and isolated subject, which is not the father, not the origin, we find a conception in Frye of the center of literary activity which is not itself verbal, not itself a part of the system of pregeneric mythoi which constitute the literary universe. How uncannily Frye anticipates and, then, crucially, rejects the discourse and thought now associated with Derrida on the question of origins cannot be overstated. Derrida writes that the "structurality of structure"

> has always been neutralized or reduced, and this by a process of giving it a center or referring it to a point of presence, a fixed origin. The function of this center was not only to orient, balance, and organize the structure— one cannot in fact conceive of an unorganized structure—but above all to make sure that the organizing principle of the structure would limit what we might call the *freeplay* of the structure. . . . Nevertheless, the center also closes off the freeplay it opens up and makes possible. . . . [A]t the center, the permutation or the transformation of elements (which may of course be structures enclosed within a structure) is forbidden. . . . Thus it has always been thought that the center, which is by definition unique, constituted the very thing within a structure which governs the structure, while escaping structurality.[37]

Now Frye:

> In the greatest moments of Dante and Shakespeare, in, say *The Tempest* or the climax of the *Purgatorio,* we have a feeling of converging significance, the feeling that here we are close to seeing what our whole literary experience has been about, the feeling that we have moved into the still center of the order of words. Criticism as knowledge, the criticism which is compelled to keep on talking about the subject, recognizes the fact that there *is* a center of the order of words.
>   Unless there is such a center, there is nothing to prevent the analogies supplied by convention and genre from being an endless series of free associations, perhaps suggestive, perhaps even tantalizing, but never creating a real structure. The study of archetypes is the study of

literary symbols as parts of a whole. If there are such things
as archetypes at all, then, we have to take yet another step,
and conceive the possibility of a self-contained literary
universe. Either archetypal criticism is a will-o'-the-wisp, an
endless labyrinth without an outlet, or we have to assume
that literature is a total form, and not simply the name
given to the aggregate of existing literary works.[38]

The center is simply desire: "the energy," as Frye defines it, "that
leads human society to develop its own form. . . . an impulse toward
expression which would have remained amorphous if the poem had
not liberated it by providing the form of its expression."[39] Human
desire (Frye's conception is Sartrean) is the absence of form or structure—a "lack" which causes form or structure to come into being
while remaining itself unconditioned by law, a "lack" standing outside
of structurality as an unmodified and unmodifiable metaphysical *ding
an sich*. Desire is the origin, the center, the point of presence which in
Derrida's terms limits the free-play of structure, or which in Frye's
terms makes archetypal analysis more than a will-o'-the-wisp, more
than an "endless series of free associations." Desire is the deepest
human center of governance; it is not the property of a single, differentiated subject, but the intersubjective force which impels all
activity of expression, all civilizing humanization and ordering of an
indifferent and stupid nature. By remaining free of all transformation,
as a kind of secular *primum mobile*, itself unmoved, desire is the sure
ground, the guarantee of Frye's ultimate humanism. And, finally, because it is the "still center," desire, as a mode of wishing, sanctions a
"real structure" as the fulfillment or *telos* of wishing. This metaphysics
of desire is in sharp contrast to Derrida, whose conception of the sign
as "difference" posits a simultaneous past-oriented (retentive) nostalgia
and a future-oriented (protentive) yearning—a kind of desire, to be
sure, but one that will find no fulfillment in a center beyond discourse.

Frye's basic theoretical conceptions are unremittingly spatial: he
realizes that the system he proposes can stand only if the structure is
"real," if it can stay closed, coherent, and self-contained. All of which
is to be compared to Derrida's subversion of "real structure," his
placing of the center within the field of free-playing transformation—
in other words, his radical temporalizing of verbal activity which keeps
structures "open": in an important sense, not structures at all. Frye's
entire literary universe (the "real structure") stands isolated in its
autonomous space, the river of time running far distantly beneath it;
it is a system of rich but limited possibilities of modal deployment and
combination, available to all writers as a simultaneity of options no

matter what their moment in time or place in space. "Whether the context is Greek, Christian, or undefined," he tells us in a very typical moment, "tragedy seems to lead up to an epiphany of law, of that which is and must be."[40] That is probably true—who would disagree with Northrop Frye about the over-all shape of a literary mode?— but it is also impoverished, as Hartman, Wimsatt, and Krieger have noted in separate critiques. Frye's notion of tradition, to borrow some appropriate words from Michel Foucault, "makes it possible to rethink the dispersion of history in the form of the same."[41] More specifically, his conception of generic history, though it highlights the constraints imposed upon, say, Ezra Pound (who would, by attempting the long poem, necessarily be imposed upon by Homer, Virgil, Milton, and other athletes of epic intention), ignores the more immediate and local constraints (imagism, economics) pressuring Pound's writing. Frye's system predisposes the critic not to perceive the freshness of trans-formation; it has difficulty accounting for individuality in expression, for ruptures and discontinuities; and it refuses without qualification to recognize the constraining and determining effect of nonliterary forces upon the literary universe. Hartman's charge (at bottom a charge of aestheticism), that Frye ignores real time, that he does not account for the distinctive voice—two sides of the same coin—is a just criticism, though as with most criticisms of Frye, it is made from a standpoint outside his set of assumptions. For Hartman's perspective on tem-porality is the Bergsonian one which regards all Viconian (cyclical, ritualized) historicisms like Frye's as betrayals of history.[42]

3

The closure of Frye's "real structure," a system impervious to the movements of unritualized time, is guaranteed through the de-ployment, at various junctures in the argument, of the strategies of dualism. Typical of the romantic mind from its earliest days (the first paragraph of Shelley's "Defense" is a *classicus locus*), what is inter-esting about these dualistic habits in Frye's work is the gentlemanly casualness with which they are introduced, the ease with which he as-sumes that the reasonable among us will share his assumptions. Thus, he tells us, "poetic thought" is something "quite different, of course, from other kinds of thought";[43] we are warned not to "impose on litera-ture an extraliterary schematism"[44] because doing so would only cause to recede into the unreachable distance what, presumably, we are all after, "a theory of literary meaning" (distinguishable, one supposes, from "ordinary meaning").[45] The unique discourse of literature is closed off (it is centripetally directed) from all that externality which is attended to by the "centrifugal," "descriptive," and "assertive" qualities of ordinary writing.[46] Frye assumes what he does so casually not because he is above tough philosophical analysis but because the reigning theoretical assumptions of his critical times posited just those sorts of dualisms and the implicit privilege of the literary that always goes along with them. Frye's casualness is intended to tell us that the reasonable of all times and places believe what he believes; in fact, his tone conveys what literary critics in the 1950s, in the Anglo-American mode, thought an eternal verity. There is nothing in his assumptions per se that any thinker in the symbolist tradition would find repugnant. In setting the literary, as a mode of discourse and a "body of vision" with which the poets are entrusted, against all other modes of thought and discourse (all jammed together under the roof of the extraliterary), Frye links his *Anatomy* with the Kantian tradition, which in its residually defensive and embattled intentions wanted to secure a unique place for literature and the other arts in a Western culture that has seemed to the romantic sensibility not to need aesthetic values and even (to some of the alienated poets and their more alienated defenders) to be hostile and condescending to the arts.

There are moments in the *Anatomy* when Frye's problematic understanding of himself as literary scientist, with critical principles which stand free of ideology, is productive. His acute demonstrations of the provincialism of the New Critics, who assert the universal applicability of ideas which manifestly grow out of the limited reach of symbolist-ironic literature, is a case in point. Many "current critical assumptions," he says, "have a limited historical context. In our day an ironic provincialism, which looks everywhere in literature for complete objectivity, suspension of moral judgments, concentration on pure verbal craftsmanship . . . is in the ascendant." His overall conclusion is that "no set of critical standards derived from only one mode can ever assimilate the whole truth about poetry."[47] It would be very difficult (and unnecessary) to withhold one's admiration for the urbanity and cool justice of his judgment upon the New Criticism.

But for all his objectivist or scientific intentions, Frye's principles have themselves a "limited historical context," and the charge of provincialism is easy to level against him. Some dozen pages after he so neatly places the New Criticism, he embraces another, and more fundamental, set of symbolist principles. In all "literary verbal structures final direction of meaning is inward," we are told, because in literature "questions of fact or truth are subordinated to the primary literary aim of producing a structure of words for its own sake, and the sign-values

of symbols are subordinated to their importance as a structure of inter-
connecting motifs." Frye goes on to define the realm of the literary as
one which grants citizenship only to the "autonomous verbal structure": "Wherever we have an autonomous verbal structure we have
literature. Wherever this autonomous structure is lacking, we have
language, words used instrumentally to help human consciousness
do or understand something else."[48] With his reliance on the New-
Critical shibboleth and cliché ("autonomous verbal structure," "a
structure of words for its own sake") and with his open condescension
toward the instrumental, the cognitive, and the descriptive functions
of literature, how obvious it is that Frye is a post-Kantian provincial
himself who derives his fundamental views from the German idealist
tradition—despite the implication that he, unlike the New Critics, is
not confined historically to a single mode, that he has a transcendent,
global perspective, a God's-eye-view of the entire literary universe.
Could anyone before Kant have so resolutely, so confidently defined
literature in the way Frye has done? The easy absolutism of his definition of literature, and particularly of his contention that the "poet's
intention" is "directed towards putting words together, not towards
aligning words with meanings,"[49] is profoundly formalistic and almost
unimaginable before Kant. I think it likely that theorists and critics
in the mimetic tradition, from Plato and Aristotle on down to Samuel
Johnson, as well as most of our contemporaries of historicist persuasion, whether pre- or post-structuralist, would consider Frye's characterization of the poetic intention as powerful evidence of—let me
appeal to Johnsonian rhetoric—a high and frenzied madness.

    In its clean severance of the literary mode from the centrifugal
responsibilities to describe and to assert, Frye's explanation of the
value of the "autonomous verbal structure" is more fundamentally
Kantian, via Schiller and Oscar Wilde, than any New Critic would
have cared to attempt. Though critics like Ransom and Brooks often
speak the language of romantic isolation, they are not (Kermode and
others to the contrary notwithstanding) content, as Frye is content, to
cut literature away from a cognitive function. Another shibboleth of
the New Critics—one worth remembering, given recent attempts to
portray them as life-denying formalists—was that literature gives a
"special kind of knowledge" of nonliterary, nonlinguistic phenomena.
Though in the end the New Critic cannot justify that claim, and probably is trapped in an aestheticism of his own, still it was his intention
to give literature the cultural relevance of a cognitive role. For Frye
all claims for literature's power of "existential revelation" are really
only unself-conscious indulgences in the fallacy of "existential projec-

tion."[50] Over and over he tells us that literature is made exclusively out of other literature, and that the literary universe is a representation not of the way things are, but of the ways of human desire.

So though Frye and the New Critics share some common philosophical backgrounds, there is a sense, as Krieger has urged, in which they are "utter alternatives" in the modern critical tradition,[51] with Frye representing a modern version of the Renaissance (Platonic) modes exemplified by Sidney and Bacon, and the New Critics linking up with (broadly) Aristotelian commitments to this world. With his interest in the way a "mature" poet's discourse is a reflection of the ambiguous and complicated textures of human affairs, Cleanth Brooks could never have written this statement: "The reason for producing the literary structure is apparently that the inward meaning, the self-contained verbal pattern, is the field of the responses connected with pleasure, beauty. . . . The contemplation of a detached pattern, whether of words or not, is clearly a major source of the sense of the beautiful, and of the pleasure that accompanies it."[52] Now if we note Frye's addendum, a few pages later, that proper contemplation of art involves "a complete surrender of the mind and senses to the impact of the work as a whole, and proceeds through the effort to unite the symbols toward a simultaneous perception of the unity of the structure,"[53] we have Frye's elegant little compression of the Kantian aesthetic. The isolation of art as "self-contained verbal pattern," free from cognitive and ethical consequences, is nothing other than Kantian "purposiveness without purpose." The idea that we yield up our selves, that we lose our knowing, willing, and hedonic propensities in the "aesthetic experience," is precisely what Kant meant by "disinterested contemplation" and "disinterested satisfaction," and what Eliseo Vivas describes, in a recent neo-Kantian reformulation, as "rapt, intransitive attention"[54]—a special kind of pleasure in which, to go back to Kant's language, our mental powers engage each other in a "lively" and "indeterminate" activity of "play," to no end except an "internal feeling" of "harmony."[55]

Like a number of neo-Kantians before him, and despite his talk of "detached pattern," Frye stands a long distance from the severe formalism and isolationism postulated at points in Kant's aesthetic. Kant considered "delineations *à la grecque*, foliage for borders or wall papers" and "many sea shells" and music "without any theme"—most excellent nonutilitarian things—to be ultimate examples of "free beauty" (which he contrasts with the "adherent" beauty of human forms).[56] It is the experience of "free beauty" (a tellingly redundant term in idealist poetics) which provokes a perfect internal freedom in the auditor's mental faculties. From Schiller to Cassirer, and from Frye to Herbert Marcuse, the belief is that though he set things on the right footing by declaring art autonomous, Kant also badly emasculated its cultural powers. Neo-Kantians have grander plans. Frye seizes upon the basic Kantian postulates, and particularly on the idea that the experience of art is an experience of freedom from all determination, cognitive, moral, and hedonic. In terms startlingly familiar to readers of Schiller's *On the Aesthetic Education of Man*, he declares that the proper experience of literature is man's ultimate goal as a creature of culture, since in it we are freed from externalities of all kinds, including the externality of externalities, time and the natural order of things. We are born into nature and time—they constitute what Frye calls our "environment." But our environment does not satisfy us; it makes us feel only distance and isolation. So we build our "homes" out of the imagination, we create civilization, the purely human order of things.[57] It is literature alone which provides us with the vision of the goals of civilization, a vision of the work which must be done if we are finally to be freed from our environment. In Schiller the statement of that vision tends to be utopian; in Frye we find the ideal of the classless society often articulated as the true goal of "liberal education," by which he means *literary* education, an ideal descended from Schiller.

Once the dated philosophical jargon of German idealism is cleared out of Schiller's theory, what we find is the contention dear to aesthetic idealists that the ability to experience the aesthetic state is coincidental with our achievement of human being. The arguments of Kant and Schiller (this is especially clear in Kant)[58] assume the "middle state" of man, to recall Alexander Pope's terms and the metaphysical schema of the chain of being. Enlightenment humanist perspectives are accepted by the German idealist philosophers, who then join them to the aestheticist concerns of modern poetics in declaring that our human definition, our difference from the physical world below us on the chain and the angelic orders above, is achieved by our capacity to experience beauty. With Kant and Schiller is born the most visible philosophy of poetics down through Frye: aesthetic humanism. The "consummation of his humanity," as Schiller puts it, depends upon man's ability to free himself from all determinations.[59] In the "midst of the awful realm of powers" (he means "nature") "and of the sacred realm of laws" (he means "moral imperatives," divinely sanctioned) "the aesthetic creative impulse is building unawares a third joyous realm of play and of appearance"—here we are, finally, in the uniquely human arena—"in which it releases mankind from all the shackles of circumstance and frees him from everything that may be called constraint, whether physical or moral."[60] What is it in the work of art, properly approached, that ensures our "release" from the "shackles of circumstance," we are obliged to ask Schiller; and the answer is the work's autonomy—his term is "self-dependence"—a quality that is grounded in its fictionality. The key is to dispense "with all assistance from reality," to create art or to experience it with pure "indifference towards reality."[61]

It is not difficult to hear echoes from Schiller's warnings about the dangers of art simulating reality or in some way requiring reality for its operation, in Frye's strictures against "existential projection." Nor is it hard to see in Frye's well-known preference for romance and comedy, alongside, as always, his consistent denigration of modes which assume externality (satire and tragedy), Schiller's version of freedom as the release from the "constraints" of time and circumstance. Haunting the humanist tradition from Schiller to Frye is the spector of a deterministic vision which, by deriving human being wholly from the historical or the natural order, appears to deny us the power to build our "home" freely in culture. To simulate reality, in Schiller's and Frye's humanist views, is to deny man his only way to achieve the distinctively human status which would effectively elevate him over, as it isolates him from, the order of things.

There are any number of vantage points from which to assess the historical moment of Frye's system, and his concept of "existential projection" is one of them. The existential projection of irony, he tells us, is perhaps existentialism itself, a projection which he claims the New Criticism especially indulges in. The New Critic ought to recognize that the ironic vision of ambiguity and tension in human affairs is only a vision, a projection of the fearful underside of human desire, ultimately a vision with dark demonic roots and not a reflection of existential reality.[62] Yet Frye himself appears to have assumed the descriptive authenticity of the vision of irony, and to have done so because it represents precisely the state of unfreedom, in the awful realm of powers, against which his poetics is directed: "The work of imagination presents us with a vision not of the personal greatness of the poet, but of something impersonal and far greater: the vision of a decisive act of spiritual freedom, the vision of the recreation of man."[63] That "decisive act of spiritual freedom"—a phrase which neatly sums up the meaning of imagination in Frye's neo-Kantian heritage—bristles with such urgency because it is an act directed against a real state of "bondage, frustration, or absurdity," to cite terms from his description of the ironic anti-hero.[64] The important passage on this contradiction in the *Anatomy* occurs in his problematic description of demonic imagery: "Opposed to apocalyptic symbolism is the presentation of the world that desire totally rejects: the world of the nightmare and the scapegoat, of bondage and pain and confusion; the world *as it is* before the human imagination begins to work on it and before any image of human desire . . . has been solidly established. . . ."[65] More clearly yet, in the first sentence of his description of the "mythos of winter": "We come now to the mythical patterns of experience, the attempts to give form to the shifting ambiguities and complexities of unidealized existence."[66] The worlds of satire and irony are centripetal constructions, not imitations—his system demands that he argue that point. And yet the demonic image becomes, in his account of it, clearly centrifugal, referential to "the world *as it is* before the human imagination begins to work on it." To put it another way, the literary patterns or mythoi of satiric literature (say, parodic or inverted quest-romance) may be, as patterns, referential only to the self-contained literary universe; but these satiric forms, he is saying, order the real content of everyday life which he describes in New-Critical and existential terms as "the shifting ambiguities and complexities of unidealized existence."

So despite all of his scientific claims, Frye's cyclic arrangement of the mythoi, and his endless enumerations of phases and subphases, are thoroughly hierarchical and judgmental in character. The real desideratum in Northrop Frye's world is freedom, the shedding of all constraints, and the pecking order of the modes is structured according to the fullness of freedom each mode is thought to image forth. In the first essay of the *Anatomy*, "Historical Criticism: Theory of Modes," Frye classifies fictions, with an assist from Aristotle, according to the "hero's power of action, which may be greater than ours, less, or roughly the same."[67] (One page later he makes this equation: the hero's "power" is his "freedom.") The list of five types of hero is arranged in descending order. At the top is the hero as divine being, who can do what he pleases: his freedom is unqualified. Then comes the romance hero who moves in and out of the natural order; in his world the "ordinary laws of nature are slightly suspended." As we move fully into history witnessing the diminishments of heroic power, down through high mimetic and low mimetic modes, at the bottom of the list we find the fully imprisoned anti-hero of the ironic mode who, as unfree, seems less than human: "If inferior in power or intelligence to ourselves, so that we have the sense of looking down on a scene of bondage, frustraton, or absurdity, the hero belongs to the *ironic* mode."[68]

In his second essay, "Ethical Criticism: Theory of Symbols," the order of freedom is an ascending one with the "descriptive" and the "formal" phases of symbolic structure both in some way accountable to nature. Accountability means that nature is assumed, in these two phases, to have an independent existence which provides the patterns for all commentary that would assign meaning to the poem (and not rest with the formalistic exercise which refuses to "allegorize" and remains satisfied with the poem as a "literal" structure whose compositional features form interlocking patterns). Even in the penultimate phase of symbolic structure, the archetypal, where we enter the literary universe proper—poems imitate other poems—we yet must assume, Frye points out, the unity of nature and *its* phasal structure. It is not until the final "anagogic phase" is reached that the shackles of circumstance and all constraints are thrown off, as time and nature are consumed in an apocalyptic conflagration which reminds us (if ever we needed reminding) of Frye's Blakean commitments. The self, which was "circumstanced"—I shall insist, with the help of Robert Frost, on the image buried in the adjective—the self which was "contained" by time and the natural order, that self suddenly achieves an unconditional freedom: not freedom "from" but freedom "pure," a freedom no longer qualified by the presence of an exterior and potentially coercive order. In the anagogic phase time and nature are ingested: "nature becomes not the container, but the thing contained."[69] The poet speaks from the "circumference," holding within himself all time and nature: "The anagogic view of criticism thus leads to the conception of literature as existing in its own universe, no longer a commentary on life or reality, but containing life and reality in a system of verbal relationships."[70] Frye then explains what the higher aestheticism is really all about. In contradistinction to the usual sort of aestheticism, which celebrates the closed sanctuary of the single work, "a tiny palace of art looking out upon an inconceivably gigantic 'life,' "[71] Frye offers a view in which a gigantic palace of art contains all life within, with not even a tiny little something left outside. The subject-object problem has been solved in favor of the poets with a vengeance that few outside the mythopoeic tradition would seriously entertain.

In the third essay, "Mythical Criticism: Theory of Myths," Frye returns to the hierarchical arrangement of the first essay, beginning with comedy on top, followed by romance, then tragedy, and, finally, in the "wintry celler,"[72] as Wimsatt once phrased it, those twins of human constriction, irony and satire. With its inevitably happy ending, comedy epitomizes the triumph of human desire over actuality: "Happy endings do not impress us as true, but as desirable, and they are brought about by manipulation."[73] What is defeated is a cruel and (Frye's redundancy gives away his obsession) an "arbitrary law."[74] The typical movement of comedy is from "law to liberty"—a movement best illustrated by Shakespearean comedy, the mythos which more clearly than all others illustrates the "archetypal function of literature in visualizing the world of desire."[75] Tragedy, on the other hand, is reduced to the issue of freedom (or, more accurately, the loss of freedom). If comedy pushes us upward in a transcendent move away from the circumstances of real society and real time, then tragedy presents us with the reverse action, a resolute move from an Eden of freedom, of vast potential quickly lost, downward into the order of things, into the hands of fate, the gods, chance, and the severe vision of an "epiphany of law": "just as comedy often sets up an arbitrary law and then organizes the action to break or evade it, so tragedy presents the reverse theme of narrowing a comparatively free life into a process of causation."[76] Any tragic mythos, according to Frye, is a reenactment of the great Fall which, with St. Augustine, he reads as the act which creates time and all its entanglements, all the complications and frustrations of an "unidealized existence."

4

In 1967 in *Validity in Interpretation* E. D. Hirsch, mounting an attack on the romantic mystique of a unique literary discourse and unique literary values, properly added Frye to his list of offenders by charging him with making literature the elite and privileged basis of the true anthropology. Grounded as it is in a nonreferential discourse with no obligation to the real state of sublunary nature, Frye's literary universe is open to the charge of elitism that Hirsch and the structuralist group have brought against it. Since the literary universe is the formal container of all human and humanizing desire, the literary critic becomes, necessarily, the privileged interpreter of that universe, and all so-called liberal, humanistic education is collapsed under the rubric of literary education. And yet for all the familiar romantic, dualizing habits of mind (the source of his elitism) that we can find in Frye, at the base of the system we can locate a powerful monistic urge, as Meyer Abrams noted in a review of the *Anatomy*,[77] a monism which emanates from Frye's center of all centers: human desire. Anterior to all discourse, desire is the motivation of our impulses to make form, not just in literary ways, but in all the ways that we attempt to humanize our inhuman environment.[78] The primal human act in Frye's system, and a model for all human acts, is an "informative," creative act which transforms a world that is merely objective, set over against us, in which we "feel lonely and frightened and unwanted," into a home.[79]

Frye's key distinctions (which presuppose that consciousness may be mimetic as well as creative) between linguistic structures which are "coherent" and those which are "correspondent" with external reality, between literary and nonliterary, nonreferential and descriptive, centripetal and centrifugal—all these distinctions in the end must be collapsed under the rubric of aesthetic humanism: all human acts are creative (hence centripetal, literary, and nonreferential). No human act, no human discourse can be mimetic. With a suspect generosity we welcome as poets our colleagues from other disciplines—a point that is made clearly in Frye's not-so-tentative conclusion.

With other idealist thinkers, having once identified "art" with a creative act of mind, then having universalized that act as the characteristic act of human (i.e., humanizing) consciousness, as neo-Kantians generally do, Frye has left no authentic ground upon which the literary or the aesthetic can stand as "unique" modes of consciousness, since all acts of consciousness are aesthetic. The chimera of the distinction between the centripetal and the centrifugal now revealed in his final chapter, no human discourse can be excluded from the palace of art. In Frye's book we see the entire neo-Kantian aestheticist movement brought to its logical conclusion: from the holistic holiness of the single poem, to the privileging of the entire canon of all literary objects as the literary universe, to the highest of all aestheticisms (the term now becomes meaningless) in which every act of making is glorified as art.

> The argument of our last essay . . . led to the principle that all structures in words are partly rhetorical, and hence literary, and that the notion of a scientific or philosophical verbal structure free of rhetorical elements is an illusion. If so, then our literary universe has expanded into a verbal universe, and no aesthetic principle of self-containment will work.[80]

Frye then raises this important question: "is it true that the verbal structures of psychology, anthropology, theology, history, law, and everything else built out of words have been informed or constructed by the same kind of myths and metaphors that we find, in their original hypothetical form, in literature?"[81] The answer is a comfortable "yes," even though he is aware that what he proposes must be crippled by his very logic, be itself a metaphor, just another myth. Literary discourse is now distinguished from other discourses by its priority, not by its mythic character; literature is the ur-source of all myths, the father of all discourses.

Frye is not daunted. All discourses are "verbal constructs," he tells us, "and the further we take them, the more clearly their metaphorical and mythical outlines show through."[82] We must force him to add criticism to his list of mythic discourses—and especially the criticism which gives us the idea of a literary universe. And so he finishes the *Anatomy* by destroying his vast system, including its so-called scientific basis. Or is it that Frye wishes us to understand that his critical discourse somehow escapes metaphor, as Ishmael alone escaped the white whale, so that his critical discourse alone can claim the privilege of being an objective report on the state of affairs in the literary universe? All of his distinctions and arrangements, and even the basic import and value of his literary universe, appear to be dissolved in the generalized Nietzschean illusionism which he announces in his final pages, as he anticipates the new Nietzschean rhetoricians at Yale.

The key to the "situation" of Frye's own discourse is his vision of an uncoerced self; it is a vision generated by a thoroughly despairing and alienated understanding of the possibilities of historical life. For Frye actual history can be nothing but a theater of dehumanization, a place of bondage and torture. A number of contradictions aside, the move is spiritually coherent from his neo-Kantian view of freedom (and its celebration of the creative mind) toward his prefiguring of the recent rhetorical interpretation of Nietzsche (and its celebration of nonmimetic figuration). For what is celebrated in both instances is a fantastical, utopian alternative to the perception of a degraded social existence: a human discoursing free of all contingency, independent of all external forces, a discoursing empowered by unconditioned human desire. The consistency of Frye is the consistency of an idealism *in extremis*. *Anatomy of Criticism* is poised crucially in 1957, looking at once backward to traditions in poetics of which it is the culmination, and forward to postmodernist responses to those traditions.

Two

If we forget that fictions are fictive we regress to myth (as when the Neo-Platonists forgot the fictiveness of Plato's fictions and Professor Frye forgets the fictiveness of all fictions).

Frank Kermode, *The Sense of an Ending*

The final belief is to believe in a fiction, which you know to be a fiction, there being nothing else, the exquisite truth is to know that it is a fiction and that you believe in it willingly.

Wallace Stevens, *Opus Posthumous*

. . . you will often hear it said that the age of the world we live in is particularly bad. I am impatient of such talk. We have no way of knowing that this age is one of the worst in the world's history. Arnold claimed the honor for the age before this. Wordsworth claimed it for the last but one. And so on back through literature. I say they claimed the honor for their ages. They claimed it rather for themselves. It is immodest of a man to think of himself as going down before the worst forces ever mobilized by God.

Robert Frost, Letter to *The Amherst Student*

Versions of Existentialism

The vogue of Northrop Frye in the United States from the time of the publication of his *Anatomy of Criticism* in 1957 through the middle 1960s is difficult to overestimate. Just recently, by publishing *Northrop Frye: An Enumerative Bibliography*, the Scarecrow Press bestowed the bibliographer's highest honor on Frye by making him the only contemporary critical theorist to have a book-length bibliographical study devoted entirely to his writings and writings about him. Even a casual perusal of the Frye bibliography turns up some awe-inspiring facts. In the category of "Writings about Frye's Criticism," which includes essays published in scholarly journals and substantial discussions in books (but not reviews), we find 129 items. Frye's books—there were thirteen by 1974, the year the bibliography was brought out—have drawn 348 reviews, with the *Anatomy* garnering fifty-eight. With further digging we discover that in 1965 the English Institute, in an ultimate act of homage, devoted a session to Frye which eventuated in the publication in 1966 of *Northrop Frye in Modern Criticism*, a book which collects major statements from leading American critics: Angus Fletcher, Geoffrey Hartman, Murray Krieger, and W. K. Wimsatt. And a mere twelve years after its publication in English one could, if one were so inclined, and so talented, read the *Anatomy* in French, German, and Italian.[1]

Wimsatt's response to the Frye phenomenon is caustic and amusing, and, given his keen historical sense for developments in critical theory, an illuminating measure of Frye's impact on the American critical landscape. In response to Chairman Krieger's mandate to write critically, skeptically, but "respectfully," Wimsatt says, in his opening paragraph: "As I always write respectfully of literary theorists, I do not find this stipulation irksome. I think I have written in its spirit. I would add the reflection that, as the devil's advocate is not called in until the prospect of canonization is imminent, and furthermore as it is extraordinary that such proceedings should take place at all during the lifetime of the candidate, I believe the honor of the occasion can be in little danger."[2] Though Wimsatt proceeds immediately to the attack, at some length, and in decidedly devilish detail, in an effort to forestall the elevation of Frye to critical sainthood, it turns out that canonization was not imminent after all. Eulogy—or perhaps its ritual opposite, the debunking of the recently deceased, recently mythologized hero—was more properly in order. For the English Institute volume of 1966 reads now, with the hindsight a decade provides, like an ironic memorial (only Fletcher was celebratory) to a critical career that had reached stardom and then, more quickly than anyone might have predicted in the middle 1960s, lost its claim to center stage. Frye would continue to elaborate (and water down) in a series of books the position he had set forth with such rigor in 1957, but the avant-garde theoretical imagination in America (when not in pursuit of Georges Poulet and modes Continental) was beginning to become fascinated with Wallace Stevens, and soon the language of fictionalism was to displace the language of myth criticism. Frye, no "connoisseur of chaos" (a phrase from Stevens we must remember) was unceremoniously tossed "on the dump" (another phrase from Stevens) with other useless relics.

It is perhaps even more difficult to overestimate the vogue of Wallace Stevens in the 1960s. No young academic coming out of graduate school in the middle of the decade with an advanced degree in literature could claim critical sophistication unless he could discourse knowingly, off the cuff, on "supreme fictions," the "gaiety of language," and the "dialectic of imagination and reality." No mature literary intellectual could be comfortable unless he could move smoothly into such ponderous conversation. Not long after the poet's death in 1955 the Stevens industry began to prosper such that it eventually swallowed whole all competition in the criticism of modern poetry. Between 1960 and 1969—or beginning roughly with Frank Kermode's little book—

we were inundated with a concordance, a bibliography, three collections of scholarly essays, two pamphlets, fifteen critical books (or about twice as many as were published on Robert Frost), about a hundred essays in scholarly journals, over forty doctoral dissertations (not counting those only in part on Stevens), and frequent admonitions from Harold Bloom that Stevens was the great modern poet, the culmination of the romantic spirit, and the true alternative to Pound, Eliot, and Auden, his hated New-Critical writers. All of this in the space of ten years.[3] But the clearest sign of all of Stevens's ascendancy was the publication in 1967 by Frank Kermode of a brilliant new cultural synthesis, *The Sense of an Ending: Studies in the Theory of Fiction*, a book which, as it related traditional apocalyptic thought about beginnings and ends to novelistic plot-making and a general (epistemological) theory of fictions, picked up the story of modern criticism where *Romantic Image* had left off ten years earlier.

1

To what extent Kermode's themes and biases are controlled by the poetics of Wallace Stevens is perhaps best attested to by the absence in *The Sense of an Ending* of any substantial, frontal discussion of Stevens himself. The poet is present in one of the epigraphs preceding the first chapter, and he is present in a closing quotation— Kermode gives him the last words of the book. But most tellingly he is present in the book's texture and rhythm, in words and phrases from his poems and essays which Kermode repeatedly and skillfully weaves into his sentences at key points in the argument. Stevens need no longer be confronted directly because, Kermode appears to have assumed, by 1967 his poetic theories and the very tone of his thought are givens within the long tradition of postromantic epistemology which begins with the reorientation of the knowing subject effected by Kant and is later radicalized in directions that Kant would never have approved. Nietzsche, Hans Vaihinger, William James and the American pragmatists, José Ortega y Gasset, and Jean-Paul Sartre (particularly in important early books, *The Psychology of Imagination* and *Being and Nothingness*) are the chief figures in a post-Kantian line which, in its ultimate extension in Sartre, concludes in an odd mixture of Kantian and anti-Kantian themes. But Stevens assumes such proper prominence in *The Sense of an Ending* because he is the culmination and summary representative of what I am going to call the conservative fictionalist tradition in modern poetics and philosophy. It is a tradition which captured the American theoretical imagination because it appeared to offer a clean break both with Frye's grander aestheticism and with the isolationists of the image represented by the New-Critical tradition. In *Romantic Image* Kermode had shown us that since Kant and Coleridge we were sunk in aesthetic isolationism; the *Anatomy* had not rescued us but, rather, had pushed us down deeper. With its unspoken purpose of radically undermining Frye's premises, *The Sense of an Ending* would show us the way out of the closed literary universe.

The epigraph that Kermode chooses from the late long poem "An Ordinary Evening in New Haven" gives us access to several of the postulates of conservative fictionalism:

> a more severe,
> More harassing master would extemporize
> Subtler, more urgent proof that the theory
> Of poetry is the theory of life
>
> As it is, in the intricate evasions of as,
> In things seen and unseen, created from nothingness,
> The heavens, the hells, the worlds, the longed-for lands.[4]

The ground of Stevens's lifelong obsessive irony toward his poetic vocation is that he is just such a harassing and severe master who is incapable of extemporizing urgent (or any other kind of) proof "that the theory/Of poetry is the theory of life." Against an irrepressible will to identify the projections of desire, those "longed-for lands," with reality itself, he sets a critical self-consciousness which incessantly subverts and dismantles his fictions and shows them for what they are: "intricate evasions of as." So the agonists of a poetics of supreme fictions are opposed in this way: a fictional thrust generated out of the great voids of desire (a "nothingness") and bodied forth through the metaphoric modes of language (the creative power of "as" and "like") is confronted with the "as it is," and in such confrontation the fictions of desire are unveiled as evasions of a truth which is generally represented in Stevens as everywhere and always hostile to human being. Implicitly identified with the "as it is," or nonlinguistic state of things as they are, "truth" and the classical conception of reality are often called into question by Stevens as fictions. At the close of *Notes toward a Supreme Fiction,* in a moment of apparent ontological breakthrough and contact, he "names" reality "flatly" his "fat girl."[5] But with exquisite self-consciousness of metaphor he tells us that he "finds" her (a realist's favorite verb) only in "difference" (a key poststructuralist term that carries the most devastating criticism yet known of realism, traditional conceptions of representation, and mimetic poetics). The "fat girl" is no more than a "rational distortion." Yet his point (there is no "literal" or "proper" meaning by which to judge metaphoric deviance) may be set aside. The main tradition of Stevens criticism is correct: "truth" and "reality" are terms in Stevens that *tend* to stand for that objectively knowable lump of thereness—a conception close to what Frye calls our "environment"—which awaits metamorphosis on the blue guitar.

The structure of Stevens's thought and of the entire fictionalist theoretical tradition on its conservative side is radically dualistic and very often paranoid:

> From this the poem springs: that we live in a place
> That is not our own, and much more, not ourselves. . . .[6]

Reality, as alien being, is a "violence" which ever pressures us, as he put it in a well-known formulation,[7] and the imagination is the response of our subjective violence which presses back against an inhuman chaos. Imagination makes space between us and chaos and thereby grants momentary release from sure engulfment, madness, and death. With reality so horribly privileged, fictions may be understood as heroic evasions, but they may also be seen as pitifully unheroic lies: perhaps the projections of a secular humanism's man-god; or perhaps just the escapist fantasies of those without sufficient courage to face the facts. Stevens had difficulty deciding whether his was a poetics of courage and high risk, or simply a poetics of cowardice; this indecision generates a highly playful, self-conscious, and hypothetical sort of discourse which constantly tests both stances as it oscillates between belief and skepticism, fiction and reality, the longed-for lands and chaos. But Stevens's dominant tendency to align truth and reality with an inhuman chaos "outside" human consciousness and human discourse produces an antipoetics whose constant lament and wearisome message is the futility of all human effort. The young man may dance nakedly in a ring on a Sunday morning, but the older man, increasingly denied delights of the flesh, and increasingly aware of the tragic meaning of the pigeon's flight, "downward to darkness," turns repeatedly to self-ironic celebration of the illusory efficacy of the human imagination. In the wake of a certain reading of Nietzsche, romantic humanism rushes toward its finale of despair.

Stevens is not quite the dramatic alternative to Frye that he appeared to be a decade or so back. Both Stevens and Frye imply systems of last-ditch humanism in which human desire, conscious of itself as "lack," to cite Sartre's term, and conscious of the ontological nothingness of its images, confronts a grim reality which at every point denies us our needs: "not to have is the beginning of desire/To have what is not is its ancient cycle."[8] Our "environment" is alien, but—here is the silver lining in this dark cloud—its very alien quality beckons forth our creative impulses to make substitutive fictive worlds. Yet the difference of Frye and Stevens on the pivotal place of desire is as impressive as their coincidence. In Frye's system desire finally overwhelms ("swallows") all exteriority. Sometime not very long after the primal face-off of consciousness and the inhuman environment, consciousness takes over. Reality in itself, after it receives its initial "formal" humanization, is put forever out of play and—in spite of some inconsistency on the point in his discussion of satire and demonic imagery—comes to occupy the peculiar limbo state of the Kantian *ding an sich*. (Though out of reach, it is yet reality, somehow, which confers the value of freedom upon the constructed worlds of desire.) Hence again the justice of Meyer Abrams's charge of monism: Frye's is a one-term system which permits literary structures to draw upon, imitate, and displace one another, but never to move outside of the literary universe. In Frye there is no exit from what Stevens called the "world of words."

If Frye is the better neo-Kantian, then Stevens is much the truer existentialist. Frye's dominant theme is the celebration of the potentially unqualified freedom of the mind's structuring capacities, as in its anagogic phase the poetic consciousness ingests the natural order of things; Stevens's dominant theme is the stubborn independence, the final freedom of being from mind and the priority of natural existence over consciousness. As he puts it in "The Connoisseur of Chaos": "The squirming facts exceed the squamous mind. . . ."[9] Stevens's poetics is a two-term system where fiction and reality engage in endless and complex play in which one term, while open to qualification by the other, always successfully resists subsumption by its opponent. So that if Frye's mythic structures are perfectly "closed" to existential reality, then Stevens's fictions would appear to be "open"—which is a way of saying that Frye's myths are spatially isolated, while Stevens's fictions participate in and are subject to the flowing of time. (The title of the second section of *Notes toward a Supreme Fiction* is "It Must Change.") What presumably guarantees the openness of fictions to time is the severe and harassing master, self-consciousness, the governing third force in Stevens's system which enables desiring consciousness to step away from itself and watch its fictive projections fail to enclose the real in its transformative vision. Frye lacks this principle of self-consciousness: Kermode charges him with forgetting the "fictiveness of all fictions." With Stevens self-consciousness is a key to his vogue, for in it, or so it seemed, the tenacious hold of aestheticism on the American critical mind was finally broken as fictions were opened to all the contamination of unliterary temporality, to history in an inclusive sense.

2

In its theoretical portions *The Sense of an Ending* gives us direct, though not always intentional, access to the problems as well as the perspectives of a conservative fictionalism. It does so most starkly, perhaps, in its contradictory impulses to unite fictive satisfactions with cognitive necessities. One way of grasping the fundamental difficulties of the position that Kermode is summing up is to notice his floating valuation of those key terms that appear to generate the entire position. At one level of implication the basic antithesis of fiction and reality results in the granting to fiction of apparently good things like structure, order, a concordant temporality, and a world of pure contemplation where all ideas can be entertained without consequence because their ideological nuances are neutered by the play of the fictive mode itself. (The latest generation of Yale New Critics will call this the self-deconstructive quality of the poetic text.) Against these values of "fiction" stand the qualities of "reality": disorder, chaos, a discordant temporality without beginning or end, and a world of praxis where ideas always embody the consequences of repressive ideology. Yet no sooner is this neoidealist, fictive act of consciousness privileged as an act of freedom from the determining forces of reality, than it is quickly deprivileged by an existentialist investment which sees fictive arrangements of being as impoverished in the face of being itself. Fictions become lies, fantasies, pregiven paradigms whose imposition upon experience constitutes a massive act of "bad faith," a turning of human being into an illusion of what Sartre called the *en soi*.

Early on Kermode tells us that "I shall be talking not only about the persistence of fictions but about their truth, and also about their decay. There is a question, also, of our growing suspicions of fictions in general. But it seems that we still need them. Our poverty—to borrow that rich concept from Wallace Stevens—is great enough, in a world which is not our own. . . ."[10] And again: "Right down at the root, they [fictions] must correspond to a basic human need, they must make sense, give comfort."[11] Everywhere fictions are charged with this double and generally self-contradictory mission: to discover the truth of the "*real*" as well as to "escape"; to "recognize" and "pay adequate respect" to "real" time, the time of the world, *and* to inform mere successiveness ("one damn thing after another") with the Aristotelian literary necessity of temporal beginning, middle, and end; or, finally, in a most exquisite contradiction, to assert a right to an "arbitrary" and "private" norm—what is a private norm?—while maintaining a responsibility to communication.[12] Now we know that though the truth is sometimes consoling it is not in its nature to be so, especially in a binary system in which we find the eternal opposition of fiction and reality. For Kermode (he is more single-minded on this than Stevens) reality is no fiction: it is the given which we do not create and cannot really change, but which we may discover if we can somehow slough off our fiction-making consciousness. Reality is truth *because* we do not create it; our fictions are lies just *because* they are constructions of our consciousness. In a system where all is fiction except reality, it is inevitable that our highest values will be aligned with what we take to be the real, because fictions, in this view, cannot in an ultimate analysis stand up as "serious." However much we may need and value them, fictions will never quite be respectable unless they do what in their very nature they cannot and must not do: give us some sort of mimetic access to the real.

Kermode's difficulties with fictions are not peculiarly his, but are endemic to his tradition. Nor is he unaware of these difficulties: when he reminds us of the "operational validity" of the gas chambers he underscores dramatically the dangers of the pragmatist's solution to the question of truth.[13] His major move (in his silent debate with Frye and mythical thinking) is an attempt to convert his epistemological problem into an advantage by claiming, in so many words, that the contradiction within the fictionalist position is its greatest strength. In the rigorous idealism of Kantian theorists of myth and symbolic form, all questions of exteriority and of extrasubjective constraints are put out of play. Kermode, by contrast, wants to claim that fictions, properly projected and properly understood, manage to convey those values of temporal openness which keep us in touch with common experience (they "make sense") while also achieving the immensely satisfactory concordances of beginnings and ends which close fictions off from "reality" (by which Kermode appears to mean a temporality without beginning or end).[14] Though at one point he explicitly cites as a source for fictionalism Kant's notion that the knowing subject "prescribe[s] laws to nature,"[15] he cannot be a faithful Kantian (nor would he want to be) and must insist, in his key distinction between fiction and myth, that we somehow retain the freedom to step outside of the law-giving action of consciousness and the paradigms it imposes upon things. This "stepping outside" occurs in an act of self-consciousness, in which mythic structures are taken apart—presumably by the myth-maker himself, in the very process of myth-making—and shown to be fictions. The self-conscious myth-maker is a fictionalist capable of writing *King Lear*, while the unself-conscious myth-maker is a moral degenerate capable of a violent anti-Semitism. Kermode puts it this way:

> We have to distinguish between myths and fictions. Fictions can degenerate into myth whenever they are not consciously held to be fictive. In this sense anti-Semitism is a degenerate fiction, a myth; and *Lear* is a fiction. Myth operates within the diagrams of ritual, which presupposes total and adequate explanations of things as they are and were; it is a sequence of radically unchangeable gestures. Fictions are for finding things out, and they change as the needs of sense-making change. Myths are the agents of stability, fictions the agents of change. Myths call for absolute, fictions for conditional assent.[16]

It is not difficult to see in this passage the fictionalist's bill of particulars against Northrop Frye. Fictions are heuristic devices, lenses which we freely put on and take off. Myths are full-fledged Kantian structures: like the forms of sensibility, time and space, or like the twelve categories of understanding, myths are the irremovable lenses of vision which determine the shape of the phenomenal world. Because of our freedom to remove ourselves from fictional perspective we can hold fictions *as fictive*, we can self-consciously assent to them on a conditional basis; whereas with myth (again on the analogy of the Kantian categories) we have no choice but to assent absolutely, since we are locked into the categories of myth as culturally and historically transcendent universals which posit exhaustively the possible modes of human desire.

As for the justice of Kermode's charge that myth posits a "sequence of radically unchangeable gestures," we need only recall Frye's Viconian recurrences—his fixed set of characters, his firmly stipulated modalities of plot, and, once again, this definition of tragedy: "Whether the context is Greek, Christian, or undefined tragedy seems to lead up to an epiphany of law, of that which is and must be."[17] The modesty of "seems" in Frye's statement is betrayed by the prognostication that his formula will reach into as yet "undefined" cultural contexts. Myths are essentially conservative, they are "agents of stability," while fictions with their presumed ability to engage a world outside themselves are radical "agents of change." But the distinction is drawn too sharply: mythic and fictional structures alike derive from an expressive, or formative act of consciousness, and for this reason fictions are as closed off, *as fictions*, from mimetic access to the real as myth is. Fictions and myths are alike nonmimetic creations of order. The real distinction lies not in the fiction per se as a vehicle of cognition, but in the self-conscious way it is held, in the overall intentionality within which fictions are given to us. There is something misleading and even cruel in Kermode's citing of anti-Semitism (a projection of death onto others) as his example of mythical thought and *King Lear* (which involves us in our own end) as the example of fictional thinking. For anti-Semitism can be held fictively, as well, as long as one encases the virulence in tonally playful discourse—attaches an "as if" here, a "so to speak" there—and as long as one does not attempt to consummate one's fictions about Jews by murdering six million of them. It is the principle of self-consciousness and not anything in the structure of the fiction itself which is the true desideratum. Self-consciousness is the ultimately privileged agent that presumably frees fictions from the inhuman (constitutive) tendencies of mythicism—it permits us to reform temporality along the comforting literary lines of Aristotelian necessity while in the same act it encourages us to recognize the real time of the world in its frightening and unredeemable successiveness. Self-consciousness, in other words, draws the line between wish and actuality and in so doing (so this argument runs) confers the desired moral quality of humaneness upon us since it ensures that in the long run we will let the "other" be in its otherness.

It is characteristic of conservative fictionalism in its theoretical maneuvers to set up an apparently rigid dualism of fiction and reality and then attempt to break down that dualism in an act of self-consciousness. Kermode's treatment of temporality as *chronos* and *kairos* is an example of this theoretical strategy.[18] As "passing time," as "time which shall be no more," "pure successiveness," *chronos* is the sort of time "which we feel to be the chief characteristic in the ordinary going-on of time." As a "norm" of reality *chronos* is the truth of a world without beginning or end. *Kairos,* as Kermode puts it in an unguarded moment, is an "escape" from mere chronicity. We turn to *kairos,* or "fictive time," because *kairos* is time "filled with significance," charged with meaning derived from its relation to both origin and end. But as usual Kermode cannot be satisfied with a simple dualism: *kairos* as such is fantasized time, mere escape from the truth of *chronos*. *Kairos* cannot in itself satisfy the mature mind: "Men in the middest make considerable imaginative investments in coherent patterns which, by the provision of an end, make possible a satisfying consonance with the origins and with the middle. . . . But they also, when awake and sane, feel the need to show a marked respect for things as they are: so that there is a recurring need for adjustments in the interest of reality as well as of control."[19] The problems of a conservative fictionalism continue to multiply: we initially make fictions because reality and truth are not satisfying and fictions supply us with comfort, "give some show of satisfaction to the mind, wherein the nature of things doth seem to deny it." But a person of psychic competence and clear-sighted vision (Kermode's terms are "sane" and "awake") apparently "needs" truth and reality ("the nature of things") as much as he "needs" fictions. Kermode's easy mixing of references to Kant, Nietzsche, and Francis Bacon is probably the best indication of the ambition of fictionalist theory as well as a sign of the violent contradiction that it tries to keep together.[20] At some point truth and reality, however terrifying, are comforting as well. Like fictions in general, *kairoi*, "historical moments of intemporal significance," must be opened to the time of the world. To live in the time made by novels, to escape existential time, where (in Sartre's words) "what I was is not the foundation of what I am, any more than what I am is the foundation of what I shall be": to do this is to sink into the inauthenticities of *mauvaise foi*.[21]

3

It is perhaps worthwhile to step back for a moment from Kermode's distillation of the themes and contradictions of conservative fictionalism and take another look at the philosophical crisis out of which fictionalism was born. Probably the first thing to be noticed is that the source generally cited for the position, Kant's "Copernican" revolution in epistemology, though it likely made the position inevitable, is misleading in the longer perspective. The ultimate source for this philosophical problem, as for most, is the Platonic privileging of being over the lies of poetic thought; the commonplace segregation of fiction and reality since Plato proves well enough that poetics has great difficulty escaping the ancient opposition. It must be granted that Kant's assault on ontology appeared to give the advantage to the fictionalists in their long-standing argument with the Platonists: Kant elevated the human subject in the cognitive process as he banished realist perspectives in ontology and epistemology, and Kermode picks up on this when he notes the "law-giving" powers of consciousness. But in the long run Kant intended no radical philosophical move, though he may have implied one, as Nietzsche would urge with not a little relish.[22]

Kant's knowing subject is not a historical being. The act of creating the phenomenal world from the formal categories of consciousness is governed by the intersubjective and cross-cultural nature of those categories and (by implication) of the consciousness which houses them. Determined by the structural nature of consciousness, and not subject to the tamperings of history, volition, and feeling, Kant's phenomenal world, though it may not be supported by the sort of being imagined in classical ontology, claims the prerogatives of reality in the classical sense. It is permanent; it is the normative context against which (as truth) all of our perceptions are measured. Among all of the productions of consciousness it occupies the place of the real. Within these epistemological perspectives Kant's aesthetic, at those critical points where it meditates on the function of art, is not much more than a happy repetition of Plato's attack on mimesis. When he terms the representation of imagination, in its aesthetic phase, an "aesthetic idea,"[23] he means for us to recall the key distinction of *ideas* and *concepts*. The latter as "forms," because they find adequate "content" in the sensuous manifold, yield the cognitive shapes of experience; the former, as forms of pure reason ("rational ideas") which cannot be satisfied in time, and cannot be adequately filled out with the sensuous data of "intuition," point beyond the limits of experience and are, from these perspectives, "fictions" in the sense that they produce no cognition of the phenomenal world. In the cognitive privilege given to the "concept" over the "idea" we see the surreptitious back-door entry of ontological realism into Kant's system: the concept gives knowledge because, as a realist would insist, its formation begins in, and is respectful of, a passive reception of the manifold.

At the very base of his epistemology, therefore, Kant's consistent strategy of dividing each portion of the cognitive process into a privileged *a priori* and an empirical dimension is reversed. For though intuition has its pure side (the forms of space and time are prior to experience and an initial basis of organizing the manifold), the true origin of cognition is a "perception" in the passive sense, "a certain affection of the mind" mediated by our sensibility. In other words, pure intuition is an organizing force without a mission unless it has something to organize. As "form" the concept must be a perfect fit for the synthesized sensory data which is offered to it. As "content" the synthesis of sensory data must be perfectly contained and exhausted by the form into which it is directed. Because they have this mutually conditioning, dialectical, or interdeterminative relationship (what Kant meant by "schematization"), the concept is not empty and the percept not blind. The "rational idea" (God, freedom, immortality), to extend the metaphor, *is* empty because it is many sizes too big for the sensory data it would envelop; and the "aesthetic idea" is epistemologically blind because as an unconstrained sensory synthesis, an exuberant reveling in the senses, it bursts through the conceptual frame which would contain it and give it phenomenal focus.[24]

By aesthetic idea, then, Kant means something close to a pure spontaneity, an unconditioned synthesis of sensory data which does not owe subservience to the concept. An aesthetic idea is the formal product of an act of consciousness which, in his words, is "free" and "independent of natural determination."[25] So Kant's statement that the aesthetic idea "occasions much thought, without however any definite thought, . . . any *concept*, being capable of being adequate to it"[26] is not covert urging, as some have suggested, prophetic of the neo-Coleridgean claim that art yields a special kind of knowledge; it is merely a reminder, clarified perfectly by its systemic relation to the first *Critique*, which says that art yields no knowledge and is by its very nature incapable of so doing. What makes art itself denies art the honor of being a form of knowledge.

Despite the claims of a number of neo-Kantians—particularly those impressed by Ernst Cassirer's epistemology of symbolic forms—Kant's actual legacy to modern poetics clearly contradicts the apologies for poetry often made in his name. The imagination, he says in the third *Critique*, is "very powerful in creating another nature . . . out of the material that actual nature gives it." But my ellipsis deliberately omits what neo-Kantians tend to forget: Kant's insertion of self-consciousness, his awareness of metaphoric overextension, communicated by "as it were" (*gleichsam einer andern Natur*), which would rule out flatly special ontological status for art.[27] The alternative nature is a fiction in the debilitating sense handed down to us from Plato and neoclassical aesthetics: "We entertain ourselves with it [*wir unterhalten uns mit ihr*] when experience becomes too commonplace and by it we remold experience. . . ."[28] In telling us that art does not *mold*, but rather *remolds*, Kant trivializes what those in his tradition would empower against a culture all too ready to denigrate fictions as a holiday from our "serious" transactions with the world. His intention of isolating the distinctive character of the aesthetic experience was admirable, but his analysis resulted in mere isolation. By barring that experience from the truth of the phenomenal world, while allowing art's fictional world entertainment value, he became the philosophical father of an enervating aestheticism which ultimately subverts what it would celebrate.

The "nature" created by the imagination (the quotations around the term indicate not only that it is Kant's term but also that he intends for us to take it "only" as metaphor, as deviation from a "proper" meaning), this "nature" "surpasses" actual nature; but in Kant's system it is that which is surpassed (the phenomenally "real"), that which is "remolded," that is privileged as normative, as essentially untouched by the fictions of imagination. The place "outside" of art encloses, defines, and judges fictions as pleasant lies generated out of boredom, fantasies which briefly block out the phenomenal reality to which we all, as serious, rational persons, shall return when we regain our courage. Kant could not have revealed the intention of his aesthetics more candidly than when he termed the "free play" of the imagination "arbitrary" and the activity of understanding "lawful."[29] Poetry, which he regarded as the strongest expression of the aesthetic movement of imagination, "declares itself to be mere entertaining play of the imagination . . . it does not desire to steal upon and ensnare the understanding."[30] Perhaps a way of glossing Kant's view of poetry is to say that within poetic discourse the faculty of self-consciousness comes overtly into the game, and as it does (this is poetry's great strength) it declares play to be only play, fiction to be distinct from reality, and "understanding" to be uncontaminated by the vision of imagination. In its sensuous feigning of the rational ideas, those mythological conceptions of metaphysical totality and finality like God, the soul, and the noumenal world, Kant's aesthetic idea institutes within its auditor an unresolvable dialectic of guilt and desire that will characterize the entire conservative tradition of fictionalism: "guilt" because we recognize our indulgence in art as mere play, a holiday from the real business of our cognitive and ethical life; "desire" because the aesthetic idea is a representation of that for which we eternally yearn but can never have in human time—a way it will never be.

It is common among poststructuralists to cite Nietzsche's later writing in such texts as *Beyond Good and Evil* and in the posthumously published notebooks, *The Will to Power*, as a radicalization of the Kantian insights—prefiguring a move beyond humanism—which calls into question the privileged place of the categories and the phenomenal reality which they posit. In poststructuralist perspectives, Kant's epistemological categories are judged as elitist fictions whose function it is to suppress (as fantasies, as entertainment) alternative modes of consciousness. Paul de Man has recently argued that even *The Birth of Tragedy* is no existentialist document but a full anticipation of *The Will to Power*.[31] Yet the earlier Nietzsche occupies a secure place in the tradition of conservative fictionalism. In *The Birth of Tragedy* the opposition of Apollo to Dionysius is a homological reflection of Kant's opposition of aesthetic idea to phenomenal reality. The crucial turn in post-Kantian thought represented by *The Birth of Tragedy* is a turn back to ontology—and to an ontology of terror at that.

For the Dionysian impulse, as Nietzsche tells it, makes reference to the ground of being itself and unveils its truth. The Dionysian artist shows us that "hidden" at the "core" of all things, just beneath the "veil of Maya," of "fair illusion" imposed by Apollonian consciousness to protect us from the dreadful wisdom of Silenus (best not to have been born; second best, to die quickly), hidden by means of illusions "strenuously and zestfully entertained," is "original pain," the "ever-suffering," chaotic and "contradictory" nature of things.[32] It is the function of the Apollonian artist to distance us psychically from dangerous commerce with the ground of being. (Kermode echoes Nietzsche this way: "It is not that we are connoisseurs of chaos, but that we are surrounded by it, and equipped for coexistence with it only by our fictive powers.")[33] But the word is "distance," not "banish," for banishment occurs only much later in Nietzsche's story when Socrates, or more precisely, the Socratic principle, exiles Dionysius and thereby condemns us to the grand self-delusion of theoretical man who lives by the idea that his thought has priority over being, that rational consciousness may "correct" and finally do away with the primordial condition of original pain, "the eternal core of things."[34] The "fair world of Apollo and its substratum, the terrible wisdom of Silenus . . . mutually require one another."[35] Cut loose from a dialectical "co-existence" with Dionysius, Apollo leads us into self-blinded illusion, illusion which does not know itself to be illusion. Apollo, then, minus the self-consciousness forced upon him by the paranoid awareness of "perpetual military encampment," by the "titanic and barbaric menace of Dionysius," gives birth to Socrates.[36]

We are permitted the pleasures of Kant's "aesthetic idea" and Nietzsche's Apollonian impulse only so long as we do not, in Nietzsche's words, become "pathological,"[37] or, in Kant's words, allow our understanding to be "ensnared," or, in the style of Stevens and Kermode, allow our self-consciousness of fiction as fiction to be extinguished in absolute assent. For Nietzsche, Dionysian vision is the necessary normative context out of which the judgment of fiction's fictionality issues, just as the perspectives of phenomenal reality in Kant isolate the aesthetic idea as aesthetic idea. But there is this difference: in early Nietzsche, the Dionysian judgment upon fiction, since it is delivered from being, from a presumed purchase upon the "core of things" (Kant's inaccessible ding an sich), can claim an even more repressive privilege for itself than Kant could claim for the phenomenal. In a classic strategy of existentialist thought, Dionysian being (chaos, the irrational, pain, evil, the loss of the principium individuationis) is given priority over the clean well-lighted places of Apollonian thought. In Nietzsche's analysis of Raphael's Transfiguration, the figures toward the bottom of the painting—contorted, helpless, full of pain and despair—assume the burden of truth and reality; while the transcending Christ, with eyes massively dilated, and face transfigured by a consciousness of grace, becomes an antithetical image to everything else in the existential landscape of the painting: this Christ must represent the fantastical lie of Christianity.[38] But whether from a Kantian awareness of phenomenal reality, or a Nietzschean vision of the irrational foundation of things, the fiction is finally trivialized. At its best the fiction may claim the honors of self-consciousness, of knowing its own epistemological and ontological worthlessness. What serenity, we need to ask ourselves, can we purchase from a self-consciousness of the impotence of fantasy in the face of truth? In the paradigmatic shift from Kant's idealism to Nietzsche's existentialism we begin to understand the urgency (if not the logic) with which modernist poets and theorists speak of fictions: Kant had suggested that phenomenal reality might become boring—"commonplace" [alltäglich] was his word. In Nietzsche something more is at stake.

4

In the late 1940s and through the 1950s Jean-Paul Sartre had an appreciable impact on American writers of fiction; Norman Mailer, even in his most recent phase, continues to characterize himself an "existentialist." Sartre has had, however, but two major disciples in literary theory in this country: Murray Krieger and Paul de Man. Beyond reinforcing (in tandem with Albert Camus, who was easier to grasp) a thematic criticism with a certain vaguely felt tragic sense of life, and beyond providing a few catch words and phrases that the au courant in the years of Dwight Eisenhower and John Kennedy could not do without, Sartre's major early work has not made much of a difference in the general practice of literary criticism in the United States, even though the key text, L'Imaginaire (1940), was available in English as early as 1948 as The Psychology of Imagination. And his major late work, the Critique of Dialectical Reason, has yet to figure in contemporary American debate on literary theory.[39] "Nausea," "anguish," "pour soi," "en soi," "freedom," "nothingness," "existence precedes essence"—such terms, and the affective ambience which they evoke, seem now either antiquated, the lingo of a previous century, or embarrassingly self-pitying, or both. The Sartre of the brilliantly "situated" historical criticism of the last sections of What is Literature?, the Sartre of Marxian disposition in the Critique of Dialectical Reason, may yet enjoy a triumphant day in America, but the earlier writer is as quaint now as the attitudes of the generation who matured with Joseph McCarthy and the Bomb, and who elected (at their most liberal) politicians of tough cool who copied out certain significant quotations from Ernest Hemingway.

It is unfortunate that the earlier Sartre did not make the impact on American literary critics that he deserved to make, because his early work is as mature and unflinching an articulation of conservative fictionalism as we have. For it is in Sartre that we can see more clearly than any place else how fictionalism, even when overtly tied to existentialism, is not the break with aestheticism and its principles of enclosure that Kermode thought it to be. Fictionalism, when held honestly, is a resolute aestheticism which brought certain nineteenth-century philosophical traditions to a conclusion. Just how central *The Psychology of Imagination* is to fictionalism and to Sartre's early thought emerges with the full exposition of his existential phenomenology, *Being and Nothingness*. And vice versa: Sartre's fundamental distinction between those two antithetical regions denoted by the title, the *en soi* (nonhuman being) and the *pour soi* (human reality, consciousness), can be seen, from the perspectives developed in the earlier book, as the culminating opposition of a philosophy which might better be called existential aestheticism. For the definition of the *pour soi* rests on a notion of freedom that owes more to Kant and Schiller than it does to its obvious sources in Hegel and Heidegger.

In a would-be modification of the traditional dualism that we have seen asserted about fictions and reality, Sartre asserts the phenomenological objectivity[40] (as intentional object) of the "not me," a move which fundamentally characterizes his existentialism against idealist and empiricist philosophies. But in his claim that the phenomenon is "transcendent," that the "being of the phenomenon . . . surpasses the knowledge which we have of it" ("the foundation of being . . . cannot itself be subject to the percipi; it must be transphenomenal"),[41] and in his desire to avoid the phenomenalist error, Sartre appears to place the *en soi* in a partial hiddenness and to institute a severe Cartesian dualism between consciousness and an *out there* that is *out of reach*. Contrary to the premises, derived from Husserl and Heidegger, of his phenomenological assault on the dualisms of traditional philosophy ("none of them is privileged,"[42] he tells us), Sartre, in a tortured argument, appears to reprivilege that world behind the scene which with Nietzsche he had thought to have forever banished. He replaces the dualism of being and appearance with a dualism of the "finite and the infinite":

> Although an object may disclose itself only through a single *Abschattung*, the sole fact of there being a subject implies

> the possibility of multiplying the points of view on that *Abschattung.* . . . What appears in fact is only an aspect of the object, and the object is altogether *in* that aspect and altogether outside of it. It is altogether *within*, in that it manifests itself . . . as the structure of the appearance, which is at the same time the principle of the series. It is altogether outside, for the series itself will never appear nor can it appear. Thus the outside is opposed in a new way to the inside, and the being-which-does-not-appear, to the appearance.[43]

Sartre's phenomenology forces him to reject classical ontology—his standpoint is within "appearance"—but his existentialism, more strongly felt, compromises his Husserlian heritage. Commitment to the priority of being over consciousness demands that being not be wholly subject to consciousness as the condition of its revelation; being *must* be banished, in some crucial part, behind the scene. If the whole of "appearance" cannot appear—this is his version of the classical "outside"—by what right can he call it "appearance"?

Sartre is aware of the problem and that is why he defensively inserts into his argument the following remark: "That does not mean that being is found *hidden behind* phenomena. . . ." Yet that is what in essence his argument does mean and what is implied by the naked contradiction of his conclusion: "What is implied by the preceding considerations is that the being of the phenomenon although coextensive with the phenomenon, cannot be subject to the phenomenal condition. . . ."[44] That which is not subject to the phenomenal condition cannot, at the same time, be coextensive with the phenomenon; a phenomenologist who is not really a secret ontologist cannot know what is not subject to the phenomenal condition. The carefully formulated phenomenological dualism of finite and infinite gives way to a more traditional (realist) ontological formulation, a slippage perhaps best explained by Sartre's desire to have it both ways, to avoid what he saw as the idealist error of Husserl (who made the being of the phenomenon absolutely subject to the phenomenal condition) while at the same time orienting himself within the Husserlian standpoint. So consciousness, an empty spontaneity for Sartre, not only in its intentionality implies a world ("consciousness in its inmost nature is a relationship to a transcendent being —a non-conscious and transphenomenal being"), but this transphenomenal being, which he calls the in-itself, has for its primary characteristic a quality of never revealing itself completely to consciousness: the for-itself and in-itself are "two closed totalities."[45] Not quite closed, however; despite his Cartesian severities, Sartre, like most dualists, cheats a little and tells us everything that we need to know but presumably cannot know about the in-itself. The subtitle for *Being and Nothingness, An Essay in Phenomenological Ontology,* contains an oxymoron which seems resolvable, in the end, in classical directions.

The massive, opaque thereness of the in-itself, in all of its fearfulness, comes out of hiding in the imagery of *Nausea.*[46] In moments reminiscent of conventional romantic vision when the "veil is torn away," the antihero, Antoine Roquentin, is shocked out of the quotidian sleep of his consciousness into a new awareness of the "viscous puddle of existence" which "floods over" and beyond the grasp of consciousness and its naming power; objects simply "spring up," they start "existing in your hand." It is in these experiences (*Nausea* is organized around such moments) that we recognize that "existence had suddenly unveiled itself. It had lost the harmless look of an abstract category." What we come to grasp in the moment of unveiling is that the rationalistic maneuvers of consciousness and the linguistic perspectives which they enforce are tricks that keep the truth hidden: "the world of explanations and reasons is not the world of existence." We recognize that our spatializing habits of closing things off from one another in neat little conceptual boxes have blinded us. The basic image is of the loss of our autonomy and of our human difference from a suffocating ontological flow, from the "soft monstrous masses"—an image perhaps ultimately evocative of sexual violation: "Existence is not something which lets itself be thought of from a distance; it must invade you suddenly, master you, weigh heavily on your head like a giant motionless beast. . . ." With all private spaces penetrated, we come to feel our contingency (*pour soi*), come to feel that we are "in the way," that human reality is always perilously on the verge of being swallowed up, or of falling back into nonhuman reality (*en soi*).

If being in-itself is so massive a priority, how does the for-itself arise, and what is it? Again Sartre's metaphors are helpful: the for-itself is a "primitive upsurge" from the in-itself, a "cleavage" or rupture in the in-itself.[47] Being in-itself, as pure identity, "full positivity"—it is wholly what it is—mysteriously gives birth to a type of being (the for-itself) which is different from itself, is what it is not.[48] The for-itself is being not in possession of its essence,[49] a "lack," a "nothingness," a "hole" in being which Sartre calls freedom and which he believes to be the foundation of human reality.[50] As freedom, human reality is necessarily a "permanent rupture in determinism," a disengagement from being in-itself which forces human reality to exist in a perpetual state of "indetermination."[51] In its "refusal of the world" human being disrupts the causal chain: "Being can generate only being and if man is enclosed in this process of generation only being will come out of him. . . ."[52] What we call human reality is not so enclosed: it rises to the status of the for-itself as it retires into a nothingness (the foundation of all acts of negation) beyond the in-itself, as the sort of being that is "fissured": the "being of consciousness does not coincide with itself in a full equivalence."[53] Unlike being in-itself, which in an important image is evoked as a plenitude, "a perfect equivalence of content to container,"[54] a space utterly full, the for-itself is captured in an image of radical temporality: it is being always on the way to itself. The act which defines human reality as the putting into question of being by being is an act which can occur only from outside the in-itself, only from outside the naturalistic prison in the nothingness that is freedom. Unlike the German romantics whose themes he has extended, Sartre tells us that there is no staged process, no "education," in the sense that Schiller and Frye attach to the term, whereby human reality comes into being as freedom. Human reality is freedom, all at once, and it is always poised against and outside of the in-itself which is a realm of perfect unfreedom, of full determination: "Man does not exist *first* in order to be free *subsequently*; there is no difference between the being of man and his *being-free*."[55] But in telling us this about freedom (that it has no derivation), Sartre drops his metaphor of "upsurge" and returns to a presiding metaphor of dualism which does not require the in-itself to be an "origin."

In "The Love Song of J. Alfred Prufrock" the protagonist says that he should have been a "pair of ragged claws/Scuttling across the floors of silent seas." It is a moment of Sartrean nostalgia, of the primordial desire of consciousness to fill its "lack" or "hole" with being, to complete itself in permanent fixed essence: "What the for-itself lacks," Sartre concludes, is the impossible (Hegelian) combination, "itself as an in-itself."[56] We return to what is basic to Sartre's thought: a metaphorics of desire which posits a lost origin and an eternal yearning for its recovery. Sartre is so difficult, so obscure at this level because he is juggling two (though not equiprimordial) origins. The for-itself as lack seeks the plenitude of the origin: the "upsurge" wants to fall back into its matrix. The for-itself is itself, however, a kind of origin, the "origin of temporality." Lack, or desire, as origin of temporality, is poised just a hair the other side of the motion that it sets going, not really subject to it but determining it as a directedness. The for-itself appears also *to be* radical temporality in that it is defined everywhere in Sartre as the movement of possibility, the being, in Heidegger's terms, which is always ahead of itself, without origin or end—never a container.[57] Temporality is not a "law of development which is imposed on being from without."[58] But Sartre's definition of desire as the "origin of temporality"—a "nothingness which separates human reality from itself is at the origin of time"[59]—is precisely a "law of development which is imposed on being from without." Like the "fictions" within the conservative tradition which must always, at bottom, be read as evasions, so the for-itself must inevitably live inauthentically because it seeks to terminate its purely temporal status by achieving primordial spatiality as an in-itself, a totality which in its plenitude would banish the desiring being which exists as temporal possibility.

Unself-conscious *mauvaise foi*, however, is an impossibility: we will always be aware in some corner of our consciousness that we cannot be what desire prompts us to be, and that our temporality is irredeemable. We do not live in a temporality with concordant beginning, middle, and end, though we may and do, as Kermode argues, project fictions in such terms. Insofar as desire (Sartre foreshadows Frye here) stands outside of temporality as origin and governor of the movement of temporality—in the sense of the "classical center," as Derrida calls it, which, situated outside of structurality, may govern structurality without being subject to it—then Sartre's key philosophical contention is contradicted: desire is absence, an essence without "content" which precedes existence and drives human being teleologically to the promised end of the in-itself—ironically, to nonhuman being. Nowhere is the contradiction more clearly in evidence than in Sartre's explanation of the emergence of freedom in anguish; his best illustration is the situation of writing:

> I discover that the permanent possibility of abandoning
> the book is the very condition of the possibility of writing
> it and the very meaning of my freedom. It is necessary
> that in the very constitution of the book as my possibility,
> I apprehend my freedom as being the possible destroyer
> in the present and in the future of what I am. . . . The book
> . . . is conceived neither as necessary nor contingent. It
> is only the permanent, remote meaning in terms of which
> I can understand what I am writing in the present, and
> hence, it is conceived as *being*; that is, only by positing
> the book as the existing basis on which my present, exist-
> ing sentence emerges, can I confer a determined meaning
> upon my sentence.[60]

If we substitute, as Sartre appears to be encouraging us to do, the for-itself for "what I am writing in the present," and, further, if we substitute the in-itself for the plenitude of meaning called "the book," then it must be concluded that desire imposes closure or "determination" upon the for-itself, upon what is presumably a "permanent disruption in determinism." A "perpetual state of indetermination" is forced by the nature of the for-itself (as yearning) to live in self-conscious bad faith, knowing that the fulfillments of desire are fictions which compromise our human reality, and that the processes of existential choice-making, in writing or in other areas, are teleologies which close down the free-play of possibilities and subvert our anguished freedom as writers and other beings-in-the-world. To return to Kermode's terms: we make fictive *kairos* in order to exclude the reality of *chronos* that is forced upon us, but we fail, and we know that we fail.

Looking back to it from *Being and Nothingness*, we can recognize Sartre's account of the image and of imaginative consciousness in *The Psychology of Imagination* as the link between his existentialism and aestheticist traditions out of Kant. With unrelenting candor Sartre tells us what many in the tradition of conservative fictionalism only imply: that the fiction, or image (which he equates with beauty), is essentially unsatisfying. In a move typical of the isolationist habits of Kant and the neo-Kantians, he segregates imaginative consciousness first from conception (which produces the abstracted, or rational universe) and then from perception.[61] The latter is an existentially authentic, though limited form of cognition which takes place in a world that is "overflowing," "brimming over"[62]—a world whose characterization both recalls significant imagery from *Nausea* and foreshadows the description of transphenomenal being in *Being and Nothingness*. In perception we have an awareness of a richness of being which, because it must always exceed our cognitive powers, motivates us to *keep on* perceiving in an effort to fill out our limitations, and to make firmer contact with that world, at the periphery of perception, that is constantly "brimming over." Imaginative consciousness, however, "suffers from a sort of essential poverty": the image "teaches nothing, never produces an impression of novelty, and never reveals any new aspect of the object. . . . No risk, no anticipation: only a certainty."[63] And it is in the nature of imaginative consciousness to be aware of this impoverishment. In a nihilating act it posits the image as "non-existent"; to say "I have an image" is equivalent to saying "I see nothing."[64] In order to have an image of a tree I must first banish into nonbeing the tree of perception. Such a mode of consciousness (like the *pour soi*) enjoys, in a phrase from *Being and Nothingness*, a fundamental "right over the real."[65]

The image is further distinguished, in romantic fashion, from the sign, as the unarbitrary is distinguished from the arbitrary, the full from the empty, and an internal relationship between signifier and signified from an external relationship.[66] We recognize the dualizing habits of the romantic theorist who would privilege while distinguishing imagination from "ordinary" consciousness, symbol from allegory. Sartre does not surprise us when, later, he tells us that the "image is symbolic in essence."[67] But the imaginative consciousness knows that the fullness of the image is purchased in the act of annihilating the real; that is why it "knows a certain fullness together with a certain nothingness."[68] The fullness of the image is a fullness of illusion, not of being. The image for Sartre is (to cite Kermode's term from *Romantic Image*) "different," and in its difference it possesses all of the qualities ascribed to it by a long line of romantic thinkers—all but one: it is drained of the ontological worth given to it by a Coleridge or a Schelling. The image, like the fiction, as Sartre stresses over and over again, is a mode of thinking and as such must be devalued in the face of being. It has no environment, it is independent and isolated—but through lack, not through fullness; it acts on nothing and nothing acts on it. It is *without consequence* in the full sense of the term."[69] How clearly in Sartre's fictionalism does Plato enjoy his last revenge.

Our conventional expectation is that an existentialist will devalue the image, and Sartre never disappoints us. The debunking of the image, in fact, is a central motif in *The Psychology of Imagination*, particularly in the last hundred pages or so. In the imaginative act, Sartre tells us, "there is always something of the imperious and the infantile, a refusal to take distance or difficulties into account."[70] The image is "transcendent" and "eternal" (not good things for an existentialist devoted to *chronos*), a "congealment," not an "overflowing."[71] In comparison with the real object, the imaginative one appears "thinned" (and is) because "it has not fed on the inexhaustible depths of the real"; "the real and the imaginary cannot co-exist by their very nature."[72] Sartre's answer to fictionalists like Kermode who comfort themselves with the notion that fictions (unlike myths) make discoveries "in the middest" is that the imaginary is simply "ruined" by the real. Here is Sartre at his most unkind:

> it [the image] is not only an escape from the content of the real . . . but from the form of the real itself, its character of *presence*, the sort of response it demands of us, the adaptation of our actions to the object, the inexhaustibility of perception, their independence, the very way our feelings have of developing themselves. This unnatural, congealed, abated, formalized life, which is for most of us but a makeshift, is exactly what a schizophrenic desires.[73]

And here is Sartre at his most ethical: "In every person we love, and for the very reason of its inexhaustible wealth, there is something that surpasses us, an independence, an imperviousness which exacts ever renewed efforts of approximation: The unreal object has nothing of this imperviousness."[74] Posited out of the nothingness of our desire, fictions are recognized as the inauthentic constructions that they are. To choose to live in them is to choose to be defined by an emblem of the in-itself; it is to choose bad faith and perhaps even schizophrenia. Even so our desire continues to generate fulfilling images, even as we continue to discard them; this process of generating and discarding goes on until death, the final fulfillment of the desire of the for-itself to be the in-itself.

And yet the imagination's negation of the world is richly cherished by Sartre as the act which, because it is capable of positing reality as a synthetic whole, proves that we are free from it, that we have a point of vantage outside of the in-itself. Our taking of perspective from the vantage of nothing is the "going-beyond" which is freedom itself, "since it could not happen if consciousness were not free. Thus to posit the world as a world or to 'negate' it is one and the same thing."[75] The fruit of negation, of "producing the unreal," is that "consciousness can appear momentarily delivered from 'being-in-the-world' . . . which is the necessary condition for the imagination."[76] So it is the imagination, as Kant and so many of his followers taught, which enables us to transcend *Alltäglich*, to "escape from actuality, our preoccupations, our boredoms . . . our worldly constraints."[77] It is imagination which saves us from being "crushed," "run through" by the real; it is imagination which is the "necessary condition for the freedom of empirical man in the midst of the world";[78] it is imagination which explains that mysterious statement in *Being and Nothingness* that the for-itself is a "permanent rupture in determinism." More enthusiastically even than his very enthusiastic romantic forebears, Sartre declares, toward the end of *The Psychology of Imagination*, that imagination is not one among a number of functions within consciousness (despite the implications of his earlier analysis of perception and conception) but the foundation of consciousness, an *a priori* of perception and conception. As the nihilating power itself—we put the world of perception out of play in order to imagine—the imagination is born in that original nihilating withdrawal from the world, the "rupture" in the in-itself which allows human reality as consciousness to come into being.[79] On the penultimate page of *The Psychology of Imagination*, Sartre takes up a position that recalls Johnson, Dowson, and company:

> an entranced consciousness, engulfed in the imaginary,
> is suddenly freed by the sudden ending of the play, of the

symphony, and comes suddenly in contact with existence.
Nothing more is needed to arouse the nauseating disgust
that characterizes the consciousness of reality. . . . the real
is never beautiful. Beauty is a value applicable only to the
imaginary and which means the negation of the world
in its essential structure.[80]

The existential-phenomenological rhetoric of this Continental philosopher cannot mask the constant theme of the conservative fictionalist
who would like to leave the living to the servants, but who couldn't
respect himself if he did. I have called this the posture of existential
aestheticism; probably a better term in view of Sartre's more critical
side is, simply, guilty aestheticism.

5

Much of what we call modern (as opposed to postmodern)
in literary thought is indebted to the existentialist premises of Nietzsche
and Sartre. In Hans Vaihinger's *The Philosophy of "As If"* (in some
ways a definitive work which remained in obscurity until Kermode and
the vogue of Stevens discovered it for literary criticism), the point of
departure is fundamentally conservative Nietzschean, though all along
the way Vaihinger develops ideas that are radically fictionalist, in the
mode of Nietzsche's later writings. In spite of his good Kantian insistence that nothing can be known about reality in itself, Vaihinger
proceeds to tell us that the basic fictive or inventive activity of human
consciousness is called into play by the "assaults" upon it of a "hostile
external world": "under the compulsion of necessity, stimulated by
the outer world, it [consciousness] discovers the store of contrivances
that lie hidden within itself. The organism finds itself in a world full
of contradictory sensations . . . in contradiction and opposition consciousness awakes, and man owes his mental development more to his
enemies than to his friends."[81] "Hostile," "enemy," "assault"—the
paranoid style of fictionalist thinking in the existential mode is clear,
and it is a style taken up by a number of important modernist writers.
According to Wallace Stevens the world is a "violence" which presses
in upon us; a "preposterous pig" which must be remade, "lock, stock,
and barrel," according to W. B. Yeats; a "black and utter chaos," in
the words of Robert Frost.[82] Sartre tells us that consciousness of the
real arouses "nauseating disgust"—and, correlatively, that the real
is *never* beautiful. Instances of these notions in modern writing could
be multiplied *ad infinitum*. Kermode reflects the tradition when he implies (after Roquentin) that being is a nominalistic chaos, antagonistic

to the categories of consciousness; picking up a term from Stevens, he
tells us that reality is "poverty," that *our* world is more complex, more
difficult to live in, more frightening, more ugly, more disordered, than
the worlds of our ancestors, or of their ancestors, and certainly of *their*
ancestors. At one point he catches himself and says that it is of course
absurd to claim a uniquely terrible historical privilege for ourselves,
but later in his book he falls back into precisely that absurdity when he
tells of the terrors of "modern reality."[83] Such self-congratulation about
the plight of being a modern, such arrogance, and such self-pity is
forced upon Vaihinger, Yeats, Stevens, Sartre, Kermode, and a legion
of others by the initial opposition of fiction to reality: the posture may
be untenable, as Kermode senses, but it is the enforced conclusion of
his tradition. And it is testimony to the pervasive influence of the
position that the idea of reality as a chaos is, since Nietzsche, a casual
assumption, one of modernism's characterizing shibboleths.

Robert Frost, who was both in and out of the position, wrote one of
its most subtle critiques:

> . . . we don't need to know how bad the age is. There is
> something we can always be doing without reference to
> how good or how bad the age is. There is at least so such
> good in the world that it admits of form and the making of
> form. . . . When in doubt there is always form to go on
> with. Anyone who has achieved the least form to be sure
> of it, is lost to the larger excruciations. . . . The artist[,]
> the poet[,] might be expected to be the most aware of such
> assurance. But it is really everybody's sanity to feel it and
> live by it. Fortunately, too, no forms are more engrossing[,]
> gratifying, comforting, staying than those lesser ones we
> throw off, like vortex rings of smoke . . . a basket, a letter,
> a garden, a room, an idea, a picture, a poem. . . . The back-
> ground in hugeness and confusion shading away from where
> we stand into black and utter chaos; and against the back-
> ground any small man-made figure of order and concen-
> tration. What pleasanter than this should be so? . . . we
> look out on [it] with an instrument or tackle it to reduce it.
> . . . we like it, we were born to it, born used to it and have
> practical reasons for wanting it there. To me any little
> form I assert upon it is velvet, as the saying is, and to be
> considered for how much more it is than nothing. If I were
> a Platonist I should have to consider it, I suppose, for how
> much less it is than everything.[84]

Frost prefaces the passage with his wickedly ironic remark about
self-congratulatory modern pessimists: "It is immodest of a man to

think of himself as going down before the worst forces ever mobilized by God." And yet he slips back into the solemn posture of *The Birth of Tragedy* when he speaks of the "larger excruciations," the "background in hugeness and confusion," the "black and utter chaos," only to distance himself again in the playful mode of later Nietzsche with his shrewd observation: "What pleasanter than this should be so? . . . we like it, we were born to it, born used to it, and have practical reasons for wanting it there." The implication is clear: this finely self-critical representative of the tradition is telling us that like too many other modernist writers he has a need (of which he is not always critical) to project a myth of unbearable chaos as the enabling condition of the modern sensibility, a need to cultivate an alluring paranoia by constructing a starkly agonistic image of the self's confrontation with its world. The myth of chaos feeds the myth of radical creativity which has tempted many since Coleridge. More and more the modernist writer has seemed to require a horrifying world (note Frost's rhetorical overkill: "utter chaos") as the *raison d'être* for serenity-giving fictions of a structured cosmos. If form, order, and satisfaction can have objective ground (if *contra* Sartre, the real *can* be beautiful), then in the logic of conservative fictionalism there is no need for fictions—no need for "creative" artists!

Moreover, in this account of him, the alienated postromantic artist becomes an exemplary figure of courage and health who teaches us that our making of gardens, baskets, rooms, and the like are acts similar to his (though, of course, less exalted), acts which may purchase some sanity for us. In a world bereft of form, form-making becomes the ultimate value, and artistic types necessarily an intellectual elite. By a route very different we have arrived once again at Frye's destination of aesthetic humanism. Above all let us remember that Frost's metaphors are decidedly aestheticist. Like rooms (or "aesthetic ideas," or Apollonian constructions of order), poems are tight little enclosures which we enter in order to close ourselves off from the ugly sweep of history. Fictions do not engage being, nor do they discover it. The closing sentences of the Frost passage are typical of the self-conscious opposer of fictions to reality who accepts the Platonic denigrations and then with some nostalgia goes ahead and indulges himself anyway.

Perhaps now the contradictions in *The Sense of an Ending* can be illuminated, or at least reinforced by the tradition within which the book is located. We see again that self-consciousness is basic. Kant implied its ever-vigilant presence in the creative act when he told us that the understanding is not "ensnared" by play; Nietzsche believed that Apollo and Dionysius required one another; Frost's nostalgic glance at Plato tells us what he thinks about fictions; Stevens asserts that the "exquisite truth" (an interesting term for a fictionalist) is the awareness of the fictiveness of all fictions; and Hans Vaihinger attempts to distinguish fictions from scientific hypotheses by claiming that in the consciousness of fictionality we maintain an "as if" posture of mind and do not "seek" reality through procedures of empirical verification—to use a term important to neo-Kantians, we stay "contemplative," we resist *praxis*.[85] In a world in which it is hard to escape the activities of *fingere* we find that "reality" is not a fiction and that the acts of self-consciousness, so far from being acts of making, are revelatory in that they yield truths about the nature of fictions themselves and their presumed relationship to reality.

One of the difficulties with the opposition of fiction and reality is that it severely and unnecessarily narrows artistic options by enforcing an all-too-predictable dialectic. Reality is horrible; it drives us into satisfying worlds of our own making. But the poet, with his prized faculty of self-consciousness, knows his fictions not to be "true"; however unsatisfactory reality may be, as a mature and sane individual (who will not dwell in fantasy) the poet is forced to "open up" his fictions to reality and to face the hard truth. Once he has done *that*, his sense of the real is renewed, but such renewal is (how could it be otherwise?) a terror-inspiring occasion. The poet is driven back to fiction-making— and so on and so forth. The point is that with reality ontologically privileged, the poet will always be driven to self-ironic critique of the process of fiction-making. Yet that same privileging of the real is a privileging of "the horror"; in an effort to preserve his being, so goes the logic of conservative fictionalism, the poet will necessarily be driven back to fiction-making.

Another difficulty is that in his self-conscious recognition of a gulf between fictive discourse and being, the poet forges another link to his not-so-distant aestheticist kin by holding up a sign that says "No road through to action." In dealing with the "great men of early modernism" (Kermode means primarily Yeats, Pound, Eliot, and others who played with fascism), "we have to make very subtle distinctions between the work itself, in which the fictions are properly employed, and *obiter dicta* in which they are not, being either myths or dangerous pragmatic assertions."[86] To return to one of Kermode's illustrations: the unself-conscious or innocent mythicist and pragmatist might murder Jews, but the fiction-maker's self-consciousness will keep him from doing that because it will keep him from all *doing*, saving as well as murdering. We run into this interesting contradiction: the same fiction-maker who privileges "reality," and in so doing would appear to be making himself invulnerable to the charge of aestheticism (the sin of loving *kairos* at the expense of *chronos*), appears to privilege fictive discourse against all other kinds of discourse by appealing to a basically aestheticist principle of enclosure (fictions "properly employed"). The counsel of self-consciousness in the aestheticist mode does not urge the uncovering and bringing to bear of alternative perspectives which in dialectical interplay might offer constraints to the excesses and blindnesses of single-minded ideology. The counsel of aestheticized self-consciousness is, rather, paralysis and despair. From a valid perception of the difficulty of humane vision and humane action, it leaps to the metaphysical conclusion that all perspectives, no matter how subtly, how flexibly managed, are inherently vicious, and that moral security lies only in withdrawal from action and refusal of all points of view except the view that no view is any good. Self-consciousness of this sort is the modernist intellectual's rationalization of his alienation and impotence.

This specially endowed, fictive literary language, because it is washed clean of mythic and pragmatic reductionist tendencies in the poet's self-consciousness, permits the poet to say anything he pleases, no matter how repugnant. Since his playfulness has presumably placed him beyond the domain where linguistic acts are regarded as *acts* with practical implication, the poet can never be charged with moral irresponsibility. Self-consciousness, then, by producing an awareness of the fictiveness of fictions, produces the knowledge which saves us from being caught up in the net of moral relations. Somewhere along the line, however, we must ask ourselves whether this late version of aestheticism is sufficient protection against the claims—moral, social, political—that can be levied on the discourse of intellectuals, or, an easier question to answer, whether a tiny community of *literati*, cherishing the insulation afforded by their brand of self-consciousness, has ever, can ever, or should ever want to make aestheticism operative in the world.

We are going to have to ask ourselves whether the aestheticist principle of self-consciousness is anything more than special pleading which confers, when present, sanity and broad-minded enlightenment—the ability to play with all ideas—and madness and narrow-minded viciousness when it is not (as when Pound made those broadcasts). In the fictive mode the moral imperatives of ideas are supposedly neutered. Though it is true that self-consciousness of this sort tends to inhibit action, it is not a psychic posture that can be maintained for long; not even intellectuals of neo-Kantian cast live on intransitive contemplation alone. Aesthetically isolated discourse, if there is such a thing, joins the mainland of social language eventually. And when it resists it is either dumped as irrelevant, or dragged in by those who would be educated by literature. With its perverse transformation of Sidney's dictum ("the poet nothing affirmeth"), the poetics of self-consciousness may not be much more, as Sartre suggests, than an apology for infantile behavior which must be judged accordingly because it is not being attributed to the legitimately irresponsible—that is, to the insane, to the senile, to children.

One last difficulty. Self-consciousness enjoys the ultimate privilege in the tradition of conservative fictionalism not only because it confers fictionality but also—the foundation of the first—because it is thought to perform the magical act of mediating between fiction and reality. It not only declares reality off-limits to fictive (playful, nonreferential, operationally invalid) discourse, but while doing this it enables us to "find out," it somehow teaches us something about reality by telling us that fictions are *not* mimetic. Like all strictly formulated dualisms, however, the fiction-reality antithesis cannot be mediated without at the same time destroying the antithesis itself, and thus destroying what confers the opposed values of fiction and reality, and the traditional ontological opposition conveyed by those terms. The very best that self-consciousness can do is to point to the empty space, the nothingness stretching out endlessly in "front" of fictions. It cannot say where that empty space becomes filled with something called reality—something which would not be mediated by fiction, or consciousness, or self-consciousness. It can only tell us that fictive discourse may not traverse that space. In other words, what I have been calling conservative fictionalism points both to radical fictionalism and to the mythicism of Frye's "Tentative Conclusion" where reality in itself is ruled strictly out of bounds.

Conservative fictionalism may not, in the end, be much more than radical fictionalism without the courage of its insights. The same Nietzsche who celebrates the Dionysian realm as reality, the true substratum of being, calls both "reality" and (more significantly yet) the very notion of antithesis into question in later works. The move is clearly predicted even in *The Birth of Tragedy* when he speaks warmly of the "extraordinary courage and wisdom of Kant and Schopenhauer." The "current optimism," writes Nietzsche (he means the rationalistic complacency that reality is knowable and even corrigible through logic), was subverted by Kant when he showed how the supposed laws of understanding serve only to raise "appearance—the work of Maya— to the status of true reality, thereby rendering impossible a genuine understanding of that reality: in the words of Schopenhauer, binding the dreamer even faster in sleep."[87] The way is open for the later Nietzsche's harsh treatment of Kant and for Jacques Derrida's proposals of the method of deconstruction and of "differance" (as the replacement of "antithesis").

Once the Kantian turn from realism is made there is no way to disguise our "inventions" with the mask of "discovery," no way back to an uncritical position. The ultimate source of epistemological discovery in conservative fictionalism, the act of self-consciousness, achieves its privilege by virtue of the supposed ability of intellect to criticize itself from the standpoint of a true reality-in-itself which is the guarantee of absolute knowledge. Without a reality-in-itself, self-consciousness could not escape the fictionality of a situated, finite perspective, could not become the perfectly uncontingent perception it is said to be. Without a reality-in-itself to which to anchor its judgment, self-consciousness could not enjoy the perception of an antithetically related fiction and reality. But in *The Will to Power* Nietzsche puts this question to the celebrators of self-consciousness: "how should a tool be able to criticize itself when it can use only itself for the critique?"[88] What, more specifically, is this reality-in-itself? In a powerful essay on *The Will to Power*, Paul de Man has shown that Nietzsche found it to be nothing more than the most necessary of all fictions, a fiction of our deepest need for a stable and permanent substratum,[89] a context of constancy, regularity, and similarity, and of the entity which is identical with itself (this latter the foundation of traditional logic). In so many words, this classical conception of reality is what we require and what we have fashioned out of our will to survive and to master. To affirm the objectivity of these classical attributes of the real is to affirm that there is unmediated knowledge of the real; this, writes Nietzsche, "is certainly not the case." "Because we have to be stable in our beliefs if we are to prosper, we have made the 'real' world a world not of change, but one of being." "The principle of identity has behind it the 'apparent fact' of things that are the same. A world in a state of becoming could not, in a strict sense, be 'comprehended' or 'known'. . . ."[90]

The best evidence for internal contradiction comes finally from conservative quarters: while pursuing what he takes to be "reality," Kermode unwittingly concedes the radical point when he says that in the cognitive function of "making sense" the fiction corresponds not to the objective structure of things but to a "human need."[91] (Great hunger is a poor judge of the lasagna.) Self-consciousness may, perhaps, mediate fiction and reality as the difference between fictions, but it may not mediate the antithesis between illusion and being because such an antithesis is itself a construction. It used to be standard procedure among historians of theory to see the Kantian critique of Western philosophy as the decisive enabling act which brought into existence modern poetics from Coleridge to Mallarmé and Cleanth Brooks; and certainly it was the intention of the neo-Kantians to call into question the categories of naive representation and referentiality. But despite all efforts to defeat the referential for literary language, in the very notion of the fiction that has dominated the modernist mind we see the emergence of a position that not only fails to escape the uncritical stance but is constituted by it. In its deployment of the principle of antithesis the modernist mind reveals its fundamental metaphysical proclivities.

Three

But every thought is also simply a thought. It is that
which exists in itself, isolatedly, mentally. Whatever
its objects may be, thought can never place them, think
them, except in the interior of itself.

Georges Poulet, *The Interior Distance*

Speaking must have speakers, but not merely in the same
way as an effect must have a cause.

Martin Heidegger, *On the Way to Language*

The fact that nonpresence and otherness are internal
to presence strikes at the very root of the argument
for the uselessness of signs in the self-relation.

Jacques Derrida, *Speech and Phenomena*

Versions of Phenomenology

In the fall of 1952, after teaching for almost twenty-five years at the University of Edinburgh (1927–1951), Georges Poulet began his tenure at the Johns Hopkins University as chairman of its French department. Poulet's first volume of *Etudes sur le temps humain* had appeared only three years before—a very late bloom by typical American academic norms. But the Hopkins literary intelligentsia, attuned with its customary clarity to stirrings on the Continent, scored a coup by identifying an emerging international figure in literary-critical circles on the eve of his very important American career and vogue. In the space of about ten years the Johns Hopkins University Press brought out *Studies in Human Time* (1956) and *The Interior Distance* (1959) (which was the second volume of *Etudes*). A third book, *The Metamorphoses of the Circle* (1966), displayed more clearly than anything Poulet had written before how compatible were his interests in the secret places of consciousness with the reigning Hopkins humanist methodologist, A. O. Lovejoy, and his pursuit of the history of ideas.

A year after Poulet's arrival at Hopkins there occurred another event of some moment to historians of contemporary theory. Fresh from completing his Ph.D. at Harvard with a dissertation entitled *Symbolic*

Imagery in Six Novels of Charles Dickens, a young American, J. Hillis Miller, after a year's stint as an instructor at Williams College, moved on to Johns Hopkins, as assistant professor of English, where he formed a friendship with the new chairman of the French department that was to have lasting effect on the careers of both men and on the postformalist American critical imagination. We have it on Miller's testimony that his friendship with Poulet transformed his critical orientation; the dissertation that was strikingly New-Critical in attack and scope became, after five years of revision closely supervised by Poulet, *Charles Dickens: The World of His Novels* (1959).[1] It was the first explicit "criticism of consciousness" written by an American. Given the distance, temporal and (as it appeared in the late 1950s and early 1960s) methodological, between the dissertation and his first book, Miller's next two books—*The Disappearance of God* (1963) and *Poets of Reality* (1965)—came with a rush and coherence that suggested a new methodology now fully grasped in fullest ardor.

By the mid-sixties American critics in search of alternatives to the New Criticism, and not satisfied with the options offered by Northrop Frye, or by the votaries of Wallace Stevens and supreme fictions, could find in Miller an avant-garde approach whose critique of formalist criticism seemed beyond cavil. At last, with this bold entry into consciousness, the assault upon our stubborn and protean tendency to assume an aestheticist posture and dwell endlessly on the linguistic minutiae of a text to no end seemed to be successful. And more: in a series of expository (and quietly polemical) essays on behalf of Poulet and the so-called Geneva group, Miller provided the kind of mediation needed by the American critic of English and American literature, whose command of French and interest in the French tradition is not particularly keen. Miller's distillations of phenomenological principles were xeroxed and eagerly read, and kept handy for easy reference to the critical controversy about whether or not Georges Poulet was really a phenomenologist. (Those in the know in the mid-sixties were quick to point out that any resemblance between Poulet and phenomenology was strictly coincidental.) If backhanded compliments by Geoffrey Hartman, Murray Krieger, and Paul de Man[2] do not sufficiently make the point that Poulet and phenomenology (or whatever it was he was doing) had caught on in the United States, then we need only recall the imprimatur of the Harvard University Press on Sarah Lawall's exposition, *Critics of Consciousness* (1968), with its chapters on Albert Béguin, Marcel Raymond, Poulet, Jean-Pierre Richard, Jean Rousset, Jean Starobinski, Maurice Blanchot, and—an inclusion which speaks much—J. Hillis Miller.

From about 1966, or with the appearance of *The Metamorphoses of the Circle* and Miller's much-reprinted essay, "The Geneva School," to about 1970, with the appearance of *The Structuralist Controversy* (Hopkins had struck again!) and Miller's disquieted, symbolically entitled "Geneva or Paris: The Recent Work of Georges Poulet" (*University of Toronto Quarterly*), the Poulet vogue was intense and commanding. The overall effect was a significant (if partial) transformation of the American critical landscape by the contemporary European philosophical muse. Though Poulet was himself no phenomenologist, and showed little interest in those who thought they were, the great curiosity in his work here had the effect of opening the way for the American critic to Continental modes of philosophy which attentive readers could glimpse at the distant perimeters of Poulet's writing. The impact of Husserl, Heidegger, Sartre, and Maurice Merleau-Ponty, though difficult to judge at this point, and still being felt in the United States, has but one parallel in the Anglo-American tradition: that of Kant and the German idealists, via the mediations of Coleridge, upon Emerson and some now forgotten American transcendentalists. If the parallel should hold up, and it gives every appearance of doing so, then American critics will be contending with a neo-Husserlian tradition for some time to come. In the meanwhile in our centers of higher critical dialogue the talk is all of structuralism, poststructuralism, and Jacques Derrida; Georges Poulet and phenomenology, once so disruptive to critical traditionalists in this country, have lately begun to assume the safe and comforting look of the last traditionalism.

1

The scandalously short-lived nature of recent critical movements may give some advantage of perspective to their would-be historians. In an important letter to Miller dated 25 November 1961, a letter knowingly cited by the cognoscenti of theory in the late sixties as proof of the vast difference between phenomenology and Poulet's quest for pure consciousness, Poulet reveals more than his obvious Cartesian affinities.

> I should readily consider that the most important form of subjectivity is not that of the mind overwhelmed, filled, and so to speak stuffed with its objects, but that there is another [kind of consciousness] which sometimes reveals itself on this side of, at a distance from, and protected from, any object, a subjectivity which exists in itself, withdrawn from any power which might determine it from the out-

side, and possessing itself by a direct intuition. . . . As you
have seen, in this I remain faithful to the Cartesian tradition.[3]

Poulet's commitment to the *cogito*, or subject which possesses itself
directly, without gap, lag, or mediation, in a "moment" before or above
time, is very clear here and in countless other places in his work. But
his explicit reference to Descartes, and Miller's confidence, helpful to
a point, that Poulet's commitment to consciousness distinguishes his
work from all criticism presupposing Husserlian conceptions of intentionality, these obscure the most significant historical issues.[4]

Poulet is not a throwback to seventeenth-century France and its intellectual climate. He is a typically modernist thinker constrained by
a formalist discourse that became an underground matrix for the "discursive practice"[5] of poets, philosophers, novelists, linguists, and the
sort of advanced thought that emerged in Flaubert, Mallarmé, Yeats,
Croce, Frost, Saussure, and Husserl himself (with whom Poulet presumably shares no essential thought). If he is a throwback, then it is
to the turn of the century formalist intellectual climate (however odd
it may be to speak of this critic as a formalist given his distaste for all
formal matters understood in the narrow sense). The connection among
these writers generally surfaces in the expressed need to escape the
privilege granted to exteriorities of all sorts by the religion of scientism.
This need is often expressed in the yearning to establish the radical
freedom and self-sufficiency of one's discipline (it is like a world
unto itself), a yearning more often than not accompanied by railings
against the enemies of freedom: Darwin, literary and philosophical
realists and naturalists, and anyone else overly impressed with evolu-
tionary metaphors and the methods and ideals of late-nineteenth-century science. If there were turn of the century rules of "discursive
practice" which silently governed the thinking and discourse of avant-
garde writers, they were rules which permitted obsessive articulation
of the fear of determinism, loss of human potency, and weariness with
temporality and all of the things of time co-opted by the connoisseurs
of exteriority. Hence the other side of aestheticist–avant-garde fears:
the charisma of transcendence and autonomy and those psychologies
of irredeemable isolation which tucked the subject safely away behind
the thick walls of personality. We see such psychologies surfacing in
texts as divergent as Walter Pater's *The Renaissance*, William James's
Principles of Psychology, and F. H. Bradley's *Appearance and Reality*.
It is within formalism understood in this way, as a metaphysics of isolation, that Poulet fits most comfortably.

Saussure's break with nineteenth-century linguistics in the first decade of the century, as Emile Benveniste has shown us, lay precisely in his discovery of language *(langue)* as a self-governing system free from the historical determinants that had dominated the philological study of language as *parole*.[6] Merely to state the issue in those terms is to recall Flaubert's "book about nothing, a book dependent on nothing external, which would be held together by the strength of its style, just as the earth, suspended in the void, depends on nothing external for its support, a book which would have almost no subject. . . .";[7] it is also to recall the coincidental efforts of Clive Bell in 1913 (in his book *Art*) to isolate the nonrepresentational elements of art as the proper purview of aesthetic theory, and of the Russian formalists to do something of the same for poetics. Such recollections may cast some historical illumination on Benedetto Croce's attempt to locate within interior space the utter singularity of intuition as its aesthetic quality, and then his effort to protect the aesthetic with the metaphysical fortress of his inside-outside distinction which relegated to irrelevance all communicative activities of "externalization."[8] To recall Croce, Saussure, Bell, and Flaubert in these ways is, inevitably, to recall Mallarmé's search for an "immaculate" discourse, purified of all external references, and the comically illuminating arrogance (and defensiveness) that he directed toward all naturalistic approaches: the difference between naturalism and poetry, he once wrote, is like the difference between a "corset and a beautiful throat."[9] And, one last example, it is to recall the young Yeats in 1898, speaking of the "autumn of the body," of writers "struggling all over Europe" against "externality," of writers who were "beginning to be interested in many things which positive science, the interpreter of exterior law, has always denied. . . ."[10] Following (and quoting) Mallarmé through the mediation of a mutual friend, Arthur Symons, Yeats's fundamental alternative was not the misty transcendentalism he sometimes flirted with in occultist circles dominated by Madame Blavatsky and McGregor Mathers, but the idea of self-sufficiency itself expressed as the desire to set up poetic discourse as a system: " 'to make an entire word hitherto unknown to the language.' "[11] When Yeats decides that the value of Mallarmean purity of discourse is the achievement of "disembodied ecstasy,"[12] his historical context constrains us to read etymologically and to understand that such ecstasy is the sort not contingent upon *bodies* and the "external" laws to which bodies are normally subject.

For all its austerities, Husserl's phenomenology, especially in its programmatic declaration in *Ideas*, shares more of the yearnings of the young Yeats and Georges Poulet than may initially meet the eye. When reinserted into its intellectual culture (*Ideas* was published in 1913),

Husserl's celebrated and debated *epochē* and its corollary, the eidetic reduction, become just the sort of intellectual strategies, just the sort of
rhetorical moves against the partisans of exteriority which Mallarmé,
Yeats, and Saussure would have instantly found congenial.[13] With one
stroke the *epochē* (the abstention from the natural standpoint) banishes the privileged position, assumed in late-nineteenth-century
thought, of the physical universe as the origin of what the Darwinists
of Husserl's youth called the epiphenomenon of consciousness. When
we suspend the natural standpoint (not only the priority of the natural
world but of the *embodied* ego), what Husserl believes to be a prior
ground of being comes to light: *"a new region of being"* in *"absolute
uniqueness"*[14] (we note the redundancy) is revealed in its autonomy and
transcendental independence from the natural world. This implies that
consciousness seen from the natural standpoint, seen (again we note the
etymology of his choice) as "incorporated"[15] psychophysical action, is
bracketed along with all of the "accidental," "individual," and "contingent"[16] qualities of being which are burned off in the reduction to the
eidos, or essence of an intentional object. Free from nature and the natural, individual ego,[17] Husserl makes it clear that phenomenological
method (and its object, the phenomenological residuum, what is left
after the *epochē* and the eidetic reduction) is a triumph over *"all sciences
which relate to this natural world."*[18] The qualification of the statement
disguises the audacity of his claim. For the triumph is, by the norms of
his intellectual culture, quite simply a triumph over all known sciences.
The purpose of the breakthrough to pure intentional consciousness and
its object, the *eidos,* is to shift philosophical research to its own formal
ground and to keep it trained on its proper intrinsic objects. "Man has
wooed and won the world, and has fallen weary. . . . He grew weary
when he said, 'These things that I touch and see are alone real,' for he
saw them without illusion at last and found them but air and dust and
moisture."[19] That is Yeats's prelude to his own aestheticist effort at abstention from natural being. Here is Husserl, in uncharacteristically
energetic tones, in tones too exultantly rhetorical, in discourse too filled
with verbal overkill to be taken philosophically straight, but perfect to
expose the theatrics of early modernist intellectual scrimmaging:

> Thus *all sciences which relate to this natural world,* though
> they stand never so firm to me, though they fill me with
> wondering admiration, though I am far from any thought of
> objecting to them in the least degree, *I disconnect them all,
> I make absolutely no use of their standards, I do not
> appropriate a single one of the propositions that enter into
> their systems, even though their evidential value is perfect, I*

take none of them, no one of them serves me for a founda-
tion. . . . all theories and sciences, positivistic or otherwise,
which relate to this world, however good they may be,
succumb to the same fate.[20]

The Husserlian phenomenologist stands approximately in the place of
Kant's auditor in the aesthetic experience. Freed from seeking the determinants of what is given directly to consciousness because he is
freed from the natural ego immersed in (Husserl's word, repeating
Kant) "interested," willing, hedonic activities, Husserl's phenomenologist is released into the "disinterested" (how easily he picks up the
neo-Kantian shibboleth) kind of seeing that enables him to "describe
adequately what he sees, purely as seen, as what is seen and seen in
such and such a manner."[21]

My point is this: Miller's evidence for Poulet's antiphenomenological,
anti-intentionalist conception of consciousness is suspect because it is
excessive. The rough stance that emerges from the letter of 25 November 1961 is certainly Cartesian, but it serves the modernist literary intellectual's flight from nineteenth-century scientific method and pre-
tension. It is a Cartesianism whose true intent is not the rejection of
phenomenology but of a philosophical determinism which to a certain
type of sensibility (Poulet's, for instance) can only seem crude and
frightening. In Poulet a strange and frightened Cartesianism at once
seeks and claims an isolated, privileged, and transcendent space of
human consciousness—as the goal of critical reading—and yet appears
to grant, at the same time, the coercive power of objectivity over the
interior subject and the shocking vulnerability of interiority to a vora-
cious exteriority. The agonistic situation of the subject is projected
dramatically by Poulet: we are to seek a free consciousness, one that is
not "overwhelmed," not "filled" and "stuffed with its objects," a consciousness that is "at a distance from, and protected from, any object";
a consciousness "withdrawn from any power which might determine it
from the outside." The letter to Miller ends: "in this I remain faithful to
the Cartesian tradition." Poulet might have more faithfully placed himself historically by suggesting that he remains true to a French symbolist
tradition which, accepting an irreparable subject-object division,
chooses the transcendent subject while relegating the object to Claude
Bernard, Emile Zola, and other symbolist enemies. When he writes in
The Interior Distance that "Every thought, to be sure, is a thought *of*
something,"[22] his phrase "to be sure" grants the phenomenological
point only in order to move on to what he considers a deeper issue.
Though no phenomenologist would agree that one has a choice in the
matter of intentionality—consciousness is intentional or it is not—

Poulet's construction remains valuable as a key to a version of Descartes which seeks to catch the *cogito* in its original, free, untouched, transcendent moment, before it becomes forever dispersed in the world, before all interior selfhood is drained off into exteriority.

2

Though he will occasionally complicate the act of reading, on rare occasion even fall into a kind of despair ("criticism seems to oscillate between two possibilities: a union without comprehension, and a comprehension without union"),[23] Poulet has on the whole produced one of the happiest bodies of contemporary criticism. His project of mimetically duplicating the *cogito* is grounded in a consistent anti-Nietzschean stance which demands that critical readers sacrifice the willing and dominating drives of the self in an act of immolation inspired by Christian and Kantian themes. No critical will to power here; no desire to pump up the critical misreader by inserting him into the territory of intrapsychic warfare, where as poet *manqué* he may join Milton, Wordsworth, and the other worthies in the game of repression. Though he would later change his mind under structuralist pressure, Miller's earliest description in 1963 of Poulet's criticism as an "act of vigorous self-dispossession," of "Christian self-effacement," and a "twentieth-century equivalent of a seventeenth-century book of devotions," is an accurate rendering of Poulet's programmatic statements, of what Poulet has always said, early and late, *he* thought he was doing.[24] And it is the programmatic Poulet, more than the practicing critic, who has fascinated the American audience.

For all of his breaks with Anglo-American methodology and old-line historicism, French and American style, Poulet's central appeal in the United States may ultimately lie in his self-effacement, and perfect openness to the other, the critical reader becoming a transparency who presents the thought of others without distortion. As the vogue of the New Critics and Northrop Frye before him would appear to have demonstrated beyond question, we have tended to honor more than most the fiction of the objective, nonideological critic who—as a "receiver" of the truth—is fair to all and has malice toward none. It is a staple of the Kantian side of the modern critical tradition to value the beautiful as that mode of experiencing objects which escapes the constraints and determinants that attend human experience at large. Beginning with Kant's third *Critique* and moving through Coleridge, Schopenhauer, T. E. Hulme, John Crowe Ransom, Eliseo Vivas, and Murray Krieger, the achievement of the properly aesthetic experience (which is an experience not to be confused with but to be isolated from knowledge and desire) is dependent on a theology of self-dispossession, on the emptying of the self of all of its worldly contents and inclinations until all that remains is, in words of Poulet which close the Kantian argument, "a kind of inner vacuum which would be informed by the thought of the other."[25] The line is unbroken: the would-be objectivism of the New Critic is replaced by the would-be (nineteenth-century) hermeneutical scientism of Northrop Frye, which is in turn replaced by the critic as perfect self-dispossessing lover—a recurrent metaphor in Poulet which links him to Ransom, whose ontological critic is similarly characterized.[26]

The presiding image of the open and generous critic in Poulet is blatantly sexual. After the initial move, in which the book is found "opening itself" (it "welcomes me" with "unheard of license"), the sexual roles are reversed and the critic assumes a conventional female posture.[27] The "humble" and "passive" reader is "completely" "opened" to the presence of a *cogito* that is "active" and "potent," a *cogito* that "forces" itself, "takes hold of," "appropriates" and "fills." There is a "strange invasion of my person"; "without selection—completely at random," various cogitos "poured their contents," "warm and confused," into me.[28] (The metaphor of the reader as "inner vacuum" is perhaps not entirely exhausted by the Kantian theory.) If Poulet almost never questions his ability to make perfect spiritual love it is because all of his chances to recover the originating *cogito* rest there, on his supposed transcendence of individuated will, of situated being-in-theworld (in Heidegger's unitary sense of the phrase). Anything less than transparency would disclose the critic's mediating presence as an agent of deferral that would throw the greatest doubt over the possibility of retrieving the subject (which even Poulet will admit exists, before the act of reading, at a distant remove). Poulet and his friends Paul de Man and J. Hillis Miller have recently attempted, in an environment now hostile to Poulet's decided inclination toward a criticism of identification that would recover the origin of expression, to construct a changing, increasingly sophisticated ("problematic") critic of consciousness who could hold his own theoretical respectability in the company of Lévi-Strauss and Derrida. But the evidence points to an unpuzzled quester for the *cogito* who has not been much fazed by what recent critics have had to say about difference and deferral.

The distance between critic and the inaugurating *cogito* he would reach is filled, according to Poulet, with exteriority or objectivity, terms which include, depending on where we look, "things" in the world described by the writer, all historical, biographical, and bibliographical information about him, all of the literary forms which he employs, and, ultimately, even discourse itself. The *cogito* is the "invisible face of the moon"[29]—but the metaphor is somewhat deceptive, since from what we perceive of the revealed subject in discourse we may predicate nothing at all about the hidden subject that we do not perceive. The privileged moment of the *cogito*, when in an act of self-consciousness the self is revealed to itself in all of its Cartesian purity, with all *res extensa* expelled, is defined with a dualistic rigor which would appear to deny entry even to the purest of spiritual lovers. But I have reversed Poulet's sexual metaphor. It is the hidden *cogito*, veiled behind discourse, things, and literary genera, which somehow penetrates through the veil, into the open consciousness of the critic. It is the *cogito*, which by definition must refuse all determination, all contact with worldliness (Poulet speaks of it as "uncontained presence," as "fundamental indeterminacy," and, in a moment of extreme idealism, as "anterior and posterior to any object"),[30] it is this *cogito*, active and potent, which somehow makes its way into discourse, through discourse, out the other side, and into the pure receptivity of the critic's "inner vacuum." The *cogito* which exists "in itself, isolatedly, mentally," in the "interior depth" of the subject,[31] "withdrawn from any power which might determine it from the outside,"[32] somehow becomes involved with discourse without, at the same time, being constituted by it, or being distorted, deferred, or touched by the differentiating medium of linguistic signs.

Poulet's candid treatment of the *cogito* becomes a prime example of what Derrida meant by the transcendental signified, or classical center, which enjoys the high privilege of governing structurality, the shape of a text, while remaining itself always outside the structural field, subject to no conditions. Derrida's major point about the history of metaphysics is stunningly authenticated by the coincidence of Poulet, Husserl, and Croce. In his study of Husserl's theory of signs, *La Voix et le phénomène* (1967, translated as *Speech and Phenomena*, 1973), Derrida uncovers in the *Logical Investigations* an attitude toward the sign remarkably close both to Poulet's relegation of discourse to the realm of the objective and to Croce's refusal to assign the activity of externalization any theoretical import in the expressive process. Three divergent philosophical directions merge in the difficult concept of the "phenomenological voice":

> It is not in the sonorous substance or in the physical voice, in the body of speech in the world but in the voice phenomenologically taken, speech in its transcendental flesh, in

the breath, the intentional animation that transforms the body of the word into flesh, makes of the *Körper* a *Leib*, *geistige Leiblichkeit*. The phenomenological voice would be this spiritual flesh that continues to speak and be present to itself—*to hear itself*—in the absence of the world.[33]

The phenomenological voice, in other words, is something like a culminating example of the logocentrism that has ruled Western metaphysics and that holds that writing is a representation of the acoustical images of speech, which, in turn, are an attempt to represent a silent, unmediated, and self-present meaning lodged in consciousness. Husserl's distinction between the sign as indication (*Anzeichen*) and the sign as expression (*Ausdruck*) is a distinction essentially between outside and inside;[34] between communication itself and intention to speak (*vouloir dire*, as Derrida insists); between the entanglement (*Verflechtung*) or "contamination" of the verbal medium understood as writing —what Croce termed "externalization," or Poulet the objectivity of discourse, with emphasis on the sign as object—and the purity of the intentional animation of meaning understood as breath (*anima*).[35] Though there is for Husserl, Derrida tells us, a "*de facto* necessity of entanglement internally associating expression and indication," the possibility of a "rigorous distinction of essence" must not be forgotten.[36] Poulet understood that possibility and the necessity of achieving a clean severance even as he would admit that at a certain level of analysis the subject is deeply immersed in forms.

What is finally isolated by Husserl and Poulet is not the expressive sign itself but the preexpressive, silent, "self-presence of the present in the living present."[37] It is a moment in "solitary mental life,"[38] anterior to discourse and time, in which discourse becomes irrelevant; a moment in which, presumably, there is no need for discourse because the speaking subject is immediately present to itself without gap in the transcendence of the present. To insert the sign here would be to cut up the subject, make it nonidentical with itself by introducing a representation which generates lag, or distance, or nonpresence (ultimately death) and difference "in the heart of self-presence"; the sign would constitute the sort of deferral that normally obtains in discourse understood as indication or externalization.[39] The "self-presence of the present in the living present" is presence itself, which, grasped as presence-to-consciousness-without-gap, is the cornerstone of metaphysics. The archive[40] of presence is just this sort of consciousness. So what Croce called an intuition, Poulet the "invisible face of the moon," and Husserl the "living voice," is what Derrida aptly describes as the "unshaken purity of expression in a language without communication. . . . By a strange paradox, meaning would isolate the concentrated purity of its *ex-pressiveness* just at the moment when the relation to a certain *outside* is suspended."[41] But this "strange paradox" is nothing other than the "phenomological project in its essence"[42]—and, we ought to add, its despair. The predicament of Husserl is the predicament of Poulet and of all radical idealisms. (Somewhere in the distant background of all of this we hear echoed Shelley's remarks about composition and the "fading coal" of inspiration.) Derrida's analysis should finally force us not only to reconsider conventional categories of demarcation within the history of philosophy, but, at the very least, to rethink Poulet's own antiphenomenological self-characterization. Poulet may not be a phenomenologist, but the exquisite irony (if we credit Derrida) is that neither is Husserl. "The lived experience of another is made known to me only insofar as it is mediately indicated by signs involving a physical side"[43]: that is Derrida articulating what he takes to be Husserl's dilemma, but it is a sentence that might just as easily have appeared in the preface to *The Interior Distance*.

Poulet's vacillating attitude toward this relation of *cogito* and discourse reflects the traditional ambiguity of the classical center as phenomenological voice. The *cogito* is separateness, point of departure, origin, source, unreachable anteriority; but it is also the "construction that causes all elements," a "principle of multiple developments which arranged themselves within a time line," and, in a telling allusion in a recent statement translated for *Diacritics*, the "thread of Ariadne which unrolls from the threshold of the labyrinth."[44] In the paper delivered at the Hopkins symposium on structuralism, Poulet threw a number of potentially hostile respondents off guard by declaring that language is not otherness, or exteriority (as he had always claimed) but that which constitutes the interior universe: "thanks to the intervention of language," as he put it, the critic has access to other consciousnesses.[45] In another passage, in which he appears to have digested Emile Benveniste's extensions of Saussure, he declares that the "subject which presides over the work can exist only in the work."[46] But at the end of the essay the bouquets he has tossed to the partisans of structuralism seem but diversions to prepare the audience for his traditional position, now restated with an enthusiasm vigorously renewed by apparent concessions. In the last paragraphs of the Hopkins paper Poulet recalls a visit to the Scuola di San Rocco in Venice where he found assembled a great number of Tintorettos. He recalls looking at all of the paintings when suddenly, in a moment typical of his literary criticism, he felt that he had reached the

common essence present in all the works of a great master,
an essence which I was not able to perceive, except when
emptying my mind of all the particular images created by the
artist. I became aware of a subjective power at work in all
these pictures, and yet never so clearly understood by my
mind as when I had forgotten all their particular figurations.
. . . What is this subject left standing in isolation after
every examination of a literary work?[47]

Before answering his question Poulet grants that there is "in the work
a mental activity profoundly engaged in objective forms," but that "at
another level" (he does not say deeper or more fundamental, but that
is what he means) we find "forsaking all forms, a subject which reveals
itself to itself." He does not appeal explicitly to any Platonic scheme
when he speaks of this subject which forsakes all forms, which is
"exposed in its ineffability and in its fundamental indeterminacy," but
this "subjectivity without objectivity" is pure, *original* metaphysical
substance, while all objectivity and all subjects involved in objectivity
are passing appearances.[48]

At the beginning of the Hopkins paper Poulet had implied a severe
critique of the precious aestheticist critic by relegating to him vases,
statues, and other spatially enclosed objects which deny us access and
seem to stand at an inhuman remove, imperially isolated from human
commerce. The shortcomings of that analysis of the spatial arts aside,
we might find it ironic that Poulet's own position—that the special
appeal of the book is that it welcomes us into the privileged space of
the subject—is a refusal of history (literary or otherwise) even more
extreme than anything antihistorical we may locate in Frye and the
New Critics. Through subjectivity's "fundamental indeterminacy"—
which is to say its fundamental freedom from the constraints and
conditions of human history—Poulet proposes, via a criticism of consciousness, another perhaps even more direct route to aestheticism.
Miller's change of stance from casual New Critic to critic of consciousness, and the corresponding change of taste that that implied for the
American critical audience, are not surprising and dramatic shifts when
the transition is seen in historical perspective as a move from an
aestheticism which celebrates the free-standing, closed poetic object
to an isolationism which celebrates a free-standing, closed subjectivity.

3

Poulet's resolute privileging of an ahistorical subjective
space, access to which is permitted by the proper cherishing of books,

has become an embarrassment to those of his American champions who have since passed into structuralism and beyond. The theoretical changes of J. Hillis Miller and Paul de Man are perfectly illustrated in their attempts to salvage their recent critical pasts by dragging Poulet with them into what Edward Said aptly termed "linguicity."[49] The most forthright example of this turn from phenomenology to its structuralist critique is Miller, who candidly recounts his identity crisis as he moves from the thoroughly sympathetic exposition of the criticism of identification in 1963 and 1966[50]—when he had no difficulty with the concepts of "presence" and "center"[51]—to the troubled essay of 1970, "Geneva or Paris," in which Poulet's taking "language for granted," as a "perfectly transparent medium," which Miller once understood as a virtue, now makes him uneasy; "All the apparent assumptions of Poulet's criticism are interrogated by Derrida and found wanting."[52] But, thanks to Derrida, the extremities of a true identity crisis are avoided. Poulet is only *apparently* wanting; the new Miller tells us that "Poulet's exploration of the *cogito* of each of his writers leads to the recognition that the *cogito* is the experience of a lack of a beginning, of an irremediable instability of the mind."[53] Suddenly Poulet begins to look, in Miller's latest analysis, not at all like the privileger of the silent origin (as phenomenological voice which is identical with itself) but like a connoisseur of *écriture* and the absence of presence.

Paul de Man's essay on Poulet of 1969, which is tellingly entitled "The Literary Self as Origin," and which appears to have influenced Miller's recent thoughts on the subject, is an even better guide to the changing critical times, perhaps for the very reason that it is so massive a distortion of Poulet's position. De Man's sentimental claim here, and everywhere, is that the hidden insights of a writer are carried by fortuitous intuitions, to which the writer himself is blinded by the systematic and rational character of the program which he consciously puts forth. De Man believes that he has access, in a writer, to the "depths and uncertainties that make up his more hidden side."[54] In this instance he means the discovery that the "subject that speaks in the criticism of Georges Poulet is a vulnerable and fragile subject whose voice can never become established as a presence."[55] Though de Man is willing to admit that it takes a "certain amount of interpretive labor to show that his criticism is actually a criticism of language rather than a criticism of the self," the admission is marred by the fact that "interpretive labor," with its naively archeological suggestion of uncovering buried truth, is not a phrase that de Man's avowed position (that there are no privileged positions) can really allow him.[56] The surprising claim that Poulet's criticism is of language, not of self, that Poulet is always "open-ended, problematic," "constantly putting his thought into question,"[57] is rooted in the idea that the place of the origin as genetic source is subordinated to a Derrida-like use of a center which does not escape structurality. The *cogito* as transcendental signified is relegated, de Man believes, to the fringes of Poulet's writing so that a center that is subject to free-playing signification, that is utterly temporal, that does not borrow its stability from outside sources, can dominate:

> when [the point of departure] . . . acts as center, it no longer functions as a genetic but as a structural and organizing principle. . . . it serves as a coordinating point of reference for events that do not coincide in time. This can only mean that the center permits a link between past and future, thereby implying the active and constitutive intervention of a past. In temporal terms, a center cannot at the same time also be an origin, a source. . . . "Source" and "center" are by no means *a priori* identical.[58]

If in de Man's retrieval of hidden insight we sense not genuine discovery but Derridean imposition—each and every programmatic statement of Poulet was deluded with respect to his true inclination—we will have to grant that on occasion Poulet sounded vaguely disturbed about his Cartesian orientation. But he never put his thought "into question," as de Man says. Poulet remains confident that in the move from a single Tintoretto to the viewing of many Tintorettos at the Scuola di San Rocco, the critic is primed to make the wondrous leap across the void separating the subject "profoundly engaged in objective forms" from the ineffable and indeterminate subject that is the other side of the moon, the principle that (as soul) animates the *corpus* but cannot be spatially enclosed within it. When James Edie suggested to Poulet that he could not call the subjectivity of Tintoretto indeterminate and still be sure that it was Tintoretto's pure consciousness he had discovered (rather than Leonardo's),[59] he made a point which anticipates de Man: that Poulet's thesis, because it is a contradiction in terms, *implies* a criticism of structure or language. (This is not the same as saying, with de Man, that Poulet *practices* a criticism of language.) Edie and de Man make more theoretical sense than Poulet, but as readers of his system they are deficient; they tell us more about themselves, and changes in critical history, than about Poulet because they willfully ignore his repeated desire to move through language and through temporality. Generally a careful student of the tricky voice of metaphor, de Man misses what Poulet tells us about his method when he speaks of the *cogito* as the "thread of Ariadne which unrolls from the threshold of the labyrinth." Situated at the *threshold*, which is to say neither "outside" nor "inside" (more of this shortly, in Heidegger), the *cogito* is freed from the maze of time which it has produced. It may be that Poulet ought to have called us into the labyrinth of history, but in fact his intention was to lead us out so that his dream of perfect communion might be realized.

The consciousness that Poulet finds behind the book is "no different from the one I automatically assume in every human being I encounter except in this case the consciousness is open to me, . . . thus the greatest advantage of literature is that I am persuaded by it that I am free from my usual sense of incompatibility between my consciousness and its objects."[60] The substratum of aestheticist ideology has always been the alienation that theorists of romanticism have talked about. It provides a metaphysical rationale for isolationism, as forthrightly articulated by William James in 1890 when he stated that the "most absolute breaches in nature" are those between persons, between thoughts that are "owned" by different consciousnesses.[61] From Pater to T. S. Eliot no idea is more obsessively reiterated than that of the inaccessibly walled-off island of consciousness, unless it is the idea of the poem similarly described in splendid isolation. Reading, for Poulet, is quite simply the redemption of such tragic isolation—a way of contacting others, of entering into community denied to him by the determinate and distinctly exteriorized groupings of everyday life. It is the special task and privilege of Poulet's reader to enter a rare community situated in original space where self-present cogitos exist above the fissures of time, in a relationship of mutuality, closed off from all dispersions and differences. It is a community whose reason for being should be well understood by Frye and other neo-Kantian partisans, who believe that literature's highest moment comes when it throws off the shackles of our alienated social circumstances.

4

The historic destiny of phenomenology seems . . . to be contained in these two motifs: on the one hand, phenomenology is the reduction of naive ontology, the return to an active constitution of sense and value, to the activity of a *life* which produces truth and value in general through its signs. But at the same time . . . another factor will necessarily confirm the classical metaphysics of presence and indicate the adherence of phenomenology to classical ontology.

Jacques Derrida, *Speech and Phenomena*

The effect of Jacques Derrida's attack on Husserl's theory of signs in *La Voix et le phénomène* is to force us into a reappraisal of the whole phenomenological movement. After Derrida we cannot avoid asking whether there is such a thing as phenomenology: whether the attack, in the name of intentionality, on the dualistically isolated, self-sufficient, and enclosed substance of Descartes's subject is anything but the most self-deluded of antimetaphysical moves in the history of philosophy which succeeds only, as Derrida shows in the case of Husserl, in re-instituting a Cartesian minimum under the guise of the "phenomenological voice." If Derrida is anywhere near the truth on Husserl, then Poulet's explicit rejection of phenomenology in the letter to Miller sets him off from Heidegger, Sartre, and Merleau-Ponty only in that the latter three are less aware of their true inclinations. With a keener self-consciousness they too might have written "in this, as you see, I remain faithful to the Cartesian tradition." In the wake of Derrida, Poulet appears more philosophically clear-sighted than he is generally given credit for. While others were lumping him crudely with the phenomenological movement, Poulet made the point about himself that Derrida would come to make about the tradition that developed from Husserl.

In the extraordinarily formidable introduction to *Being and Nothingness* ("The Pursuit of Being"), Sartre sets forth some fundamental conditions of his phenomenological method. His intention, as he states it, is to replace philosophy's embarrassing traditional dualisms (interior vs. exterior, being vs. appearance, potency vs. act—in which the first term of each antithesis is privileged) with the monism of the phenomenon which reduces the existent to the "series of appearances which manifest it."[62] Drawing on Heidegger's critique of the traditional handling of "phenomenon," and in particular on his critique of the negative and wholly privative meaning of the term that emerges most fully in Kant, Sartre insists that the "appearance," in his reorientation of things, "becomes full positivity; its essence is an 'appearing' which is no longer opposed to being but on the contrary is the measure of it."[63] What this means is that the "phenomenon can be studied and described as such, for it is *absolutely indicative of itself.*"[64] Sartre offers a literary example which speaks to the issues that concern Poulet and his structuralist revisionists: "We shall refuse . . . to understand by 'genius'—in the sense in which we say that Proust had genius' or that he 'was' a genius—a particular capacity to produce certain works, which was not exhausted exactly in producing them. The genius of Proust is neither the work considered in isolation nor the subjective ability to produce it; it is the work considered as the totality of the manifestations of the person."[65] So there is no indeterminate subject tucked away behind language, untouched by being and time; nor even, apparently, a wish that there was: "The appearance does not hide the essence, it reveals it; it *is* the essence. The essence of an existent is no longer a property sunk in the cavity of this existent; it is the manifest law which presides over the succession of its appearances, it is the principle of the series . . . the well-connected series of its manifestations."[66]

In an attempt to refine his neat textbook definition of phenomenology, Sartre subverts himself by creating a fatal gap inside the phenomenon, so that what was presumably a thoroughly unitary affair now becomes fissured. The phenomenon, it turns out, is not "absolutely indicative of itself" because the "principle of the series," the "well-connected series of its manifestations"—the so-called "manifest law" of the phenomenon which "presides over the succession of its appearances" is by no means manifest. Sartre acknowledges the problem: the principle, the law, the well-connectedness in the phenomenon is not given to consciousness, is no appearance, in fact, but an interpretation whose object is situated behind the phenomenon. Of course Sartre denies that his new dualism carries any of the useless ontological freight that his phenomenological method was designed to jettison. In a passage that I have already examined in chapter 2, he puts it this way: "the existent in fact cannot be reduced to a *finite* series of manifestations since each one of them is a relation to a subject constantly changing. Although an object may disclose itself only through a single *Abschattung*, the sole fact of there being a subject implies the possibility of multiplying the points of view on that *Abschattung*. This suffices to multiply to infinity the *Abschattung* under consideration."[67] The being of the phenomenon (Sartre characterizes it as the "being-which-does-not-appear") is "transcendent" and can never be given even to that hypothetical, changing subject whose perspectives are multiplied to infinity.[68] For at every point out *to* infinity, what is given is given phenomenologically as an *Abschattung* for a finite human subject, for an existent, in other words, who is still subject to the human and temporal conditions of revelation. But *at* the point of infinity, beyond every finite perspective possible, the "being-which-does-not-appear" is grasped—how could Sartre avoid the logic?—by a transcendental subject. His conclusion is contradictory. Since the transphenomenal being of the phenomenon is not subject to the phenomenal condition, is never given to a human subject, it cannot, despite his disclaimer, be coextensive with the phenomenon; it cannot be "full positivity" unless it is subject to the phenomenal condition. After the most rigorous intellectual effort Sartre has come around to a position (against his explicit intention) that is similar to what Poulet openly embraces. Anxious to avoid the idealistic reduction of being to a constituting consciousness, Sartre's existential depriviliging of consciousness leads ironically to the proposal of a world-behind-the-scene. More and more, Poulet's elusion of the labyrinth of time appears not idiosyncratic, but normative for contemporary criticism.

5

If there has been one philosopher–literary critic in the twentieth century who has seemed not to succumb to temptations to transcend history, it is Martin Heidegger.[69] From *Being and Time* (1927) down through his late essays on poetry, his attack on the various forms of dualism that have engaged philosophers and literary theorists since Descartes has been relentless. Both thematically and methodologically Heidegger's antidualism—with its attendant metaphoric strategies for subverting the traditional view of the subject as free substance, floating somewhere in the ethers above time and human society—is a unifying principle for work done both before and after the so-called "turn" or reversal *(die Kehre)*. From a certain perspective, the celebrated turn —if that is what it truly was—is of no significance; the later, poetic Heidegger is simply the fulfillment of a project begun in *Being and Time*. To describe the *telos* of Heidegger's career thus is to suggest— not incorrectly, however crudely—that he is an archromantic in the German tradition whose quest is for a unity of human being with its world that almost defies the normal capacities of discourse. Hence his notion of *Dasein*, generally misunderstood, via Sartre, as "human reality"; hence the frequent concatenated expressions ("being-in-the-world" [*in der Welt sein*] is the pivotal one) aiming to convey a unitary phenomenon which translations tend to fragment; hence the difficult metaphoric consequences of certain key terms, early and late, such as "world," *physis*, *logos*, "appropriation," "difference," and "spanning." But in the time-honored nineteenth-century fashion of the German idealists, he fights dualism with the weapons of a dualistic and aestheticized terminology that would divide human experience into the beautiful and the mundane. For "mundane" in Heidegger read *das Man*, the inauthentic "one" who moves anonymously through the socially determined necessities of "everyday life" *(das Alltägliche)*; for the Kantian "beautiful" substitute "being as such."[70] In Heidegger the "ontological" (as the being or ground of entities, being which, though not itself an entity, permits entities, as their context, to be encountered as such) is pitted against the "ontic"[71] (entityhood and the traits of entities, the realm of inquiry for scientists, dogs, donkeys, and other object-mongers). The "historicality" of human being is pitted against the "world-history" of objects.[72] The "phenomenon" is re-defined (with powerful Hegelian resonances) as the proper purview of the ontologist—as showing forth, "self-blossoming emergence," "self-manifestation, self-representation, standing-there, presence"[73]—all of this against inherited concepts of the phenomenon as veil, illusion, privation behind which is hidden being that does not show itself or shine forth, never emerges, and is always inaccessible to consciousness.[74] While in theory, as Stephen Bronner has argued, the ontological and the ontic are inseparably bound, from the point of view of Heidegger's practice they are absolutely differentiated and give rise to two distinct types of knowledge:[75] science, which deals with the ontic level of existence, and philosophy, which deals with the ontological, the "ground of grounds" (Grund des Grundes)[76] of our freedom, of authentic Dasein, and of our transcendence of the everyday life of das Man as ontical (objectlike) subject.

That Heidegger's attack on the spatialized, isolate self aligns him with romantic values and perspectives we can, at this juncture, take safely for granted. The interest lies in the differences within that continuity, in Heidegger's existentializing and historicizing of human being. To the end of exposing some differences I offer passages from three texts: Schelling's "On the Relation of the Plastic Arts to Nature," Emerson's Nature, and Heidegger's analysis in Being and Time of the worldhood of the world (which he acknowledges owes a methodological debt to romantic concepts of nature) and his metaphoric gloss on that worldhood, the analysis of tool and its context in the "workshop." I begin with Schelling, who insists that the question of the nature of nature is anterior, logically, to the classical injunction that it is nature that art must imitate:

> But what should this broad general proposition profit the
> artist, when there are almost as many differing views
> of it [nature] as there are modes of life? Thus, to one,
> nature is nothing more than the lifeless aggregate of an
> indeterminable crowd of objects, or the space in which,
> as in a vessel, he imagines things placed; to another, only
> the soil from which he draws his nourishment and support;
> to the inspired seeker alone, the holy, ever-creative
> original energy of the world, which generates and busily
> evolves all things out of itself.[77]

The first two options cited by Schelling are variations on the single theme of Cartesian dualism: nature as lifeless *res extensa*, opposed to all subjectivity. This is the theme of Coleridge's world without imagination, where "all objects (as objects) are essentially fixed and dead"[78]— what he describes in "Dejection: An Ode" as the "inanimate cold world" of the "loveless ever-anxious crowd." It is the theme of Poulet's alien object-world through which the critic of consciousness must journey in order to get to the promised land of the *cogito*. It is the notion, finally, of "world" as defined by what is called common sense: "world" as collection of things the whole of which is equal to the sum of its parts, a locus of human being in which human being is in the world as (to cite Heidegger's echo of Schelling) water is in a glass[79]— the world as the "space" in which, "as in a vessel," things, human beings among other things, are "placed." Within such assumptions one can only act practically—which a romantic lexicon would gloss as voraciously, egocentrically: we can invest things with value, we can *use* nature as the soil from which we draw "nourishment and support." The alternative is to reject Cartesianism and its utilitarian consequences altogether for another set of assumptions (theological, transcendental, decidedly monistic) which would establish nature as origin and ground, an all-embracing totality within which the isolation of subject and object may have some analytic but no real value, a unitary context within which subject and object are interdependent. In this view of nature—the one that Schelling clearly favors—the structure of relationality itself is more primordial than things actually in relation.

Schelling traced epistemologically the movement from the crowd of objects and purely utilitarian relations to the "holy," as movement in consciousness from reason and intellect to "intuition." Romantic writers tended to enthrone this perception and then assign it exclusively to artists and poets; Emerson is especially lucid on the point. Provided that the appropriate surnames were substituted, the passage that follows from *Nature* (1836) could be interpolated with ease into Schelling's text:

> When we speak of nature in this manner, we have a distinct
> but most poetical sense in the mind. We mean the integrity
> of impression made by manifold natural objects. It is
> this which distinguishes the stick of timber of the wood-
> cutter from the tree of the poet. The charming landscape
> which I saw this morning is indubitably made up of some
> twenty or thirty farms. Miller owns this field, Locke that,
> and Manning the woodland beyond. But none of them

> owns the landscape. There is a property in the horizon
> which no man has but he whose eye can integrate all the
> parts, that is, the poet. This is the best part of these men's
> farms, yet to this their warranty-deeds can give no
> title.[80]

Schelling's crowd of objects is given a Kantian ring by Emerson with the phrase "manifold of natural objects"; the relation of pure utility is repeated in the illustration of farming (and one notes the choice of Locke); the notion of nature as object ("twenty or thirty farms") is set against the nature (here called "landscape") which embraces both subject and object. What is very clear in Emerson is that the move, obsessively interesting for the romantic mind, from the practical (with a clear economic implication) to the aesthetic is a move from working, willing, and ownership ("property," the warranty-deed) to a mode of being characterized by pure contemplation; from property as *private property* to "a property" as a quality revealed by vision but located neither in vision (as *in* a subject) nor *within* the fenced-off boundaries of this or that farmer's property. What is also interesting in Emerson's text is that though he has no recourse to the holy, he manages to save the values of the holy for the aesthetic: as perfect uselessness, the aesthetic is found outside the realm of working and of private property. It is transcendent not in the sense that it partakes of the noumenal (though Emerson will make that claim frequently) but because it achieves a perfect apartness, a freedom ("none of them owns the land-scape") by virtue of its unprivatized and materialistically unlocatable being. No matter how men work, or where they work, or under what conditions they work, or what purposes working serves, the landscape as a realm of vision remains what it is: it simply abides. The revenge of the aesthetic is that it can negate the values of private property, the economic privileges of ownership, and all of the conditions that attach to ownership. But it is a revenge itself conditioned by the hated practical world, a revenge which operates within the perspective of alienation: from an economically alienated position of impoverishment, the poet becomes property-rich in the sense that he becomes landlord and master of timeless imaginative territory ("a property . . . which no man has but he whose eye can integrate all the parts"). The poet assumes a new kind of alienation, an alienation which permits the aesthetically elite to play in the imagination, a world of freedom beyond and above the practical world where, from this exalted perspective, workers and owners, those who serve private property and those who have it, are alike slaves, alike ensnared in a vicious process.

Though Heidegger's search for a relational context that would resolve Cartesian difficulties is no less committed than Schelling's and Emerson's—and considerably more extended and detailed—his point is a would-be reversal of theirs, and as such a perfect illumination of what it means to call his phenomenology "existential" (rather than transcendental after Husserl), or his romantic orientation historical rather than idealistic. An important clue is his distinction between the kind of being that is "present-at-hand" (*Vorhandensein*) and the kind of being that is "ready-to-hand" (*Zuhandensein*): a distinction between what is merely there, for no purpose (at hand but not *to* the hand, not "handy") and what is there usefully, invested with value, good for something: preeminently, the tool.[81] What Heidegger does, in essence, is to reverse the typical romantic ranking of the aesthetic over the utilitarian, the contemplative over the active life. This reversal is a key to his understanding that human being is fundamentally and immediately to be found in praxis, in its ceaseless concern with and management of things; in other words, human being is fundamentally worldly, and fundamentally temporal—not eternal, not transcendent of the quotidian routines of the work-a-day world. (With his stress on praxis it becomes immediately apparent why Heidegger must reject Husserl's *epochē*; in effect, it is the rejection of the idealistic implications of the *epochē* which characterizes his phenomenology as existential.)

Tools[82] have a "proximity"[83] to human being that items of *Vorhandensein*, nonuseful stuff, whether natural or artifactual, can never have. Tools exist in the "neighborhood"[84] of human being, they have been brought close in the exercise of concern, not in a spatial sense, as when I say the ashtray is close to my hand, but in a spiritual sense which we discover when an indispensable instrument with which we do our work, and which enables us to further our projects, for some reason malfunctions. The malfunctioning of the tool necessarily entails a loss of human being in the sense that it shuts down the realization of certain human possibilities. It is the tool, not the romantic's affectively invested natural object, which belies the isolation of subject and object, which unveils human being as neither inside nor outside. "World" (*Welt*) rather than "nature" in the Schellingian or Emersonian senses is the region (*Gegend*) of *Dasein*; it is the inclusive, all-embracing totality understood now as a culturally determinate instrumental complex. The items within this relational context called world reveal *Dasein's* investments of value: those things ready-to-hand which have been given assignment or reference, a quality which is never discernible scientifically as a property or trait in the ontic sense (as in a trait of a spatially locatable object), a quality which, as it reveals the concerns of *Dasein*, reveals its purposes, its possibilities, in the work it would do.

This totality of assignments, or "workshop"[85] (Heidegger's most illuminating metaphor for what he intends by *Welt*) establishes the being that *Dasein* may achieve, given the media available to human work at any given juncture of human history; and the work that is *done* is a "world-building," which "is history in the authentic sense," since it is through "world-building" that human being in its various manifestations is disclosed and brought to light.[86] The obsessive metaphors in Heidegger of "proximity," "nearness," and what is obscurely translated as "deseverance" (*Ent-fernung*)—a "bringing close," "*an essential tendency towards closeness*"[87]—together with the metaphors of the "region" or "neighborhood" of *Dasein*, are probably as precise ways as he could have hit upon to express the notion of a subject which is not enclosed substance but is in-the-world, unfolds through its intentional acts which are not only *in* time but, in some primordial sense, establish human temporality as such. The metaphors of "region" and "neighborhood" suggest that *Dasein* is at once self-present and spread out in and through the objects of its concern, not bound up spatially at a distance from all objects. This "spread out" and self-present quality of *Dasein* is what Heidegger means by world in the expression "being-in-the-world." *Dasein* is a constitutive structure of world, and its being-in (*in-sein*) refers to its fundamental involvement, its intentionality; but world is, in turn, the basic constitutive structure of *Dasein*. The circular, unitary, reciprocal involvement of subject and object in Heidegger's thought is not evidence of a logical failure to keep things properly sorted out and properly placed in their lexical bins, but rather of the contrary: of a conviction that *Dasein* and world as ontological, not ontic, are never to be interpreted with categories drawn from the ontic spheres of *res extensa*, never to be reduced to the subject-object model that tends to dominate the history of Western thought (another reciprocative model, but one which involves "subject" with "object" as just another kind of *res*). As instrumental totality, as field of human activity, world is not only the context or ontological ground which permits entities to come forward and be seen, but also the context of the discoverer of entities. World is the "there" of *Dasein*, and *Sein* is the being of the world. Human being is both center and circumference.

Heidegger's elevation of the instrumental over the natural is his way of uncovering the worldhood of the world. While the nature of nature is not and must not be fully historical, the worldhood of the world is human in a way that nature can never be. As the workshop, the world is a place especially amenable to farmers like Miller, Locke, Manning, and other owners or laborers, and is to be contrasted to the holy ground of Schelling or the landscape of Emerson, which are places inaccessible to those unable to shut off will, action, and making. For Emerson the experience of vision is nothing less than the destruction of our social condition: "The name of the nearest friend sounds then foreign and accidental: to be brothers, to be acquaintances—master or servant, is then a trifle and a disturbance."[88] To enter the world for Heidegger is to enter history (apparently), while to enter the landscape is to transcend it. But in his analysis of the cognitive "lighting up" of world—as distinguished from our preoccupied, concernful, and undifferentiated living in the world—Heidegger reverts, in his privileging of the broken tool (Zuhandensein which ceases suddenly to function, becomes Vorhandensein) to the reprivileging (in the mode of Kant, Coleridge, and other progenitors and practitioners of modernist aesthetic thought) of aesthetic contemplation and of the moment of willess, intransitive vision. The useless, broken tool pulls us up short, pulls us out of action and out of the chain of transitive acts demanded by the workshop (the entire chain of referential assignments, the instrumental complex which conditions every individual assignment of work). In its broken, useless condition the tool has been "made strange" (romantic and formalist theories dovetail easily with Heidegger at this point), has had its film of familiarity stripped from it: Shelley would recognize both the strategy and its goals.

Neither an ontical concept which "signifies the totality of those entities which can be present-at-hand within the world,"[89] nor a subjective concept in the Cartesian sense of res cogitans, world is uncovered for consciousness by the broken tool. We become aware of the tool as tool when we are awakened from the sleep induced by the smoothly functioning tool which, in its perfect utility, disappears into its functioning. Equipment, Heidegger reminds us, is never encountered in isolation; it always belongs to a totality of equipment; it is essentially something with reference to something else, something-in-order-to (etwas um-zu). "Equipment—in accordance with its equipmentality—always is in terms of [aus] its belonging to other equipment: ink-stand, pen, ink, paper, blotting-pad, table, lamp, furniture, windows, doors, room."[90] But the being, or world, of equipment, its totality of context, its successive assignments of the in-order-to taken as a unified whole, is, as long as equipment remains in good order, withheld, inconspicuous, unobtrusive: hidden from consciousness. Only when equipment fails, when the hammer can no longer be used for hammering, does the world announce itself to us: "In conspicuousness, obtrusiveness, and obstinacy, that which is ready-to-hand loses its readiness-to-hand in a certain way. . . . It does not vanish simply, but takes its farewell, as it were, in the conspicuousness of the unusable. Readiness-to-hand still shows itself, and it is precisely here that the worldly character of the ready-to-hand shows itself too."[91] With the breakdown of equipment, at *that* very moment we become witnesses to an ontological shift or transition. To put it another way: at the point of "farewell," in a privileged time of the "between" neither purely ontological nor purely ontic, we experience a moment of revelation which would unite the two separate levels of being on their fundamental ground. This context of equipment which has been lit up with the disturbing of the referential assignment of the tool is nothing less than a "totality of involvements," a workshop which is constitutive of the ready-to-hand in its readiness-to-hand, and is "earlier" than any single item of equipment (as, for example, a farmstead is prior to its various utensils or outlying lands). The workshop becomes both origin and end:

> But the totality of involvements itself goes back ultimately to a "towards-which" in which there is *no* further involvement: this "towards-which" is not an entity with the kind of Being that belongs to what is ready-to-hand within a world; it is rather an entity whose Being is defined as Being-in-the-world, and to whose state of Being, worldhood itself belongs. This primary "towards-which" is not just another "towards-which" as something in which an involvement is possible. The primary "towards-which" is a "for-the-sake-of-which."[92]

6

The so-called turn or reversal from the phenomenological ontology of *Being and Time* to the later essays on language and poetry, via the "Letter on Humanism," is subverted by the common aesthetic method which guides the analysis in both periods of Heidegger's writing. The difference is that the later Heidegger places more and more faith in the possibilities of poetry, and specifically in the possibility that poetic language would deliver and open up the human world, and, more extremely, that poetic language *alone* would deliver on the promise of phenomenological ontology. The bridge between early and late Heidegger is "The Origin of the Work of Art" (*Der Ursprung des Kuntswerkes*), and the bibliographical history of this piece is a clue to the value that he placed upon it.[93] Given initially as a single lecture at Freiburg in the fall of 1935 (just a few months earlier he had given the lectures that would constitute *An Introduction to Metaphysics*) and repeated at Zurich in January of 1936, "The Origin of the Work of Art" was expanded into three lectures which were delivered in Frankfurt late in 1936. This latter set of Frankfurt lectures found its way into print, initially, in *Holzwege* (1950), an edition which itself, through the 1950s, went through several printings and changes. Finally, "The Origin of the Work of Art" was printed separately by Reclam of Stuttgart, with an introduction by Hans-Georg Gadamer, but only after the text of *Holzwege* had been once again revised. The obviousness of the point does not detract from its significance: the long-term care that Heidegger lavished on this text on aesthetics claims for it something like a governing place in his canon.

The newly prominent term in Heidegger's vocabularly is *Kunstwerk* and it takes its place in relation to readiness-to-hand and presence-at-hand thus: *Kunstwerk-Zuhandensein-Vorhandensein*. What had seemed a simple opposition in *Being and Time* of the ready-to-hand and the present-at-hand is reconceived, with the entrance of the third term, as dialectical activity. As in *Being and Time*, the middle term, equipment, assumes an ontological priority in the interpretaton of everything that is. In its equipmental character equipment helps us to pry open the work of art, since both display a functional relation of form to matter, while in its "thingy" character, which derives from presence-at-hand, the stuff of which equipment is fashioned, equipment helps us to comprehend the dimension of the work of art as "earth."[94] (More later on this difficult concept.) Whereas in *Being and Time* Heidegger left us with the impression that when one came upon failed equipment one simply was arrested, lifted out of the flow of *praxis* into the frozen attention that allowed one vision of the complicated interrelated human investments of "world," in "The Origin of the Work of Art" he seems to be saying that only art can help us to that kind of awareness, that the phenomenological grasp of being does not happen fortuitously but only through artistic mediation. Heidegger insists so strongly on the last point, in fact, not only in "The Origin of the Work of Art" but in a number of the later essays, that it is not a violation of the spirit of his philosophy to call it an inquiry into aesthetic ontology, rather than phenomenological ontology, provided that Heidegger's kind of aestheticism is understood to route us, at least by intention, deeper into the human world, not away from it.

He cites as example a painting by Van Gogh of a pair of peasant shoes set against a background of undefined space.[95] His main point is that the painting is *technē* which, in his etymology, means not craft or technique, but a mode of knowing, a bringing into the light, unconcealedness—what the Greeks called *alethēia*. What is brought into

the light is not the subjectivity or personal world of the artist—
Heidegger was no protocritic of consciousness, in spite of rumors to
the contrary—nor a representation of some real or ideal entity, but
the truth of the being of the entity. In the terminology of *Being and
Time*, art opens up the *ontological* ground of the merely ontic. Neither
by description, nor by observation of the process of making shoes,
nor by a report on their actual use do we encounter *alethēia*, but by
bringing ourselves before Van Gogh's painting. So the painting functions as failed equipment had functioned earlier: it gives us entry to
the world that supports peasant shoes; it makes them appear as such—
as *peasant* shoes.

Though he sentimentalizes his analysis of Van Gogh by writing that
the person who wears the shoes "knows" without noticing or reflecting all of the things that the painting tells the critical interpreter, in
general Heidegger avoids the romantic idealization of the folk. As he
develops the issues it is clear that he means it when he says that truth
must happen in art, and only in art; it seems impossible that he means
to imply that the complicated processes of concealedness-unconcealed-
ness, of the intimate opposing of world vs. earth, and of the difficult
function of the rift (*Riss*) are all grasped silently and unself-consciously
by folk intuition. We may stop our gliding consciousness when we
encounter the broken hammer, or we may simply toss the hammer
away and get a new one without experiencing the opening of a world.
The implication is that in art, insofar as we bring ourselves before it,
"world" will force itself upon us: "the equipmentality of equipment
first genuinely arrives at its appearance through the work and only
in the work."[96] Truth "happens" in the work: "In the work of art
the truth of an entity [its ontological support] has set itself to work.
'To set' means here: to bring to a stand. Some particular entity, a pair
of peasant shoes, comes to stand in the light of its being. The being
of the being comes into the steadiness of its shining."[97] The art work
thus becomes a uniquely honored example of what was defined in *Being
and Time* as phenomenon ("showing forth") and *logos* ("making manifest").[98] In the terms of the pre-Socratic story that Heidegger tells in
An Introduction to Metaphysics, the art work becomes the privileged
mediation, the healing connection uniting what has been torn apart
by the history of Western metaphysics (ontotheological thought). The
dualisms we know now as inside and outside, subject and object,
thought and being, the pre-Socratics understood as a single totality
of being which displayed itself not as nature (an object which stands
apart from thought and discourse, and which then needs to be represented in thought conceived as logical thinking or rationality), but

as *physis* ("the power that emerges . . . the process . . . of emerging from the hidden," a "shining appearing") and *logos* (the primal gathering principle, a discourse which is a "collecting collectedness" of being understood as *physis*).[99] Art defeats these divisions, these fallen duplicities of Western philosophical thought. The continuity of Heidegger's metaphors tells us that in the idea of the work of art he brings together and unifies the concepts of phenomenon, *logos, physis,* and *Schein*. The Descartes-denying, unitary notions of world and phenomenon, *logos* and *physis*, reach their culmination in an aesthetic neatly prefigured in this passage from *Being and Time*, which banishes what Nietzsche called the world-behind-the-scene: " 'Behind' the phenomena of phenomenology there is essentially nothing else; on the other hand, what is to become a phenomenon can be hidden. And just because the phenomena are proximally and for the most part *not* given, there is need for phenomenology. Covered-up-ness is the counter-concept to phenomenon."[100]

It is not that art brings into the light of *alethēia* that which lurked hidden on the other side of phenomena, just beyond the reach of consciousness. Art's disclosures do not penetrate phenomena in order to dredge upon noumenal realities and bring them before our awareness. After *Being and Time* Heidegger argues again and again that there is need for art to unconceal what is covered-up, what is given to consciousness but does not shine and show forth the being of its being, what is given as mere thinginess or mere equipment, what in its easy reliability puts our phenomenological awareness into a state of stupor and half-wakefulness. Art strips the film of familiarity from our everyday world, it discloses the ontological radiating through what is merely ontic (the object which, as object, is fixed and dead). Outside of art, Heidegger seems to be saying, the realm of consciousness is phenomenologically underpowered, it is a realm of obscurity, of things dimly and dully apprehended in their entityhood (when they are apprehended at all), a realm of slipperiness and elusiveness where nothing stands steadily or forthrightly as what it is. Outside of art we see shoes; inside we see the world of shoes, the entire context within which their work is carried out.

The point of Heidegger's attack on the Cartesian subject becomes ultimately clear in his essays on art, poetry, and language when he repeatedly attacks the expression theory as a model of artistic origin which "presupposes the idea of something internal that utters or externalizes itself"; which presupposes that expression is an activity controlled by an individuated, univocal subject in isolation; and which presupposes that what is presented in expression is the perspective, the consciousness, the inner personal world of a single expressive agent.[101] That sort of model, loosely Wordsworthian, was canonized for a whole generation of scholars as the romantic view by Meyer Abrams in his monumental studies; it was articulated repeatedly under the guise of the *cogito* by Poulet; it was indulged in by Heidegger himself in his discussion of Georg Trakl and the "site"[102]—the poetic statement which remains unspoken, unspeakable, the "ever more hidden source" of everything that does get said. That sort of model, which is of the essence of common sense, and which has lately been under severe attack by structuralist and poststructuralist thinkers, was opposed with great energy by the antihumanist strain within romanticism itself which believes, with Heidegger, that in great art "the artist remains inconsequential as compared with the work, almost like a passageway that destroys itself in the creative process for the work to emerge."[103] That setting up of the artist as a passageway, or passive medium, has innumerable echoes in romantic thought on both sides of the Atlantic and all over the Continent, on down to its great contemporary elaboration in the *Anatomy of Criticism*. What Heidegger shares with this tradition is not the vaguely Christian, vaguely Eastern contempt for the subject that we find in Shelley or Schopenhauer or Frye, but a radical claim that the subject does not exist at the deeper levels of philosophic analysis. Art confirms for him that being-in-the-world is not personal or private being-in-the-world; that the idea of the worldhood of the world, as the structural dimension of *Dasein* which emerges in the analysis of failed equipment and great art, is fundamentally a suprapersonal structure, an "open relational context,"[104] which discloses cultural and historical being (not the trivialities of personal selfhood):

> The *world worlds*, and is more fully in being than the
> tangible and perceptible realm in which we believe
> ourselves to be at home. World is never an object that
> stands before us and can be seen. World is the ever-
> nonobjective to which we are subject as long as the paths
> of birth and death, blessing and curse keep us trans-
> ported into Being. Wherever those decisions of our history
> that relate to our very being are made, are taken up and
> abandoned by us, go unrecognized and are rediscovered
> by new inquiry, there the world worlds. A stone is world-
> less. Plant and animal likewise have no world; but they
> belong to the covert throng of a surrounding into which
> they are linked. The peasant woman, on the other hand,
> has a world because she dwells in the overtness of beings,

of the things that are. Her equipment, in its reliability,
gives to this world a necessity and nearness of its own.[105]

By interpreting creation as the "self-sovereign subject's performance
of genius,"[106] modern subjectivism (as Heidegger calls it) necessarily
trivializes world by making it a kind of private property, rather than
the common land of *Dasein*, a neighborhood or region of human being.

The notion of world is deepened when Heidegger elaborates it against
a second crucial concept, that of earth *(Erde)*. If equipment is a mediating term between *Kunstwerk* and what is called *Vorhandensein*, then
the thinginess of equipment must as well cast light upon the work of art.
A possible objection to Heidegger's analysis, at this point, might be that
it merely repeats the analysis of failed equipment and the emergence of
world in the moment of vision triggered by that failure. One might
argue that art only makes more easily available what is frequently available (though hidden to deadened consciousness) in our everyday world,
if only we would pay the proper sort of Kantian attention to the things
about us. Such an objection has no force when the notion of earth is put
alongside that of world, and the two are seen as an "intimacy of opponents"—when "world" and "earth" are perceived as set into design
in the figure of the rift *(Riss)* which unveils world and earth in their
deepest intimacy of disconnection.[107] As this aspect of his theory is
elaborated, the term *Kunstwerk* emerges as a dialectical synthesis which
captures the world-opening quality of broken equipment and the world-
resisting quality of *Vorhandensein*, or what is called the "self-
closure"[108] of earth. The work of art "sets up" a world, but it "sets
forth" the earth: *"The work lets the earth be an earth"*[109] is the way
Heidegger phrases it. What he means by this is not that the work is
realistic in its portrayal of nature, but something far more familiar to
readers of neo-Kantian aesthetics. In "The Origin of the Work of Art"
earth is a reference to the aesthetic medium: the sculptor's stone, the
painter's pigment, the poet's language, the architect's rock and wood.
The aesthetic handling of medium is in brilliant contrast to the handling
of medium as equipment: "Because it is determined by usefulness and
serviceability, equipment takes into its service that of which it consists:
the matter. In fabricating equipment—e.g. an axe—stone is used, and
used up. It disappears into usefulness. . . . By contrast the temple-work,
in setting up a world, does not cause the material to disappear, but
rather it causes it to come forth for the very first time and to come into
the Open of the work's world."[110]

So we have the familiar formalist distinction of utilitarian and aesthetic values, of a medium which must be made unobstrusive if it is to

be useful, if it is to mediate, and of a medium cherished for its own sake, set forth in its irreducible sensuous reality, as good in itself, thrusting itself upon our attention. But earth thus set forth, unconcealed from its hidden place in reliable equipment, remains in all its immediacy a mystery; unlike world which is an "opening," earth "denies us any penetration," it is that which is "by nature undisclosable, that which shirks from every disclosure and constantly keeps closed up."[111] The setting forth of earth is a paradox in that earth is brought into the Open only in order that it may announce itself as "essentially self-secluding," forever closed to the gaze of "technical-scientific objectivation"[112]—but not closed (apparently) to the gaze of Heidegger. Earth against world, *Vorhandensein* against *Zuhandensein*—in the distant background Hegel's in-itself against the for-itself: an existentialist thematic shapes up. If world (clearly a cultural category) is the "self-disclosing openness of the broad paths of the simple and essential decisions in the destiny of an historical people,"[113] then earth begins to look like the representation of an existential category, the overriding existential category: the unendurable "in-itself" whose perfect resistance to consciousness foregrounds the agonies of human finitude and isolation. Heidegger speaks of earth as a "jutting in"[114] which (though he does not say so) would appear to force *Dasein* to authentic self-confrontation, or to flight.

The question, then, is of the relationship of world to earth. It is not a relation of the empty unity of opposites unconcerned with one another. What Heidegger means by the intimacy of their opposition is in part clarified by his dramatic metaphors of invasion: the uninvadable earth, closed off to penetration, penetrates world. Always active in the making of world, *Dasein* is passive vis-à-vis earth. And whereas *Dasein* is familiar with the world, reciprocal with it as an intimate dwelling place or home, the rhythms of earth are alien to *Dasein*. As the difference or "between" of world and earth, *Dasein* becomes the dialectical ground of their intimate disconnection. The difficult relation of world and earth is further clarified by the metaphors of the rift and the open;[115] they reveal the nature of truth in art, which is not simply a truth of the open, the clear, the worldhood of the world lit up for our gaze, but a doubleness of clearing and obscuring, a truth of the simultaneity of unconcealing and concealing. "Truth is un-truth, insofar as there belongs to it the reservoir of the not-yet-uncovered, the un-uncovered, in the sense of concealment. In concealedness, as truth, there occurs also the other 'un-' of a double restraint or refusal."[116] The truth of being, then, is not to be aligned with the unveiling of the worldhood of the world—an impression left by *Being and Time*. Heidegger's much-repeated metaphors of lighting up and clearing need to be placed alongside the equally significant patterns of images, generated from the metaphor of earth which cannot be found in *Being and Time*, of ultimate, unredeemable hiddenness: "Truth is present only as the conflict between lighting and concealing as the opposition of world and earth."[117] Thematically truth is apprehended as the conflict of the cultural and the existential on the field of *Dasein*; structurally it is made to appear in art through figure and centrally through the rift—another figuring of the "between" which constitutes the cleft that keeps world and earth apart in a design that "measures" and "bounds"[118] their apartness in *Dasein*. In Heidegger's difficult metaphor the open, like *Dasein* itself, is both center and circumference. As center it gathers all beings to it and makes them appear coherently as beings-in-the-world; and yet it is circumference, as well, an encirclement of beings, itself encircled by the impenetrable earth. The open is the open by virtue of the closed which surrounds it.

The existential thematics of early Heidegger is in some part obscured by the proliferation in the late essays of a series of terms which are semantically slippery and are made even more difficult because of the metaphoric weight they must carry. These terms variously tend to emphasize a principle of gathering: in the early work *logos* is "original collecting collectedness," the "primal gathering principle," *world* is "relational context," and *rift* is a figure of gathering into intimate opposition. To these early terms must be added the master concept of the late essays, language, and the entire series of its metaphoric interpretations as the "house" of being; as the "neighborhood" of *Dasein*; as "appropriation"; as the calling of beings into "presence" and "nearness" (and their counterconcepts, "scattering," "distance" and "absence"); as that which "bids" and "invites"; as "gathering," "assembling," "letting-stay"; and those late variants on rift, "difference," "measure-taking," "threshold," "dimension," and "spanning."[119]

Neither expression nor mimesis, in its appropriating activity language (no activity of man) gathers human being into its region, grants it an abode, makes it possible for human being to dwell familiarly. Those same appropriating and invitational powers which draw and call man into humanness extend into the ontic realms, and by so doing bestow thinghood by gathering things into the nearness of *Dasein*. The gathering of things is always a gathering into the proximity of *Dasein*, and proximity to *Dasein's* concernful being is what bestows worldhood. The themes of late Heidegger remain much what they were in *Being and Time*; the difference is that the burdens have been shifted to language. If we now add to the metaphoric patterns of gathering and proximity the entire pattern that unfolds from the notion of the rift—

dif-ference, measure-taking, threshold, dimension, and spanning—what we see is something like the completion of the thought elaborated in "The Origin of the Work of Art." The allegory of cultural man's conflict with himself as existential man (world vs. earth) is repeated, then varied upward as a conflict between existential man and the supernatural (earth vs. sky); and both themes are constituted linguistically with the sort of rifting or threshold moment now called dif-ference: "The dif-ference is the bidder. The dif-ference gathers the two [world and thing] into the rift that is the dif-ference itself."[120] But the dif-ference is also the threshold, "the ground-beam that bears the doorway as a whole. It sustains the middle in which the two, the outside and the inside, penetrate each other. The threshold bears the between."[121] And dif-ference (like the notion of bridging) is also gauging, dimension-taking, "the middle for world and things" which "metes out the measure of their presence."[122] And, lastly, dif-ference is the spanning of *Dasein* between earth and world, earth and sky: "Man does not undertake this spanning just now and then; rather, man is man at all only in such spanning."[123]

Jacques Derrida's criticism of Heidegger is just; Heidegger's key theme is a humanistic one, carried quietly by the notion of proximity.[124] If early metaphors of gathering emphasize a drawing into the nearness of human beings, then late metaphors do not reject this thought but rather supplement it. In spanning, in bridging, in taking measure, even in the dif-ference, human being is thrown outward. The activities of drawing in and of throwing outward, in the end, however, have the single effect of the *spreading out* of the human, the measuring of all things from an anthropocentric center. Thus the Derridean charge that Heidegger is the last humanist, not the destroyer of the *anthropos*. And we probably should add to this critique that Heidegger's existential humanism celebrates as its ultimate category of value the aesthetic; for it is only poetry, he tells us repeatedly in the late work, that can gauge man's measure by unveiling the difference of the between. The lesson of Heidegger is a consistently tragic one. Unlike the German idealists behind him, and unlike the apocalyptic humanist Northrop Frye, for whom all things are solvent in the human imagination, Heidegger emphasizes that though there are many worlds there is only one earth—mysterious, mastering, and intransigent before our human projects. Earth cannot be liberated into the region of *Dasein*. Or to put it in his terms: man undertakes spanning, but he does not accomplish it. The dif-ference is not *spanned*; *Dasein* moves within the isolating boundaries of earth and sky.

7

> The fact that Heidegger does admit a form of "authentic" historicity in his system is not really relevant.... Heidegger tends to belittle historicity as "vulgar"; and his "authentic" historicity is not distinguishable from ahistoricity.
>
> Georg Lukács, *Realism in Our Time*

> ... I soon realized that Heidegger's concreteness was to a great extent phony, a false concreteness, and that in fact his philosophy was just as abstract and just as removed from reality, even avoiding reality, as the philosophies which at that time had dominated German universities, namely a rather dry brand of neo-Kantianism, neo-Hegelianism, neo-Idealism, but also positivism.
>
> Herbert Marcuse, "Heidegger's Politics: An Interview"

If Heidegger's romantic exaltation of poetic language as ontological revelation places his thought as yet one more, perhaps culminating, repetition of a visionary theory of the poet, then his account of what he calls the "historicality" of *Dasein*, so far from accommodating his romanticism to time and culture, goes a very long way toward subverting the foundational concept of world, the primary intention of which is to offer a viable alternative to transcendentalist evasions of the labyrinth of history. His well-known insistence on the "thrown" or "situated" character of human being, and his repeated claims for the historical relevance of poetry and of his philosophical method, need to be tested against the theory of historicality set forth in the penultimate chapter of *Being and Time*. In any interpretation of what Heidegger intends on this issue, it is probably worth keeping in mind that the theory of *Dasein's* historicity comes at the conclusion of a lengthy examination (it is the bulk of *Being and Time*) of the existential structures of *Dasein*, which is sometimes separated out from the method of that treatise and relegated to its thematics. Care and concern, anxiety and fear, being-towards-death, authenticity and inauthenticity, thrownness, falling, projection, guilt, conscience, mood, resoluteness, and everydayness—those structures as a group, but preeminently being-towards-death, form the determining context for an interpretation of *Dasein's* historicality.

The primary task in getting at historicality, Heidegger believes, is to describe some sort of "connectedness" between birth and death. As might be expected, he challenges traditional concepts which describe history as something that happens to human being: he sees behind such notions an amalgam which posits human being as a substance, a plan or essence given before time, which "stands in history," and at the same time becomes the passive plaything of circumstances and events. Against this sort of thought Heidegger wants to claim that *Dasein* is *"not 'temporal' because it 'stands in history'* "—as a ship rides the waves of the ocean, in it, but not in it—*"but that, on the contrary, it exists historically and can so exist only because it is temporal in the very basis of its Being."*[125] *Dasein* does not stand *in* history as an object in a container, nor can it ride history without being essentially touched by it: it is history—in Heidegger's terminology—it is "historizing," an idea distinguished from the "world-history" of cultural objects which have a pastness that keeps them past, as reliques of another age.[126] "World-history" happens to equipment; equipment is constituted by circumstances and human need. *Dasein,* on the contrary, since it can never be *Zuhandensein,* can never be past in that sense. Because *Dasein* is reciprocally involved with *Welt, Dasein's* pastness cannot be that of objects which are "innerworldly" (*innerweltlich*), that is, spatially encounterable. As a way or possibility of being, a relation to being (in other words, not ontic), *Dasein* can never, in a sense, be past at all. Though individual human beings clearly become past and cease to exist, the structural possibilities for *Dasein*, its various existential modes of being, continue to exist as a sort of continuing, universal storehouse of human options which are always open and which may be repeated. In fact, it is our peculiar fate to repeat (in the sense of fetching again, retrieving), and the only question for Heidegger is whether such repetition will be authentic or inauthentic. The distinction of historicality and world-history, in its echo of a number of key terminological dualisms, will turn out to be the most suggestive clue to Heidegger's difficult analysis. For the distinction will carry the meaning that we have seen already emerging in the conflict of existential and cultural *Dasein* and the consequent assignment of priority to the existential.

The question, I believe, is this: what quality of historicity is truly being assigned to *Dasein* if its "historizing" is understood wholly under the aegis of existential categories? Don't existential categories tend to be empty of detailed historical and social content? Isn't what Heidegger calls authentic historicality finally quite unhistorical? As "thrown," *Dasein* presumably finds itself submitted to a world. And yet in its true project it is the task of *Dasein* to transcend the world-historical, public implications and constraints of its thrownness. *Dasein* achieves such transcendence in the proper anticipation of death, which drives out every accidental and provisional possibility of *Dasein*, every possibility that is generated by the particular local textures and coercive forces of social institutions unfolded and unfolding in a culture. We know of Heidegger's protracted analysis of human being in its relations to instrumental complexes, but his analysis of interhuman relations in a social dimension is philosophically denigrated as "public-ness" (*Offentlichkeit*), an inauthentic realm of chatter and shirking ruled by *das Man*. "Heidegger forwards no analysis of the roots of *Offentlichkeit*, linguistic or otherwise—and for good reason," Stephen Bronner has written.[127] *Das Man* can only cover up *Dasein*. Few would deny his point that earth juts death into world, and that the ultimate context of world is an existential one (that, perhaps, is why it is a basically uninteresting point). But his existentialism is an escape from the real implications of his master metaphor of world as a *workshop*. For the metaphor demands that world be placed not in an existential context but within a frame of economic and political power wherein the purposes of the tool might be more profoundly interrogated. What, and who, really, "supports" that pair of peasant shoes?

"Only being free *for* death gives Dasein its goal outright. . . . This is how we designate Dasein's primordial historizing, which lies in its authentic resoluteness and in which Dasein *hands* itself *down* to itself, free for death in a possibility which it has inherited and yet has chosen."[128] Of course by accidental possibilities Heidegger means not coercions generated socially, economically, and politically, but existential inauthenticities like comfortableness and shirking. Yet his limiting of the accidental and the provisional to such existential possibilities is itself a way of blocking out of consideration what his theory of historicality manifestly must avoid: the submission of *Dasein* to constitutive social structures. Heidegger is clear about this:

> If Dasein, by anticipation, lets death become powerful
> in itself, then, as free for death, Dasein understands itself
> in its own *superior power*, the power of its finite freedom,
> so that in this freedom, which "is" only in its having
> chosen to make such a choice, it can take over the *power-
> lessness* of abandonment to its having done so, and can
> thus come to have a clear vision for the accidents of the
> Situation that has been disclosed.[129]

By taking over its own thrownness and abandonment, *Dasein* takes over, in a modest way, its own situated being; its being free for death means, in a circumscribed but irreducible sense, that *Dasein* is, simply, free.

In the transcendence of the powerlessness of abandonment, in the transcendence of the determinates of situation, we can locate Heidegger's alliance with the German idealist tradition which he thought to have put behind him. (No chance, of course, for the full-throated celebration in the mode of the Schillers and Marcuses of the utopian vision of freedom.) In its repetition (as a retrieving) of a possibility of existence that has come down to us ("going back into the possibilities of the Dasein that has-been-there"), *Dasein* makes a "reciprocative rejoinder" to the possibility of that existence that has-been-there: "*Authentic Being-towards-death—that is to say, the finitude of temporality—is the hidden basis of Dasein's historicality.*"[130] Avoiding, therefore, the fragmentations of daily life, the ways it is "driven about," *Dasein* wants to come to itself, not by attaining to some transcendent essence—for there is none—but (the effect is the same) by opting authentically for a culturally transcendent set of possibilities for being-in-the-world: "If it wants to come to itself, it must first *pull itself together*"— Heidegger recalls his principles of gathering with full force at this point—"from the *dispersion* and *disconnectedness* of the very things that have come to pass."[131] The injunction is fundamentally the idealistic one to unify; at all events, wrote Coleridge, who was nothing if not idealistic, the imagination must struggle to unify. *Dasein* must "*pull itself together, and think up for itself a unity in which that together is embraced.*"[132]

Such is authentic historicality: free from the constitutive powers of the "they," from the world-historical, from the powers that speak silently through institutions, and from the ideologies which surround and give a *telos* to human workshops, *Dasein* luxuriates in its *superior power,* in its escape from the dispersing forces that scatter human being through various levels of ensnaring relations. "Dasein is constituted in Historicity," Marcuse has argued, "but Heidegger focuses on individuals purged of the hidden and not so hidden injuries of their class, their work, their recreation, purged of the injuries they suffer from society."[133] Even to set up the problem in the way that Heidegger does, to suggest a unity and wholeness just the other side of history which becomes dispersed or fragmented in time, is a fundamentally idealistic way of mythologizing a narrative of human being. In this mythology, the "thrown" character of being-in-the-world, a supposedly primordial condition, becomes a falling from unity, a secondariness. *Verfallen* retains the stubborn theological implication of The Fall. In its disposition to recover unity from dispersion, Heidegger's philosophy is fundamentally nostalgic and world-weary. It is a last-ditch defense of the concept of man as a unified and gathered totality, secure in his neighborhood, existentially limited, of course, and confined by the biological trap, but in the freedom for death, free at the very heart of its being.

Four

history tells us that there is no such thing as
a timeless essence of literature, but under the rubric
"literature" (itself quite recent, moveover) a process
of very different forms, functions, institutions, reasons,
and projects whose relativity it is precisely the historian's responsibility to discern. . . .

Roland Barthes, *Critical Essays*

the capital sin in criticism is not ideology but
the silence by which it is masked. . . .

Roland Barthes, *Critical Essays*

Uncovering History and the Reader: Structuralism

One of the most startling events in the reception of structuralism in the United States occurred when a blue-ribbon committee of the Modern Language Association agreed to award the James Russell Lowell Prize for 1975 to Jonathan Culler's *Structuralist Poetics*. Anyone working in a literary department (and particularly in an English department) in the late sixties and early seventies could not have missed the repeated cries of outrage and disbelief directed at the news of the latest French barbarism. Very few could have predicted, in the wake of the Hopkins conference on structuralism of 1966, that the Lowell prize of '75 would be awarded to a book about an intellectual movement which (in the language of the structuralists) denied special privilege to literary discourse.

It might of course be argued that the MLA, by honoring Culler, was merely recording a dispassionate judgment. Structuralism, whatever its final merits, was not just one among a number of odd Continental flirtations with exotic modes of thought. It had, after all, since the late fifties and the earlier writing of Claude Lévi-Strauss, captured almost every serious intellectual center in Europe, and in the last five or six years in the United States had become an obsession (albeit a *bête noir*) for anyone even mildly concerned with the recent course of critical theory and its traditional history, and with the pedagogical rationale of literary and other humanistic disciplines. Though he was not the first on the scene (he was preceded by Fredric Jameson and Robert Scholes), Culler's was arguably the most accessible and fullest exposition of a group of writers whose main intellectual preoccupations made them appear to be at once fascinating, difficult to approach, and yet somehow only of marginal importance to scholars trained in conventional humanistic ways.

In orderly and comprehensive fashion, in the first part of his book Culler described the basic ideas of Saussure, Barthes, Lévi-Strauss, Roman Jakobson, and A. J. Greimas. In a second part, he extrapolated a model from structuralist principles designed to make the reading of literature as a whole (in his words) a "coherent and autonomous discipline."[1] Thus structuralism, which prior to Culler's interpretation had never been understood as having primary bearing on literary disciplines, was converted wholesale by him into a literary methodology of global implication. And in a third and concluding section he had dispensed with an apparent lunatic fringe of the new French thought, led by Jacques Derrida and centered in *Tel Quel*. To sum it up: Culler had performed a sterling service for contemporary intellectual historians by explaining a movement of huge international import, and then had made that movement workable for American literary scholars: reason enough, perhaps, to award him the Lowell prize.

If that is the reason. A certain nagging question continues to demand attention. How did a professional organization as conservative as the MLA so easily manage to insulate itself from the rampant paranoia in this country toward recent French thought? It is said that abominations are often fascinating, but Conrad's perception surely will not explain why the MLA granted its imprimatur to Culler. Nor does the objectivist argument (the corporate consciousness of the American literary establishment recognizes excellence when it sees it, so though we reserve the right to disagree with you, we will honor the force of your scholarship) suffice, despite the lip-service we like to give it. Culler's book has practically single-handedly mediated (and constituted) our understanding of structuralism, not because his work is demonstrably more acute than, say, Jameson's, but because his mediation rests on intellectual principles easily recognizable and very dear to the traditionalist American critical mind. Culler has made structuralism safe for us, and the MLA prize represents not merely the applause of his scholarly peers, but, as well, an ideological nod of recognition.

1

Both before and after making his major statement on the relevance of structuralism to literary criticism in a chapter entitled "Literary Competence," Culler introduces a number of crucial, and much-debated, recent critical issues in ways, calculated or not, that go far toward softening the impact of the new French thought. First of all, he gives us a convenient handle on (while thoroughly domesticating) Saussure's pivotal distinction between *langue* and *parole* by referring us to Noam Chomsky's parallel distinction between *competence* (the grammatical system we have internalized) and *performance* (actual linguistic behavior).[2] Second, he broaches the touchy subject of the *subject* with the sort of craftily balanced phrasing that has the appearance of both asserting and denying the status quo: "Individuals choose when to speak and what to say (though those possibilities are created and determined by other systems), but these acts are made possible by a series of systems which the subject does not control."[3] Now, though that statement in substance wipes out the supports of the free Cartesian *cogito* deployed by Poulet as well as essential elements in existential phenomenology, it does so in grammatically subordinate status. What is placed up front is the relatively trivial (and questionable) philosophic point that the individual can choose when to speak. Rhetorically viewed Culler's statement has the effect of saying that the isolate subject is simultaneously of supreme importance and of supreme unimportance. The bleaker deterministic point which Continental structuralists have never shied from stating in the bluntest fashion (one thinks of Roland Barthes's announced desire to "amputate" literature from the individual)[4] is somewhat deflected without being denied, and the collectivistic political and social implications of structuralist thinking, which in his earlier writings Barthes met head on, are diverted. Third, Culler shrewdly searches out a primary contradiction of structuralist thought: cultures are posited as diverse and heterogeneous, yet the practice of Lévi-Strauss in anthropology or of Tzvetan Todorov in literary criticism is precisely in the opposite direction, toward universal and uncontingent grammars of myth and narrative structure.[5] But he yet proceeds, both in the analysis of Lévi-Strauss and in his presentation of "literary competence," on the implied assumption of a unified Western culture[6] that permits literary readers the easy luxury of never having to question whether the systematic models with which we might "master" (a favorite word) diverse texts represent an adequate response to the systems of force which constrain the production of the text. The idea of the unity of Western culture, and its corollary, that history is a repetition of the same, tends to promote historical hubris: history is what we say it is. And "we?"—"we are nothing other than our systems of reading and writing."[7]

In the concluding paragraph of *Structuralist Poetics* (it has the tone of a peroration), Culler asserts the time-honored Socratic goal of Western humanistic education: the highest knowledge is self-knowledge, because that kind of knowledge will set us free.

> We read and understand ourselves as we follow the operations of our understanding and, more important, as we experience the limits of our understanding. To know oneself is to study the intersubjective processes of articulation and interpretation by which we emerge as part of a world. He who does not write—he who does not actively take up and work upon this system—is himself "written" by the system. He becomes the product of a culture which eludes him.[8]

If that statement causes us to look again at the meaning of what we saw Culler place in grammatical subordination (acts of speaking are made possible "by a series of systems which the subject does not control"), if it causes us to ask how, since "we are nothing other than our systems of reading and writing," we can possibly avoid becoming mere products of a culture, then it should force us as well to ask another question: What does it mean to celebrate self-knowledge, when all that we can know is the self? Of what quality and value is self-knowledge when it is acquired in an enclosed intersubjective space which permits no access to anything that is "other" to that which is generated by present cultural systems?

A fourth and final strategy for defusing the general structuralist intention of resituating literary discourse, from its place apart, back within discourse at large, is reiterated several times through the first part of *Structuralist Poetics:* I refer specifically to Culler's conclusion to the analyses of Jakobson and Greimas, to what he decides about the value of linguistics, and metaphors drawn from linguistics, for literary scholarship and its procedures. Linguistics, may, he writes, "provide a general focus," but it "does not . . . provide a method for the interpretation of literary works."[9] Culler's book, then, performs the intellectually useful act of telling English-speaking critics what they need to know about formidable Continental sources of structuralist thinking, while at the same time providing the comforting reassurance that the governing conceptual framework of structuralism may be safely ignored.

I think it is fair to ask, now, whether in the discussion of literary competence Culler has moved critical theory much beyond where

Frye's *Anatomy* had left it in 1957. The following remarks, for example, from Frye's "Polemical Introduction," fit the argument for literary competence perfectly:

> . . . at no point is there any direct learning of literature itself. Physics is an organized body of knowledge about nature, and a student of it says that he is learning physics, not nature. Art, like nature, has to be distinguished from the systematic study of it, which is criticism. It is therefore impossible to "learn literature": one learns about it in a certain way, but what one learns, transitively, is the criticism of literature. Similarly, the difficulty often felt in "teaching literature" arises from the fact that it cannot be done: the criticism of literature is all that can be directly taught.[10]

A structuralist would not disagree with Frye's statement (though he would want to substitute "reading" for "criticism" and "writing" for "literature"). Moreover, the structuralist would approve of Frye's rejection of the realism of such traditionalist approaches as the New Criticism: working within a neo-Coleridgean heritage, the New Critic tends, first, to ascribe, *a priori*, special objective properties to literary discourse (it is inherently ambiguous, or symbolic, or organically whole), and then, with circular logic, to describe the critical act as consisting in the location, that is, the *finding* of those qualities, wherever they may be. While noting his debts to Frye, Culler also notes his differences: "Few have put the case for poetics more forcefully than Frye, but in his perspective . . . the relationship between poetry, the experience of poetry and poetics remains somewhat obscure."[11]

The problem, however, may be one of contradiction rather than of obscurity, for in much of his elaboration Frye tends to treat the "literary universe" (the system or *langue* which conditions individual literary performances) less as a heuristic critical postulate, with its parentage in Vico and Blake, and more as objective truth, an ontological ground of deep structures which can be mirrored in critical reading. And the question that Frye never consistently answers according to the theoretical dictates of his "Polemical Introduction"—is structure or system a creation of the critical enterprise, or does it sit latently under the whole range of Western literary texts?—is fudged by Culler as well. Thus we note the vacillation of the following: "The work has structure and meaning because it is read in a certain way, because these potential properties, latent in the object itself, are actualized by the theory of discourse applied in the act of reading."[12] The Nietzschean perspectivism that Culler gives with the one hand—a work has structure because it is read in a certain way—is quickly taken away by the second part of the sentence which speaks of structure as latent in the object itself. (Theoretical consistency would require that Culler say that structure is latent in the reader, not the object; I take his inconsistency not as a sign of intellectual looseness, however, but as a sign of a more fundamental intention.) If literary structure is the intuitively *internalized*[13] grammar of literary discourse, then it must be a reflection in the act of reading of what is *externally* there in writing; and what is externally there in writing, by that argument, must assume coercive force by becoming a norm for what E. D. Hirsch calls validity in interpretation: literary structure is independent of readers' systems and an objective measure of their critical acumen.

Two rigorous structuralist principles—(1) that the self is an intersubjective construct formed by cultural systems over which the individual person has no control; and (2) that the text is a kind of formless space whose shape is imposed by structured modes of reading—are compromised seriously by Culler and in both instances in traditionalist ways. Thus in *Structuralist Poetics* it is never clear that Culler has not relinquished two stubborn traditionalist principles: (1) that the individual self at its higher pitches of self-consciousness can cut itself free of cultural determination; and (2) that the properties which distinguish types of discourse inhere in discourse itself as ontological substrata. What he calls the "critical piety" of believing that "meanings are always implicitly and objectively present in the language of the poem" is indulged by Culler himself.[14]

The argument for literary competence proceeds largely with these ambiguities left unresolved. At pivotal places, however, resolution is purchased when Culler presses the conservative side of his theoretical disposition. For by literary competence he does not mean only to repeat the unobjectionable notion that to read literature successfully we need to acquire a training and a method different in some part from that demanded by other disciplines. When he speaks of literary competence as an "autonomous discipline" he means to posit, as Frye had done some twenty years earlier, that the conventions which we use to read literary texts derive from a conceptual framework uniquely compatible with the literary experience. Frye, we recall, eschews the help of Jungian psychology and the neo-Kantian philosophy of symbolic forms, not by denying the obvious conceptual parallels from the work of Jung and Cassirer, but by suggesting that Jung and Cassirer are unnecessary because criticism as a scientific and systematic discipline can go it alone on its own conceptual basis, since the necessary concepts are intrinsic to the discipline. Like Frye, Culler denies the structuralist vision of an interdisciplinary methodology and the integration of the various humanistic fields; he pushes literary criticism into the sort of isolationism which a variety of aesthetic idealisms since Kant (the New Criticism being only one instance) have declared as their primary theoretical intention. In Culler's words: "a structuralist poetics would claim that the study of literature involves only indirectly the critical act of placing a work in situation. . . ."[15] As he goes about defining a structuralist poetics, that seems to be true. A question worth raising is whether the notion of a "structuralist poetics" is a theoretical oxymoron.

It is a question that Culler is not interested in posing. His is the pursuit of an "intrinsic" reading (Jameson's word),[16] a term that should recall the philosophical pivot of René Wellek and Austin Warren's *Theory of Literature* (1949) and the hard distinction they draw between intrinsic and extrinsic approaches to texts. Though Wellek and Warren did not enjoy the benefit of structuralist perspective—discourse does not contain properties apart from a system of reading "which assigns structural descriptions to the objects in question"; a literary taxonomy, therefore, "should be grounded on a theory of reading"[17]—still Culler's major points about literary competence do not seriously conflict with the mainstream formalist principles canonized by Wellek and Warren. Even though he rejects the objectivism of the New Critics, Culler's thinking tends to promote objectivist values. The disciplinary exclusionism of a structuralist poetics, its refusal to place a work "in situation," resembles the crippling antihistoricism of idealist criticism. But "antihistoricism," though a familiar complaint of more traditionally trained historicist scholars, is not an accurate charge to level at the older formalists, nor is it an accurate characterization of the brand of structuralism made available to us by Jonathan Culler. In fact there is a fairly well-specified idealistic theory of history in a New Critic like Cleanth Brooks, and it is a theory in its formal dimension pretty much respected by Culler.

I am referring to Eliot's vastly influential notion of a tradition of "unified sensibility," explored at length first in Brooks's *Modern Poetry and the Tradition* (1939). The tradition of unified sensibility has its origin in the unified Europe of Dante; its rich plenitude is in evidence in the great Elizabethan dramatists and the metaphysical poets; a fall from such unity is marked in Milton, Dryden, and the eighteenth century; and a recovery is noted in Keats and the poets of Eliot's generation (many of whom were personal friends of Brooks). Brooks's thesis posits (by his own admission) an eternal[18] writing, motivated by an ideal, integrated consciousness, and informed by a single set of temporally persistent linguistic conventions (the extended metaphor, the studied uses of paradox, wit, irony, and ambiguity). In a later book which heavily influenced the classroom procedures of a generation of English teachers, *The Well Wrought Urn* (1947), Brooks offered the even more accessible (and pedagogically serviceable) thesis of historical process as simple repetition (no fall from unity of sensibility is indicated) by isolating the prime intellectual and linguistic features of "the tradition" in a poet from each significant era of English poetry. The major consequence of this New-Critical definition of poetry as a uniquely endowed kind of discourse is the minimization of change, difference, and discontinuity in literary history and the concomitant stressing of stasis, repetition without difference, and continuity. (On this point, the Russian formalists, as Jameson persuasively argues,[19] who have yet to make a decisive impact on our literary thought, part company with the Anglo-American New Critics with whom they otherwise share a number of theoretical perspectives. The conception of "defamiliarization," or making strange [*ostranenie*], is no stranger to critics who cut their teeth on Coleridge's and Shelley's claim that poets strip away the film of familiarity from habitual perception, but the Russian formalists' model of literary history as discontinuity is foreign to us.) The effect, at any rate, of this emphasis in Brooks on repetition and continuity is to project historical time as an unproblematic eternal now (we might recall certain phrases from Eliot's "Tradition and the Individual Talent"); to force our sense of what constitutes us in the present to be perfectly constitutive of the past; to turn our sense of currently active conventions of literary discourse into transcendental structures (e.g., a literary universe); to assume that cultural and historical variations, though undeniable, are differences that make no difference. In other words, to adopt the historical assumptions of a Brooks is to ensure the most prized value of idealist criticism: the freedom and autonomy of literature.

Within Culler's structuralist framework the inherent properties of discourse are translated from their realist place in Brooks's theory into products of systems of reading, but this epistemologically more tenable position at once reaffirms the autonomy of the literary experience (rather than of the literary object) and enthrones an aggressive intersubjective will to mastery which substitutes what is currently in force for historical exploration. If we ask Culler if there is any useful distinction to be drawn between the conventions which readers manipulate, now, in order to "produce" the text and those conventions which may in fact have stimulated and driven the author's intention; if we ask him whether there is a useful distinction to be made between reading a text and writing one; if we ask him if the reader's system of production is to be understood as only heuristic, his answer in each instance is "no." Thus: "One can think of these conventions not simply as the implicit knowledge of readers but also as the implicit knowledge of authors."[20] Granted that we *can* think of these things as identical, why in fact *should* we, especially when we remember that the reading self is essentially a formation of the cultural systems of the reader's times?

Even more serious objections can be raised against Culler's claim that "The conventions of poetry, the logic of symbols, the operations for the production of poetic effects, are not simply the property of readers but the basis of literary forms."[21] Culler's structuralist caution is now subverted: the effects that readers produce are mirrors of the text ("the basis of literary forms"), of what is apparently residually there in the text, independent of the reader's consciousness. But this is the sort of contradiction that apparently can be borne, because it produces a result fatally enticing to critics like Culler, Frye, and Hirsch, that of making the critical enterprise a science that can guarantee the validity of critical reading. Culler's belief that the reader and the writer are instances of the Same leads to the comforting consequence of Brooks's position which assumed that Eliot and Donne are instances of the Same. And whereas Brooks mainly ignores the fact that readings are mediations, that reading, in Culler's allusion to Barthes, "is not an innocent activity"[22]—it occurs in time and hence is subject to all the hazards and deviances of temporal location—Culler explicitly addresses this fact of our reading experience only in order to structure the respective temporal situations of writer and reader so that the fact of "situation" becomes a nonproblem. Understanding is no dialogue; there is only the self, and understanding must be equated with mastery: "Any work can be made intelligible if one invent appropriate conventions," he writes:[23] a point that anyone who has spent time in the classroom knows is all too sadly true.

Just who is this competent reader upon whom Culler bases his theory? He is not, as we have seen, the individual, Cartesian subject, but an interpersonal "I," an ideal formed by purely literary norms or constraints. The powerful constitutive forces of the historical process (political and economic contexts, class differences, and so on) are somehow—Culler never tells us how—blocked out. They have no force. With the reader thus isolated, we are prepared to understand what he means, in the following statement, by "ideal reader," by "we," and by the phrase "the institution of literature": "The question is not what actual readers happen to do but what an ideal reader must know implicitly in order to read and interpret works in ways which we consider acceptable, in accordance with the institution of literature."[24] Culler's reader is a sophisticated fund of a particular kind of knowledge, but whether or not his "generalized knowledge of literature" is anything more than a grand tautology; whether his knowledge can make any cognitive contact with texts; whether the "literary institution" is so impregnable and monolithic a thing as Culler makes it out to be; whether the reader, so defined, can be judged to be a believable member of the human race, as opposed to a member of an elite club of professors of literature—all of these are open questions.

2

Structuralism has its distant progenitors in Marx, Nietzsche, and Freud, but the single most influential source of what we know as structuralism (including *Structuralist Poetics*) is Ferdinand de Saussure's *Course in General Linguistics*. The *Course* is a problematic text if for no other reason than that the form in which it presents its author's views is not the author's but those of his most grateful students. Saussure's text is the reconstruction and synthesis of his editors (Charles Bally, Albert Sechehaye, and Albert Riedlinger) of the fullest sets of notes compiled by students who took Saussure's lectures in general linguistics at the University of Geneva over the academic years 1906–07, 1908–09, and 1910–11. The editors tell us that they also made use of all manuscript materials at their disposal, "including the personal notes of F. de Saussure."[25]

Awareness of the textual origins of this fundamental work of structuralist thought ought to have encouraged a more cautious approach to its themes. Systemic symmetry and architechtonic fullness are not really its virtues, yet the text has often been cited and summarized (in his recent book on Saussure Culler does this)[26] in ways that suggest that its basic points follow one another in perfect rational lucidity of succession. Saussure's big ideas are easily identifiable: the seminal distinctions of *langue* and *parole*, of the synchronic and the diachronic, of paradigmatic and syntagmatic; the recovery from earlier philosophical traditions of the notion of the arbitrary nature of the linguistic sign, and the assiduous pursuit of its consequences in the notion of "difference"; and, finally, the idea of "structure" itself. American students of structuralism can appreciate the efforts of Culler, Jameson, and Robert Scholes, among others, to spell out Saussure's general conceptual frames and pin down the essential meanings of his most significant distinctions. But with the sterling exception of Jameson, too many American and Continental commentators have treated the *Course* as if it were a book of undeniable axioms, unknown before the Geneva lectures, with no parallels in the theories of other disciplines, with no constraining historical context of its own, and as if the master had satisfied himself, with no afterthoughts, on all of the major problems. This implicit attribution of ease and clarity at the origin has tended to produce a dogmatism in structuralist writings which not only narrows Saussure's thought but also denies a certain richness that is there.

In 1954, one of Saussure's most acute interpreters, Emile Benveniste, established a perspective on Saussure's major advance in linguistics which has never been challenged. Benveniste explained that "the approach which characterized linguistics during the nineteenth century and at the beginning of the twentieth was exclusively historical. History as the necessary perspective and successivity as the principle of explanation, the splitting up of language into isolated elements and the laws of evolution peculiar to each one of them—these were the dominant characteristics of linguistic doctrine."[27] In specific terms, what Saussure was rejecting was an unsatisfying experience with history itself, as Jameson has argued,[28] a rejection that made itself felt in a positive way in the setting up of the antihistorical principle of system, or synchrony, as the first principle of his linguistic theory. Historical philology takes as its object actual linguistic behavior (speech or *parole*) and then submits that object to a study of the only kind of causes available to the nineteenth-century historicist: which is to say external causes such as "geographical barriers, migration and population shifts"[29] and all the accidents of temporal life to which linguistic behavior is subject. Saussurean linguistics, on the other hand, takes language as a complete system, a "perpetual present," in Jameson's words,[30] the coherence of whose being is somehow internal to the system itself. Language, Saussure argued, considered as system (*langue*), is "comparable to a symphony in that what the symphony actually is stands completely apart from how it is performed."[31] Since language "is a system that has its own arrangement," Saussure can say that his "definition of language presupposes the exclusion of everything that is outside its organism or system."[32]

It would seem fair, then, to conclude, as Benveniste has done, that Saussure's advance over historical philology was to move from an external approach to the isolated linguistic phenomenon (an atomistic linguistics) to an internal concern with a freestanding whole (structural linguistics). Benveniste's definition of structure seems faithful to Saussure's intention: "By structure is meant, especially in Europe, the arrangement of a whole in parts and the demonstrable coherence of these reciprocally conditioned parts in the whole. . . ."[33] And from this view of linguistic phenomena as existing in a conditioning "field," it appears to follow (this is a point made by both Benveniste and Jameson) that "the legitimacy of diachrony, considered as a succession of synchronies, is thus reestablished"; "the temporal model proposed by Saussure is that of a series of complete systems succeeding each other in time."[34] This structuralizing of linguistics, and its extension, the structuralizing of temporal processes, result in a historicism of models (a point emphasized by Benveniste, Jameson, Culler, and other commentators on Saussure, and supported by numerous passages in the *Course*).

Though his work in *The Prison-House of Language* is much indebted at several points to Benveniste, Jameson makes a number of original contributions to Saussurean commentary, not the least of which is his setting of the idea of system in the intellectual context of the late nineteenth and the early twentieth centuries. Jameson points out that though the idea of system is an antihistorical one, Saussure's antihistoricism has a rich history in formalist claims for "pure" poetry.[35] This point can be expanded. The ideas of the French symbolists, the English aesthetes, the critical thought of T. E. Hulme (which would feed the Anglo-American New Criticism), the aesthetics of Croce and Clive Bell, the vitalism of Henri Bergson, the earliest phenomenological disquisitions of Husserl on the *epoché*—each of these aesthetic and epistemological perspectives, each in its distinctive manner, sets forth an ideal of disciplinary autonomy or self-sufficiency presumably guaranteed by an explicit bracketing, to cite Husserl's key term, of extrinsic conditions and causes. Thus whether what is in question is the symbol, or the image, or intuition, or existential particularity, or the intensive manifold, or significant form, or the intentional grasp of essences, in every case what is established is a formalistic purity which transcends such encircling determinates as nature, various historical environments, rational consciousness, and the discursiveness of so-called ordinary discourse. With this setting in mind, and recalling the language of Saussure's and Benveniste's definition of system, it does not require advanced knowledge in the history of criticism to understand that romantic theories of organicism stand in the not-so-distant background of Saussure's idea of system (he himself appeals to the metaphor of the organism).[36]

If such historicizing of Saussure succeeds in locating the structuralist revolution within a long modernist reaction against positivism and the bugaboo of science, it will have to be acknowledged that Saussure's formalism is not merely another example of the idealistic nostalgia for absolute freedom as an alternative to the determinist vision of later nineteenth-century religions of science. For one thing, Saussure's notions of *langue* and of system are profound determinisms,[37] and, as such, refusals of nineteenth-century idealism's celebration of imagination as the human center of things, of free consciousness as the *sine qua non*. And in spite of his appeal to the organic metaphor, Saussure owes no debt (unlike Coleridgean organicism and its fulfillment in Crocean intuitionism) to a neo-Kantian metaphysics and he has no use for a substantialist view of discourse: the symbol, the image, the organic poem, and the intensive manifold all assert at some level a natural rather than an arbitrary view of the so-called "literary" sign. The romantic theory of literary language as dynamic *energeia* (a process of expression originating in imagination) forces an ultimate natural reference of literary discourse to a parallel metaphysical process of spirit unfolding from the "I am" (Coleridge's ground of grounds, substance as noumenal energy). In its affirmation of a wholly relational and differential view of discourse as system, Saussure's thought recollects Nietzsche in that it constitutes a rigorous antihumanism at least in intention (*pace* Jacques Derrida). Recent structuralist and poststructuralist assaults on the human center as origin (especially in its phenomenological formulation) are heavily in Saussure's debt. "No one now," as Benveniste has written, "seriously raises the question of the monogenesis or polygenesis of languages, or, in a general way, that of absolute origins. . . . At no moment of the past and in no form of the present can one come upon anything 'primordial.' "[38]

Structuralism as we know it takes off from this heavily counterhistorical and counterphenomenological side of Saussure's notion of system. Hence the repeated stress on classification and on the universal narrative model which produces the *parole* of actual narratives and which transcends not only the individual will but also cultural differences and historical changes. Recent structuralists see the distinctions made between synchrony and diachrony, between *langue* and *parole*, not as attempts to set up dialectically related oppositions, but as Platonic hierarchies which devalue historical and existential contingencies in order to grant ultimate privilege, as Plato did, to temporally transcendent forms. And if the work of recent structuralists too often seems to indulge a life-denying rationalism, it must be admitted that their Platonic sanction is granted by a number of apparently position-taking passages in the *Course*. Thus: "speech is many-sided and heterogeneous . . . we can not discover its unity. Language, on the other hand, is a self-contained whole and a principle of classification."[39] Or this: "In separating language from speaking we are at the same time separating:

(1) what is social from what is individual; and (2) what is essential from what is accessory and more or less accidental. Language is not a function of the speaker. . . ."[40] Or this: "the distinguishing characteristic of the sign—but the one that is least apparent at first sight—is that in some way it always eludes the individual or social will."[41] Or this: "diachronic events are always accidental and particular."[42] Hence the heavily weighted rationalism (and urgency) of Saussure's central directive: "from the very outset we must put both feet on the ground of language [langue] and use language as the norm of all other manifestations of speech," because language "is a system whose parts can and must all be considered in their synchronic solidarity."[43] Recent literary structuralists understand Saussure to be saying in such passages that the systemic dimension of language is all that is open to human intellection, all that can be known.

Structuralism in this sense can be understood as a flight from romantic irrationalism and various epistemologies of intuitionism that culminate in the later philosophy of William James and in Henri Bergson. Perhaps the most extreme expression of this platonized Saussure is Todorov's assumption of a universal grammar: "This universal grammar is the source of all universals and it gives definition even to man himself. Not only all languages but all signifying systems obey the same grammar. It is universal not only because it informs all the languages of the universe, but because it coincides with the structure of the universe itself."[44] The precise notion of langue (as "the ensemble of linguistic possibilities or potentialities at any given moment")[45] is turned by Todorov into a metaphor which does some traditional metaphysical work. And though more philosophically cautious than Todorov, and despite his critique of linguistics as a mode of discovery, Culler likewise pushes Saussure in a similar direction by making langue over into a system of reading which, within a given cultural frame, absolutely governs interpretation—just as the concept, within rationalist traditions, tyrannizes the particular.

Among Saussure's American expositors, Jameson has been very hard on this antihistoricist thrust in his theory. Jameson puts the issue succinctly when he writes: "Once you have begun by separating diachronic from synchronic . . . you can never really put them back together again. If the opposition in the long run proves to be a false or a misleading one, then the only way to suppress it is by throwing the entire discussion onto a higher dialectical plane, choosing a new starting point, utterly recasting the problems involved in new terms."[46] Though Jameson is willing to admit that the structuralist attack on

the Cartesian subject is a deeply anti-idealistic impulse and carries a
fundamental awareness of the collective character of human existence,
The Prison-House of Language is unified, among other ways, by an
insistent charge that Saussure and his structuralist progeny suffer from
a failure of historical consciousness that stems from the hierarchizing
of synchrony and diachrony. (Edward Said makes a similar point when
he writes that recent French critics have focused on the fixity of "structure" to the neglect of the processes of "structuring.")[47] Of course,
when Jameson says that the entire discussion needs to be thrown onto
a "higher dialectical plane," he means to bring forward the notion of
"dialectic" itself. The difference between Culler's and Jameson's treatment of Saussure is that one likes what he sees while the other does not;
both, however, agree as to what is essentially there.

But given the textual problems of the *Course* there may not be much
value in positing its essence. It may be more useful to bring against the
Platonic passages in the *Course* other statements which do throw the
discussion onto the plane of dialectic and which in fact attempt to
integrate synchrony and diachrony. Thus: "speech has both an individual and a social side and we cannot conceive of one without the
other. . . . Speech always implies an established system and an evolution; at every moment it is an existing institution and a product of
the past."[48] Or: "execution is never carried out by the collectivity.
Execution is always individual, and the individual is always its master."[49] Or, most unmistakably: "Language and speaking are then interdependent; the former is both the instrument and the product of
the latter"; but the sentence immediately following muddies the waters:
"But their interdependence does not prevent their being two absolutely
distinct things."[50] Yet by the argument advanced in the opening chapter of the *Course*, the absolute distinction of *langue* and *parole* is wholly
a product of a certain type of analysis: interdependence, by that same
argument, would seem to be a fact of the being of language. If at "every
moment" speech "is an existing institution and a product of the past,"
then synchrony and diachrony are, by virtue of the nature of language
itself, "together" and we do not need a theory, as Jameson thinks,
to tell us that that is so. At any rate, it is clear that the recent structuralist inability to come to terms with the diachronic and executive
dimensions of discourse has led to the Platonic pursuit of the taxonomy or model as transcendentals. Perhaps with a somewhat revised
notion of system and history as an integrated and dialectically controlled field of linguistic phenomena, we may return to the *Course*
prepared to understand anew what Saussure may have been emphasiz-

ing in his discussion of the arbitrary quality of the sign, in his distinction between syntagm and paradigm, and in the fecund discussion of difference.

First the notion of the sign. Saussure's bipartite definition of the sign as an acoustical-psychological entity which "unites, not a thing and a name but a concept and a sound image"[51] defers from the outset the ontological question of the relationship of language and reality in itself. The sign, then, which is a combination of concept (signified, *signifié*) and sound-image (signifier, *signifiant*), is "arbitrary" in two senses. First, the bond between signifier and signified is not a natural bond—nothing in the nature of things forces the choice of a particular sound-image upon a linguistic community in order that it may represent a particular concept; and second (this is implied), the bond between sign as a totality (the bonded entity of signifier and signified) and the real thing is arbitrary, as any casual comparison of different languages will indicate ("Since I mean by the sign the whole that results from the associating of the signifier with the signified, I can simply say: *the linguistic sign is arbitrary*").[52]

At this point, as Benveniste has noted, a potential confusion arises over Saussure's use of the term "arbitrary." Benveniste's point is that since neither an individual nor a given collectivity within a particular culture is free to associate at will just any sound-image with a given concept, the connection between the two is not arbitrary: "on the contrary, it is necessary."[53] The connection between signifier and signified is so intimate and so instantaneous that there is no question even of isolating a perceptible, defined act of connecting; the act of connecting is unthinkable, and were it otherwise Saussure would fall into the trap of positing the signified as a prelinguistic mental entity. Benveniste believes that by allowing the term "reality" to creep into his analysis (the total sign is arbitrary with respect to the thing), Saussure has unwittingly indulged ontological hunger and in the process has ignored the cultural matrix of the sign.

Benveniste may have made too much, however, of very little. Saussure can speak for himself on this issue. After stipulating that the notion of symbol posits the "rudiment of a natural bond between the signifier and the signified," he writes this: "The word *arbitrary* also calls for comment. The term should not imply that the choice of the signifier is left entirely to the speaker (we shall see . . . that the individual does not have the power to change a sign in any way once it has become established in the linguistic community); I mean that it is unmotivated, i.e., arbitrary in that it actually has no natural connection with the signified."[54] The main points of Saussure and Benveniste are the same because both argue explicitly for a bond between signifier and signified that is culturally necessary; both insist on a bond between the sign as a totality and the real that is from the hypothetical natural point of view arbitrary or unmotivated; and, as I understand them, since neither claims to possess unmediated ontological knowledge, both seem to agree that from the point of view of language (from an inspection of different languages) an ontological substratum, a common world of real objects, is indicated as a universal fiction of language. It is this fiction which more than anything else reinforces our sense of the arbitrariness of the bond between signifier and signified. Strictly speaking, in other words, we do not (and cannot) "know" that such a bond is arbitrary, since all of our knowledge of "reality in itself" is a representation of language.

Though Saussure's general point is as old as the beginnings of Western philosophy, the story of Western philosophy demonstrates how easily the point is forgotten. Jameson underrates the persistence of the naturalistic error when he writes that Saussure's linguistics strikes down the peripheral theory of a few poets.[55] The mainstream of aesthetic modernism (even the structuralist Todorov draws from it when he tells us that linguistic structure is a mirror of the structure of the universe) has primarily characterized itself not by its misleading propaganda against science and philistinism that the aesthetic world is a thing wholly apart, but by its claim that the aesthetic world plumbs the nature of things; and the pivot of this claim is the prior ontological claim for a natural bond between signifier and signified, and between sign and thing. At key moments in Coleridge and Hegel on symbol, in Croce and Hulme on the expressive image, in the New Critics on metaphor, and in a myth critic like Philip Wheelwright on depth language, what is indicated is a theory that language in the aesthetic mode overcomes the arbitrariness of ordinary discourse by achieving ontological participation. The underlying significance of such participation appears to be the freeing of "aesthetic" writers from temporal and cultural constraints.

In contrast, by emphasizing, with apparently incontrovertible evidence, the arbitrary nature of the sign, Saussure's linguistics situates discourse, literary or otherwise, in its true home in human history, and by so doing subverts the formalist *telos* of timelessness. To designate the sign as arbitrary is simultaneously to call attention to it as a temporal and cultural production. His paradoxical claim that the sign is both immutable and mutable is at once a recognition of the powerlessness of the individual subject, his passive and repressed status within a linguistic community, and a reminder of the vast and frightening force of human collectives to seize discourse for the ends of power. Since there is no natural bond between signifier and signified, since the basis of the connection is traditional and irrational, language is the most flexible of institutions, the most open to appropriation.[56]

A second Saussurean distinction that needs reconsideration in historicist light is that between syntagmatic and associative (or paradigmatic) relations within any given "language-state."

> In discourse, on the one hand, words acquire relations
> based on the linear nature of language because they are
> chained together. This rules out the possibility of pro-
> nouncing two elements simultaneously. . . . The elements
> are arranged in sequence on the chain of speaking. Com-
> binations supported by linearity are *syntagms*. The syntagm
> is always composed of two or more consecutive units. . . .
> Outside discourse, on the other hand, words acquire
> relations of a different kind. Those that have something in
> common are associated in memory, resulting in groups
> marked by diverse relations.[57]

As an example of the syntagmatic grouping Saussure cites the sentence as something like an ideal type.[58] Paradigmatic groupings are necessarily freer, for associative relations may be established on the ground of a common radical, or a common suffix, or by way of analogy of the concepts signified, or simply by similarity of sound-images. Thus in the paradigm, "There is at times a double similarity of meaning and form, at times similarity only of form or of meaning. A word can always evoke everything that can be associated with it in one way or another."[59] To sum up the main difference: the syntagm "suggests an order of succession and a fixed number of elements," while "terms in an associative family occur neither in fixed numbers nor in a definite order."[60] The syntagm, then, is a determinate thing, whereas the paradigm is by definition indeterminate and indefinite. Jameson contends, and I think he is correct, that the distinction between syntagm and paradigm is a disguised form of the enabling opposition between diachrony and synchrony, *parole* and *langue*, which generated Saussure's entire theory: the determinate syntagm is temporal whereas the indeterminate paradigm is a transcendental. Saussure's investment in yet another crippling dualism once again pushes his theory in Platonic directions. According to Jameson: "The originality of Saussure's point of departure returns to limit his results: for that initial repudiation of history, which at the very outset resulted in an inability to absorb change into the system as anything but a meaningless and contingent datum, is now reproduced, at the very heart of the system itself, as an inability to deal with syntax as such."[61]

But, again, I do not think that Jameson's critique applies as much to Saussure as to those who believe that they follow his linguistic counsel. For though it may be true that the logic of Saussure's discovery of system will force him to grant priority to the paradigm, the facts of discourse would seem to throw the emphasis on the syntagm. In *actual* verbal discourse the syntagm necessarily exerts controlling force upon the reader's consciousness. Since actual discourse is nothing if not syntagmatic, the syntagm fixes the process of reading within a determinate historical matrix that closes off the infinite proliferation of a paradigm which reaches "outside discourse" proper, though its first term is necessarily fixed within a syntagmatic structure. Saussure's discussion of syntagmatic and associative relations allows us to judge the truncated linguistics of the older group of Yale New Critics and of the newest Yale New Critics whose work is motivated by the so-called poststructuralism of Derrida. Both groups are in pursuit of an unconstrained paradigmatic method of interpretation. With the *Oxford English Dictionary* close at hand, both types of critic—the poststructuralist more radically, with a total commitment to the open-endedness of the paradigm—fail to credit the coercive power of the historical determination and cultural enclosure of semantic potential mediated by the syntagm. In *Theory of Literature*, Wellek and Warren can in one breath, almost, knowingly cite the precise sense in which Andrew Marvell's "vegetable love" is historically fenced-in and then add that it is valid to lay over Marvell a mid-twentieth-century meaning that could not have been available to the poet.[62] Similarly, in a number of instances in their recent essays, J. Hillis Miller and Geoffrey Hartman pursue the syntagmatically alienated word through the history of the West. The final effect of both criticisms is to promote the idea that all meaning is eternally present in an unrestrained free-playing discourse, that the differentiations of time and culture have no effect. I assume that if we could put the question bluntly and directly to a Todorov, or a Brooks, or a Hillis Miller: do you believe in something called "poetry" with a capital letter—a sort of transcendental form against which all actual poems are mere approximations?, the answer would be "no, in thunder!" And yet the undeniable historicist implication of a negative reply—there are only discrete *poetries*—has rarely guided the work of these exemplary modernist critics.

The final Saussurean idea that needs reconsideration in the light of historicist method is the problematic notion of difference. In order to set up its implications I cite Jameson again, this time on the necessary condition for historicity: "a genuine historicity is possible only on condition this illusion of an absolute present can be done away with, and the present opened up again to the drift from the other ends of time."[63] If one way of describing the character of contemporay critical theory, particularly its theory of history, might be to point to its repeated affirmation of an absolute presence, a transcendental or ideal space which draws all contents homogeneously to itself, from Brooks's tradition of unified sensibility, to Frye's suggestion of the unmoved fixture of desire, to Poulet's pretemporal Cartesian *cogito*, then an antithetical way of describing the intention (if not the achievement) of recent movements in Continental philosophy would be to say that they have been concerned to denigrate absolute presence as an illusion. Thus Heidegger's and Sartre's antisubstantialist insistence on *Dasein* or *pour soi* (descriptions of human reality which affirm its radical temporal character, its condition of being bereft of a given prehistorical core of unchanging content, its condition of being always-about-to-be); thus the structuralist insistence that the subject is a cultural construction; and thus the poststructuralist meditation of Derrida, with its Saussurean subtilizing of Sartre's notion that existence precedes essence, and its intention of reclaiming the thickness of discourse by banishing the center that sits outside the forces of discourse, which are rarefied by the center. Saussure must be credited with lending linguistic authority to such contentions. On the basis of his discussions of the arbitrary character of the sign he comes to these compelling conclusions: "If words stood for pre-existing concepts, they would all have exact equivalents in meaning from one language to the next; but this is not true"; so, "Instead of pre-existing ideas . . . we find . . . *values* emanating from the system. When they are said to correspond to concepts, it is understood that the concepts are purely differential and defined not by their positive content but negatively by their relations with other terms of the system. Their most precise characteristic is in being what the others are not."[64] The arbitrary and differential qualities of both signifier and signified are two sides of the same coin. In a series of passages which have much informed Derrida, particularly his essay "Differance," Saussure draws out these implications of difference:

> Signs function, then, not through their intrinsic value but through their relative position. . . .
>
> This is even more true of the linguistic signifier, which is

not phonic but incorporeal—constituted not by its material substance but by the differences that separate its sound-image from all others. . . .

Everything that has been said up to this point boils down to this: in language there are only differences. Even more important: a difference generally implies positive terms between which the difference is set up; but in language there are only differences *without positive terms*. Whether we take the signified or the signifier, language has neither ideas nor sounds that existed before the linguistic system, but only conceptual and phonic differences that have issued from the system. The idea or phonic substance that a sign contains is of less importance than the other signs that surround it.[65]

Despite Derrida's pinpointing of an embarrassing contradiction in Saussure, the effect of which is to reinstate the transcendental idea of an absolute presence (I shall deal with this problem in the next chapter), it would have to be admitted, even by Derrida, that the primary intention of Saussure's linguistics (neatly summarized by the phrase "differences *without positive terms*") is to destroy absolute presence and by so doing institute an ineradicable temporality, a "genuine historicity." Though Jameson will not credit Saussure's linguistics as the basis of historical method, it is clear that "differences *without positive terms*" does open the present to the "drifts from the other ends of time." Such an idea of difference punctures the mystifying notion of a transcendental signified—a signified which is said to exist positively and independently of a signifier and which would command the relational or lateral play of signifiers at a untouchable distance from discourse—and it punctures the persistent notion of a Cartesian subject (the key modernist version of the transcendental signified) which as pretemporal phenomenological voice could direct the play of differences without, in turn, being directed by such play. By virtually ignoring the role of the syntagm; by not following through on the implications of Saussure's statement that the synchronic and the diachronic are interdependent (Culler says that signs "require an ahistorical analysis");[66] and by not sufficiently assessing the radical temporality established by the idea of difference, contemporary structuralists have directed their inquiries into the status of discourse toward goals that seem at odds with the aims of the father of structuralism. In so many words Saussure has told us that the constraining context for the various languages of man is the context of history, that "human" and "history" are pretty much synonymous terms. It might be persuasively argued that the difficulty with Saussure is that his work is mainly negative—that he wipes out transcendentalist directives without supplying the positive. But to fault Saussure for that is surely not to say that he disallows historical inquiry, but only to say, at most, that his work was incomplete.

3

If Saussure can be credited with providing the major methodological assumptions for contemporary structuralists, then Claude Lévi-Strauss must be credited with pushing Saussurean thought to the center of European intellectual activity in the early and middle fifties. Since 1963, when *Structural Anthropology* made its initial American appearance, a steady flow of translations has made Lévi-Strauss's vast anthropological studies available to an English-speaking audience. Historians of structuralism, from the early synoptic work of Donato and Said, through Jameson, Culler, Scholes, and Terence Hawkes, have not hesitated to assign fundamental significance to his ideas. Given the distance of Lévi-Strauss's discipline from the normal concerns of literary scholars, it is no surprise that what has attracted the literary community to his work are those of his theoretical pronouncements which have seemed most transposable to the problems of literary interpretation. His concern with the global reach of myth as a type of discourse and thought was bound to ring bells with an American literary-critical group that had so recently and so warmly received the work of Northrop Frye. The continuity of Frye and Lévi-Strauss has been more impressive to us than their philosophical differences.

A reader just coming off an encounter with Frye's *Anatomy* and picking up Lévi-Strauss's essay on the Oedipus myth would find at the theoretical heart of the essay a statement which he would have no difficulty in situating within Frye's assumptions. I refer to the following:

> Myth is the part of language where the formula *traduttore, tradittore* reaches its lowest truth value. From that point of view it should be placed in the gamut of linguistic expressions at the end opposite to that of poetry, in spite of all the claims which have been made to prove the contrary. Poetry is a kind of speech which cannot be translated except at the cost of serious distortions; whereas the mythical value of the myth is preserved even through the worst translation. Whatever our ignorance of the language and the culture of the people where it originated, a myth is still felt as a myth by any reader anywhere in the world. Its

substance does not lie in its style, its original music, or its syntax, but in the *story* which it tells. Myth is language, functioning on an especially high level where meaning succeeds practically at "taking off" from the linguistic ground on which it keeps on rolling.[67]

The emphasis in this statement on myth as deep structure, as universal narrative model which frees itself from temporal and cultural contingencies and which is intuited ("felt") by "any reader anywhere in the world," recalls the eternal present of Frye's literary universe and his postulation of its plenitude of narrative modes. But with this difference: Lévi-Strauss is willing to grant the conservative aestheticism which Frye rejected, for in poetry, he is saying, the formula *traduttore, traditore* has full application ("Poetry is a kind of speech which cannot be translated except at the cost of serious distortions"). Yet in the very act of granting validity to the aesthetic approach in the criticism of poetry, Lévi-Strauss has denied aestheticist criticism (and poetry) scientific value because unlike myth they are not universal in scope. Without directly saying so, he attributes something very like objective ontological worth to myth. He puts it this way: "Myths are anonymous. . . . When the myth is repeated, the individual listeners are receiving a message that, strictly speaking, is coming from nowhere; this is why it is credited with a supernatural origin. It is therefore comprehensible that the unity of a myth should be projected onto a postulated center. . . ."[68]

The philosophical premises for this notion of myth are most fully explored in the introduction ("Overture") to *The Raw and the Cooked*. Wishing to bring order out of chaotic cultural data and thereby demonstrate the "universal significance"[69] of his study of the South American Bororo myth, Lévi-Strauss postulates, if not a center (a term he restricts to either a supernatural origin or a Cartesian subject), then an empirical plenitude that seems more than hypothetical, a totality of cultural data which, if it could be grasped, would guarantee an "ultimate state" of anthropological knowledge. Lévi-Strauss indulges in such scientific hubris ("totalization," as it will come to be called after Derrida's critique of his work), paradoxically, when he claims the humility of his project:

> But I do not hope to reach a stage at which the subject
> matter of mythology, after being broken down by analysis,
> will crystallize again into a whole with the general appear-
> ance of a stable and well-defined structure. Apart from the
> fact that the science of myths is still in its infancy, so that
> its practitioners must consider themselves fortunate to

> obtain even a few tentative, preliminary results, we can
> already be certain that the ultimate state will never be
> attained, since were it theoretically possible, the fact still
> remains that there does not exist, nor ever will exist, any
> community or group of communities whose mythology
> and ethnography . . . can be known in their entirety.[70]

Contrary to what Lévi-Strauss believes he is saying, what his statement denies is the practical, not theoretical, possibility of that "ultimate state," since nowhere in the statement does he deny that there exists a coherent totality of ethnographic material which, if it could be gathered, would reveal objective unity. This totality would function as an origin or center which would stand outside the structures fashioned by the mythographer and would govern their ultimate shape. The contemporary literary theorist looking to affirm the autonomy of the literary institution would have no difficulty accommodating this aspect of Lévi-Strauss to Frye's literary universe. But about two pages later Lévi-Strauss revises the totalizing drift of his thought:

> There is no real end to mythological analysis, no hidden
> unity to be grasped once the breaking down process has
> been completed. . . . The unity of a myth is never more than
> tendential and projective and cannot reflect a state or a
> particular moment of the myth. It is a phenomenon of the
> imagination, resulting from the attempt at interpretation;
> and its function is to endow the myth with synthetic form
> and to prevent its disintegration into a confusion of op-
> posites. . . . Since it has no interest in definite beginnings
> or endings, mythological thought never develops any theme
> to completion: there is always something left unfinished.
> Myths, like rites, are "in-terminable."[71]

This qualification is not productive, however, because it is submerged in a dominant universalism and objectivism. For though Lévi-Strauss here appears to deny unity, or origin, or totality, or absolute presence as the ground of analysis, and though, unlike Frye, he explicitly raises the vexed Nietzschean question of interpretation—a question which I take to be constituted by the concerns of temporal and cultural differences and what Derrida calls the "white" mythologies of discourse—in his elaboration of his assumptions he stresses something else: what Paul Ricoeur has called a "Kantism without a transcendental subject."[72]

With the help of Saussure, Lévi-Strauss defines his project as the effort to write "an outline of the syntax of South American mythology," a synchronic project which will not be "confined within the frontiers already established by historical investigation."[73] The goal is to demonstrate the operation of a monolithic determinism that would

> reduce apparently arbitrary data to some kind of order, and
> to attain a level at which a kind of necessity becomes
> apparent, underlying the illusions of liberty. . . . the ap-
> parent arbitrariness of the mind, its supposedly spontan-
> eous flow of inspiration, and its seemingly uncontrolled
> inventiveness imply the existence of laws operating at a
> deeper level. . . . In allowing myself to be guided by the
> search for the constraining structures of the mind, I am
> proceeding in the manner of Kantian philosophy. . . .[74]

Though he will go on to state his differences with Kant—he claims to assume neither universal forms of human understanding nor a transcendental subject—he ends where Kant did: with an assumption of universal forms of consciousness which function as an eternal geometry, or transcendent center, that underwrites "a pattern of basic and universal laws."[75] The coincidence of Kant and Lévi-Strauss is pinned down for us if in every instance of the word "myth" in the following statement we substitute the phrase "the categories of human understanding": "I therefore claim to show, not how men think in myths, but how myths operate in men's minds without their being aware of the fact. . . . it would perhaps be better to go still further and, disregarding the thinking subject completely, proceed as if the thinking process were taking place in myths. . . ."[76]

It is this Kantian urge to guarantee the universal value of his anthropological procedures that undercuts the distinction in *The Savage Mind* between *bricoleur* and "engineer." As part of a larger effort to distinguish magic and modern science as two modes of scientific thought, and with the intention of rescuing magic from its usual relegation to the crude and unsophisticated, Lévi-Strauss insists that *bricolage* is not "primitive" but "prior."[77] As one of his translators notes, *bricoleur*, though it has no precise English equivalent, may be understood as a "Jack of all trades or a kind of professional do-it-yourself man"[78] who must make do with what is at hand:

> the "bricoleur" is . . . someone who works with his hands
> and uses devious means compared to those of a craftsman.
> The characteristic feature of mythical thought is that it
> expresses itself by means of a heterogeneous repertoire
> which, even if extensive, is never the less limited. It has to

> use this repertoire, however, whatever the task in hand
> because it has nothing else at its disposal. Mythical thought
> is therefore a kind of intellectual "bricolage". . . .[79]

In contrast to the engineer, who defines his means in terms of a particular project, and who subordinates each of his tasks to the "availability of raw materials and tools conceived and procured for the purpose of the project," the *bricoleur's* universe of instruments "is closed
and the rules of his game are always to make do with 'whatever is at
hand,' that is to say with a set of tools and materials which is always
finite and heterogeneous because what it contains bears no relation to
the current project, or indeed to any particular project, but is the contingent result of all the occasions there have been to renew or enrich the
stock or to maintain it with the remains of previous constructions or
destructions."[80] The point of the distinction is that " 'the engineer'
is always trying to make his way out of and go beyond the constraints
imposed by a particular state of civilization while the 'bricoleur' by inclination or necessity always remains within them."[81]

Lévi-Strauss's distinction between *bricoleur* and engineer is an extention of Saussure's definition of the sign. The engineer represents
a naive view of linguistics, a scientific thinker with a mystified conception of the signifier as a transparency which looks out upon a
freestanding signified (the engineer is "trying to make his way out of
. . . the constraints imposed by a particular state of civilization"); the
bricoleur, on the other hand, would instinctively understand that all
signifieds are historical productions, within a closed and finite field, of
the differential play of signifiers that are at hand, and that they bear
no motivated relation to a signified totality (or final project). But
the gap between theory and practice is huge. Despite the affirmation of
myth without origin, despite the preference for the *bricoleur*, Lévi-
Strauss's actual anthropological work is that of the engineer, as Derrida
has argued, whose practice is commanded by the engineer's yearning
for universality. In the attempt to free himself from the "constraints
imposed by a particular state of civilization," Lévi-Strauss ignores
cultural heterogeneity (Culler has made this point). Lévi-Strauss is the
synchronic Platonist that Saussure never was, and nowhere is that more
in evidence than in his duplicitous employment of "binary opposition"
which, in Jameson's words, is both an "underlying structure" and a
"method of revealing that structure"[82] (a criticism of Lévi-Strauss
that pretty much amounts to a definition of the engineer's project).
The commitment to interpretation which chiefly distinguishes Lévi-
Strauss from Frye is only verbal; as readers, both present themselves

as transparencies, innocents who somehow elude the clutches of perspective.*

4

Perhaps because his subject, in contrast to Lévi-Strauss, Foucault, or Derrida, has often been literature and the problems of its interpretation, Roland Barthes is easily the best-known representative of the new French point of view. Sentence by sentence, Barthes's books are lucid, their organization generally elegant, and, we shouldn't underestimate this factor, most of them can be read in an evening. Many of his pieces have the appeal of timely exposition: articles defining structuralism and myth, brief overviews of recent critical movements in France, a long essay summarizing the main features of Saussure's *Course*. And Barthes has made his thought available: no ivory-tower intellectual, he has brought recent theoretical debate to the *TLS*, and has made brilliant connections between semiotics and the movies, wrestling, cooking, political sloganeering, advertising, fashions in clothes, stripteasing, cars, photography, toys, and margarine.

Barthes has been a visible writer on the Continent for almost thirty years, but his work has come to the United States all in a rush. In not much more than a decade his translators have flooded us with *Writing Degree Zero, Elements of Semiology, Mythologies, On Racine, Critical Essays, S/Z, The Pleasure of the Text, Sade, Fourier, Loyola,* and a book about himself. We register the fact of our inundation, but as of yet we have not raised the question of what Barthes fundamentally represents. Structuralism? Poststructuralism? Psychoanalysis? Existentialism? Political engagement? He has been pinned with all of these labels and perhaps for that reason alone some suspect him to be an intellectual drifter, blowing in the winds of contemporary criticism. As far as I know, no one has accused him of consistency. Barthes's

---

* The most candid statement of this idea in contemporary theory is made by Hayden White, whose structuralism is worked up explicitly through Kenneth Burke and Northrop Frye. White contends that, though discourse is inevitably shaped by a writer's commitments to a precritical linguistic protocol (a dominant trope), *his* readings of such discourse are given from a value-neutral point of view—a self-consciously ironic perspective which, by virtue of its self-consciousness, moves beyond irony and all other constitutive tropes. (See *Metahistory: The Historical Imagination in Nineteenth-Century Europe* [Baltimore: Johns Hopkins University Press, 1973], pp. ix–xii, 426–34). Self-conscious irony, however, is probably only the essence of irony, the irony of irony, not its transcendence. See chapter 2, above, for a critique of this very issue.

career, though far too complicated to assess in any adequate way here, may be limned for its commanding perspectives and turns. I find essentially one major change of stance, signaled by the publication in 1966 of the as yet untranslated *Critique et verité*. After that, much of his work is in the mode now associated with Derrida and *Tel Quel*. Before that, Barthes's work is held together by a profound commitment to the historical nature of discourse. It is this earlier Barthes who most interests me, because it is the earlier Barthes who is the most effective antidote to the Platonic aridities of Lévi-Strauss and the American mediation of structuralist ideas.

One of the key terms of recent French criticism, *écriture* (loosely translated as "writing") was put into the contemporary critical lexicon in *Writing Degree Zero*, and in a sense which is now virtually ignored. *Ecriture* is set off from *language* ("a corpus of prescriptions and habits common to all the writers of a period") and *style* (the "reflex" of a writer's art, a "closed personal process," "the product of a thrust"— biological or biographical—"not an intention").[83] *Ecriture* is essentially the product of choice, "the imposition of something beyond language," and beyond style, "which is both History and the stand we take in it."[84] Barthes's early brush with existentialism is evident in his distinction. For whereas neither language nor style are the products of choice —they operate as necessity, together they "map out for the writer a Nature"—*écriture* represents a free commitment in which the writer manifests and communicates "a state of happiness or malaise," and in which he "links the form of his utterance which is at once normal [as language] and singular [as style] to the vast History of the Others."[85] Barthes's existentialism, however, is not sentimental. If the purer Sartrean background is evident in the rejection of deterministic schemes (*écriture* shows the writer "clearly as an individual because this is where he commits himself"), then this apparently free commitment is made deeply problematic when Barthes insists that the act of freedom is at the same time "an act of historical solidarity."[86] And when he adds (in anticipation of the concern with intertextuality) that all *écriture* "still remains full of the recollection of previous usage, for language is never innocent," whatever the "need for a free language," when he insists that *écriture* remains stubbornly a "trace," a sort of verbal memory, and that the writer inevitably becomes "a prisoner of someone else's words," it is evident that Barthes is rejecting the easy existentialist cant of freedom, and that he is submitting *écriture* to the informing powers of historical matrices.[87] The theme of *écriture* in *Writing Degree Zero* constitutes a double rejection: first, of the neoclassical poetics which poses writing as a transparent, natural discourse that evades temporality; and

second, of a symbolist poetics which in a "violent drive towards autonomy destroys any ethical scope," and in so doing attempts to turn its
back on society.[88] The rejection both of modernism and of the view that
modernism itself rejected encourages us to grasp in the notion of
écriture the fundamentally historical being of discourse.

In the light of this emphasis on *écriture*, we might read Barthes's exposition of Saussure in *Elements of Semiology* as, at the crucial points,
an effort to make the *Course in General Linguistics* more immediately
responsible to social concerns. Leaning on the revisions of Saussure
made by Brøndal, Barthes first pushes to the foreground a resolutely
dialectical conception of the relationship of *langue* and *parole*, and then
with the help of Louis Hjelmslev's enlargement and redistribution of
Saussure's terminology he tries to turn the synchronic thrust of *langue*
in a direction of increasing responsibility to particularly, historicity,
and the processes of acculturation. Within *langue* itself "Hjelmslev distinguishes three planes: i) the *schema*, which is the language as pure
form. . . . this is Saussure's *langue* in the strictest sense of the word. . . .
ii) the *norm*, which is the language as material form, after it has been
defined by some degree of social realization, but still independent of
this realization . . . iii) the *usage*, which is the language as a set of habits
prevailing in a given society. . . ."[89] Concrete speech in itself, or isolated
individual performance, is relegated, as is the structuralist wont, to a
realm of the unknowable, nominalistic particular. And in keeping with
the overall structuralist intention of focusing on collective realities, or
interconnected fields of relations, the social concept of "usage" is
awarded a privileged place in linguistic analysis.

To this discussion of Hjelmslev's neo-Saussurean handling of the
relationship of language and speech, Barthes appends the notion of
idiolect (" 'the language'," in Martinet's phrasing, " 'inasmuch as it is
spoken by a single individual' ").[90] While agreeing with Jakobson's
critique of the idea (" 'private property in the sphere of language does
not exist' "—hence "the idiolect would appear to be largely an illusion"),[91] Barthes nevertheless wishes to retain a version of the idea
which would "correspond roughly to what we have attempted to describe elsewhere under the name of 'writing.' We can say in general that
the hesitations in defining the concept of idiolect only reflect the need
for an intermediary entity between speech and language (as was already proved by the *usage* theory in Hjelmslev), or, if you like, the need
for a speech which is already institutionalized but not yet radically open
to formalization, as the language is."[92] It is this combined notion of
idiolect and usage as institutionalized speech that informs Barthes's
semiological extension of Saussure's linguistic model. The semiological

system, unlike *langue* in its basic sense, is a second-order discourse built upon the model of language; and unlike *langue* it is elaborated "not by the 'speaking mass' but by a deciding group. In this sense it can be held that in most semiological languages, the sign is really and truly 'arbitrary' since it is founded in artificial fashion by a unilateral decision; these in fact are fabricated languages, 'logo-techniques.' The user follows these languages, draws messages (or 'speech') from them but has no part in their elaboration."[93] Barthes's examples are the languages of the fashion, automobile, and furniture industries.

The immense force of his point is perhaps matched only by the near universality with which it has been resisted, in the contemporary critical theory community. By reminding us of the artificiality and undeniably arbitrary status of semiological systems—and we can add to his examples the discourse of literature and of literary critics—Barthes reminds us not only of their unnatural status (they are modes of discourse given to us neither by God nor by the nature of things) but also of the much-avoided (because uncomfortable) corollary that these systems are put into operation, put into force *by force*. Vast, diffuse, and nearly anonymous "deciding groups," establishments of power, in so elaborating the perimeters and structures of a language, define our ways of thinking and behaving and our norms of value: the individual has no say, and neither does that sentimental construction called "the people." After Barthes, the various formalist notions of a free and unconstrained self, and of a free, autonomous literary language, are revealed for what they are: the fantasies of the repressed and—in the political extension worked through in *Mythologies*—the prized ideals of bourgeois culture.

In the preface to *Mythologies* Barthes makes this statement on the origin and intention of his collection:

> The starting point of these reflections was usually a feeling of impatience at the sight of the "naturalness" with which newspapers, art and common sense constantly dress up a reality which, even though it is the one we live in, is undoubtedly determined by history. In short, in the account given of our contemporary circumstances, I resented seeing Nature and History confused at every turn, and I wanted to track down, in the decorative display of *what-goes-without-saying*, the ideological abuse, which, in my view, is hidden there.[94]

Among the many essays in *Mythologies* which demonstrate what Barthes is talking about, I offer one as exemplary: his devastating analysis of a well-known exhibition of photographs which in the late fifties and early sixties quickly became a great coffee-table favorite of the socially enlightened, *The Family of Man*.[95] The aim of the exhibition, Barthes says, "was to show the universality of human actions in the daily life of all the countries of the world: birth, death, work, knowledge, play, always impose the same types of behavior; there is a Family of Man." Therefore, what might "originally pass for a phrase belonging to zoology . . . is here amply moralized and sentimentalized . . . [into an] ambiguous myth of human 'community' . . . ." And cunningly so: for "first the difference between human morphologies is asserted . . . [and] the image of Babel is complacently projected over that of the world." But, then, from all this acknowledged diversity,

> a type of unity is magically produced: man is born, works, laughs and dies everywhere in the same way; and if there still remains in these actions some ethnic peculiarity, at least one hints that there is underlying each one an identical "nature," that their diversity is only formal and does not belie the existence of a common mould. Of course this means postulating a human essence, and here is God re-introduced into our Exhibition: the diversity of men proclaims his power, his richness; the unity of their gestures demonstrates his will.

The photographs together with their accompanying quotations (primitive proverbs, verses from the Old Testament) proclaim an "eternal wisdom, a class of assertions which escape History" and which actively work "to suppress the determining weight of History; we are held back at the surface of an identity, prevented precisely by sentimentality from penetrating into this ulterior zone of human behavior where historical alienation introduces some 'difference,' which we shall here quite simply call 'injustices'." Barthes's intention is not to deny the obvious, that there are natural facts like birth and death and hunger, but to affirm that "if one removes History from them, there is nothing more to be said about them; any comment about them becomes purely tautological. . . ." The point is this: "Whether or not the child is born with ease or difficulty, whether or not his birth causes suffering to his mother, whether or not he is threatened by a high mortality rate, whether or not such and such a type of future is open to him: this is what your Exhibition should be telling people, instead of an eternal lyricism of birth."

But it was the purpose of the exhibition to hide such considerations under "the decorative display of *what-goes-without-saying*." This masking of ideological abuse under the guise of nature is the primary intention of myth as a semiological system of communication and social usage. Barthes's notion of myth is not only, then, fundamentally at odds with Cassirer's, Frye's, and Lévi-Strauss's theories of myth as universal narrative structure grounded in the structure of consciousness; it points out, in effect, that theirs are yet further confusions of nature and history. (Though he would reject the idea that he is confused, Frye would have to admit that in the *Anatomy* he overtly grounds his system in universal natural processes.)[96] As Barthes puts it, "mythology can only have an historical foundation, for myth is a type of speech chosen by history: it cannot possibly evolve from the 'nature' of things."[97] So as a formal linguistic system, myth is part of semiology, and therefore requires, in part, that the analyst of myth be equipped with Saussurean perspectives. But myth is also an expression of intentional force, and for this reason is a part of ideology and demands that the analyst not be content to describe linguistic structures but be willing to take the further step required of a historical science and study "ideas-in-form."[98] The mythical intention is not, strictly speaking, hidden—were it so myth could not be efficacious, and would not have what Barthes calls an "imperative, button-holing character."[99] Rather, the ideological motive is put forth in the dress of reason and nature. Myth naturalizes motives as it insinuates into the consumer's consciousness (this would hold equally for the consumer of literary criticism and the consumer of Exxon gasoline) a system of values as a system of facts. In Barthes's view the chief energizing force behind myth is bourgeois culture which succeeds in making itself nearly anonymous by cloaking its purposes in the twin images of Nature and the Eternal Man.[100] A key sentence in Barthes's sociology, "The status of the bourgeoisie is particular, historical: man as represented by it is universal, eternal,"[101] may be rewritten in order to align much contemporary literary theory with its social context and to suggest that formalist thought is an expression of bourgeois values: "The status of formalism is particular, historical: poet and poetry as represented by it are universal, eternal."

What is unclear in Barthes's account is how the mythologist (not the one who makes myth but the one who takes it apart, who unveils its ideological intention for what it is) escapes being himself constituted by bourgeois values. Barthes's explanation seems weak and question-begging. He tells us that the mythologist is by definition on the Left, that his revolutionary intention "announces itself openly as revolution and thereby abolishes myth."[102] But we may ask how this can be so, especially when within structuralist assumptions the self must be seen as the construction of the cultural system that surrounds it, and, more specifically, of the bourgeois cultural system of value within which, by admission, Barthes finds himself embedded. How does the revolutionary mythologist escape being appropriated by bourgeois norms? Barthes says that such freedom is achieved by an act of self-consciousness. That may be the case. Yet in allowing us to believe that such self-conscious-ness may produce an unproblematic innocence of self, he indulges in the very bourgeois myth that he is concerned to explode.

This issue of the reader's share in the interpretive process is one which Barthes will increasingly attend to in his later books, and in ways increasingly debilitating for the richly historical intention an-nounced in *Mythologies*. In the appendix to his study *On Racine* he outlines a program for the writing of literary history that would pre-sumably not be enervated from the outset by the formalist isolationism suggested by his title, "History or Literature?" But in the final para-graphs of this piece, Barthes's equation of historical being with the "utterly subjective," in its recollection of a traditional epistemological model, would seem to deny the critic access to knowledge.[103]

To his credit, I think it is the very strength of his revisionist program that emphasizes the weakness of his conclusion. Working again the anti-Cartesian vein of structuralism, Barthes tells us that a new literary history cannot get off the ground without first overcoming the " 'cen-tralizing' privilege granted the author" by traditional historicism (Sainte-Beuve is a lonely exception, he thinks, because he "had the astonishing merit of describing a true milieu, in which no single figure is privi-leged").[104] Barthes describes traditional literary history as author-centered, "a series of monographs, each of which, almost without ex-ception, stakes out an author and studies him for himself; history here is merely a succession of individual men."[105] Even the most casual perusal of the tables of contents of books that are presented as literary histories will confirm his point that traditional historicism, in its grant-ing of privilege to the author, is largely driven by the idealist notion that the so-called major writer is one who transcends his times, that history is a succession of autonomous great men. (At this level of Barthes's inquiry, the antagonism between "critics" and "historians" disappears as both take modernist poetics at its word: literature creates a "world" of its own.) Barthes's wish, on the other hand, "To amputate literature from the individual!" is buttressed by the strategy that authors "be considered only as participants in an institutional activity that transcends them individually."[106]

I extrapolate the following set of imperatives, from his book on Racine, for the would-be historical critic: (1) The writer's contemporary audience must be studied with the goal of determining both its social configuration and its intellectual training. (2) The critic's academic situ-ation, within a structure of higher education where fortresslike walls isolate the various areas of humane learning from one another, must be radically questioned. Barthes is persuasive on this matter: "Racinean scholarship is, on the whole, university scholarship; such works can therefore not transgress, without using limited subterfuges, the very forms of higher education: on the one side philosophy, on another history, and beyond, literature. . . . the object of research itself remains predetermined by an obsolete scholarship."[107] (3) Instead of assuming that the discourse of the major writer is unique, the critic's research should be directed by the ample evidence of historical collectives of literary language and a collective literary mentality. (4) As a corollary to the last directive, the question of the relationship of so-called major and minor writers must be raised again, but not on the conventional assumption that such a relationship is not significant. And (5) the discipline of literary theory must itself be historicized; one compelling implication of this is that we would begin to see contemporary literary theory as a product of a contemporary situation, rather than, as is our Hegelian custom, the achievement of ultimate methodological sophistication in the final and fullest revelation of the Idea of Literature. A history of literature must at the same time be a "history of the very idea of literature,"[108] and it needs now to be reconducted on the assumption that the ontology of literature is historical (there is no literature with a capital letter). As Barthes writes: "literature's very being, when restored to history, is no longer a being. Secularized . . . literature becomes one of those great human activities, of relative form and function. . . . In other words, literary history is possible only if it becomes sociological, if it is concerned with activities and institutions, not with individuals."[109] Taken either singly or as an ensemble, these proposals have the effect of a single directive which would encourage us to understand the title of Barthes's essay "History or Literature?" as a deliberate ironic posing of false alternatives. Literature and theories about its nature and value are symbiotically related activities, heavily weighted by complicated institutional intentions; they are not essences with *a priori* status whose identities are only approximated in the temporal activities of finite beings.

The collection of essays published under the title *Essai Critiques* in 1964 and translated in 1972 provides the most convincing evidence that Barthes's career through the fifties and early sixties was unified by a desire to bring to the foreground of theoretical debate the historical ontology of both literary and critical discourse. *Critical Essays* provides, as well, indications in its last few pieces of a change that would be fully voiced in *Critique et verité* (1966, a slashing response to Raymond Picard's attack on *Sur Racine*) and in the best-known later works, *S/Z*,

The Pleasure of the Text, and *Sade, Fourier, Loyola.* A number of the
pieces in *Critical Essays,* especially those on Brecht, reiterate the themes
of most concern to Barthes in the fifties: "the evils men suffer are in
their own hands"; "art can and must intervene in history"; "we must
have an art of explanation and no longer merely of expression"; "there
is no such thing as an 'essence' of eternal art."[110] The idea of a Brech-
tean "critical" theater highlights Barthes's Marxist debts and an underlying aesthetic of "critical realism" that appears to rely on the thought
of Georg Lukács ("according to the profoundest Marxist teaching, each
[ideological] theme is at once the expression of what men want to be
and of what things are").[111]

What these various politically inspired essays make clear is Barthes's
willingness to intermingle what Sartre (in *What is Literature?*) labored
to keep distinct as the difference of poetry and prose: a Kantian aesthetic
tradition with its celebration of an enclosed "intransitive" sort of discourse which in its self-sufficiency does not take an object; and the
tradition of engagement with its celebration of a transitive discourse
(language as a means "supports a *praxis*").[112] Barthes says "we want *to
write something,* and at the same time *we write* (intransitively). In short,
our age produces a bastard type. . . ."[113] His kind of structuralism represents a commitment to both traditions, but it is not a theoretically contradictory eclecticism. The formalism of structuralist thought (which
out of context sounds much like what used to be called New Criticism in
this country) is integrated with "responsibility." In his first *Tel Quel*
interview (1961), certain emphases must not be misread as repetitions
of formalism—when, for example, Barthes says that the being of literature lies in its processes of signification, "not in what is signified."[114]
When he says the question is one of "systems rather than objects," of
"function" not of "content," he means not to echo the New-Critical
shibboleth (literature must be, not mean) but to remind us of the Saussurean axiom that, since there are no signifieds independent of signifiers, we need "to enter the 'kitchen of meaning' " if we would grasp the
historical ontology of writing:[115]

> I have always been interested in what might be called the
> responsibility of forms. But it was only at the end of my
> book *Mythologies* that I realized this problem must be
> raised in terms of signification. . . . In other words: ever
> since the final fifty-page essay of *Mythologies,* ideas and
> themes interest me less than the way society takes possession
> of them in order to make them the substance of a certain
> number of signifying systems. This does not mean that this
> substance is indifferent; it means that we cannot apprehend

> it, manipulate it, judge it, make it the basis of philosophical,
> sociological, or political explanations without first having
> described and understood the system of signification of
> which it is merely a term; and since this system is a formal
> one, I have found myself engaged in a series of structural
> analyses. . . .[116]

The quite brief, abstract, and frequently anthologized definition of
structuralism that Barthes published in *Critical Essays* under the title
"The Structuralist Activity" is easily mistaken as a formalist document
of the old school unless it is understood within a framework of keen
social sensitivity to the ways that discourse is appropriated for the ends
of power ("the way society takes possession"). When, therefore, he
writes that the "goal of all structuralist activity . . . is to reconstruct an
'object' in such a way as to manifest thereby the rules of functioning . . .
of this object"; when he describes the structuralist activity as a type of
imitation whose goal is to render intelligible (not copy) in order "to
make certain functions appear"; and when he insists that structuralism
"seeks to link to history not only certain contents . . . but also certain
forms,"[117] he is seeking to connect structuralism to the revolutionary
consciousness that he celebrated in *Mythologies*. Structuralist activity
seeks out in forms of signification the hidden motives of power behind
the mask of what-goes-without-saying.

In a little noticed essay called "Taking Sides," which is actually a
review essay of Michel Foucault's *Histoire de la folie*, this theme of appropriation—the interested, self-aggrandizing, social possession of systems of discourse—receives its most far-reaching treatment. Barthes's
meditation on Foucault is one of the most remarkable meetings of
kindred spirits in contemporary theory. Not only does it make very
clear the drift and importance of Barthes's early career, but it yields as
well an indispensable perspective on Foucault; it suggests a continuity
between structuralism and what is called poststructuralism; and it fills
in, in so many words, the philosophical background of Edward Said's
recent work (*Beginnings* and *Orientalism*). Barthes begins in a familiar
vein: "This audacious book . . . restores to history a fragment of 'nature'
and transforms into a phenomenon of civilization what we hitherto took
for a medical phenomenon: madness."[118] What Barthes centrally insists
upon (in effect) is that Foucault's effort is to be seen as coincidental with
his own to destroy the illusion of the natural, history-transcending
identity of literature. For like literature, "madness is not the *object* of
knowledge, whose history must be rediscovered; one might say that
madness is nothing but this knowledge itself. . . ." Again, like literature,
madness is no timeless essence, but "a variable and perhaps hetero-

geneous *meaning*, according to the period. . . ." And once more: like madness, literature is the product of a faked dialogue; madness is the "pure function of a couple formed by reason and unreason, observer and observed."[119] Both madness and literature, however, are silent: the mad do not tell us what they understand about men of reason and the concept of reason, just as literature does not give its opinion about what men of criticism have said about it, or an opinion about the notion of criticism itself. Madness and literature can only be *what they are said to be*, "since there is no discourse of madness about reason" (or of literature about criticism) "corresponding to the discourse of reason about madness,"[120] or of criticism about literature. Barthes's construction of Foucault's method rehearses and enlarges his earlier "History or Literature?": "For the constitutive observation of madness [or of literature] by men of reason is very quickly seen to be a simple element of their praxis. . . . the history of madness always follows a history of the ideas of labor, of poverty, of idleness, and of unproductivity. . . ."[121] And though Foucault heatedly rejects the characterization, Barthes shrewdly calls his work "structural history," implying by the term that rare and happy blend of synchrony and diachrony. (In the next chapter I will take up again the connection between Foucault's historicism and the task of writing literary history.)

The following summary by Barthes teems with the sorts of implications that need to be attended to by literary critics:

> Without ever breaking the thread of a diachronic narrative, Foucault reveals, for each period, what we should elsewhere call *sense units*, whose combination defines the period and whose translation traces the very movement of history; animality, knowledge, vice, idleness, sexuality, blasphemy, libertinage—these historical components of the demential image thus form signifying complexes, according to a kind of historical syntax which varies from epoch to epoch; they are, if you like, clauses of what is signified, huge "semantemes" whose signifiers themselves are transitory, since reason's observation constructs the marks of madness only from its own norms, and since these norms are themselves historical.[122]

Though madness and literature cannot be defined in the traditional sense, since they "possess no transcendent content," they can be structured by a willful, interested, and highly selective "act of exclusion" (Nietzsche again), an act "which in a positive sense accounts," within a single, hierarchized relationship, for reason and madness, literature and nonliterature, included and excluded.[123] What is inside will be called sanity, truth, beauty, and goodness, and what is outside madness, false-hood, ugliness, and evil; "in the couples constituted by reason and mad-ness, by included and excluded, [poetry and nonpoetry], knowledge [or poetics] is a taking of sides. . . ."[124] The act of exclusion, which by its very nomination, as Barthes notes, accounts for both excluded and in-cluded, amounts to an act of institutionalized violence.

It is at this fruitful point that we confront the most troublesome issue in Barthes's writing. He will remind us in the essay "The Two Criti-cisms" that "history tells us that there is no such thing as a timeless es-sence of literature, but under the rubric 'literature' (itself quite recent, moreover) a process of very different forms, functions, institutions, rea-sons, and projects whose relativity it is precisely the historian's re-sponsibility to discern. . . ." (Simply put, the historical context of Racine "is not ours.")[125] In an essay published at about the same time as "The Two Criticisms" ("What is Criticism?"), with superb con-sistency Barthes notes that since critics, like authors of what is called literature, are similarly historical beings, "criticism must include in its discourse . . . an implicit reflection upon itself. . . . In other words, criticism . . . is essentially an activity, i.e., a series of intellectual acts profoundly committed to the historical and subjective existence (they are the same) of the man who performs them."[126] The purpose of this act of self-examination is apparently to put the critic in a situation of minimum self-delusion with respect to his ideology and prejudices, a situation in which he will not confuse his own historical and subjective being with an author who is not himself and a phase of history which is not his. The critic's task is "to adjust the language his period affords him . . . to the language, i.e., the formal system of logical constraints elaborated by the author according to his period."[127] So far Barthes has offered a view of history that powerfully resists the idea that tempo-rality is a repetition of the same—a view that insists on change and dif-ferences—and the sanguine thought that these changes and differences can to a reasonable extent be known, that accurate historical conscious-ness, while difficult to come by, is not out of the question. His struc-turalist formulation of the point is as follows: the being of literature lies "not in its message [the signified] but in its system. The critic is not responsible for reconstructing the work's message but only its system."[128]

But how can the critic, a historical being through and through, whose language "does not come down to him from Heaven" but is a "necessity"[129]—how can this critic, whose self is wholly a construction of the systems of his time, discover the author "according to his period"? How can he "reconstruct" the systems of constraint which produced the author but not himself? With no instruction to the contrary, we are forced to understand Barthes's use of the term "subjectivity" according to a traditional epistemological model which would stipulate that subjectivity is always a bar to knowledge. He bears out our fears when he tells us that the object of the critical act is "not to *discover* the work in question but on the contrary to *cover* it as completely as possible by its own language."[130] And if that is not clear enough, what could be more openly subversive of his historicist intention than this: "Thus begins, at the heart of the critical work, the dialogue of two histories and two subjectivities, the author's and the critic's. But this dialogue is egoistically shifted toward the present: criticism is not an homage to the truth of the past or to the truth of 'others'—it is a construction of the intelligibility of our own time."[131]

We have arrived at the phase of Barthes's career which forms the theoretical backbone of Culler's *Structuralist Poetics* and some of the recent essays of Stanley Fish. Later writings like *S/Z* and *The Pleasure of the Text* press on in this direction. Barthes uses the term "dialogue" to describe the critical act, but with his egoistic focus the term is unearned. What is called poststructuralism (it can be identified by such signposts as Barthes's latest texts, some of Derrida, and the Yale appropriation of Derrida) sometimes sinks irretrievably into the stupor of a self-satisfied solipsism. Unlike the argument advanced by Gadamer, in the thought of Barthes terms like "subjectivity," "prejudice," and "history" cancel each other and destroy the possibility of authentic historical consciousness. It is a story we have been reading for the last decade or so.

We can characterize the change in Barthes's thought signalled by *Critique et verité* as a turn toward Derridean poststructuralism. The problem with such a characterization is that it is anachronistic, for in 1966 Derrida was still an obscure young philosopher whose major publications lay in the future. Yet the reader of *Critique et verité* who forgets the precise chronology of recent French criticism must be excused if he hears Derrida in Barthes's contention that literary language constitutes what will be called a *mise en abyme,* a discourse by nature *without a nature* and (in opposition to practical language) "unsituated," "without contingency," something like a "pure ambiguity." Supported by an "empty meaning," such discourse is without "bottom."[132] If we sense that Barthes is looking in two directions at once—toward a Derridean critique of discourse without center, and backward to a familiar romantic distinction between a free aesthetic discourse and the practical, end-directed, end-controlled language of quotidian man (shades of the aestheticist revulsion before Victorian moralism), then by 1970, with the publication of *S/Z*, in the United States his most notorious work, there can be no question that Barthes has adopted wholesale a Derridean perspective and vocabulary. He has thrown over his historically disposed structuralism for something called "difference." "This difference is not, obviously, some complete, irreducible quality . . . it is not what designates the individuality of each text, what names, signs, finishes off each work with a flourish; on the contrary, it is a difference which does not stop and which is articulated upon the infinity of texts, of languages, of systems. . . ."[133] The temporally determinate syntagm is replaced by "the infinite paradigm of difference";[134] the ideologically committed notion of *écriture* gives way to the "writerly" text, to Writing. And the reader, no longer a consumer, becomes "a producer of the text":

> the writerly text is *ourselves writing* before the infinite play
> of the world . . . is traversed, intersected, stopped,
> plasticized by some singular system (Ideology, Genus,
> Criticism) which reduces the plurality of entrances, the
> opening of networks, the infinity of languages. The writerly
> is the novelistic without the novel, poetry without the
> poem, the essay without the dissertation, writing without
> style, production without product, structuration without
> structure. But the readerly texts? They are products (and
> not productions), they make up the enormous mass of our
> literature.[135]

This distinction between the "writerly" and the "readerly," which is clearly indebted to Derrida's notions of free-play and decentering, is a distinction not between the objective properties of two different kinds of discourse but between two ways of taking texts. One way (the "classical") is to take the text as determinate (via *cogito*, or archetype, or historical matrix, or moral imperative), the other, as indeterminate— in Barthes's words, as a mode of interpretation, in the Nietzschean sense, which "posits the image of a triumphant plural, unimpoverished by any constraint. . . ."[136] The writerly text is constituted as "a galaxy of signifiers, not a structure of signifieds; it has no beginning; it is reversible; we gain access to it by several entrances, none of which can be authoritatively declared to be the main one. . . ."[137] Several more echoes of Derrida ("nothing exists outside the text," no center, no signified to which to anchor an "ideology of totality")[138] make the point: Barthes's rejection of structuralism is a metaphor for the rejection of any and all critical theories which are committed to the finitude or closure of the text—and he makes no distinction between the kind of theory committed to traditional modes of ontological closure and that committed to the secularization or historicizing of the being of literature. It matters not to Barthes, these days, whether the determinacy of a text is guaranteed by normative forces whose being is wholly temporal (and transient) or whether such determinacy is eternally guaranteed by a timeless force outside the discourses of history.

So in place of the traditional book Barthes puts the "text," by which he and a number of recent French thinkers mean something like "open writing," what is called, alternatively, "textuality," "intertextuality," or Writing. These terms signify not what in common usage is called a "text," nor a given corpus of texts, but all writing taken as a self-conditioning mass whose limits cannot be known. Each single text (in the common usage) is an "entrance into a network with a thousand entrances; to take this entrance is to aim, ultimately, not at a legal structure of norms and departures, a narrative or poetic law, but at a perspective (of fragments, of voices from other texts, other codes), whose vanishing point is nonetheless ceaselessly pushed back, mysteriously opened. . . ."[139] Such detachment of Writing as textuality from all determinates amounts to the contemporary linguistic fulfillment of the Hegelian dream of absolute freedom. For like Hegel's Spirit, Writing "exists *in* and *with itself.* Matter [or, for our purposes, the traditional concept of the text] has its essence out of itself; Spirit is *self-contained existence.* . . . Now this is Freedom, exactly. For if I am dependent, my being is referred to something else which I am not: I cannot exist independently of something external [like a transcendental signified]. I am free, on the contrary, when my existence depends upon myself."[140]

If we ask Barthes how Writing or the "writerly" text (as a putatively unconstrained mode of reading) can possibly be produced by a human reader, whom he describes (as late as *Critique et verité*) as a systematized or cultivated subjectivity (i.e., derived from culture) and subject, therefore, to enormous constraints—if we ask how this reader can possibly begin to produce writing as textuality, he gives us no satisfaction. The problem is ignored as he pursues, in *The Pleasure of the Text,* without awareness of contradiction, the twin goals of private, sexual, "asocial" bliss (*jouissance,* "coming") and the "revolutionary" destruction of a bourgeois ideology which he aligns with values of responsibility and seriousness (again, shades of the 1890s). This presumably subversive (anarchic?) text of bliss (a variation on what was called the "writerly" text) somehow undoes all of those various ideological systems which fight for repressive hegemony over discourse and which, when successful, impose a "ruthless" topic (when power is on the side of a particular ideology) and transform discourse into nature, or what-goes-without-saying.[141] The most powerful motif in *The Pleasure of the Text*, in fact, is a political one: Barthe's text of bliss, in its "edged" or "seamed" character, is said at many points to unsettle all ideologies.[142] This text of bliss must throw off the isotropism of classical writing and become "atopic." Through deployment of principles of "absolute instability" and "logical contradiction," it "undoes nomination" and thereby becomes unpredictable and free of all centered systems of meaning.[143] But since all blissful experience so engendered remains locked up in what Barthes (echoing the neo-Kantian, Eliseo Vivas) calls an "absolutely intransitive" experience of erotic silence, to which no discourse, no concept, no system can be adequate or even minimally accessible—and most especially since such experience cannot, by definition, be "taken over by any collectivity" (Barthes is quite insistent about this latter point), his revolutionary intention is nothing more than empty rhetoric.[144] That Barthes's various techniques of subversion might themselves be conventions is never questioned; perhaps because such questioning would reveal them to be those well-worn instruments of what Lukács called the ideology of modernism.

The blissful text's subversiveness, Barthes claims, lies in its ability to elude the dominance of ideological systems (sociolects) like Marxism, Christianity, capitalism, or whatever, and it accomplishes this by destroying utterly "its own discursive category, its sociolinguistic reference. . . ."[145] But, how is *that* achieved? The general answer is that the text of bliss suspends all signified values, all of the so-called good causes through the "simple effect of polysemy" which would make the ideological commitment of a literary dialect "dubious from its origin."[146] All who are familiar with the American New Critics recognize the strategy (though Barthes's is a more radical commitment to polysemy than what we remember in William Empson). And a second strategy— the calling of ironic attention to the fictiveness of ideological systems— will recall Frank Kermode's *The Sense of an Ending:* "The text needs its shadow: the shadow is *a bit* of ideology, *a bit* of representation, *a bit* of subject . . . subversion must produce its own chiaroscuro."[147] In these ways the text undercuts its traditional medieval and Renaissance epistemological function and becomes an instance of purest textuality: "*Text* means *Tissue:* but whereas hitherto we have always taken this tissue as a product, a ready-made veil, behind which lies, more or less hidden, meaning (truth), we are now emphasizing, in the tissue, the generative idea that the text is made, is worked out in a perpetual interweaving. . . ."[148] As sheer interweaving, as web without a centering spider, free-play without closure, endless galaxy of liberated signifiers, the text destroys itself as veil, lens, or mirror—and unburdens itself of the cognitive weight that these traditional epistemological metaphors are meant to bear.

The text so liberated becomes the site of what Barthes believes to have been repressed "by nearly every philosophy":[149] pleasure without responsibility to ends and values beyond pleasure's own free-standing being. The text "is (should be) that uninhibited person who shows his behind to the *Political Father*."[150] "That is the pleasure of the text: value shifted to the sumptuous rank of the signifier."[151] The pleasure of the text is the pleasure of the therapeutically relieved self. Barthes's latest work is something like an ultimate gearing-up of the Kantian engine; as a seeker of pleasure in isolation from social, cognitive, and ethical dimensions of selfhood, he reaffirms the fragmented personality upon which Kant erected his aesthetic system, while turning his back upon those ideologies in force which produce that fragmentation. Poststructuralist hedonism may be the most extreme expression of a theory that art exhibits "purposiveness without purpose."

5

At the conclusion of an essay on the act of reading which focuses on two examples from Henry James and T. S. Eliot, Walter Benn Michaels, a younger American critic who is indebted to the perspectives of structuralism, draws out for us this lesson: "What these two accounts, taken separately or together, demonstrate about literary criticism is not exactly clear. Perhaps they are best understood as reminders that reading, whatever it is, can never be neutral, reminders that will seem supererogatory only as long as we ignore the disingenuously normative role neutrality plays in the theory and practice of literature."[152] Perhaps at this moment in contemporary theory Michaels's point can be taken for granted, however shocking it might seem within the context of traditional theory. But if, as Michaels argues, and I believe he is correct, traditional theory represents the abuse of neutrality as a principle of interpretation, then much of what has been written recently in the wake of structuralism represents the abuse of partiality. Barthes says that the capital sin in criticism is not ideology but the silence by which it is masked. Recent theory is very quick to acknowledge openly its commitments, its historicity, the fact that it is not innocent or "value-neutral"; the capital sin of this sort of honesty and self-consciousness appears to be the belief, always unstated, that the mere acknowledgment of the interested quality of the act of reading somehow protects the reader from all other sins. I want to examine briefly three approaches to the interested reader that have acquired some notoriety: the first, broadly structuralist, is represented by Stanley Fish's essay "Interpreting the *Variorum*"; the second, phenomenological, via Husserl and Roman Ingarden, is represented by Wolfgang Iser's "The Reading Process: A Phenomenological Approach"; the third, also phenomenological, this time via Heidegger and the German hermeneutical tradition, is represented by Hans-Georg Gadamer's *Truth and Method*.

Fish's first principle is both neo-Kantian and neo-Saussurean: the sense or meaning of a text does not inhere objectively in a text. The assumption that he stands most opposed to is "that there *is* a sense, that it is embedded or encoded in the text, and that it can be taken in at a single glance."[153] (That last clause is directed at a straw man; not even the most naive traditionalist believes that!) Fish opposes naive realism (the reader's mind is a mirror reflection, a neutral report on an objective state of affairs), a position that has stubbornly held on in traditionalist theory by the telling claim that it is common sense and therefore need not be stated, much less discussed. (In philosophical history the position of naive realism has never had a serious proponent.) But from this rejection of naive realism Fish leaps to an equally naive idealism: aside from presently operating contexts for reading, there are neither textual nor historical constraints on the reader's consciousness; the text itself is radically indeterminate—though how a critic of Fish's disposition can allow himself that objectivist claim is never made clear. The rejection of realism leads in Fish's argument to the structuralist notion that any meaning of the text is wholly a construction of the reader. Hence it follows that all interpretations, since they cannot be matched to an objective norm, are equally arbitrary, equally available but not (Fish adds this twist) equally acceptable.

Having turned his attention from a phantom structure of the text itself to the "structure of the reader's experience"[154] (the only thing open to inquiry, yet *how* open, we wonder, since such structure would itself need to be interpreted, etc., etc.?), Fish raises the important question: *"Who* is this reader?" The answer is the "informed or at-home reader" who is our contemporary and a member of "a community made up of those who share interpretive strategies."[155] "This, then, is my thesis: that the form of the reader's experience, formal units, and the structure of intention are one, that they come into view simultaneously, and that therefore the questions of priority and independence do not arise."[156] And, in another statement of the thesis: "To construct the profile of the informed or at-home reader is at the same time to characterize the author's intention and vice-versa, because to do either is to specify the *contemporary* conditions of utterance. . . ."[157] The acceptable or good reader, in this view, is the one who manipulates strategies of reading now in fashion (the condition of community acceptance). In this way Fish can account for agreement and a reasonable stability in interpretation:

> The notion of interpretive communities thus stands between an impossible ideal and the fear which leads so many to maintain it. The ideal is of perfect agreement and it would require texts to have a status independent of interpretation. The fear is of interpretive anarchy, but it would only be realized if interpretation (text making) were completely random. It is the fragile but real consolidation of interpretive communities that allows us to talk to one another....[158]

Fish is difficult to argue with on his own intellectual ground; moreover, he is perhaps the most artful rhetorician among contemporary critics. It may not be altogether inappropriate, however, to suggest that considerations of some other intellectual contexts will point to weaknesses in his thought. First of all, like Culler's, Fish's reader is purely literary: his membership in a community of literary critics somehow cancels out the forces that shape his political, social, or ethnic status. But any theory that is based on the idea that the reader is a constituted and constituting entity yet refuses to assess the consequences of our memberships in nonliterary communities is by definition drastically incomplete. A literary community walled off from larger enclosures of social structure and historical process is a repetition of aestheticist isolationism. At the very least Fish might have pointed out that the consolidated interpretive community he is talking about is situated on the northeastern seaboard of the United States, and that most of its members are "at home" in the English departments of Yale and Johns Hopkins.

Second, it is not the case that the only alternative to naive realism or objectivism is Fish's brand of intersubjective idealism, which not only denies the objectivity of knowledge in the absolute sense of the term "objective," but also appears to deny that there is anything *to be interpreted.* Are the various intentional objects of the interpreter's consciousness equally indifferent? Do epics, lyrics, and novels form one homogeneous soupy texture? Texts are not merely indeterminate for Fish but they are indeterminate in the same way—a text is a kind of empty container waiting to be filled with meaning. Presumably, once we have pinned down the interpretive strategies of a given critical community, we will know in advance what it is going to say about a particular text. The act of practical criticism becomes in this view a redundant and monotonous application of theory: there can be no surprises. Hillis Miller's Stevens, de Man's Rousseau, and Fish's new version of Milton will merge on a blurred and hazy horizon, and Miller, de Man, and Fish themselves will suffer a similar fate as critical identities. The vast and varied past of cultural and authorial intention is collapsed into the single identity of what Fish calls the contemporary conditions of utterance. Like Culler again, he posits an intersubjective idealism which amounts to a solipsism that wipes out the past as it promises the oldest of Western maxims—know thyself—in its most emasculated form, directing us to know ourselves in the absence of dialogue. As an act of making, literary criticism is self-expression which would elevate the critic to the status of romantic poet. If we accept this, the next step is to make a comparative judgment: whose acts of self-expression shall we prefer to read, Wordsworth's or Fish's? Or, more fairly, which body of criticism understood as self-revelation will interest us over the long haul, Samuel Johnson's or Stanley Fish's? Fish's theory of interpretation encourages such comparisons because it forbids any inquiry into the historical process which deposits countless traces of the past on that putatively enclosed environment called "contemporary conditions of utterance." The reading selves of a Johnson or a Fish are not simply determined by an isolated contemporary moment.

The second example of a theory of reading that I wish to discuss, that of Wolfgang Iser, does not recast history in the image of contemporary conditions of utterance, though it recognizes such conditions and takes them into account. For Fish there is one reality, the now of our interpretive community; for Iser, two: the reader in his times, the writer in his. And whereas Fish works within a traditional subject-object model—he reverses the conventional emphasis in order to celebrate readerly activity—Iser's theory of reading attempts to revise the model itself: subject and object are coordinates within the integrated medium of what Husserl defines as intentional consciousness. Working with Ingarden's extension of the Husserlian insight, Iser offers this overview of the process of reading:

> . . . Roman Ingarden confronts the structure of the literary text with the ways in which it can be *konkretisiert* (realized). The text as such offers different "schematized views" through which the subject matter of the work can come to light, but the actual bringing to light is an action of *Konkrietisation*. If this is so, then the literary work has two poles, which we might call the artistic and the aesthetic:

the artistic refers to the text created by the author, and
the aesthetic to the realization accomplished by the reader.
From this polarity it follows that the literary work cannot
be completely identical with the text, or with the realization
of the text, but in fact must lie halfway between the two.[159]

Iser's theory has the virtue of recognizing that the text, as at least a
partially determinate and coercive force (it offers " 'schematized
views,' " it "imposes certain limits on its unwritten implications"),[160]
commands the reader to move into a history that is not a mere repetition
of contemporary conditions of selfhood. But the text is also partially
indeterminate: it has what he calls "gaps," its schemas and outlines
need to be filled out by realizing acts of the reader's imagination.[161]

In his elaboration of a phenomenological theory of reading, Iser
moves closer to Fish's structuralism than we might have anticipated,
and in the process appears to forsake his phenomenology for the conventional subject-object model and some straightforward hedonistic
values. The best of authors (Iser cites Laurence Sterne) deliberately
leave their texts open and incomplete: "If the reader were given the
whole story, and there were nothing left for him to do, then his
imagination would never enter the field, the result would be the boredom which inevitably arises when everything is laid out cut and dried
before us."[162] The true purpose of reading is not to know the text (however knowledge and the discipline of acquiring it may be defined),
but to experience ourselves as active, creative, and free agents; and
the author, by leaving gaps, encourages us to have such experience:
"Herein lies the dialectical structure of reading. The need to decipher
gives us the chance to formulate our own deciphering capacity—i.e.,
we bring to the fore an element of our being of which we are not
directly conscious."[163] Thus "no author worth his salt will ever attempt
to set the *whole* picture before his reader's eyes. If he does, he will
very quickly lose his reader, for it is only by activating the reader's
imagination that the author can hope to involve him and so realize
the intentions of the text."[164] Perhaps because Iser defines authorial
intention as the desire to help the reader to avoid boredom by experiencing the joy of his activated deciphering capacity, he is unin-
terested in asking what a text is and what a reader is. In numerous
places in his essay Iser defines the reader as an autonomous and private
individual (in violation of Husserl's *epochē* he speaks of "individual
disposition," of the "individual mind of the reader with its own particular history of experience, its own consciousness, its own outlook").[165]
He ignores both author and reader as cultural constructions. So from

a theory which in its beginnings appeared to promise movement in a historicist direction, we end with a theory centered in the delights of the personal reading subject.

One of the most serious efforts in contemporary theory to recover history for textual interpretation, Gadamer's *Truth and Method*, stands outside the structuralist tradition proper. Gadamer's premises derive from Heidegger's *Being and Time*, and the specific points he makes on behalf of hermeneutical theory are elaborated within a critique of traditional hermeneutics which fills out some very difficult, elliptical statements in section 32 of Heidegger's early treatise. Gadamer's main exhibit of traditional hermeneutics, the thought of Friedrich Schleiermacher, represents the most widely accepted (though implied) theory of interpretation persisting in contemporary literary theory, through the New Critics, Frye, and Poulet. In traditional hermeneutics reading is assumed to be "a divinatory process, a placing of oneself within the mind of the author . . . a recreation of the creative act. Thus understanding is a reproduction related to an original production. . . ."[166] As "immediate, sympathetic and conatural," understanding becomes a transparency through which authorial intention is fully recovered; the interpreter, in this view, becomes absolutely contemporaneous with his author.[167] Gadamer then goes on to link this sort of hermeneutics of innocence to its apparent progenitor: the Kantian aesthetics of genius which claims that imaginative thought is a "free construction and the free expression of an individual being."[168] As its proper hermeneutical complement, therefore, the Kantian aesthetic demands an equally free, equally innocent interpreter. For reasons well understood by phenomenologists as well as structuralists, Gadamer must reject the innocent interpreter because all understanding, he writes (citing Heidegger), is a forestructuring process, and the primary question that must be confronted is this: "What is the special virtue of the historical consciousness—as against all other forms of consciousness in history—that its own relativity does not destroy the fundamental claim to objective knowledge?"[169] Gadamer's response, in contrast to too much of recent French thought, is cognitive, not hedonic.

Simply put: history for Heidegger and Gadamer is no closed, completed, and foreign object from which we stand detached, but, in the Hegelian mode, an ongoing and embracing process: "history is not only not completed," Gadamer writes, "but we stand within it as one understanding, as a conditioned, finite link in a continuing chain. . . ." He repeatedly reverts to metaphors of a hugely inclusive totality, of a never-ending river, of a large, nourishing earth, in order to suggest the reciprocal involvement of past and present. Hence: "history does not belong to us [as individuals], but we belong to it." Or: "we always stand within tradition, and this is no objectifying process, i.e., we do not conceive of what tradition says as something other, something alien. It is always part of us, a model, or exemplar, a recognition of ourselves." Or: "Understanding is not to be thought of so much as an action of one's subjectivity, but as the placing of oneself within a process of tradition, in which past and present are constantly fused." Or:

> Time is no longer a gulf to be bridged, because it separates, but it is actually the supportive ground of process in which the present is rooted. Hence temporal distance is not something that must be overcome. This was, rather, the naive assumption of historicism, namely that we must set ourselves within the spirit of the age, and think with its ideas and its thoughts, not with our own, and thus advance towards historical objectivity. . . . [Time] is not a yawning abyss, but is filled with the continuity of custom and tradition, in the light of which all that is handed down presents itself to us.[170]

Now, if those statements appear to make the acquisition of an authentic historical understanding too easy, too sentimental, then we must add to them another series of remarks which make historical consciousness difficult and problematic. Against the continuity of custom and tradition we need to place Gadamer's awareness of strangeness and difference. He asks the tough question that Fish and the structuralists almost always skirt: "How do we discover that there is a difference between our own customary [linguistic usage] and that of the text?" In his attempt at an answer Gadamer distinguishes between foremeanings that bring us into the truth of the text and those which he calls "arbitrary fancies"—products of "limitations imposed by imperceptible habits of thought. . . ." Those anticipatory foremeanings that are not arbitrary are recognized only after a rigorous self-examination which helps historical consciousness to achieve not "self-extinction" (the goal of traditional hermeneutics) but intensified possession of itself. Since it is the "tyranny of hidden prejudices" that denies us access to historical knowledge, Gadamer's recommendation of a cleansing self-consciousness, though hardly novel, has the purpose of uncovering for us our hidden biases, "so that the text may present itself in all its newness and thus be able to assert its own truth" against our own foremeanings. But even when such self-consciousness is achieved, the interpreter is not removed to a value-free vantage point. Rather, he continues to exist and function within a "situation" which will deny him scientific certainty: "To exist historically means that knowledge of ourselves can never be complete." And this means that what E. D. Hirsch has called "meaning" and "relevance" cannot be perfectly severed, but must always, at some level, exist in indistinguishable unity. To the question how can we know we have bracketed out all of our irrelevant hidden biases, Gadamer answers, refreshingly, "we can't."[171]

It is perhaps clear by now that Gadamer is using terms like "history," "foremeaning," and "prejudice" in two senses. There is a persistent and massive flow which characterizes authentic historical time (Gadamer calls it "tradition"), and there are those inconstant, brief-lived little tributaries (arbitrary fancies, illegitimate prejudices, limited foremeanings of our present moment) which the historical consciousness often confuses with the mainstream. Legitimate foremeanings and legitimate prejudicies permit the interpreter to come into contact, always through himself, with authoritative tradition whose temporal continuity establishes a fund of historical (as opposed to ontological) universals which form the nutritive ground of authentic interpretation. This linking and exploration of the terms "authority" and "tradition" are crucial to Gadamer's theory of interpretation, for both its main strength and its ultimate (and somewhat frightening) weakness. For if the authority granted to tradition (sometimes he calls it "the tradition"!) assures the realization of his cognitive hope for historical consciousness, then at the same time it calls such consciousness into question. After Barthes's analysis of social myths and the sources of their power, and (as we'll see in the next chapter) after Foucault's parallel analysis of the repressive forces hidden behind and motivating discourse, the very concepts of authority and tradition would seem to require the kind of probing which Gadamer never supplies.

Working against what he calls the Enlightenment prejudice against prejudice, and its enthronement of universal, uncontingent reason, he argues that "authority" is neither irrational nor arbitrary, and that it provides a norm for distinguishing between legitimate and illegitimate prejudices.[172] As a ground of legitimate prejudices, authority somehow becomes a source of truth for the kind of hermeneutical understanding which has managed to place itself under its aegis. Gadamer in this way tries to rehabilitate the concept of authority which, in opposition to free reason, Enlightenment thinkers had deformed by equating it with blind obedience. The essence of true authority, he writes, is that it is based

> not on the subjection and abdication of reason, but on
> recognition and knowledge—knowledge, namely, that the

other is superior to oneself in judgment and insight and that for this reason his judgment takes precedence, i.e. it has precedence over one's own. This is connected with the fact that authority cannot actually be bestowed, but is acquired and must be acquired, if someone is to lay claim to it. It rests on recognition and hence on an act of reason itself which, aware of its own limitations, accepts that others have better understanding.[173]

He then expands the notion by moving it from personal authority to the transpersonal authority of tradition:

That which has been sanctioned by tradition and custom has an authority that is nameless, and our finite historical being is marked by the fact that always the authority of what has been transmitted—and not only what is clearly grounded— has power over our attitudes and behavior. . . . And in fact we owe to romanticism this correction of the enlightenment, that tradition has a justification that is outside the arguments of reason and in large measure determines our institutions and our attitudes.[174]

The conclusion is this: "In our understanding, which we imagine is so straightforward, we find that, by following the criterion of intelligibil-ity, the other presents himself so much in terms of our own selves that there is no longer a question of self and other."[175] Gadamer's argument encourages us to translate the phrase "criterion of intelligibility" into "the authority of tradition"; he concludes that this criterion is available to us all as a unity of human being in its hermeneutical dimension. Hence the so-called Husserlian "horizon" or closed "standpoint" of a given individual, in a given culture, in a given historical phase, is not closed but open: "It is, in fact, a single horizon that embraces every-thing contained in historical consciousness."[176]

For all its promise, Gadamer's historicist argument begs more ques-tions than it answers. If we can applaud the generous intention, virtu-ally unknown in structuralist quarters, of recapturing history for tex-tual interpretation, then we can only be stunned by the implication of what he has uncritically to say about authority, the power of tradition, knowledge, our institutions, and our attitudes. At one level the argu-ment is harmless. I refer to those times when in the privacy of our minds we conclude that X or Y is smarter, or knows more than we do about some subject. But just as soon as the argument is moved off the base of the personal, a relatively trivial concern, just as soon as Gadamer begins to speak of a "nameless" traditional and institutional authority, it is clear that the terms "knowledge" and "intelligibility" are being used (perhaps unwittingly) in a Nietzschean sense, and that the primary issue by his own admission ("tradition has a justification that is outside the arguments of reason") is power. In other words, reason is arbitrary; reason is irrational. The question of the acquisition of power is indistinguishable from the question of the acquisition of knowledge and authority. Our willingness to assent to authority is no cool act of reason but a submission to the force that defines and appropriates tradition and knowledge and encloses our cognitive reach within their boundaries. The long temporal unity of historical consciousness, the very basis of shared tradition and the bond of a community of meaning: are these determinations of established power and the effects of a massive repression? These are questions that cannot fairly be posed to Gadamer; these are questions for Michel Foucault.

Five

I was surprised that so many who had not been to prison could become interested in its problems, surprised that all those who had never heard the discourse of inmates could so easily understand them. How do we explain this? Isn't it because, in a general way, the penal system is the form in which power is most obviously seen as power? . . . Prison is the only place where power is manifested in its naked state, in its most excessive form, and where it is justified as moral force. . . . What is fascinating about prisons is that, for once, power doesn't hide or mask itself; it reveals itself as tyranny pursued into the tiniest details; it is cynical and at the same time pure and entirely "justified," because its practice can be totally formulated within the framework of morality. Its brutal tyranny consequently appears as the serene domination of Good over Evil, or order over disorder.

Michel Foucault, *Language, Counter-Memory, Practice*

What is questioned by the thought of differance . . . is the determination of being in presence. . . . The first consequence of this is that differance is not. It is not a being-present, however excellent, unique, principal, or transcendent one makes it. It commands nothing, rules over nothing, and nowhere does it exercise any authority. It is not marked by a capital letter. Not only is there no realm of differance, but differance is even the subversion of every realm. This is obviously what makes it threatening and necessarily dreaded by everything in us that desires a realm. . . .

Jacques Derrida, "Differance"

Starts w/ Derrida as antagonist of the
traditionalists - displays yale deconstructors'
distortion of Derrida that establishes Them as
The new formalists (aesthetes, etc.) - ends w/
Foucault as someone realizing the historical
implications of Derrida (features suppressed by
the yale school).

When in late October of 1966 over one hundred humanists and social
scientists from the United States and eight other countries gathered at
the Johns Hopkins Humanities Center to participate in a symposium
called "The Languages of Criticism and the Sciences of Man," the
reigning avant-garde theoretical presences for literary critics in this
country were Georges Poulet, to a lesser extent members of the "Geneva
school" associated with him, and, in the distant background, in uncertain relationship to the critics of consciousness, the forbidding philosophical analyses of Heidegger (*Being and Time*), Sartre (*Being and
Nothingness*), and Merleau-Ponty (*The Phenomenology of Perception*).
In the words of its organizers, Richard Macksey and Eugenio Donato,
the intention of the symposium and the two-year program of seminars
and colloquia that followed it was "to explore the impact of contemporary 'structuralist' thought on critical methods in humanistic and social
sciences. . . . [and] to bring into an active and not uncritical contact
leading European proponents of structural studies in a wide variety of
disciplines with a wide spectrum of American scholars."[1] Though on
the Continent the attack on phenomenology and existentialism had
long been explicitly underway, in the work of Lévi-Strauss and Barthes,

and implied in the writings of neo-Saussurean linguists, in the mid-sixties the key figures of the structuralist movement were still virtually unknown in American literary critical circles. In the year of the Hopkins symposium, which also saw the appearance of the pioneering issue of *Yale French Studies* devoted to structuralism, American criticism was still fascinated, a good decade after the waning of the New Criticism, by perspectives which never succeeded in putting to rest basic formalist principles which structuralism, at least by intent, seemed sure to demolish.

Several factors acted to guarantee the privilege of the literary realm. There was the work of Northrop Frye and Murray Krieger; the keen interest in aesthetic fictions fueled by the growing critical attention to Wallace Stevens; the forces of neo-Kantianism (with their stress on isolationist ideas generated from the third *Critique* and from philosophical sources ranging from Hans Vaihinger to Ernst Cassirer and early Sartre); and, finally, as structuralists like to emphasize, there was phenomenology's prizing of the imperial *cogito* which is situated, in Poulet's interesting phrase, at the "threshold of the labyrinth." All of these pressures (and others) continued to ensure the isolate and elite privilege of the literary, a realm—alternately called discourse or consciousness—situated just the other side of discourse at large. In the Kantian idiom that became current in this country in the 1960s, the literary was said to be essentially "constitutive," never itself constituted, never itself given inner life by what is summarily dismissed by formalists as the "nonliterary." From our present vantage point, it is not difficult to see that at the time of the Hopkins symposium Poulet was a representative of a last traditionalism, of an impulse to keep literature free from all extraliterary coercions, and that his American vogue was evidence of our susceptibility to his message that literature is an expression of a consciousness which "exists in itself, withdrawn from any power which might determine it from the outside. . . ."[2] The single rigorous native theoretical critic to stand in firm opposition to aesthetic isolationism in the past two decades, E. D. Hirsch, passed through the critical scene of the 1960s without making much of a difference. We don't necessarily have to assent to Hirsch's position in order to regret the brevity of his moment; an excellent opportunity to debate cherished formalist premises was passed up.

With the advantage of hindsight, and with the example now behind us of Hirsch's failure to significantly affect the course of American criticism, perhaps we may understand why the hopes of the organizers of the Hopkins symposium were in some ways bound to be unrealized. Essentially, Frye had anticipated the Lévi-Straussian moment for American criticism; perhaps that is why the structuralist phase of Roland Barthes's career would exercise so little dominance over our critical imagination. The edited proceedings of the symposium, collected in a volume entitled *The Languages of Criticism and the Sciences of Man: The Structuralist Controversy*, issued in 1970, and again in 1972 in paperback as *The Structuralist Controversy*, prefigured the most heated combat in our critical history, but they do not mark the beginning of a structuralist movement in our criticism. The books on structuralism by Robert Scholes, Fredric Jameson, and Jonathan Culler, among others, stand as assessments of a high cross-disciplinary road not taken. Since until very recently Poulet and the critics of consciousness continued to hold down our critical frontiers, Macksey and Donato's title, *The Structuralist Controversy*, must be judged premature. Their real historical achievement is that they predicted and shaped a theoretical controversy of the most far-reaching and elemental significance.

Sometime in the early 1970s we awoke from the dogmatic slumber of our phenomenological sleep to find that a new presence had taken absolute hold over our avant-garde critical imagination: Jacques Derrida. Somewhat startlingly, we learned that, despite a number of loose characterizations to the contrary, he brought not structuralism but something that would be called "poststructuralism." The shift to poststructuralist direction and polemic in the intellectual careers of Paul de Man, J. Hillis Miller, Geoffrey Hartman, Edward Said, and Joseph Riddel—all of whom were fascinated in the 1960s by strains of phenomenology—tells the whole story. In the space of five or six years Derrida had arrived; had attracted some extraordinarily committed and gifted students on both coasts; had spawned two new journals, *Diacritics* and *Glyph*, the first of which gives us documentary history of the growth of poststructuralism in our country, and both of which, in spite of their youth, have achieved remarkable visibility and attention. Further, the impact of Derrida inspired (under John Irwin's editorship) the overhaul of the formerly regional *Georgia Review*. And more: Derrida and his followers had managed to create a genuine controversy by solidifying an opposition party whose various constituents, until now, never have had much use for one another. The traditional historicists, the Chicago neo-Aristotelians, the specialists in American literature, the Stanford moralists, the myth critics of the Frye type, old-line Freudians, critics of consciousness (such as were left), the budding structuralists, and the grandchildren of the New Critics now gathered under the umbrella of Murray Krieger's contextualism—all have found themselves united against a common enemy in a Traditionalism which, though imposed upon them by Derridean polemic, has seemed to suit these strange bedfellows just fine. Judging by their published responses, talks (and talk) at MLA conventions, and remarks that I have over-heard in the vicinity of the departmental coffee pot at various uni-versities, it appears that the traditionalist opposition has not been able to resist expressing (not entirely without cause) condescension, smug-ness, disbelief, ironic cool, and downright anger. Predictably, its members have tended to characterize the enemy as barbarians bent on destroying all humane values (with "humane" a synonym in the tra-ditionalist lexicon for all things civilized, all things good and to be cherished). The Derrideans, for their part, and I think to their ultimate polemical disadvantage, have delighted in portraying the traditionalists as weaklings in hurried retreat (Hartman describes it as "panic")[3] from the master's hazardous and difficult message.

The prime mover of our poststructuralist controversy made his quietly subversive appearance on the American scene at the Hopkins symposium where he delivered one of the indisputably landmark essays to come out of the proceedings, "Structure, Sign, and Play in the Dis-course of the Human Sciences," an elegant attack on the traditionalist position in general, and a frontal move against structuralism in particu-lar as it was then represented by Claude Lévi-Strauss. Though in the fall of 1966 Derrida stood on the verge of achieving an international reputation (1967 would see the appearance of three of his major texts), when he delivered his Hopkins paper he was almost unknown in the English-speaking world, and in France not very much more than an ex-ceptionally promising philosopher who at age thirty-three had to his credit some scattered essays and a translation of Husserl's *The Origins of Geometry* (1962), published together with a long critical intro-duction.

It would be unreasonable in the extreme to demand that anyone at that conference should have grasped the full potential for havoc car-ried by Derrida's earliest writings, yet in a remarkable piece of intel-lectual forecasting, which he called "The Two Criticisms," Eugenio Donato did just that. Though on the whole concerned to demonstrate the theoretical opposition of phenomenology and existentialism to the structuralist movement, Donato was able to anticipate, on the basis of one of the essays that would become the first chapter of Derrida's *De la grammatologie*, two issues (heavily indebted to Nietzsche's critique of metaphysics) that would obsess Derrideans and anti-Derrideans in the early 1970s. The first was the issue of decentering, or what Derrida would call the "structurality of structure," the point of which is that there is, in effect, no "point," no origin, no end, no place outside dis-course from which to fix, make determinate, and establish metaphysical boundaries for the play of linguistic signifiers. In terms drawn from Saussure's *Course in General Linguistics* (appealed to repeatedly as the ground of structuralist thought), *langue*, as a system of discursive possibilities transcendent of any actualization of it, any *parole*, would be denied, by poststructuralists, its commanding force over a field of discourse. The second issue, implicit in some of Barthes's structuralist work, but raised to crisis pitch by Derrida, stipulated that the interpretation of any signifying chain is necessarily only another chain of signs. If the critic's discourse cannot, by these lights, enjoy the status of a transparency, or of an easy mimetic representation, then (in Donato's words) an "essential line between literature and criticism" cannot be drawn: "each sign is in itself not the thing that offers itself to interpretation but interpretation of other signs. There is never an *interpretandum* which is not already an *interpretans*, so that a relationship of both violence and elucidation establishes itself with interpretation." Donato adds—and this soon was also to be picked up in the poststructuralist debates—that "no doubt" this is an idea "we should have known since Nietzsche and Freud";[4] we can add, now, that in the United States we could have had access to that idea in the semiotics of Charles Sanders Peirce.

The Derridean perspectives which have most impressed American criticism come from a few seminal essays in translation. One of the books of 1967, *La Voix et le phénomène*, appeared as *Speech and Phenomena* as late as 1973; its immersion in technical Husserlian issues has not found for it a wide audience. *De la grammatologie* appeared not until the end of 1976; *L'Écriture et la différence* in 1978. The focus, then, has necessarily been on shorter pieces such as "Freud and the Scene of Writing," "Differance," "White Mythology," "The Ends of Man," and, most intensely, on "Structure, Sign, and Play." After Donato's groundbreaking work, the lead was taken by the current Yale group. In 1969 Paul de Man published a reevaluation of Poulet (and consequently of a significant tendency in his own critical thought), showing that Poulet's apparently unqualified commitment to a Cartesian *cogito*, as an origin outside of history and discourse, was in reality countered everywhere in Poulet's writing by a view of the *cogito* comparable with (who would have imagined it?) the critique of the *cogito* in "Structure, Sign, and Play," and with Emile Benveniste's relocation of the subject to a function of discourse: "I" is only a lexical function, a pronoun. (De Man's essay would find an influential forum in 1971 when he included it in his collection, *Blindness and Insight*.)

On the heels of de Man's essay, and owing a large debt to it, came J. Hillis Miller's final look at Poulet which, like de Man's, only this time explicitly, tied Poulet to Derrida's ideas via generous citations of the essay "Differance." Following his attack on the premises of M. H. Abrams's *Natural Supernaturalism* in 1972 in *Diacritics*, Miller assumed the burden of chief spokesman and polemicist. While de Man was publishing a series of difficult Derridean revisions of Nietzsche in 1972, 1974, and 1975, and while Hartman was establishing himself as the philological athlete of American poststructuralism with a two-part study of *Glas* in the *Georgia Review*, Miller engaged Abrams at the MLA convention and in the pages of *Critical Inquiry*, prepared a long two-part essay on Wallace Stevens for the *Georgia Review* (in the course of which he carried Stevens into the poststructuralist camp), introduced a key term for the controversy, *mise en abyme*, reviewed the state of American and Continental criticism, and inducted his Yale colleagues into the uncanny critics' hall of fame (or, depending on one's point of view, the critical house of ill-fame). In 1975, again in *Diacritics*, Miller opened the first skirmish of American poststructuralist internecine warfare when he took to task Joseph Riddel's book on William Carlos Williams, *The Inverted Bell*, for its putative misunderstandings of Heidegger and Derrida. The traditionalist response to this poststructuralist activity has been to charge it with unbridled subjectivism, relativism, irrationalism, and structural self-contradiction. But since these charges are generally made with a passion that may be perceived as rancorous defensiveness, and without substantial and rigorous argument, their validity is open to considerable doubt.

What ironically may give vitality to the traditionalist position is the work of Edward Said, which is undeniably sympathetic with many of the ideas of structuralist and poststructuralist writers. In his widely noticed overview of recent Continental developments published in 1971 in *TriQuarterly,* and since much revised and expanded in the book called *Beginnings* (1975), Said's rhetoric and tone were just of the sort to warm traditionalist hearts. Consider how the following[5] might be read as traditionalist nostalgia for the good old truths of humanism: "The eccentricity of so bleak and antihumanistic a view of man is reflected even in Foucault's prose." "If we are inclined to think of man as an entity resisting the flux of experience, then because of Foucault man is dissolved . . . into little more than a constituted subject, a speaking pronoun, fixed indecisively in the eternal, ongoing rush of discourse." "In achieving a position of mastery over man, language has reduced him to a grammatical function." "Nearly every one of the structuralists acknowledges a tyrannical feedback system. . . ." "In other words, man now lives in a circle without a center, or in a maze without a way out." "The structuralists' predicament is an accurate symptom of man mired in his systems of signification." "They are structuralists . . . because they accept their existential fate inside a language whose mode of being is pitilessly relational. . . ." "The elegance and terror of such a world view, completely confined to discourse, is a veritable nightmare utopia. . . ." If we add these following remarks: on Derrida's critique of structuralism as a "grotesque explication"; on his style as enigmatic, self-indulgent and maniacally complex; on his general thought as possessing "twisted pertinence"; on the place of his thought as a philosophy of "ontological absence," of "nihilistic radicality," and of "utter blankness," we may perhaps understand why in some poststructuralist quarters Said is considered the enemy within. In the revision of his *TriQuarterly* essay it is quite clear that his critique is not traditionalist in bias but rests on a powerful enthusiasm for Michel Foucault. But his championing of Foucault has thus far (regrettably, to my mind) not made a decisive impact, and his remarks on Derrida may contribute to a distorted understanding of him as some kind of up-dated Sartre, the newest philosopher of *le néant* who practices through the good offices of a subtilized Saussurean linguistics. Which is precisely how Krieger, who has been for years our most influential guide to contemporary criticism, has construed Derrida in the final chapter of his latest book, *Theory of Criticism* (1976).

1

In a reflection upon the changing course of his own career in the late 1960s, Roland Barthes perhaps too neatly summarized the passage from structuralism to poststructuralism:

> in the former text ["Introduction a l'analyse a structurale des recits" (1966)] I appealed to a general structure from which would be derived analyses of contingent texts. . . . In *S/Z* I reversed this perspective: there I refused the idea of a model transcendent to several texts (and, thus, all the more so, of a model transcendent to every text) in order to postulate that each text is in some sort its own model, that each text, in other words, must be treated in its difference, "difference" being understood here precisely in a Nietzschean or a Derridean sense. . . . the text . . . is not the *parole* of a narrative *langue*.[6]

A recollection of Derrida's critique (in "Structure, Sign, and Play") of Lévi-Strauss's methodological contradictions will tell us that Barthes's description of the journey to poststructuralism is too dramatically posed to function as an accurate historical account. Structuralism's employment of a transcendent and totalizing model (Paul Ricoeur describes it as a Kantian form of the unconscious) is played off explicitly in Lévi-Strauss with this description of mythographical method: "There is no real end to mythological analysis, no hidden unity to be grasped once the breaking-down process has been completed. Themes can be split up *ad infinitum*. . . . Consequently the unity of the myth is never more than tendential and projective and cannot reflect a state of a particular moment of the myth. . . . [Unity] is a phenomenon of the imagination, resulting from an attempt at interpretation. . . ." The source or "common origin" for mythological analysis, he concludes, is purely "hypothetical," a postulation of pragmatic urgency which we make in order to get work done. Mythological thought has no real ontological interest "in definite beginnings or endings," for myths, "like rites," are "interminable."[7] In a Derridean word, Lévi-Strauss is saying that myths are *acentric*. Only a few pages later, however, we find him agreeing with Paul Ricoeur that his work is a "Kantism without a transcendental subject."[8] But Ricoeur's charge points to no deficiency, according to Lévi-Strauss, since it is a description consonant with his "ambition . . . to discover the conditions in which systems of truths become mutually convertible and therefore simultaneously acceptable to several different subjects. . . ." It is his very purpose, in other words, to find a "pattern of those conditions" which would "take on the character of an autonomous object, independent of any subject."[9] Lévi-Strauss's theoretical ploy (the institution of the homology and the binary code) permits him to remain faithful to the overriding structuralist intention of avoiding the assumption of a prediscursive, centered subject. But it is clear that his need to find transcendent "conditions" and "mutually convertible" systems expresses just the sort of nostalgia for an innocent center, and for the engineer's privileged claim to unproblematic access to a structure beyond structurality, that in "Structure, Sign, and Play" and the *Grammatology* Derrida finds pervasive in his texts. On the question of the origin or center it matters not at all what name we choose to give it, for the course of Western thought, in the terms of Derrida's argument, is governed by the positing of a metaphysical presence which abides through various fictive appellations, from subject to substance to *eidos* to *archē* to *telos*, transcendentality, conscience, structure, man, or the ultimate fiction of God, the fiction of indifference itself, the fiction of "exemption" from supplement.[10]

Derrida's critique of Lévi-Strauss (whose texts sit on the fault-line between structuralism and poststructuralism) sets up the far-reaching opening statement of "Structure, Sign, and Play":

> ... the structurality of structure ... has always been neu-
> tralized or reduced, and this by a process of giving it a
> center or referring it to a point of presence, a fixed origin.
> The function of this center was ... above all to make sure
> that the organizing principle of the structure would limit
> what we might call the *freeplay* of the structure. ... the
> center closes off the freeplay it opens up and makes possible.
> ... it has always been thought that the center, which is by
> definition unique, constituted that very thing within a
> structure which governs the structure, while escaping
> structurality. ... The center is at the center of the totality,
> and yet, since the center does not belong to the totality ...
> the totality *has its center elsewhere*. ... The concept of
> centered structure is in fact the concept of a freeplay ...
> which is constituted upon a fundamental immobility and a
> reassuring certitude, which is itself beyond the reach of the
> freeplay. With this certitude anxiety can be mastered, for
> anxiety is invariably the result of a certain mode of being
> implicated in the game. ... [11]

The center, in so many words, is the creation of the "force of desire."[12]
In something like an ultimate act of wish-fulfillment, desire attempts to
establish the center beyond fictive status as objective reality, the
ground of all grounds, the metaphysical truth in itself that masters all
anxiety and grants final reassurance. In the tenth book of *The Republic*
Socrates points us elegantly to the entire Derridean critique of the center (and its related criticism of the classical sense of representation)
when he tells Glaucon that "there is no difference in reality" because
God's desire to be the pure origin (to be indifference) forced him to be
the "real maker of the real bed ... which is essentially and by nature
one only."[13]

The impact of Derrida on the traditionalist position can be measured
most precisely, I think, by his singular success in stirring up that old
unmasterable anxiety about the center. Frye's reflection on his archetypalist method in the *Anatomy* may be the most honest facing-up to
anxiety for the center that we can find in traditionalism. Criticism that
aspires to knowledge, he writes at a self-conscious moment, "recognizes
the fact that there *is* a center of the order of words." One sentence later,
however, in a passage I quoted earlier, this "fact" of the center is revealed by Frye's rhetoric as a projection of desperate programmatic
necessity, not as a constituent of objective reality:

> Unless there is such a center, there is nothing to prevent the
> analogies supplied by convention and genre from being an

endless series of free associations, perhaps suggestive . . . but
never creating a real structure. . . . If there are such things as
archetypes at all, then, we have to take yet another step,
and conceive the possibility of a self-contained literary
universe. Either archetypal criticism is a will-o'-the-wisp, an
endless labyrinth without an outlet, or we have to assume
that literature is a total form. . . .[14]

Lévi-Strauss's acentricity of mythological thought to the contrary,
Frye's reaching for a "real structure"—that is, a structure whose center
is elsewhere, beyond the structure—and his need to assume total
("totalizing") form brings him much closer to the contradiction that
Derrida finds in Lévi-Strauss than we might ordinarily think. For "an
endless labyrinth without an outlet" is a perfect figure for what Derrida
meant by decentered structure, by what he called the "structurality of
structure"; and "an endless labyrinth without an outlet" is exactly what
the traditionalist position must not countenance.

The same frightening figure of the endless labyrinth occurs in another traditionalist quarter, very remote from Frye's, and the response
is the same. In a reflection on his method, Georges Poulet asserts a
residual Cartesian sense that the self is in essence free of all external
constraints—the supreme secular instance, in other words, of freedom
itself—when he situates the *cogito* metaphorically with the spool of
Ariadne's thread. He cautions us to remember that Ariadne's thread
"unrolls from the threshold of the labyrinth."[15] The effect of Derrida's
critique of centered structure is to urge us to stay inside the labyrinth of
discourse and to become comfortable with the idea that all outlets are
illusions. To this end he concludes his book on Husserl by reminding us
that the phoneme is not the signifier of a full, transcendent inner voice
present to itself outside the mediation of so-called phonetic writing, but
the *"phenomenon of the labyrinth"* itself.[16]

"But have we not heard something like this before?" one sort of
traditionalist is justified in asking. "A Jacques Derrida might be necessary within a French critical scene which never seriously invested in the
proposals of the Ransoms and the Brookses, never came under the domination of a New Criticism in the Anglo-American sense. But in the
United States we have long heard the claim urged that the discourse of
poetry, at least, was nonreferential, that the poem itself, as the phrase
used to go, was a self-sufficient organic whole whose meanings were
perfectly coincidental with the linguistic network. And in the 1960s we
learned, with the help of the Frank Kermode, that aesthetic fictions were
sui generis; with the help of the neo-Kantians, following the proposals
of Ernst Cassirer, we realized that all modes of discourse, not only the

literary, could be thought of as autonomous and autotelic. We need not fear the labyrinth."

But we do: our investments in Cassirer, in fictions, and in the New Criticism were carefully hedged by our confidence in locating a "point of presence," a "fixed origin," outside the labyrinth. Cassirer and the neo-Kantians commanded the labyrinth by appealing to a version of Kant's *a priori*, an eternal geometry of the categories of mythic consciousness. The connoisseurs of fictions (excluding Nietzsche and the poststructuralists) invariably make appeals to "reality"—no fiction this —in order to obtain a sure ontological fix on fictive deviations, and thereby measure their force and reach. And the New Critics, despite their insistent attack on easy referentiality, in the end would seek some outlet from the maze of a self-contained discourse in covert appeals to expressive and mimetic principles of escape. Derrida's definition in the *Grammatology* of the traditional "idea of the book," as the "idea of a totality, finite or infinite, of the signifier," may be taken as a poststructuralist gloss on the New-Critical idea of "organic discourse." Derrida continues: "this totality of the signifier cannot be a totality, unless a totality constituted by the signified preexists it, supervises its inscriptions and its signs, and is independent of it in its ideality."[17] This preexistent and independent totality of the signified which supervises the play of the book's signifiers is the center that is elsewhere, the dictating referent that stands independent of the referring agencies of discourse.

When in the position-taking essays collected at the end of *The Well Wrought Urn* (a nice metaphor of the traditional book's closure) Brooks refers to the "maturity" of the great poet's attitude, he has recourse to a controlling expressive principle which is not deferred endlessly by irony, ambiguity, and wit, and which will put a stop at some point (as he believes Yeats's occult system puts a stop) to the endless possibilities for semantic multiplication which his favored verbal strategies might spur. Similarly, and from the other side, as it were, when he concedes that mature poetry is finally a "simulacrum" of the complex textures of the real, of the "facts of experience," as he puts it, he is making a last-ditch mimetic appeal to an origin beyond the labyrinth which supervises the construction of the maze.[18] So if we situate the various constituents of the traditionalist position on a continuum stretching from, at one extreme, the apparently radical New Critics, to the other extreme, the apparently reactionary old-line historicists, what we see from the Derridean vantage of decentering is in all cases a refusal to relinquish an innocent origin to the "aphoristic energy" of writing,[19] and a desire in every case to master anxiety. In all cases, a belief that poems must "mean" as well as "be" is grounded on the theory of mimesis, that there exists a signified free of the signifier, something outside textuality to which the poem must refer. It is a theory which Derrida's various Nietzschean strategies intend to explode.

2

The pivotal principle of decentering, announced in the opening paragraphs of "Structure, Sign, and Play," opens up several other Derridean themes in that essay (with its notoriety guaranteed by its inclusion in *The Structuralist Controversy*, and with its elegant compression of poststructuralist ideas, "Structure, Sign, and Play" has assumed for Derrida's American enthusiasts—at the cost of some distortion of his position—the status of a sacred essay). The first consequence of decentering is unqualified free-play; "the domain and the interplay of signification" are extended *ad infinitum*:[20] "One could call *play*," he writes in the *Grammatology*, "the absence of the transcendental signified as limitlessness of play, that is to say as the destruction of onto-theology and the metaphysics of presence. . . . this *play*, thought as absence of the transcendental signified, is not a play *in the world*, as it has always been defined, for the purposes of *containing* it. . . ."[21] So by his refusal to accept uncritically the traditional Western metaphysics of the sign, which speaks of sign as "sign of," and which requires a signifier rigorously distinguishable from a signified, Derrida collapses all signifieds within signifiers; his version of play, unlike its traditional exposition in Kant and Schiller and other theoreticians of play, wants to do without ontological anchors. In Kant free-play becomes, in the end, a negative confirmation of the categories and the phenomenal world which they posit. In a remarkable series of figures ordering the respective values of the categories and of free-play, Kant tells us that the aesthetic is "arbitrary," that it is "mere play" or "mere entertaining play," while the categories of understanding which constitute our cognitive life are "serious business." Poetry, we might recall, is the highest of aesthetic forms in Kant's third *Critique* because it recognizes, in its potential as play, a subversive force for undermining our serious business. Unlike *écriture* in Saussure, poetry is harmless because it does not, like Satan in Eden, desire to "steal upon and ensnare" our understanding.[22] In Derrida, no appeal must be made to a reality principle that would surround and close off the field of play. Unlike Kant, Derrida speaks not of a free-play *in* the world, but of a "freeplay of the world."[23]

The principles of decentering and free-play (the terms "principle," "concept," or "theme" are not technically applicable to the Derridean texts)—these so-called nonconcepts point to a third issue, touched on very early by Donato: that interpretation cannot be passive mimesis; it is the substitution, rather, by a kind of hermeneutical violence, of one chain of signifiers for another. Such interpretation, according to Derrida, can be performed nostalgically, as we hope against hope to retrieve "an origin which is free from freeplay," or with Nietzschean gusto of affirmation, "the joyous affirmation of the freeplay of the world and without truth, without origin, offered to an active interpretation. . . ."[24] Which leads to a consequence grasped cleanly, so far as I know, only by Wayne Booth: that the key value terms of poststructuralism as they are expressed by Derrida in his Hopkins essay (and pursued with erotic zeal by recent Barthes) are practical and affective, not cognitive.[25]

At the conclusion of "Structure, Sign, and Play," and pervasively in the work of Derrida's Yale disciples (Hartman, Miller, and de Man, but not entirely in Harold Bloom), a new hedonism is suggested. Terms like "joy" and "activity," and their variants, are fundamental. They recall the overt preoccupations of the nineteenth-century aesthetes with a *telos* of "pleasure" and a quest for "freedom" that have typified an astonishing variety of modern critical theories whose presuppositions are idealistic (in the Kantian sense) and whose critical practices are disposed toward one sort of formalism or another. In Brooks, it is the freedom of literary discourse from direct reference and nonliterary constraints; in Frye, the freedom of the literary universe; in Poulet, the freedom of the *cogito*; in Kermode, the severance of aesthetic fictions from ideological reference; in Culler's structuralism, the freedom of a professional community to establish interpretive norms, and so on. The fundamental aspects of Derrida's writing plainly do not sanction a new formalism or a new hedonism, but the Yale appropriation of him, I shall argue shortly, is just as plainly an ultimate formalism, a New Criticism denied its ontological supports and cultural goals, a Cleanth Brooks or a Murray Krieger raised to the nth power and so stripped of the belief that poetry offers a new kind of knowledge. The Yale Derrideans will not in the long run threaten every partisan of traditionalism, because they will turn out to be traditionalism's last formalist buttress.

When Derrida wrote that the transcendental signified "is never absolutely present outside a system of differences," that it had no natural locus but was situated as a systemic function,[26] he was pointing us to an essay that he would publish in France in 1968 and which would be translated and appended to the study of Husserl that made its American appearance in 1973. Unlike "Structure, Sign, and Play," the essay I refer to, "Differance," is extremely difficult in execution, though no less for that a formative influence upon the Yale critics. The essay's formidable quality perhaps accounts not only for its lack of currency among non-Derrideans, but also for a persistent ignoring by the Yale group of an important part of its author's intention: not merely to decenter and by so doing teach us that the aphoristic energy of writing cannot be commanded metaphysically from "outside," but also to suggest what, if not metaphysical presence, does exert informative power from inside the fields of discourse. (To be fair to the Yale group, some of the blame for the skewing of Derrida can be charged to the master himself for too much subordinating of correlative subthemes and certain consequences of difference that would suggest we might find something more valuable to do than meditate with endless repetition on the bottomless abyss of writing.)

The major theme accompanying decentering is that there is nothing outside the text, "il n'y a pas de hors-texte,"[27] a theme generated by the problematics of "differance," a neologism Derrida introduces with the assistance of the French *différer* in order to explain the duplicitous structure of signification. Differance carries two distinct significations: "On the one hand, it indicates difference as distinction, inequality, or discernibility; on the other, it expresses the interposition of delay, the interval of a *spacing* and *temporalizing* that puts off until 'later' what is presently denied, the possible that is presently impossible."[28] As we work through the essay, it becomes evident that this second signification, deferral, as the "possible that is presently impossible," is itself caught up in a movement of differentiation, for what is deferred has never been possible as the ontological ground of the sign. Or rather, it is precisely the burden of classical Western semiology, always in the service of metaphysical need for presence, to construct the sign as representation of presence "in its absence." "When we cannot take hold of or show the thing, let us say the present, the being-present, when the present does not present itself, then we signify, we go through the detour of signs. . . . The sign would thus be a deferred presence. . . . this classical determination presupposes that the sign (which defers presence) is conceivable only *on the basis* of the presence that it defers and in *view of* the deferred presence one intends to reappropriate." Thus in the classical semiology, the sign is both "*secondary* and *provisional:* it is second in order after an original and lost presence. . . . It is provisional with respect to this final and missing presence. . . ."[29] The comfort of classical thought is to believe that the "possible" is ontologically secure as center, that the "possible" sits outside the system of differences, that the possible is only *presently* impossible. Mimesis or representation, in Derrida's view of the sign, is no mirroring process which would capture in the reflections of writing an absent, self-present object, anterior to systems of representation based on the principle of difference. In the Derridean disturbance of this classical contradiction, mimesis, instead of being thrown away (a misconception of Derrida's detractors) is identified as a problematic textual maneuver (rather than a textual translation) which creates the illusion of a nonlinguistic object that is being mirrored, or, in Derrida's terms, provisionally deferred.

Despite Said's contention, Derrida's grammatological terms are not doing disguised ontological work.[30] Everywhere it is his purpose to "question the secondary and provisional character of the sign" by opposing it to a " 'primordial' difference."[31] This will mean, in effect, that the possible only presently impossible never was possible as ontological ground. The sense we have of a presence now deferred and waiting to be reappropriated is but an illusion created by the very process of linguistic deferral, an illusion continuously undercut by the cunning movement of signification as the structure of differance. *Il n'y a pas de hors-texte* must mean, then, the questioning not only of the authority of presence but also of "its simple symmetrical contrary, absence or lack." *Il n'y a pas de hors-texte* must not be read as positing an ontological "nothing" outside the text. Said's, Krieger's, Culler's, and on occasion even Miller's implications to the contrary notwithstanding,[32] Derrida's poststructuralism is not a linguistically crafty existentialism which poises writing, in Said's phrase, "just a hair beyond utter blankness."[33] Derrida is no ontologist of *le néant* because he is no ontologist.

To bring this ontologically paralyzing sense of deferral together, as Derrida does, with Saussure's reinforcing principle that "in language there are only differences without positive terms," is to enter the coincidental spaces of grammatology and *écriture:* "there is no phonetic writing. . . . Saussure had only to remind us that the play of difference was the functional condition, the condition of possibility, for every sign; and it is itself silent. The difference between two phonemes, which enables them to exist and to operate, is inaudible. The inaudible," along with other purely graphic devices such as spacing and punctuation, "opens the two present phonemes to hearing as they present themselves."[34] Differance, which belongs to "no category of being, present or absent"—it is not a new name for the "most negative order of negative theology"—is not only a critique of the metaphysical culmination called phenomenology, which identifies the center as inner, self-present voice, but also the subversion of all ontological versions of the center ("there is no presence before the semiological differance or outside of it") and the very basis of the strategy of decentering.[35] Differance so understood leads us to the figure dominating the writings of the Yale Derrideans, the figure of discourse as *mise en abyme:* in the Yale appropriation of Derrida, a figure for the setting of the ultimate formalism:

> What is questioned by the thought of differance . . . is the determination of being in presence. . . . The first consequence of this is that differance is not. It is not a being-present, however excellent, unique, principal, or transcendent one makes it. It commands nothing, rules over nothing, and nowhere does it exercise any authority. It is not marked by a capital letter. Not only is there no realm of differance, but differance is even the subversion of every realm. This is obviously what makes it threatening and necessarily dreaded by everything in us that desires a realm. . . .[36]

Then, echoing the conclusion of "Structure, Sign, and Play," Derrida writes that differance "must be conceived without *nostalgia;* that is, it must be conceived outside the myth of the purely maternal or paternal language belonging to the lost fatherland of thought. On the contrary, we must *affirm* it—in the sense that Nietzsche brings affirmation into play—with a certain laughter and with a certain dance."[37]

In a number of other places Derrida extends, amplifies, and re-iterates the problems of decentering and differance through exploration of such other grammatological terms as "trace," "supplement," "hymen," "tympan," "dissemination," and others, including "metaphor," arriving always, as he had with differance, at a point of ineradicable un-decidability. Said's description of "dissemination" may stand as a rough characterization of all of these terms: "the power of textuality to burst through semantic horizons."[38] Such terms, Derrida stresses constantly, are nonterms, nonconcepts, nonrealms, nonprinciples—were they otherwise they would institute, against all of his announced intentions, new versions of the center that is elsewhere. Were they otherwise they would become newly masked ontological terms for full presence. In its trace-structure, for example, the sign—because it is inhabited by the mark of something other than itself—tracks down tracks; con-ceived otherwise than as self-effacement, the trace would be an "in-destructible and monumental presence."[39] Similarly, "supplement" is not, as the classical position would have it, and as Derrida explains in detail in his reading of Lévi-Strauss and Rousseau in the *Grammatology,* the complement of a plenitude—an embarrassing classical contradic-tion—but a replacement that is always excessive. "What we have tried to show by following the guiding thread of the 'dangerous supple-ment,' " he writes, is that "there has never been anything but writing; there has never been anything but supplements, substitutive significa-

tions which could only come forth in a chain of differential references.
. . . And thus to infinity. . . ."[40] And metaphor, as he shows, following
Nietzsche's "On Truth and Lie in an Extra-Moral Sense," is the ultimate excess, since, properly restored to its effaced place in metaphysical
discourse, metaphor destroys the possibility of the proper, the literal,
the nonmetaphorical, and takes us into the dangerously slippery and
"abyssed" landscape of writing where it is no longer possible to delude
oneself that the metaphoric can be made decidable, can be measured
as deviation from the norm of the literal. To say of "White Mythology"
that its disquisitions make it impossible ever to know what we are
doing is, as Paul de Man reminds us in his most recent essay on
Nietzsche, precisely the point.[41] Derrida's is a "technique of trouble."[42]

The lesson of all such grammatological maneuvers is that writing is
neither provisional nor secondary but a movement in itself "abyssed"
as deeps below deeps are revealed under the force of Derridean deconstruction. *Arché* and *telos*, and anything else that would hold down,
fix, and in general *determine* the movement of signification, are dissi-
pated by a writing which, in its undecidable processes, moves against
itself and against all efforts to give its processes a reassuring certitude.
Perhaps another way to put all of this is to say that writing itself has no
context external to itself which would coerce its movements. Derrida's
summary remarks on the sign as trace and differance make it clear that
he believes that any alternative to his elaborate extention and critique
of Saussure would necessarily fall into metaphysics and thereby destroy
the differential quality of language by attempting to save the value of
full presence:

> The trace is not only the disappearance of origin . . . it
> means that the origin did not even disappear, that it was
> never constituted except reciprocally by a non-origin, the
> trace, which thus becomes the origin of the origin. From
> then on, to wrench the concept of the trace from the classi-
> cal scheme which would derive it from a presence
> or from an originary non-trace and which would make
> of it an empirical mark, one must indeed speak
> of an originary trace or arche-trace.[43]

Oddly, however, though Derrida warned that differance, as the subversion of all ontological realms, could authoritatively command nothing, the Yale critics have taken differance as a radically subversive
authority which autocratically commands, as *abyme*, the whole field
of writing, and while doing so establishes writing as a monolith itself
that forever escapes determination.

But this is to see only the negative side of Derrida (Hartman, de Man, and Miller have chosen to see little else). Other tendencies, though admittedly sometimes overshadowed by his attacks on metaphysics from Plato to Lévi-Strauss, have the effect of moving us on, after his powerfully convincing claims for decentering, in order to interrogate, from within writing, and on wholly temporal and cultural grounds, what (if not naked being) does shape and inform the play of signification. Though any effort to identify a positive thrust in Derrida's thought will, eventually, run up against his remark to Jean Hippolite that he was trying to put himself "at a point so that I do not know any longer where I am going,"[44] still a variety of statements can be marshaled for this effort from several texts available to his American audience. We can begin with his irritated response to a charge, following his delivery of "Structure, Sign, and Play," that he was a destroyer: "I didn't say there was no center, that we could get along without the center. I believe that the center is a function, not a being—a reality, but a function. And this function is absolutely indispensable. The subject is absolutely indispensable. I don't destroy the subject; I situate it."[45] Or consider this, in the paper itself, a comment on free-play the implications of which have not been emphasized: "being must be conceived of as presence or absence beginning with the possibility of freeplay and not the other way around."[46] Or the statements, too numerous to quote in full, that differance "makes the presentation of being-present possible"; that "there is no presence *before* the semiological difference or outside it" (emphasis mine); that consciousness is a "determination" and an "effect" within a system of differance, not a matrical form of being.[47] Or most clearly, perhaps, this statement: "Since language . . . has not fallen from the sky, it is clear that the differences have been produced; they are the effects produced, but effects that do not have as their cause a subject or substance, a thing in general, or a being that is somewhere present and itself escapes the play of differences."[48]

In one of the fullest of Derrida's texts now available to an English-speaking audience, *Of Grammatology*, the sign as cultural production is quietly insinuated within massive readings of Saussure, Lévi-Strauss, and Rousseau, with an important glance or two at Heidegger. Especially in the reading of Saussure the scholarly force of Derrida's argument is irresistible. He begins by linking Saussure with the dualistic models of Greek and medieval metaphysics and theology, and the moral systems these models sanction against a writing (in these lights) unveiled as a fall from the soul, conscience, the transparent immediacy of "good writing"—a fall from the signifier as inner voice coincidental with (effaced to) self-present Deity. As he takes us through these traditional

perspectives and their traditionalist elaboration: the exteriority of the
body, the evil of passions, the writing that is bad—"sin," "lie," "usurpation," "trap," "disguise," "perversion," "rape," "pathological," "tyranny," "irrational"—Derrida demonstrates with remarkable clarity
what is at stake in his proposal to shift the philosophical focus from
self-present speech to writing.[49] The point of Saussure's traditionalist
ploy is to "derive historicity, and paradoxically, not to recognize the
rights of history, production, institutions *etc.*, except in the form of
the arbitrary and in the substance of naturalism."[50] Put as baldly as
possible, Derrida's point is that once we have turned away from various
ontological centerings of writing, we do not turn to free-play in the
blue, as the Yale formalists have done. Rather, it would appear that our
historical labors have just begun. It is in the very trace-structure of the
sign, in other words, that we may locate Derrida's most fundamental
attack on the metaphysics of presence, since it is in the sign conceived
as trace that the present as an in-itself is broken up and reconstituted
as a synthesis of retentions and protentions, a relation to both as a
past and a future. Thus the "substance" or "subject" of metaphysics,
which is inevitably founded on the basis of the presence of the present,
is dispersed in an ineffaceable historicity of discourse. It is the trace-
structure of the sign that grounds what is now called "intertextuality."
John Rowe makes the point in this way: " 'intertextuality' does not indicate merely the strategy of reading one text with another, but the
fact that every text is itself already an intertextual event. . . . the text
is not itself"[51]—because the present is not itself.

   Consciousness, the subject, the presence or absence of being, apparently forever dissolved as versions of the untouchable transcendental signified, now suddenly return as they all become situated as
intertextual functions of semiological systems which do recognize the
"rights of history, production, institutions" to coerce and constrain the
shapes of free-playing discourse. Semiological systems based on the
principle of difference "have been produced," and the key questions
become what and by whom: what discharges of power, under what networks of guidance, to what ends, and in what temporal and cultural
loci have semiological systems been produced? If Derrida concludes
the project of Nietzsche, which he defines as the "liberation of the signifier from its dependence or derivation with respect to the logos and
the related concept of truth or the primary signified,"[52] then he also
suggests the initiation of a new project (in this sense he has surely
known exactly where he is going), a project already handsomely underway in the poststructuralist writings of Michel Foucault: to uncover
the nonontological reincarceration of the signifier within cultural ma-

trices which, though themselves subject to difference and change, nevertheless in their moment of power, use the signifier, take hold of it, establish dominance over it in order to create truth, value, and rationality, and then violently set these *in place* as norms, coercive contexts for expression, meaning, and sanity that claim for themselves eternality and universality, even though these norms will themselves be displaced in time by new structures of domination.

But despite this historical consciousness in Derrida, there is an emphasis in his writing which encourages the pleasure-oriented formalism of the Yale critics. Derrida's deconstructive approach has the effect of unifying an apparent diversity of Western philosophical writings by uncovering their common logocentrism. The effect of his many analyses of representative Western thinkers is to give the impression that traditional philosophical discourse is monolithically preoccupied with a formally self-sufficient set of logocentric issues, that, despite his warnings that it has been produced and has not fallen from the sky, Western philosophical discourse has eluded the multiple relations of force traversing any society, has de facto, in every instance, resisted the rights of history and its institutions. Thus Descartes's discourse, presumably offered at the conclusion of "White Mythology" as an example of an opaque metaphorics, is quickly made a transparency—a white mythology itself—which in its effacement of its own fabulous figurations offers a spendid view of a centering structure that stands autonomous in the remote distance, above all the multiplicity of Western philosophical writings: "This metaphorics no doubt has its own specific syntax," Derrida writes, "but as a metaphorics it belongs to a more general syntax, a more extensive system whose constraints are equally operative in Platonism. . . ."[53] Or, in another foray into structuralism in the *Grammatology:* "I obviously treat the Saussurean text at the moment only as a telling example within a given situation. . . . My justification would be as follows: this and some other indices . . . already give us the assured means of broaching the de-construction of *the greatest totality*—the concept of the *epistémè* and logocentric metaphysics—within which are produced, without ever posing the radical question of writing, all the Western methods of analysis, explication, reading, or interpretation."[54]

The problem with such statements is not that they are "wrong"— Derrida is utterly persuasive—but that they postulate a set of textual determinates so broad (Said has made this point well), so historically inclusive that they deny that a given text, or group of texts, is enmeshed in circumstances any different from the circumstances that enclose any other text. Our impression (and it is an impression unavoidably shaped by the Yale mediation) is that at a certain preferred Olympian level of analysis the environments (intellectual, social, political, etc.) of Plato, Descartes, Rousseau, and Lévi-Strauss are reassuringly interchangeable.[55]

Derridean deconstruction, more specifically, uncovers those rules governing the production of all Western philosophical discourse which would attempt to establish the signifier as a transparency yielding an unobstructed view of a privileged and autonomous signified (truth, reality, being). The rules of logocentrism define the sign as a provisional signifier functioning in the absence of a presence that must be reappropriated at a future point in time; they attempt to establish the priority of voice over writing (i.e., the ideality of meaning over the fallen corporeality of discourse); at all costs, logocentrism must try to protect the ideality of meaning by inventing a residence for ideality—the interior of a consciousness shielded from all exterior contaminations. It is difficult to see, on this point, why Derrida's and others' attacks on structuralism for its courting of formalism and historical aridity do not apply to Derrida as well. Derrida's deconstructive project is formalist through and through. Its synchronic desire for *"the greatest totality,"* for dialogue with a unified tradition (logocentrism), defeats its would-be historicist disposition. The charge of formalism is to a certain extent valid even taking into account Derrida's scholarly skill in demonstrating how particular terms are loaded by a writer's cultural disposition.[56] Yet his formalism is at the same time one of his greatest strengths, for it is the basis of an elegant, commanding overview matched in philosophic history only by Hegel. It is precisely this generalizing ("structuralizing") reach of his analyses that lends them their power. When, for example, he demonstrates with great power in *Writing and Difference* that structuralism, phenomenology, and formalism are all intimately reinforcing conceptions of the same Western metaphysical urge, much of the controversy in contemporary theory evaporates as proponents of these positions are suddenly revealed in the common heritage of their desire.[57]

3

Whatever the degree of personal commitment one can detect in Derrida's implication of a poststructuralist historical method that would yield a positive kind of knowledge, both the American Derrideans and their antagonists have agreed in so many words that his texts support no such implication. Beyond that they have also tacitly agreed on the essence of the message. These days the chief difference

here his critique of yale

between the avant-garde critical group and the traditionalists is that
one voices delight in Derrida's apparent message and the other a mixture of scorn, outrage, and irony, with a dash of despair sometimes
sifted in. (I say "apparent message" because I detect that much of
what is claimed in Derrida's name bears only the most tenuous relationship to what in fact he has been writing.) To Abrams's complaint
that "deconstructionist principles" make any "history which relies
on written texts" an "impossibility," Miller responded: "So be it. That
is not much of an argument."[58] And Miller is of course right. The question remains, though, whether there be sound alternatives which reject
the melodramatically narrowed either/or of the current debate.

In the broadest terms, the traditionalists have urged that historical
and critical methods can produce positive knowledge of texts and
their environments only if three premises govern our scholarly procedures. In Abrams's elegant summary these premises state (1) that
written texts "say something determinate"; (2) that such determinacy
is grounded on authorial intention, "what the author meant"; and (3)
that the properly equipped historian can mimetically approximate such
determinable intention, can produce a reading that similarly equipped
experts will agree possesses " 'objectivity.' "[59] (But by his placement
of the term "objectivity" in quotation marks we note a dangerous ambiguity in the third premise: is Abrams speaking of ontologically pure
objectivity, or of an objectivity projected onto texts by the hermeneutical norms of a professional group? If the latter, then his first two premises are not unproblematic.) The key for the traditionalists would
appear to be E. D. Hirsch's strenuous argument in *Validity in Interpretation* for a textually controlling and determinate authorial intention not
itself subject to disruption and dissipation in linguistic deferral and
multivalence: an intention, in other words, situated outside textuality.
(Hirsch's is the most rigorous argument for these ideas, though he has
been given little, and sometimes no credit at all by proponents of traditionalism.) As in Hirsch, Abrams's examples of centers of determinacy
are invariably romantic and phenomenological; his dissatisfaction with
Derrida and the deconstructionists is that they deny us "recourse to a
speaking or a writing subject, or ego, or cogito, or consciousness,"
or "voice," "and so" (here is the unwarranted leap) "to any possible
agency for the intention of meaning something."[60] Abrams agrees with
Wayne Booth that an author can earn, "by his excellence, a full authority."[61] With the exception of Hirsch, however, thus far the traditionalists have done not much more than assert the necessity of faith
in the principle of the author who may earn full authority, and then
bewail the fearful consequences of not believing. Perhaps the unad-

mirable absence of detailed argument here is a backhanded recognition, after all, that the principle of decentering is rooted in the compelling notion that in language there are only differences without positive values.

For their part, members of the avant-garde have argued that positive knowledge is not available because there is no stable ontological ground for it. We will have to learn to live with anxiety, we are told, because the certitudes and assurances given by determinate authorial intention, or by a determinate anything else, located "elsewhere," have been forever shattered by Derrida's numerous attacks on the center. Often this bad news is carried by an embarrassing rhetoric which portrays the avant-garde critic as an existential hero, courageous enough to face down his "inauthentic" urges. Criticism today, writes Hartman, is "turning grim," "far less hopeful"—even "desperate."[62] He asks, "can we tolerate and live in this verbal revel, or do we seek to end it by passing to a stage beyond, that metaphysical 'beyond' or 'real presence' which has gone under so many names?"[63] In this allusive account, the traditionalist is a Hamlet who makes his quietus with the bare bodkin of a privileged center, while the avant-gardist, or real Hamlet, chooses the labyrinth and thereby refuses hermeneutical suicide. The text, at any rate, as reified locus of determinacy, is replaced by textuality, a putative nonconcept, often figured in American Derridean commentary with much enthusiasm by the metaphor of the labyrinth. As it incorporates decentering, difference, differance, and other grammatological moves, the labyrinth places writing before us as the setting of the abyss. *Mise en abyme*, thanks to Miller and company, has become a battle cry, along with two corollary themes: that reading is no mimesis but a violence of mastery and substitution, and that history, in the models of Lovejoy and Abrams, is a chimera.

Among the many formulations of the abyss in the texts of the American Derrideans, I want to single out the following. The first is from Paul de Man's essay, "Political Allegory in Rousseau."

> The resulting meanings [of Rousseau's texts] can be said to be ethical, religious, or eudaemonic, but each of these thematic categories is torn apart by the aporia that constitutes it, thus making the categories effective to the precise extent that they eliminate the value system in which their classification is grounded.[64]

The second formulation is from Miller's essay on Stevens's "The Rock":

> The multiple meanings of the word "cure," like the meanings of all key words and figures in "The Rock," are

incompatible, irreconcilable. They may not be followed,
etymologically, to a single root which will unify or explain
them, explicate them in a single source. They may not be
folded together in a unified structure, as of leaves, blossom
and fruit from one stem. The origin rather is bifurcated,
even trifurcated, a forking root which leads the searcher
for the ground of the word into labyrinthine wanderings
in the forest of words. . . . However hard . . . [we try] to
fix the word in a single sense it remains indeterminable,
uncannily resisting . . . [our] attempts to end its movement.
Cover the abyss, or open it up, or find the bottom, the
ground of the rock, and make it a solid base on which to
build—which is it? How could it be all three at once? Yet
it is impossible to decide which it is. To choose one is to
be led to the others and so to be led by the words of the
poem into a blind alley of thought.[65]

And the third is from Hartman's essay on *Glas:*

. . . Derrida's systematic play, his *serio ludere,* is the real
issue. To call it "freeplay" seems understated. . . . For a
machine with this much play in it is either a surrealist,
erotic, morphological fantasy . . . or a language game with
so many trick-possibilities that to say there are seven types
of ambiguity is suddenly of the same order of truth as that
there are seven humours or even seven cardinal sins. The
point is not that they are without number . . . but that the
reentry into consciousness of contradiction or equivocation
through such "free-play" appears to be unbounded. . . . The
fullness of equivocation in literary structures should now be
thought about to the point where Joyce's wordplay seems
normal and Empson's *Seven Types* archaic. A 1001 nights of
literary analysis lie before [us]. . . .[66]

The single theme of these and other American formulations of *mise
en abyme* is that Derrida's denial of absolute authority, of ontological
agency as governance and closure of free-play, is equal to the denial of
all agencies and structures of authority and constraint (or "confinement," in the Foucauldian idiom). Discourse that is unbounded free-
play is discourse that is free in some absolute sense; and such freedom is
the cornerstone principle of formalist, idealist, and aestheticist positions
after Kant. This unloosening, in the fullness of equivocation, of the re-
straints of "maturity" and "reality" that New Critics typically imposed
upon ambiguity, wit, and irony represents a new formalism, then, only
in the sense that it is the older formalism with its ontological freight
thrown away: Hartman's verbal revels will not be ended. In the unde-

cidable textual moment called the *aporia*, all historically locatable thematic categories are "torn apart," in de Man's words, because the *aporia*, as the moment of decisive and divisive textual self-consciousness, makes thematic categories into self-canceling forces which "eliminate the value system" that is their presumed ground. The ground is itself ungrounded. In Miller's final turn of the screw, the abyss is itself abyssed; it is no referential device that would fix textuality's gaze on ontological nothingness. The allegorizing impulse of traditionalist criticism would appear to be at last permanently deflected. Difference is pressed into double service since it appears to guarantee at once the transcendence of discourse at large, as the uncontrollable sea of textuality, and the transcendence of its various individuated examples that we call texts, which are not really individuated, or closed, since in them we can trace countless inscriptions of other texts in the retentions and protentions of the sign.

The value of this Derridean mode of textual meditation? Hartman's rhetoric is telling: neither critic nor text can any longer be "subjected," he writes, "to a dominant subject, whether identified as author, cogito, archetype, or field of knowledge." Derrida " 'decenters' all themes or metaphors in philosophy as in literature, to reveal that nothing can be 'proper,' 'present,' 'in place.' "[67] In ours and the text's release from domination, and in our consequent move from such subjugation into full liberty, we finally enter the idealist's heaven. A younger member of the Yale group, Leslie Brisman, candidly makes the point for us when he forces upon Derrida the alien desires of post-Kantian epistemology and aestheticist sentimentality. In an essay on Swinburne, Brisman claims that both Swinburne and Derrida champion our freedom from the "metaphysics of presence and our freedom from the tyrannizing presence of the Eliotic world of objects. The point where Swinburne's verse seems to slacken its obedience to sense may be, not the more primitive bondage to sound, but the more original lordship over the world of sensate things. Poetry traces its distance from, and victory over, such things."[68] The lesson of Derridean differance, however, has never been that language releases us from a tyrannical world of sensate things. Brisman's romantic point is Hartman's, but not quite Derrida's: we win the pure experience of *joyeuse* which tragically eluded the generation of later nineteenth-century aesthetes, and in the bargain we acquire what traditional humanism always desired but always subverted in its lust for the center: true "openness of thought" before the text that is itself truly open.[69]

In the face of such claims it is perhaps permissible to ask at least two questions. Is the American Derridean's desire to experience the joy of freedom any more than a reflection (and tacit acknowledgment), as it was for Lionel Johnson, Ernest Dowson, and the younger Yeats, of a situation in which that kind of freedom is denied all around, a situation in which oppression, not freedom, characterizes social existence? Second, have the Derrideans practiced a new unfettered formalism, or have they established a new allegory founded upon the rock of a new center, a "single root," a "single sense," a "single source" of determinacy, a new transcendental signified called the abyss? In theory, the abyss is itself abyssed, and therefore cannot serve as a point of presence. But somewhere along the line a judgment will need to be made about the practice of the Derrideans; a judgment as to whether their essays on Rousseau, Nietzsche, Stevens, Swinburne, and others, do not repeat the same point, do not allegorize texts from the perspective of the *aporia*, over and over in very predictable ways, and with a heavy-handedness reminiscent of mythographic and structuralist critics.

The question is whether the American Derrideans have not established new prison-houses for the better dominance of the critical consciousness, have not shown by their example that the claim for "openness" is the purest of pieties. The following statement about the function of rhetoric, from one of de Man's essays on Rousseau, represents, in its willful flight from textures of difference, and in a rather traditional way, what the New Critics used to call the crude stance of the allegorizing mythographer: "The fact that one narrates concepts [*Profession de foi*] whereas the other narrates something called characters [*Julie*] is irrelevant from a rhetorical perspective."[70] We must no longer, with Northrop Frye, seek the deep structures of myth, but, with Paul de Man, the deep structures of rhetoric. And isn't the concluding statement of Miller's essay on Stevens a self-conscious warning to the masters as well as to the epigones? "Any such formulation, whether it is called . . . '*la dissémination*,' 'the aporia,' '*la differance*,' 'decentering,' 'deconstruction,' 'double bind,' 'cure,' '*mise en abyme*,' 'transumption,' . . . or whatever, can quickly become, like any other critical word, a dead terminology able to be coldly manipulated by epigones. . . ."[71]

Questions about the status of history in deconstructive criticism are less slippery than questions circling about the status of the abyss. On the matter of history, the deconstructionist position—despite the awesome historical learning of its Yale proponents—appears equivalent to the position of the literary know-nothing, newly reinforced with a theory of discourse that reassures him that history-writing is bunk. In Saussure's terms, the Yale Derrideans, by their refusal to credit the historical (or syntagmatic) dimension of discourse, pursue meaning exclusively in its paradigmatic form (which is by definition indefinite) and as if all meanings were at all times eternally present. The central problem with the deconstructionist position on this point is not that it attacks history and historicism as it is understood and practiced by traditionalists, but that it relegates history, in the process of attack, to the ruling Platonic conceptions of the traditionalists. In Miller's polemic against traditionalist historicism, in his review of *Natural Supernaturalism*, he accuses Abrams of assuming a primal unity for Western culture which, in spite of its modifications, fragmentations, displacements, is ultimately recoverable as an origin through the culture's major texts. Indispensable to Miller's charges are Derrida's critiques of centered structure and of the sign as differance and metaphor. Abrams, Miller is saying, cannot put his notion of the transcendental signified of Western culture into question, and therefore assumes both the virginal innocence and the perfect tyranny of the transcendental signified. Abrams can believe that the signified is recoverable because he assumes a "direct, one to one relation between a work and its 'source' "; assumes, in other words, that a text can successfully translate the signified "without loss from 'source' to 'copy,' " and that these operations of textual translation (of naive mimesis) are made possible by a ruling conception of metaphor as ornament.[72] Abrams respects the distinction between literal or proper meaning and metaphoric deviation, while rejecting the counsels of Nietzsche and Derrida that difference and metaphor are, in a nonontological sense, "primordial." Language, according to Miller, is the missing term in Abrams's argument.

Miller fired a second and most unpredictable shot against traditionalist historicism in a review of the West Coast deconstructor, Joseph Riddel. In Riddel's book on William Carlos Williams, Miller believes he discerns, underneath an immensely thick Heideggerian and Derridean overlay, a covert employment of the favorite traditionalist notion of the "literary period." This idea has its foundation in the history of ideas and its Platonic recourse to a commanding *Weltanschauung* which determines the texts of a period, differentiates these texts from texts of other periods (they have their own *Weltanschauungen*) and, most importantly, encloses a period as a separable entity for analysis. Against this recognizably traditionalist thought, for which periodization is both heuristically and ontologically valid, Miller brings this: "Each period is itself equivocal. Periods differ from one another because there are different forms of heterogeneity, not because each period held a single coherent 'view of the world.' "[73]

The sense of history suggested by the phrase "different forms of heterogeneity" might point us in the direction of the powerful antidote to Platonic historicism that we find in the writings of Michel Foucault.

But it is an alternative left unexplored by the American Derrideans, probably because the so-called nonprinciple of *mise en abyme* functions in deconstructionist commentary as a universal shield which protects texts from difference rather than opening them up to it. Whatever the abyss might mean in theory, in practice it generates a view of history remarkably consistent with a view that both de Man and Miller had entertained in earlier phases of their careers when they wrote under existential and phenomenological perspectives. In a transition statement in his essay on Poulet of 1971, Miller merges the terminologies of existential phenomenology and poststructuralism: "The human condition remains the same throughout history, de Man would argue, and the great writers of every epoch rise above the superficial configurations of thought in their ages to express in authentic language the human predicament, in particular the abysses in man's experience of temporality."[74] Nowadays great writers are said to "rise above" the thought of their times via the *aporia*, which tears up all thematic determinates; or, in Miller's words, to similar effect, "every literary text performs . . . its own self-dismantling. . . ."[75] Understood, however, as a heterogeneous form of forces, ontologically empty but historically full, dominant, and transformable, the *aporia* is not alien to the analysis that Derrida carries on in the *Grammatology*. To use the *aporia*, particularly in the anti-Derridean way that Miller does, in order to privilege literary discourse for its supposedly self-deconstructive power, is to reinstate the speaking subject as a free and unblinded authority.

The American Derrideans make an initial and potentially fruitful assumption of a heterogeneous synthesis of forces operating in time only in order to demonstrate that the essence of the "literary" lies in its power to place all such forms of force in self-destructive relation. In their power to make this happen, all texts and all writers are said to be the "same"; all historical forces are shown to be "superficial." At the essential ("essentializing") level of textuality, all texts and all writers elude domination and elude all would-be determinates of textuality and literary identity. Herein lies the essence of the "great" work, the "major" writer, and, finally, the essence of the new privilege given to literary discourse. (A rather incredible conclusion for a criticism made in the name of a philosopher one of whose major tasks has been to explain why no discourse can claim such privilege.) It is a familiar story in contemporary American criticism, for more openly professed formalists like Cleanth Brooks and Murray Krieger, employing the weapons of irony and ambiguity, had long ago told us how (in the case of Brooks) Wordsworth was actually very much like Donne, and how (in the case of Krieger) Pope was not as trapped in Enlightenment perspectives as we had thought—was, deep down, a poet of existential desolation and meaninglessness, as, in Krieger's view, all important writers are. Whether New-Critical or poststructuralist, the formalist critic is concerned to demonstrate the history-transcending qualities of the text, and whether he wields the textual cleaver of difference or that of irony, he portrays the writer as a type of Houdini, a great escape artist whose deepest theme is freedom, whose great and repetitious feat is the defeat of history's manacles. Miller candidly makes the point in his wavering assessment of the place of Stevens in American poetic history: "Stevens' 'The Rock' . . . is a thorough deconstruction of the Emersonian bedrock self. Stevens' poem . . . is an interpretation of Emerson and Whitman which undermines their apparent affirmation (though of course both Emerson and Whitman had, each in his own way, already annihilated his own seemingly solid ground). . . ."[76]

The third member of the terrible trio of issues (the abyss, history, reading) animating the current debate is that reading is not carried on by a transparent, neutral self, but is a form of creation and a will to mastery. This question about the status of the reader possesses the most potential for critical havoc, but neither side has very well defined its contours, and the Yale Derrideans have not much bothered to explore the ramifications of their essential point. It has sufficed, for the Derrideans, to spread terror in traditionalist quarters. The boundary between text and commentary is "highly fluid," according to Hartman; the idea that the interpreter can stand in some value-free space, as in a Cartesian "natural light," is but a fiction that can be easily exploded.[77] Echoing Harold Bloom, de Man tells us that there is no such thing as an accurate reading, but only misreadings of two sorts: those he calls "wrong" and those he calls "valid."[78] What purpose such traditionalist terms can serve in a poststructuralist context de Man never says, but he does define a "valid" and a "good" misreading: "By a good misreading, I mean a text that produces another text which can itself be shown to be an interesting misreading, a text which engenders additional texts. If you have a poor text, you cannot make up a very rewarding construction."[79] The shift from cognitive terms ("wrong," "valid") to ethical and practical language ("good," "interesting") is entirely consistent with the drift of American poststructuralism (freedom, joy, affirmation, the erotic pleasure of the text) and especially harmonious with de Man's Nietzschean basis—the stress on will to power in reading that Abrams presumably ignores. But this shift to affective rhetoric succeeds in generating a subject-object model (with psychologistic nuances) for the relationship of reader and text markedly similar to the one that operates in traditionalist thought. In the framework set up by de Man, it would have to be admitted that the Rorschach inkblot is a strong text, since it is capable of eliciting many "rewarding" constructions.

By their insistence on power in interpretation—we are free to "make up" rewarding constructions in a 1001 nights of literary analysis—American Derrideans give their opponents ample reasons to charge that they are simply interested in loosing upon the world the mere anarchy of the self's radically subjective potential. By their insistence on the freedom of "subjective" response, Derrideans seem to covertly acknowledge that an "objective" reading is possible, but that because they wish to shore up the autonomy of the self, they choose to ignore such a possibility. The text as a thing that elicits interesting responses is not only too vaguely defined—it is de-defined, which is perhaps de Man's real point. Such a notion of the text also emphasizes the joy and freedom of subjective response by taking away all constraints from text and reader. Does what we "make up" flow from a subjectivity untouched by society and time? Do the values of freedom and will to power surface in a historical vacuum? If not (and it would be difficult for Derrideans to argue the affirmative), then freedom is not what they say it is, there are limits to power, and *joyeuse* is tightly circumscribed by canons of interpretation.

By dialectical implication, boredom and confinement become the two great evil fates harassing the poststructuralist quest for joy and freedom. If, as Stanley Fish has suggested, echoing a sentiment of Culler at the end of *Structuralist Poetics,* one need no longer be concerned with being right, but only with being interesting,[80] then by the same argument one must fear to be oneself dulled and bored, in the process dulling and boring one's readers (for one devoting his life to literary criticism, no inconsiderable fear). The activity of the literary critic, thus aestheticized, thus "affectivized," does not isolate him from the mainstream conditions of modern society, but rather constitutes an academic elaboration and intensification of them. American poststructuralist literary criticism tends to be an activity of textual privatization, the critic's doomed attempt to retreat from a social landscape of fragmentation and alienation. Criticism becomes, in this perspective, something like an ultimate mode of interior decoration whose chief value lies in its power to trigger our pleasures and whose chief measure of success lies in its capacity to keep pleasure going in a potentially infinite variety of ways. Yet once again Kant's withdrawal of a disinterested, contemplative pleasure from the arena of duty and action and the province of knowledge reaps the final harvest of its self-destructive end. A 1001 nights of literary analysis, or psychic death—such appear to be the fearful options of the new aesthetes.

My point is that the Derrideans and their antagonists are (as Walter Michaels suggests about a variant of their debate) flipsides of the same coin. In theory the Derrideans cannot believe in a self before interpretation, but since in their practice they have celebrated the free-play of interpretation without exploring the idea that the reading self is a kind of text, itself subject to constitutive determination, they allow us to conclude that beneath the theory lies the sort of solipsistic impulse (in evidence in Hartman's meditation on *Glas*) that Hirsch, Abrams, and others charge them with. Here is Hartman engaged in a philosophical aerialism that trips him into the free fall of free association:

> Ca is homophonic with *Sa*. On the first page [of *Glas*] Derrida condenses "savoir absolu" as *Sa*. Then let us substitute *Sa* for ca. . . . But *Sa* as tachygraph, as artificial abbreviation, was already there before Derrida. . . . For *Sa* is homophonic with the abbreviation for "signifiant" when distinguished in Saussure from *Se*, the "signifié." This doubled *Sa* not only suggests that so-called absolute knowledge is as unstable as the volatile phoneme or signifier but also it makes the text of Saussure into an additional "signifié." Because of this double or false bottomed *Sa*, we can hardly keep track. . . . Ca is too sassy.[81]

Onto *Glas*, a text already well loaded with puns, Hartman imposes, from within the vast store of the echo chamber of his mind, a Saussurean overlay ("Then let us substitute. . . . For *Sa* is homophonic. . . ."). But why should "we" substitute? Because we know that Derrida knows Saussure? Simply because Saussure wrote before Derrida does not mean that he is *there* in the passage that Hartman alludes to. Where is the textual clue that suggests Derrida, not Hartman, is making a homophonic liaison with Saussure? Since Hartman believes that puns, including his own, are beyond good and evil, perhaps he is beyond censure.

The value-free, historically transcendent reader celebrated by the traditionalist is no alternative to Hartmanian revelry. Michaels has located a model for reading in Peirce that would move us on to solid ground.[82] On a different philosophical path, Gadamer's elaborations of Heidegger's dark remarks on the prestructuring propensities of human understanding offer us a model which would at once respect the radical alterity of the text while not ignoring the historicized consciousness of the interpreter. One of the things traditionalists have always demanded from theory is that it pay homage to the otherness of the text, because such otherness carries values and modes of consciousness, not necessarily our own, but nevertheless worth coming to know. Avant-gardists also conceive the text as other. At the same time, however, they have put forth a theory of reading which now appears hell-bent on dissipating otherness in our will to master it. If we refuse to retreat to a Cartesian conception of an innocent self operating in the halo of natural light, can we construct a theory of reading and textuality that would permit interpretation that can claim to produce not self-expression but knowledge? Can we devise a theory of reading that would respect and seek intratextual determinates and some participation in a history that is not purely the retrospective imposition of ourselves? Within a post-Nietzschean view of the interpreter as an agent willing dominance, can we come to recognize the text as an "event"?

4

> Different *oeuvres*, dispersed books, that whole mass of texts
> that belong[s] to a single discursive formation—and so
> many authors who know or do not know one another, criti-
> cize one another, . . . pillage one another, meet without
> knowing it and obstinately intersect their unique discourses
> in a web of which they are not the masters, of which they
> cannot see the whole, and of whose breadth they have a very
> inadequate idea. . . . they communicate by the form of
> positivity of their discourse. . . . Thus positivity plays the
> role of what might be called a *historical a priori*.

Michel Foucault, *The Archaeology of Knowledge*

We can begin to gauge Michel Foucault's relationship to Jacques Derrida and his American followers and to the sort of traditionalism represented by Wayne Booth, M. H. Abrams, and E. D. Hirsch, by briefly quizzing the difficult, sliding terms "textuality," "text," "determinacy," and "intention." Derrida and the Yale critics contend that the act of isolating a verbal sequence, and ensuing attempts at circumscribing and enclosing its semantic horizon, can be carried out only if the critic refuses to recognize the linguistic authority of Saussure's differential view of discourse and the "abysmal" consequences of this view. The view that language is a play of differences affirms that there are no isolate texts, no atomic cores that can be fenced off as untouchable private property (no poem in itself). Further, it affirms that there are no larger ranges of discursive territory whose boundaries can be securely drawn (as literature, philosophy, history, science, etc.), so that literature, for example, can be looked at as a historical continuity against a diffused "background" of other discourses whose intrusive potential can be held at a safe distance. Saussure's differential view of language (as it is mediated by Derrida) leads to these consequences because it forces us to understand that no discourse refers unproblematically to a nondiscursive object that is the ground of the discourse; discourse is the setting of the abyss *(abgrund)*; it is without ground. The formalist's "text," or the traditional historicist's discourse of "literature," as fixed paddocks of meaning, yield to "textuality"—a potentially infinite and indefinite, all-inclusive series of networks of interrelation whose connections and boundaries are not securable because they are ruled by never-ending movements of linguistic energy that recognize neither the rights of private ownership nor the authority of structuralism's centralized government of interpretive norms. In its severest terms, textuality is a fundamentally open and radically temporal affair; the larger and smaller spatialized distinctions among discourses are ontologically unsupportable.

In practice, however, a certain ambiguity has crept into the term "textuality." At one point in his analysis of Saussure—and methodologically it is a typical moment for Derrida—he says that the *Course in General Linguistics* is merely an instance of textuality that is governed by a universal *epistēmē* (Western logocentric metaphysics) which dictates "all the Western methods of analysis, explication, reading, or interpretation."[83] Against a variable and transformable sense of the *epistēmē* (archive, discursive formation, historical *a priori*) that operates in *The Order of Things* and other of Foucault's books as a force of limited historical determination, Derrida appears to offer an *epistēmē* so massive and inclusive that it occasionally functions as a transcendental of sorts, a set of textual rules, rooted out by deconstructive method, that causes all instances of textuality to repeat a specified set of textual problems. Overly enamored of Derrida's convincing argument that discourse is ontologically homeless, and unconcerned with the changing historical colorations that Derrida's analyses are able to specify (despite their similarly constrained logocentric thinking one would not mistake Derrida's Plato for his Husserl), the American Derrideans have insisted that the infinitely abyssed nature of writing is final proof of writing's freedom from would-be textual determinates.

Foucault may be understood to be attempting to situate textuality between Derrida's notion and what the Yale group have made of it. As the regulative force of writing, he believes that textuality is contextualized from within (as opposed to being governed from without by a nondiscursive ground) by a set of rules that is always subject to historical transformation. From this perspective, traditionalists like Abrams and Hirsch are not wrong to insist that a power of determinacy may play within discourse, but merely mistaken in locating such power in a freely individuated authorial intention which seeks to impose itself upon language from "outside." The *aporia* (or *mise en abyme*) in the hands of the Yale critics, or the free intention of Abrams and Hirsch, are alike strategies for denying the pressure of historical contexts and for affirming that *écriture*, or authors, "rise above" the superficialities of their times. Understood as a series of discursive formations, Foucault is saying, history is a "web" that neither authors nor writing can master. He would agree with traditionalists that unless we deploy, at least for heuristic purposes, some form of the principle of determinacy, criticism cannot offer itself as a cognitive activity, for the refusal of determinacy is the refusal of knowledge. In the several texts now available to his English-speaking audience—*Madness and Civilization*, *The Order of Things*, *The Birth of the Clinic*, *The Archaeology of Knowledge*, *Discipline and Punish*, *The History of Sexuality*, and the collection called *Language, Counter-Memory, Practice*—Foucault has put forth a number of detailed recommendations for history-writing and its philosophy, while at the same time pursuing a highly useful series of pointed attacks on phenomenological method and the traditional approach to the historicist project.

5

In the introduction to *The Archaeology of Knowledge*, Foucault distinguishes the ideals and tasks of his revised historicism from what he takes to be the assumptions and methods of an older and bankrupt approach. Under changing rubrics, this distinction preoccupies him through *The Archaeology* and other self-conscious theoretical meditations, the most important of which is the essay "Nietzsche, Genealogy, History." It is, fundamentally, a distinction between a historicist mode of writing which will give value to "phenomena of rupture, of discontinuity," and those which will celebrate the idea of "tradition" itself, and the activities of "tracing a line" and of seeking "lasting foundations." Any specification of discontinuity, he believes, would necessarily involve the deployment of concepts like "threshold, rupture, break, mutation, transformation," for the end of reconstituting, "on the basis of what . . . documents say, and sometimes merely hint at," a past "from which they emanate and which has now disappeared far behind them. . . ."[84] Foucault's neglect, at this early stage of his exposition, of the neo-Nietzschean stress on the problems of interpretation, the incessantly projective quality of an interpreting consciousness cut off (by his own argument) from the past it would recapture, I take to be strategic, a sign of his unwillingness to give in to the easy subjectivism that has barred many recent theoretical critics from history. Though American Derrideans almost universally ignore him, Foucault accepts Jacques Derrida's major points about decentering, difference, and free-play, and he accepts Derrida's banishment of ontology and attacks on representation (as straightforward mimesis) and phenomenology. But Foucault is no champion of the *aporia*, no connoisseur of *abyme*. His naked statement of his goals as a historian is not evidence of what could be (and has been) termed old-fashioned historicist naiveté, but of a passionate belief that genuine history-writing is not only possible, but is *made possible* by Derrida's revision of traditionalist thought in general and of structuralism in particular.

Foucault's attack on traditional historicism is prefaced by an analysis of what he understands to be the usual traditionalist response to the notion of discontinuity—a notion he assumes plays a major role in the historical disciplines, however they are conceived. For the classical historian, discontinuity is simply a raw given, but it is unthinkable and must be overcome. Hence, through analysis, dispersed events have to be "rearranged, reduced, effaced in order to reveal the continuity of events. Discontinuity was the stigma of temporal dislocation that it was the historian's task to remove from history." The essential job of the new Foucauldian historian is "probably this displacement of the discontinuous: its transference from the obstacle to the work itself. . . ."[85] Such revision of the role of discontinuity in the discourse of history-writing highlights a distinction between "total" history, which seeks a system of homogeneous relations, and "general" history which employs "the space of a dispersion,"[86] or what Foucault called in *The Order of Things* the *epistēmē*. This is an epistemological field which is not to be understood as a cultural totality, or "unit-idea," as Lovejoy puts it in his definition of the task of the historian of ideas. In Foucault's words: "The history of ideas, then, is the discipline of beginnings and ends, the description of obscure continuities and returns, the reconstitution of developments in the linear form of history."[87] As the space of a dispersion, the *epistēmē* provides a broadly Derridean alternative to the totalizing history that wants to draw "all phenomena around a single center—a principle, a meaning, a spirit, a world-view, an overall shape. . . ."[88] The single center, whatever name we may choose to give it, functions according to the model of a Platonic form: as an essentializing force which, by causing particular texts to become veils covering a hidden ontological realm, robs them of their identity as it annihilates differences. In his posing of discontinuous, or general history, against continuous, or total history, Foucault reminds us of how extensive his agreements with Derrida are: continuous history, he writes in an especially luminous passage,

> would provide a privileged shelter for the sovereignty of consciousness. Continuous history is the indispensable correlative of the founding function of the subject: the guarantee that everything that has eluded him may be restored to him; the certainty that time will disperse nothing without restoring it in a reconstituted unity; the promise that one day the subject . . . will once again be able to appropriate, to bring back under his sway, all those things that are kept at a distance by difference, and find in them what might be called his abode.[89]

The purpose of continuous history, then, is simply "to preserve, against all decenterings"—the allusion is to Marx, Nietzsche, and Freud—"the sovereignty of the subject."[90] Foucault's linkage, in *The Archaeology*, of phenomenology's privileged *cogito* with the traditionalist, or continuous, approach to the discipline of history clarifies the blunt rejection of phenomenology that he announced in a foreword he had penned especially for the English edition of *Les Mots et les choses:* "If there is one approach that I do reject . . . it is that (one might call it, broadly speaking, the phenomenological approach) which gives absolute priority to the observing subject, which attributes a constituent role to an act, which places its own point of view at the origin of all historicity— which, in short, leads to a transcendental consciousness."[91]

The stage is not quite set for the exposition of his alternative, for first Foucault must subvert the central conceptual strategies of traditional historicism. To this end he opens a frontal assault on *tradition* (an idea which "makes it possible to rethink the dispersion of history in the form of the same; . . . [and] enables us to isolate the new against a background of permanence, and to transfer its merit to originality, to genius, to the decisions proper to individuals"); on *influence, development,* and *evolution* (causal processes that link a succession of dispersed events through the "same organizing principle"); on *spirit* (which "allows the sovereignty of a collective consciousness to emerge as the principle of unity and explanation," and which assumes a "community of meanings"); on *oeuvre* (which posits unity grounded in a "founding subject" and its "expressive function"); on the *book* (whose frontiers are always assumed to be clear-cut, and whose internal system is thought to achieve an autonomous form that denies essential relations with "other books, other texts, other sentences," and denies, most of all, that the book is merely a "node within a network"); on the *secret origin* (which denies discontinuity and the "eruption of a real event"); on the *phenomenological voice* (which Foucault, in powerful echo of Derrida's study of Husserl, defines as "an incorporeal discourse, a voice as silent as breath, a writing that is merely the hollow of its own mark. . . . manifest discourse . . . is really no more than the repressive presence of what it does not say"); on *langue* (a "finite body of rules that authorizes an infinite number of performances," but which can never raise the diachronic issue in its bluntest form: "how is it that one particular statement appeared rather than another?"); on the familiar disciplinary *division of discourse* (as literature, philosophy, science). Tradition, influence, development, evolution, spirit, *oeuvre*, book, origin, voice, *langue*, and divisions of discourse made along the usual disciplinary lines: these are the central forces for unity and continuity within four methodologies (traditionalist historicism, formalism, phenomenology, and structuralism) which in Foucault's perspective reveal their fundamental affiliations.[92]

In a systematic effort to erase them all, Foucault would establish the new frontier of his own kind of historicism: "Once these immediate forms of continuity are suspended, an entire field is set free. A vast field, but one that can be defined nevertheless: this field is made up of the totality of all effective statements (whether spoken or written) in their dispersions as events and in the occurrence that is proper to them."[93] This "field" is what poststructuralists call "textuality," but in his interest in the "occurrence" that is "proper" to statements, Foucault tells us, in so many words, that he does not conceive of textuality as *mise en abyme*, but as that internal and informative setting of statement which is open to definition and determinacy. And to claim that much, for Foucault, is to claim that his attack on traditional historicism's conceptions of unity and continuity does not issue from an anarchistic and nominalistic alternative. Nominalism is a false alternative to traditional unity. His desire, on the contrary, is to "grasp other forms of regularity, other types of relations." For to

> reveal in all its purity the space in which discursive
> events are deployed is not to undertake to re-establish it
> in an isolation that nothing could overcome; it is not to
> close it in upon itself; it is to leave oneself free to describe
> the interplay of relations within it and outside it. . . . The
> . . . purpose of such a description of the facts of discourse
> is that by freeing them of all the groupings that purport
> to be natural, immediate, universal unities, one is able to
> describe other unities, but this time by means of a group
> of controlled decisions.[94]

Those "other unities" which are neither natural nor immediate, Foucault calls by various names: discursive formation, *epistēmē*, historical *a priori*, archive. And the kind of history-writing that deploys such conceptions he calls archaeology, genealogy, general or effective history. Most fundamentally, the discursive formation challenges the metaphysical idea of the older historicism that the discourse of a discipline, let us say that of psychiatry, or of literary criticism, is unified by virtue of its ability to attend to an essential object, "madness," or "literature," whose character is ideal: naturally and universally given, temporally and culturally unmodifiable. In his initial formulation of the point, the discursive formation sounds neo-Kantian. But it isn't: "each of these discourses [medicine, grammar, political economy] constituted its object and worked it to the point of transforming it altogether. So that the problem arises of knowing whether the unity of a discourse is based not so much on the permanence and uniqueness of an object as on the space in which various objects emerge and are continuously transformed."[95] Thus the object is constituted, but not by a set of structuring categories located in consciousness. Rather, as a "well-defined regularity," a "group of rules," a "field of strategic possibilities," a "system of dispersion," the discursive formation determines, dominates, and even overwhelms the subjects responsible for discourse.[96]

The discursive formation, as at once diffuse, anonymous, and repressive, challenges the cherished formalist principle that has vitalized so many contemporary critical systems. Discourse conceived as "fiction," "literature," the "literary universe," or "the poem itself," and the author conceived as the autonomous ground of intentionality, or *cogito*, are hereby radically constrained; no longer, in this view, are they to be conceived of as "free." To cite an example Foucault gives in *The Order of Things*: "What was common to the natural history, the economics, and the grammar of the Classical period was certainly not present to the consciousness of the scientist; . . . unknown to themselves, the naturalists, economists, and grammarians employed the same rules to define the objects proper to their study, to form their concepts, to build their theories."[97] Like its idealistic counterpart, Kant's *a priori* categories of consciousness, what Foucault calls the discursive *"rules of formation"* establish the conditions of the existence of the object. But because such rules, unlike a set of Kantian universals, have themselves only historical being, they change, they are themselves subject to appropriation, and therefore account not only for the existence of the object, but also for "coexistence, maintenance, modification, and disappearance."[98] A discursive formation exists not as a center,

a homogeneous sort of being—a unit-idea, or a transcendental consciousness—which sucks all dispersed things into its unified and homo-
genizing substance; nor does it enjoy the synchronic privilege of
Saussure's *langue*. As a historical *a priori*, the discursive formation partakes simultaneously of the synchronic and the diachronic: it rules
time, but only in time and *for* a time. It exists, therefore, as a heterogeneous or "problematic unity" which contains the elements of its own
transformation and appropriation.[99] Here is Foucault's summarizing
statement on the discursive formation which indicates just how far he
has come from idealistic and structuralist thought and the methodology
of the history of ideas:

> These systems of formation must not be taken as blocks of
> immobility, static forms that are imposed on discourse
> from the outside, and that define once and for all its
> character and possibilities. . . . As a group of rules for a
> discursive practice, the system of formation is not a stranger
> to time. . . . A discursive formation, then, does not play the
> role of a figure that arrests time and freezes it for decades
> or centuries; it determines a regularity proper to temporal
> processes. . . .[100]

In his specification of the forces at work to rule discourse and the
objects which discourse permits to exist, nowhere does Foucault write
with keener social awareness than in his discussion of what he calls
"authorities of delimitation."[101] As a diffuse and hidden conglomerate
of power—in the nineteenth century, for example, medical discourse
was situated in a network of interlocking authorities that included
penal and religious agencies— the discursive formation is a repressive
force, and in Foucault's system, primary evidence of Nietzschean will
to power as will to truth. The discursive formation is nothing other
than a subtle grouping of mutually reinforcing connections among
professional disciplines, "institutions, economic and social processes,
behavioral patterns, systems of norms," which permits the object "to appear, to juxtapose itself with other objects, to situate itself
in relation to them, to define its difference, its irreducibility. . . ."[102]
This statement of the methodological strategies of psychiatry, political
economy, natural science, grammar, medicine, or the penal code vis-à-
vis their respective "objects" has immense implications for the "object"
of the literary critic (though Foucault has not made it his business to
explore them). The literary historian will find Foucault's statement of
intention very congenial: "To define these *objects* without reference to
the *ground, the foundation of things,* but by relating them to the rules
that enable them to form as objects of a discourse and then constitute

the conditions of their historical appearance. To write a history of discursive objects that does not plunge them into the common depth of a primal soil. . . ."[103]

The point is a remarkably simple one, and it is fully anticipated in some of Barthes's texts. At some theoretical level we all credit it, but it is too rarely credited by practice. There is no essential, Platonic object—let us say a "poem"—before which the discursive practice of literary criticism must (in its construction of a poetics and the methods of procedure that such a poetics would authorize) *make itself transparent*. Like those who would be defined rational rather than mad, or truth-speaking psychiatrists rather than quacks, those who would not be excluded from the country of poets and poetry-critics will find themselves without much choice, confined within the historical determinations of truth, rationality, and the poetic. In a brilliant illustration, Foucault says that it is not enough to speak the truth—one must be "within the truth" (*dans le vrai*):[104] "what conditions did Linnaeus (or Petty, or Arnauld) have to fulfil," he writes in *The Order of Things*, "not to make his discourse coherent and true in general [i.e., without condition] but to give it, in the time it was written and accepted, value and practical application as scientific discourse . . .?"[105] The violent and repressive underside of this statement about Linnaeus is explored in "The Discourse on Language" (*L'Ordre du discours*), now available to an English-speaking audience as the appendix to *The Archaeology of Knowledge*:

> People have often wondered how on earth nineteenth-century botanists and biologists managed not to see the truth of Mendel's statements. But it was precisely because Mendel spoke of objects, employed methods and placed himself within a theoretical perspective totally alien to the biology of his time. But then, Naudin had suggested that hereditary traits constituted a separate element before him; and yet, however novel or unfamiliar the principle may have been, it was nevertheless reconcilable, if only as an enigma, with biological discourse. Mendel, on the other hand, announced that hereditary traits constituted an absolutely new biological object, thanks to a hitherto untried system of filtrage: he detached them from species, from the sex transmitting them, the field in which he observed being that infinitely open series of generations in which hereditary traits appear and disappear with statistical regularity. Here was a new object, calling for new conceptual tools, and for fresh theoretical foundations. Mendel spoke the truth, but he was not *dans le vrai* . . . of

contemporary biological discourse: it simply was not
along such lines that objects and biological concepts were
formed. . . . Mendel was a true monster, so much so that
science could not even properly speak of him. . . . It is
always possible one could speak the truth in a void; one
would only be in the true, however, if one obeyed the rules
of some discursive "policy" which would have to be re-
activated every time one spoke.[106]

The implication is that if one would not speak truth "in a void," as
Mendel did in 1865 and 1866 (with unintended Foucauldian irony, a
text in animal biology states that at the time of publication Mendel's
discoveries were unaccountably "lost sight of"[107]), or if one would
not write poetry in a void as did Robert Frost (when he achieved
magazine publication only five times between 1895 and 1912, a period
during which he wrote a number of poems later acclaimed), then one
had better assent to the rules of discursive policy by placing oneself
within the confines of those systems that determine biological or poetic
truth for one's time. To refuse to conform is to accept a place, whether
one intends to or not, alongside society's more dramatically visible
outcasts: the criminals, the insane, racial minorities, and the indigent,
who are brutally and unhesitatingly subjected to the power that divides
and silences. In "The Discourse on Language" Foucault details how
the discursive formation, wonderfully equipped with the prodigious
machinery of the will to truth, pursues its vocation of exclusion ("*prohibition, division,* and *rejection*") in order to relegate difference to
nontruth and nonhuman being.[108]

What a book like *Madness and Civilization* shows (and we should
recall that it was published before Derrida's major work appeared) is
that difficult linguistic terms like "difference" and "binary opposition"
may be applied with considerable point to the violent hierarchization
of social realities. More specifically, Foucault is concerned to demonstrate in *Madness and Civilization* how a dominant culture maintains
its status first by relegating differences to oppositions, and then via
a "ritual of division," and by "rites of purification and exclusion,"
forcefully condemns one pole of the binary contrast (the poor, the
unemployed, the prisoners, the insane) to silence in a country of confinement.[109] When the Hôpital Général was established in Paris in
1656 as a "semijudicial structure," a "power of segregation" was un-
leashed which in Foucault's later texts becomes an emblematic sign
of the determining and excluding work done by every system of
formation.[110] The cunning achievement of all such cultural systems
is that they assign natural being to those inside their versions of

truth and monsterhood to those outside. Robert Frost in the earlier phase of his career, Mendel, criminals, and the insane are alike monsters whose forced exclusion allows dominant cultural establishments to appropriate to themselves poetic truth, biological truth, rationality, sanity, social value, and well-being. Among the strategies of a discursive formation, which posit the rules for the construction of statements that can be considered *dans le vrai*, Foucault lists doctrine, educational systems, the theme of the founding subject, and the theme of a universal mediation.[111] These principles of exclusion—together with tradition, influence, development, spirit, *oeuvre*, book, origin, voice, *langue*, and the conventional disciplinary method of staking out discursive turf and of organizing the university—all are so many ways of rarefying the thick densities of discourse and of repressing those modes of discourse which cannot be sanctioned by rules of formation currently in place.

In his discussion of the prohibitive power of "enunciative modalities," Foucault illustrates his point by writing that "medical statements cannot come from anybody . . .": "Who, among the totality of speaking individuals, is accorded the right to use this sort of language? Who is qualified to do so?"[112] Or who is qualified, for that matter, to make poetic statements, or statements that will fulfil the conditions of literary criticism? To probe the source of a speaker's authority is very quickly, as Foucault shows, to discover impregnable interlocking institutions which force expression into certain thoroughly architected places of confinement. A medical doctor will have a degree from a university which is overseen and accredited by professional associations and governmental agencies; furthermore, there will be an institutional site of speaking, a laboratory, a hospital, "from which the doctor makes his discourse, and from which this discourse derives its legitimate source and point of application. . . ."[113] The analogy with the literary critic is plain. He will, at a minimum, have a Ph.D. in literature, and preferably from one of a small group of celebrated universities. He will need a university appointment or a position at a small "respected" college; a letterhead announcing his name, an M.A. degree, and his home address as Commerce, Oklahoma, will constitute a distinct disadvantage. An ambitious literary critic who desires to lodge his statements within our current sense of critical truth would seek "coexistence," as Foucault puts it, with certain other disciplines—Saussurean linguistics, anthropology in the structuralist mode, deconstructionist philosophies, and so on. And his books and articles will speak from institutionally sanctioned sites: a university press, a scholarly journal, but again this is only minimal, for to be critically *dans le vrai* in 1980 is to speak under the imprimatur of certain preferred presses and journals. Above all, certain doctrines will be paid reverence.

The analogy with the situation of the poet is harder to make, but it is nonetheless viable. Let me return to the example of Frost's early career. In order to write within the dominant sense of the poetic in the United States in the last decade of the nineteenth century and in the first decade of the twentieth, one had to employ a diction, syntax, and prosody heavily favoring Shelley and Tennyson. One also had to assume a certain stance, a certain world-weary idealism which took care not to refer too concretely to the world of which one was weary. (Among other things, I am describing "My Butterfly," one of five poems Frost did succeed in publishing before 1913.) One needed to respect, as well, a certain absolute division between poetry and prose, and, in particular, one had to avoid the mistake of E. A. Robinson and Frost: that of apparently trying to fob off as poems prosy little fragments that might better find their home in the realistic or naturalistic novel. In sheer chronological time, it was not so very long before Ezra Pound would announce, as if it were a commonly held critical dictum, that poetry must be at least as well-written as prose. But Pound's sense of the poetic was articulated in the heady times of a modernist revolution which had already successfully appropriated the poetic for its own ends, and in the process had stripped power from the honorific norms that had denied "poetry" to Robinson and Frost and would surely have denied it to Pound, Eliot, Stevens, Williams, and other voices of the "new." The dramatic rise of both Robinson and Frost after 1913 was not the result of a collective coming to good sense on the part of magazine editors, critics, contemporary poets, and other instruments of a repressive poetic discipline that had confined Robinson and Frost to speaking in a void. It is important to avoid sentimentality on this point. Strictly speaking, by Foucault's lights, Robinson and Frost were not liberated from incarceration by the modernist revolt; they were merely taken into new quarters of confinement, where under the authority of a different kind of repression their kinds of expression were granted the privilege of the poetic, even as other kinds were excluded and relegated to the status of the "old-fashioned."

6

Foucault has shown little interest in extrapolating from his philosophical outlook a model for the writing of literary history. It is clear, however, that such extrapolation would not violate the spirit of his historicism, and would usefully extend his theory into an area of literary scholarship now unfortunately relegated to the junkheap of traditionalist methodological naiveté. The text most open to extrapolation for harried literary historians is "Nietzsche, Genealogy, History," an essay which recapitulates Foucault's major assumptions and attacks while it makes a series of positive recommendations. Understood as "descent" *(Herkunft)* and "emergence" *(Entstehung),* and contrary to the desires of traditional history, genealogy is a rejection of continuity and the "metahistorical deployment of ideal significations and indefinite teleologies. It opposes itself to the search for 'origins' " *(Ursprungen).*[114] The Foucauldian genealogist, with Nietzsche, declares that there are no "immobile forms that precede the external world of accident and succession," that things have no "timeless and essential secret," no "essence." Genealogical anti-Platonism therefore "permits the discovery, under the unique aspect of a trait or a concept, of the myriad events through which—thanks to which, against which—they were formed."[115]

In the genealogical view, then, the discourse of the literary text need not be connected through a leap of historical imagination with some distant background of inert ideas which the traditional historian would claim it makes reference to. In the genealogical view the text *is* history because it is saturated in its smallest details by a complicated lineage, by a dynastic repression which provides a point of focus for the text's fundamental historical drama. Textuality for Nietzsche and Foucault may be defined as *history agonistes.* As such, Foucaldian textuality is at once burdened by its dynastic heritage *and* undecidable —not in the American Derridean sense of undecidability as *mise en abyme,* but in the more limited sense that the text's identity is rooted in an attempt to be unhistorical by annihilating both its antecedents and its constraining discursive formation. But since texts are traversed and marked by different genealogical forces and by different determinates of the "true" and the "poetic," texts are not all undecidable in the same way. Undecidability in Foucault's genealogical sense is a fact of historical struggle rather than a fact of transcendence of it.

If, as David Carroll has recently argued, the notion of the *epistēmē* which dominated *The Order of Things* is a disguised metaphysical term for the historical plenitude of textual significance that was desired by the methodologists of the history of ideas,[116] then the notion of "genealogy" in Foucault's recent work disrupts this plenitude by opening it to the changes of temporal process. The *epistēmē* is probably the weakest component of Foucault's earlier work, a reinstalling of the methodology of the history of ideas which enforces a monolithic coherence of writing, a determinism with no capacity to explain change, difference, resistance, or variation in historical discourse. The only change possible, in the theory of the *epistēmē*, is produced by cataclysmic discontinuity, a shattering of the *epistēmē* in force (and the institution of a new one) that can be accomplished only by a radically originating act of imagination. (Hence those necessary bedfellows of the nineteenth century, scientific naturalism and poetic idealism.) Genealogy is a subtler (resolutely dialectical) historicist strategy, an impure determinism which can account, at once, for the repressive force of the historical conditions of discourse (descent), and for a (continuous) *emergence* from those conditions of a newer (not new) formation of power.

The first order of business for the genealogist is the "dissociation of the self, its recognition and displacement as an empty synthesis, in liberating a profusion of lost events."[117] Foucault's phrasing recalls Miller's declaration that the concept of the literary period is better served by notions of heterogeneity than by those various ontological notions of substantial unity which underwrite the history of ideas in the mode of Lovejoy and all other efforts at "continuous history." To assert that the self is an "empty synthesis" is to echo a key point of decentering: that the self is without ontological foundation. But "synthesis" and "heterogeneity" should not be collapsed into the *aporia*—a notion which, in the hands of Miller, de Man, and Hartman, places the elements of synthesis into self-canceling opposition, and in so doing effectively converts history into a repetition of the same by dissipating the force of changing historical determinates. (Stevens, according to Miller, deconstructs the Emersonian bedrock self, but then, as his theory of the *aporia* demands that he admit, Emerson and Whitman had also deconstructed their own apparent faith in the self, and so look very much like Stevens after all; in this way the Yale Derrideans undermine the older Yale New-Critical habit of making historical distinctions at the expense of the so-called naiveté of the romantics. A worthy intention is achieved, but at the cost of wiping out historical differences altogether.) The self as synthesis is ontologically empty, but the consequence of this insight need not be abysmal, for historically the self is a full nexus of forces, Foucault is arguing, delimited by the *epistēmē* or archive of a particular epoch, and somewhat discontinuous as a synthesis with the syntheses of other epochs, though *as synthesis* it will surely contain among its constituents foreshadowings of future formations and traces of the lineage it has struggled to escape.

As the "equivalent of stock or descent," *Herkunft* is the "ancient affiliation to a group, sustained by the bonds of blood, tradition, or social class." In his attempt to analyze descent, the genealogist will not try to identify traits that are "the exclusive generic characteristics of an individual, a sentiment, or an idea. . . . rather, . . . [he] seeks the subtle, singular, and subindividual marks that might possibly intersect in them to form a network that is difficult to unravel."[118] What this means for the writing of literary history is that the historian will be loath to isolate giants like Milton for English poetry or Emerson for the American scene, who pour forth down through the centuries un-interrupted "streams" of "major" influence. Perhaps another way to put this is to say that the historian will be loath to substitute the para-digm of his literary education in "great writers of England and Amer-ica" for the processes of history itself; he will be at least willing to entertain the question of whether or not the foremost thing in the mind of a young Wordsworth or a young Frost is how to outdo Milton or Emerson. Milton or Emerson will be convenient names only for the focusing of convergences of force which no authorial will (including those of Milton or Emerson) can control or even hope to be conscious of. Awareness of the numerous subindividual marks imprinted on authors by an impressive discursive formation (as well as by a subtle and potentially life-denying lineage) will encourage the historian to cease looking in the distant past for a single heavyweight father-figure as the sole determinant of a given literary identity, will encourage him to start looking closer to home, at numerous forgotten contem-poraries whose sense of the poetic may or may not correspond with that of the emerging identity in question.

For example: it has been the habit, until very recently with the pub-lication of Bernard Duffey's *Poetry in America: Expression and Its Values in the Times of Bryant, Whitman, and Pound*, to isolate Emerson from contemporaries like Bryant, Whittier, Longfellow, Lowell, and Holmes whose poems more often than not have proved an embarrassment to twentieth-century critical sensibility. Whether it comes from Harold Bloom or traditional historians of American poetry like Hyatt Waggoner and Roy Harvey Pearce, the isolation of Emerson and an Adamic "tradition" (in Foucault's sense) running through Whitman, Stevens, Roethke, and Ginsburg produces a repeti-tious continuity which celebrates the individual authorial will ("tradi-tion and the individual talent") and which dissolves, in the process, the myriad, changing forces, poetic and otherwise, that shaped the identities of figures as culturally separated as Emerson and Roethke. In different ways the methods of Bloom, Pearce, and Waggoner have the effect of rarefying the densities of discourse. The habit of historians of Ameri-can writing is to distinguish a single defining theme (the Adamic, the romance, the pastoral, the symbolic, the world elsewhere); this strategy tends to result in a forcing of the widely dispersed events of our literary history into a single container. Foucault's method, on the other hand, would dissolve the author or theme back into the archive, or system of rules, which allowed it to function poetically. Practically speaking, such an approach would be clearly visible in a table of contents. The reader will no longer see a list of authors (as in Bloom and Pearce), but a list of relations which bring so-called minor voices together with major ones (as in Duffey). The result of such a reorientation of historical method would be an emphasis on both lineage and differences and a perception that the literary self as synthesis "is an unstable assemblage of faults, fissures, and heterogeneous layers"; such a perspective would view the literary self as the product of the "hazardous play of dominations"—some of them not at all "literary." To conclude this too hasty exposition of *Herkunft*: "The search for descent is not the erecting of foundations: on the contrary, it disturbs what was previously considered immobile; it fragments what was thought unified; it shows the heterogeneity of what was imagined consistent with itself."[119]

A second Nietzschean term that Foucault deploys with rich methodological significance is *Entstehung*, or emergence, "the moment of arising." "As it is wrong to search for descent in an uninterrupted continuity, we should avoid thinking of emergence as the final term of historical development."[120] If *Herkunft* emphasizes the moment of assured power, when, as a system of subjections, a discursive formation seems firmly in place, then in the analysis of *Entstehung* what is studied is the moment of the seizure of power, the moment of change itself (about which it has been written that Foucault has no theory). "Emergence is . . . the entry of forces, it is their eruption, the leap from the wings to center stage, each in its youthful strength. . . . No one is responsible for an emergence; no one can glory in it."[121] The genealogical study of emergence will neither credit a single figure for a revolution, nor will it sentimentalize revolution as the creation of a free space for expression. (Sloganeering writers of manifestos for the "new" who speak of liberation must be seen, in this light, as making purely strategic contributions.) Humanity "installs each of its violences in a system of rules," writes Foucault, "and then proceeds from domination to domination." Quoting Nietzsche, he describes emergence as " 'an extended battle against conditions which are essentially and constantly unfavorable.' "[122]

The analogy is this: The making of modernist poetic revolution involved an appropriation of the reigning sense of the poetic, and its system of rules, by subtly connected bodies of poets, academicians, journalists, publishers, and magazine editors, who wrote manifestos, "new" theories of poetry, disquisitions on the degeneracy of the times, and took over centers of communications, all for the purpose of returning poetry to truth and reality. Here is Foucault's general description of emergence:

> Rules are empty in themselves and unfinalized; they are impersonal and can be bent to any purpose. The successes of history belong to those who are capable of seizing these rules, to replace those who had used them, to disguise themselves so as to pervert them, invert their meaning, and redirect them against those who had initially imposed them; controlling this complex mechanism, they will make it function so as to overcome the rulers through their own rules.[123]

Whereas traditional history "aims at dissolving the singular event" into an "ideal continuity," what Foucault calls "effective history" wants to preserve discontinuity, eruption, the moment of emergence, and to seek the point of "the reversal of a relationship of forces, the usurpation of power, the appropriation of a vocabulary turned against those who had once used it. . . ."[124] Taking note of the images of aggression, discharge of power, general activism, willfulness, self-promotion, and self-aggrandizement suggested by Foucault's verbs, we are prepared to read Bernard Duffey's description of the eruption of the avant-garde in early twentieth-century American poetic history:

> Poet and poetry in the avant-garde would seek to define themselves outside the common experience and above it in an astonishing ramification of inquiry, manifesto, and publicity. The activity quickly shaped itself into waves that in bulk and complexity were unprecedented in American poetry. There would be books on the age and its cultural problems, like Brooks's and Mencken's; a proliferation of poets' essays explaining and justifying their allegiance, the capturing of reviewers' columns, the founding and multiplying of poetry magazines, the creation of critical journals, the carrying of discussion into a sophisticated and urbane journalism itself new to American publishing and the infiltrating of established publishing houses, along with the founding of new ventures.[125]

To the analysis of descent and emergence a revisionist historian needs to add, at a minimum, a third analysis, that of discursive coexistences, if he would escape the formalism of a traditional history-writing which assents (again the examples of Bloom and Pearce come to mind) to the rarefying and exclusionary boundary-drawing of conventional disci-

plines. The revisionist historian in Foucault's model would have to define the task of *literary* history as a fundamental oxymoron. The idea
of a literary history, or of an American literature, is a contradiction that
does not reveal itself as such unless we understand that the archive,
and the thick reality of discourse that it authorizes, refuses disciplinary
isolations of discourse and does not permit it to be enclosed within na-
tional boundaries (the term "America," for example, since it applies to
most of the Western Hemisphere, is not owned by the United States;
the widespread practice of using "America" and the "United States" as
synonymous terms tells a story that Foucault would recognize instantly). So our hypothetical historian of American poetry will need to
take stock of the poetic writing of other nations at some stage, and he
will need to pinpoint areas of discursive intersection where literary,
philosophical, scientific, and religious modes of writing find a point of
contact.

In forsaking the traditional terms for describing literary forms,
Duffey once again suggests a handy strategy for getting at discursive
concurrences. Whereas formal literary terms like "lyric" and "epic"
tend to sustain disciplinary coherence and autonomy, his multifaceted
substitutions ("homily," "hymn," "analogy," "prospect," "occasion,"
and "dialectic" are examples), because they are allowed to play major
definitional roles, effectively push literary discourse back under the
dominating aegis of the archive. Terms like "homily," "analogy," and
"occasion" help thicken what has been thinned by disciplinary prohibi-
tions. These terms suggest the violence that Foucault's historical *a priori*
does to the traditional sense of "discipline": "Different *oeuvres*, dispersed books, the whole mass of texts that belong to a single discursive
formation—and so many authors who know and do not know one another, criticize one another, invalidate one another, pillage one another,
meet without knowing it and obstinately intersect their unique discourses in a web of which they are not the masters, of which they cannot see the whole. . . ."[126] Duffey's displacement of conventional literary
terminology demonstrates how the historical *a priori* governing early
nineteenth-century poetry (he calls this confluence of poetic, theological, and political forces of determination "the coherence," a term that
will recall the double meaning of "discipline" in Foucault) works on
highly specified levels of style (down to image and metaphor) in order
to shape the form and texture of poetic statement. Moreover, even as
Foucault suggests that any particular archive will set the conditions not
only for statements that fall within it but for those that would transform
it altogether, so Duffey shows that Poe's expression is conditioned, as a
rejection of coherence, by the very rules of coherence. Reading Foucault

and Duffey we acquire a more precise sense than we have ever enjoyed of what it means for a modernist critic like Eliot to tell us that Poe is a forerunner of the symbolist movement, and perhaps even a more precise sense of what it means for a writer, in emotional and psychic costs, to be "ahead of his time."

The final trait of effective history, and the most problematic of the tasks before the revisionist historian, "is the affirmation of knowledge as perspective."[127] Moving directly out of Nietzsche's conception of the will to power, Foucault, by denying that historical commentary can be "universal mediation," exposes for what it is "the fiction of a universal geometry," the desire of the interpreter "to adopt a faceless anonymity."[128] "Historians take unusual pains to erase the elements in their work which reveal their grounding in a particular time and place, their preferences in a controversy—the unavoidable obstacles of their passion." "This demagogy, of course, must be masked. It must hide its singular malice under the cloak of universals. As the demagogue is obliged to invoke truth, laws of essences, and eternal necessity, the historian must invoke objectivity, the accuracy of facts, and the permanence of the past." "In appearance, or rather, according to the mask it bears, historical consciousness is neutral, devoid of passions, and committed solely to the truth."[129] The direction of Foucault's statement, with its wicked attendant ironies, is unmistakable. He has made a potentially dangerous alliance with those theorists of hermeneutical and structuralist traditions who, by assuming the Kantian "critical" position and then pushing it to an unhappy extreme, manage to subvert the notions of cognition and historical discovery so thoroughly that the specter of solipsism is resurrected once again. All we can ever hope to know is ourselves, and even to say that much in this perspective is to be an optimist: at worst our personal selves; at best the intersubjective dimension of selfhood established by professional norms of interpretive competence (as Culler argues), or the historicized self of "tradition" established in the arguments of Heidegger and Gadamer. And as if these Nietzschean nightmares were not bad enough, Foucault tells us in *The Archaeology* that "it is not possible for us to describe our own archive, since it is from within these rules that we speak, since it is that which gives to what we can say . . . its modes of appearance, its forms of existence and coexistence, its system of accumulation, historicity, and disappearance." Our own archive cannot be described, and yet "in its presence it is unavoidable."[130] It is no mystery why our leading Marxist theoretician, Fredric Jameson, has been decidedly cool to Foucault; no wonder why some have thought anarchism to be the deep message of his philosophy of history.

To give up on the problem at this point would be to confirm the suspicions in traditionalist quarters that Nietzsche is being used by Foucault, and other contemporary French and French-influenced critics, to strengthen an unadmirable urge toward pure subjectivism. But there is no way to ignore the practice of Foucault. *Madness and Civilization*, *The Order of Things*, *The Birth of the Clinic*, and *Discipline and Punish* are models of historical research and detail, and they are offered to us as knowledge, as historical discoveries, and not as the product of a hermeneutical revel danced out on one of those 1001 nights of analysis. Of course there is *perspective* aplenty in these books, and no one who reads them can possibly miss the passion and cold fury, the involvement of Foucault himself that drives the writing of at least three of these texts. The fact that the historian's consciousness is itself historicized is for Foucault, however, no bar to historical study, but its very condition.

So I choose to set aside the inhibiting (and I think unsubtle) statement from *The Archaeology* that I have just quoted, and to emphasize this from the essay on Nietzsche: "But if it [the historical consciousness itself] examines itself and if, more generally, it interrogates the various forms of scientific consciousness in its history, it finds that all these forms and transformations are aspects of the will to knowledge. . . ."[131] In so many words Foucault appears to be telling us here that even though historical cognition is itself a mediated and historicized process, and history-writing fundamentally an interchange between the past and the ineradicable presentness of a consciousness at some level discontinuous with what it would know, even blind, to a certain extent, to its own disposition, nevertheless we are not doomed to the pits of subjectivism. The historical consciousness, the will to knowledge itself, though it can never be neutralized, is itself open to historical exploration and at least partial definition. If we can admit to this, we will implicitly grant two points: (1) a perfectly objective interpretation is possible only if the interpreter is a transcendental being—that is, if he is not human; and (2) the unavoidable given of all cognitive processes—that knowledge, however we may define it, is received through a situated human consciousness that has spatiotemporal location, idiosyncratic colorations, and philosophical and sociopolitical prejudices—this is in itself no excuse to give up the labors of research or the rigors of historical self-examination and yield to the fashionable and casual historical despair of contemporary criticism. The much-touted discovery by hermeneutics and structuralism, that interpretation is problematic, and in some essential way a creative act, not a value-neutral description, must no longer be used as an excuse to abandon historical exploration (and treat all the objects of consciousness as if they were replications of one another, or, even worse, make believe that there are no objects for consciousness to mediate) and give up altogether the gathering of data and documents. What "madness" means in Foucault's book is surely in part an expression of his will to knowledge. But would anyone care to argue that it was Foucault, in 1656, who wrote the enabling charter of the Hôpital Général? Long ago we learned not to yield to the lure of naive realism. It may be that the first order of critical business before us in the 1980s is to turn off the stereophonic Sirens of naive idealism. But how is this to be done?

Perhaps it is necessary to return to Derrida and Foucault, not as philosophical antagonists, as in Said's recent conception of them, but as cooperative philosophical explorers who presume to speak with epistemic authority about the subjects they investigate. "Joy," "freedom," and "activity" (and the naive politics of liberation that generates them) are not the values that Derrida and Foucault espouse. The question is, what is the source of their authority, and the one answer that both rule out is a historical consciousness that is "neutral, devoid of passions, and committed solely to the truth." What Derrida and Foucault have done, in fact, is to uncover (their metaphor of laying bare is instructive) the presiding logocentric urges, rules, and oppositions which have guided the production of meaning from Plato to the present day. What they have done, to put it another way, is to bare the structure of historical consciousness in the West, not from the privileged point of self-present presence, which would enable them to take its objective measure, but from inside, as it were, as that structure restrains their own writing. The guiding methodological fiction (or illusion) which enables them to do their work is one that tells them that they are at the end of an era: in the right place for taking the long view, for summing up, for listing debits and credits, for casting out the old and welcoming in the new, a time and place for self-renewal. This pragmatic fiction tells them, in so many words, that they have had the luck to appear just at that point when the great systems of metaphysics that have been in operation since Plato seem to have reached a point of exhaustion. From their place "in between" the closure of metaphysics and an undecidable future (what Derrida means by our "era"),[132] they are necessarily forced from their understanding of history into deconstructive readings powerfully motivated by their historically predicated alienation from the metaphysics of presence.

The readings of Derrida and Foucault are correct, then, not in some absolute sense, since they are powerless to totally expunge logocentric passion from their own discourse, but because they have acquired in their struggle with history a more intimate and self-conscious grasp of the logocentric structures of constraint than have any of the thinkers of their philosophical heritage. Of course (one would hope this goes without saying) even more lucid readings of the history of Western thought may well be produced in the future. There will be further revisions. And their value will rise or fall not because a new theorist will have found a way to do objective interpretation, as Hirsch would have it, nor because he will fulfill the Marxist confidence of Antonio Gramsci that *all* the traces of history that mark the interpreter can be inventoried,[133] but because our hypothetical theorist's revised reading will necessarily work through what Derrida and Foucault have done, and will have subjected their texts to deconstruction.

Despite what he says about "free-play" in the *Grammatology* (that it destroys a metaphysics of presence), Derrida more typically emphasizes that deconstruction is not free-playing, joyful destruction but a dismantling that enables a more intimate kind of knowing. So it is not a matter of throwing away the Western tradition and its reasonable orders, since that tradition and its reason is just about all that we have, and are likely to have. The difficulty with Foucault's phrasing of the historicist's problem of interpretation is that it makes it appear that individual historians are embroiled in local and very limited controversies which constitute their understanding and thereby force them into subjective irrelevance. Derrida's phrasing of the problem is preferable: we are constituted most fundamentally not by local prejudices (which can be shed) but by an unavoidable logocentric structure, the universal constraint of Western thought (roughly translated in Foucault as the structure of exclusion). "The unsurpassable, unique, and imperial grandeur of the order of reason, that which makes it not just another actual order or structure (a determined historical structure, one structure among other possible ones) is that one cannot speak out against it except by being for it, that one can protest it only from within it. . . ."[134] It is a matter of questioning this order from within the order itself; it is a matter of creating an internal disturbance;[135] it is a matter, then, of strategic questioning of reason by reason, of the metaphysical tradition with the very tools that that tradition has given us (there being no other to work with). In other words, there will be no welcoming in of the new, no self-renewal in the naive sense of those terms, no replacement of the tradition. The liberated "openness of thought" which Hartman sees represented by Derrida tells us something about Hartman's desire, and his mode of appropriation, but little about Derrida. Our historical guilt cannot be redeemed because in some ineradicable ways we will continue to commit the crime. Since the revolution against Western metaphysics and the myriad discourses that it supports (most of which would not be ordinarily characterized as metaphysical) can only be made from within traditional metaphysics, it is not a question of releasing oneself into an unrepressive new order (there are none), but of generating a writing that exceeds, by questioning them, the values most dear to the tradition. What Foucault calls "effective history," then, is not a new historicism, but the old one disturbed, questioned, its duplicities and its techniques illuminated. Our contemporary historicity may perhaps be no more, or less, than the deconstructive project in its strangely divided identity: decadent and phlegmatic, and yet bravely energetic and full of hope; paralytic and corrosively self-ironic, and yet awesomely productive and full of assurance.

Part Two

The American Scene: Four Exemplary Careers

Six

If we share Arnold's loss of faith, we can go either of two ways: we can view poetry as a human triumph made out of our darkness, as the creation of verbal meaning in a blank universe to serve as a visionary substitute for a defunct religion; or we can—in our negation—extend our faithlessness, the blankness of our universe, to our poetry. . . . Stubbornly humanistic as I am, I must choose that first alternative: I want to remain responsive to the promise of the filled and centered word, a signifier replete with an inseparable signified which it has created within itself.
Murray Krieger, "Literature vs. Écriture"

more than most theorists, I have worked in accordance with what counter-positions (to mine) in the history of theory and in the work of my contemporaries have forced me to take account of, but to co-opt them, to incorporate them without undoing my own construct, (if I may be dangerously candid) to see how much of them I could swallow without giving myself indigestion.
Murray Krieger, "Theories about Theories about Theory of Criticism"

—Is thinking impossible without arbitrary signs? &—how far is the word "arbitrary" a misnomer? Are not words etc part & germinations of the Plant? And what is the Law of their Growth?—In something of this order I would endeavor to destroy the old antithesis of Words & Things, elevating, as it were, words into Things, & living Things too.
Coleridge, Collected Letters of Samuel Taylor Coleridge

Murray Krieger's Last Romanticism

Not long after the publication of his first book, *The New Apologists for Poetry*, in 1956, Murray Krieger became recognized as a pioneering figure in the United States for the discipline called literary theory, which our academic establishment had hitherto always relegated, at its most generous, to fringe status. Thanks in no insignificant part to a series of books that he published after *The New Apologists* (*The Tragic Vision*, 1960; *A Window to Criticism*, 1964; *The Play and Place of Criticism*, 1967; *The Classic Vision*, 1971; and *Theory of Criticism*, 1976), the discipline of theory has almost become a standard component in the graduate training of literary scholars. Three professional honors awarded to Krieger coincide with the burgeoning prestige of theoretical study in this country: in 1963, the University of Iowa gave him a chair in literary criticism—the first of its kind in the United States; in 1974, he was made a University Professor for the nine campuses of the University of California; and in 1975 he founded at California's Irvine campus the well-known School of Criticism and Theory. Given his long-standing preoccupation with the traditional history of his discipline and its contemporary offshoots and negations, Krieger's career becomes in a number of important ways a miniature history of what has happened theoretically in the contemporary scene.

Since Krieger himself has taken considerable pains in *The New Apologists for Poetry* to demonstrate the ambiguity of T. E. Hulme's vigorous antiromanticism, and since Hulme has always figured as a prime source of his theoretical perspectives, Krieger will not be surprised by the title of this overview of his work. He might, however, be dismayed by the attribution of a romanticism that is not only unambiguous but also the desperate finish of a theoretical tradition opened by Kant, Coleridge, and company. By calling Krieger's romanticism unambiguous I do not mean to imply that it is unqualified or that it is naively full of hope. It makes no "transcendentalist" claims (as the Coleridges and Shelleys understood the word); it is not "visionary" in the sense intended by older or more recent scholars of romanticism; it has only the most peripheral interest in nature. His is the romanticism, rather, of a mid-twentieth-century urban intellectual much shaped by attitudes that may be loosely gathered under the rubric of existentialism, especially as it was defined by William Barrett's *Irrational Man*; hovering around the edges of everything Krieger writes—sometimes sitting at the very center of his work—we sense the decisive influence of post–World War II reflections on the horror. It is a romanticism substantially, though not totally, indebted to the goals that the New Critics appeared to be pursuing but never reached. These and other qualifications aside, Krieger's romanticism is continuous with its early-nineteenth-century sources and has remained steady in its thrust—this despite the anxiety that the position appears to have caused and continues to cause him.

So that we may gain a point of entry into Krieger's poetics let me simplify complicated issues in romanticism by segregating threads within nineteenth-century thought which are often intimately entangled and even philosophically interdependent. The ancient ontological puzzle of the relationship of the particular to the universal can serve as a way of coming at a problem that troubled deeply a number of romantic poets. Is the poet, in Emerson's lucid and hopeful phrasing, a "representative man" who sums up us all, a complete man among partial men whose expressive discourse tells us who we really are and helps us to transcend our isolating particularity by showing us the community of our human being? The great writer, Emerson tells us, is like, or ought to be like (the imperative is always implied) an Andean volcanic mountain, "a Chimborazo under the line, running up from a torrid base through all the climates of the globe, with belts of the herbage of every latitude on its high and mottled sides. . . ."[1]

But if the Chimborazo is a metaphor for the great expressive hope of the romantics, then their worst fears are carried by metaphors of isolation, by images of the poet as a "solitary singer" (to lift a phrase from Whitman's tragic mood). These fears are realized by an irredeemably alienated figure who identifies his poetic power with his isolation, and who can even celebrate his isolation as the source of his power. This kind of poet prizes and cultivates the particularized subjectivity that the Wordsworths, Emersons, and Schopenhauers scorned as "mean," "trivial," and destructive of human community. This isolated creature, so pleased with its own isolation, must be judged from the Emersonian perspective as the demonic ideal of later-nineteenth-century symbolists and aesthetes. Here is Mallarmé on the point: "We are now witnessing a spectacle . . . which is truly extraordinary, unique in the history of poetry: every poet is going off by himself with his own flute and playing the song he pleases."[2] Mallarmé thought he could explain this artistic situation with a sociological observation that those unlikely allies of the symbolists, Marx and his inheritors, would commonly make: "the essential and undeniable point is this: that in a society without stability, without unity, there can be no stable or definitive art. From that incompletely organized society—which also explains the restlessness of certain minds—the unexplained need for individuality was born. The literary manifestations of today are a direct reflection of that need."[3]

Whether or not Mallarmé's Marxist insight on the source of alienation is a sufficient and necessary explanation, poets and theorists, both before and after Mallarmé, but increasingly after him, have conceived themselves as isolated rather than integrated, as islands unto themselves, rather than as parts of the mainland. And this conception of the poetic character, more than any other single factor in critical history since the romantics, has determined the course of what is called "modernist" thinking about the nature and function of poetry. From the very beginning of his career as a literary theorist, with the publication in 1952 of *The Problems of Aesthetics*, the anthology he co-edited with his mentor Eliseo Vivas, to the present, Krieger has been a self-conscious, agonized, and, in part, an unwilling connoisseur of postsymbolist aesthetic isolationism, and thus a superb representative of the neo-Coleridgean mainstream of modern theoretical criticism.

1

The "artist in isolation" is often located, thanks to Frank Kermode, as a post-Mallarmean species flourishing luridly in the gardens of *fin-de-siècle* aestheticism. But the prototype for this exotic creature can be found everywhere earlier in the nineteenth century, in those numerous self-portraits of artists who, even while they suffer the painful alienation of their difference from other human beings, receive the special dispensations of such difference by being granted (at least this is the common rationalization of their unhappiness) a unique vision of the truth. To put things that way, roughly in Kermode's terms, is probably enough to remind us of the alienated modes of thought at the theoretical base of romanticism. From the outset, and in powerful conflict with the more integrational forces in romantic aesthetics (the poet is a "man speaking to men"), we hear the voices of isolation which declare the poet set off from all others by the dubious gift of an unusually intense, unusually fine sensibility. Krieger's tactic in *Theory of Criticism* is representative of this critical tradition. After conceding that there are all sorts of forces at work to forge the writer's identity into communal shape ("he brings with him . . . whatever his society and its history have made of him, including his language and the peculiar literary heritage that his culture has provided to shape his writing habits"), Krieger yet insists that the task of the writer who would be authentic is to distance himself from all that is common in order "to make what comes out [of the creative process] essentially different, a sovereign object independent of its genesis."[4]

There never has been any poverty of theoretical texts in the last century and three-quarters to explain the alienated situation of the writer. The irony of many of these texts is that they attempt to demonstrate their theories not so much by the power of their arguments, but by the posture of their various rhetorics. We have heard over and over again, and in many different critical idioms, how symbol must be set against allegory; the secondary imagination against the primary; intuition and feeling against reason and logic; poetry against science; the aesthetic realm against the moral and the cognitive; the self-consciously fictive against the naively referential—and, in Krieger's post–New-Critical idiom, the artist against the nonartist, poetic discourse against ordinary discourse, aesthetic values against all other kinds of values. Kant (that tripartist) aside, a respectable generalization about romanticism would emphasize the obsessive dualism of its way of looking at the world.

For all of its demystifying and democratic predispositions toward matters social and aesthetic, at the center of romantic thought there is also (as Harold Bloom has not yet tired of telling us) a powerful elitism. This elitism, put forward in the guises of creative genius and

various other ideals of originality, would claim that artistic actvity—
by definition something that artists alone may engage in—is the most
deeply humanizing activity; the difficulty is that "we," mankind at
large, we nonartists, are by this reckoning excluded from the community of the most human sorts of beings. (Thus do the poets and
their defenders take revenge upon the practical, "insensitive," and
technical-minded society that excludes them.) Just what particular
mix of literary, philosophical, social, and political ingredients brought
this aesthetic theory into being in critical and literary history since
about 1790 or so has been illuminated by the controversies of recent
decades. What needs exploration is the extent to which Krieger's neo–
New-Critical poetics, what he has called "contextualism,"* has remained a prisoner to the kinds of thinking and terminology that can
be traced to romantic isolationism, and, beyond Krieger, the extent to
which the puzzles, quandaries, and dead ends of contemporary American theory are indebted to this kind of thought.

Without reducing Krieger's twenty-five odd years of activity as a
critical theorist to his earliest work in the prefaces of the anthology of
1952, with hindsight we can see in evidence there, in his (and Vivas's)
very conception of the basic problems of aesthetics, the assumption
of post-Kantian isolationist thought. Thus the important consideration in the definition of art is not the traditional one of art's relationship to other human activities and the world of nature, but—a point
taken too much for granted by too many theorists since Kant—the
ways in which art is awesomely independent of nature and other "non-
artistic" human processes. When Krieger turns to the mental processes
which produce a work of art, his speculation is directed toward the
ways "in which the mental activities of the artist are the same as, or
different from, those of the non-artist."[5] His focus is on difference,
and the difference is said to lie in the literally creative act performed
by the artist, by which it can be claimed (without declaring the poet
a God who can work *ex nihilo*) that in a significant way the artist brings
something new into the world which cannot be reduced to an object
of imitation, a moral exemplum, etc. When the created work happens
to be literary, the abiding question is always: how is the discourse
of the literary work different in kind from "ordinary discourse" (a

---

* Neither the dictionary meaning of "context," nor the philosophical sense
of the term given to it by Stephen Pepper, are Krieger's meanings. "Contextualism" as a poetics would seal off the poem from nonpoetic "contexts"; the
proper "context" for anything *in* the poem, in Krieger's argument, is only
the poem itself.

term which generally functions in Krieger's writing as an umbrella covering pretty much everything repugnant to romantics). When Krieger and Vivas pose the problem of the function of art, they make it clear that they prefer the view that art can be of special value to society if, and only if, we see it functioning *sui generis*, to please itself, so to speak. And, predictably, after setting out the problems of aesthetics in this fashion, we find Krieger leaning decidedly toward Vivas's neo-Kantian definition of the aesthetic experience which, to make a long and brilliant tale very short, concludes in favor of truth in labeling: when Vivas calls an experience "aesthetic" he is prepared to distinguish it from the moral, the cognitive, and the hedonic as an experience within which we find ourselves with all of our normal "interests" terminated, all self-consciousness sloughed off, intransitively enclosed in "rapt attention."

So there we have it: in an act of consciousness "unique" to the artist, an art object is "created" which, given our proper attention to it, will afford us a "unique" kind of human experience. Through this experience, somehow, we are to return—finally Krieger wants to break out of all the isolationist traps he has set for himself—to the human world somehow specially endowed, epistemologically freshened by an aesthetic experience, to perceive in a "unique" way, to enjoy "the unique view of the world which can come with the purely poetic experience."[6] Before finessing the fragmentation and alienation of his own society by telling us that now it is possible, as it was not before, to make "nice theoretical distinctions among the modes of human activity," he grants—with the nostalgia typical of a certain kind of modern temperament—the essential point: the "integrated quality" he finds in classical and medieval cultures is probably the "mark of the greatness" (I choose to understand "greatness" here as "health") of those ages.[7]

Krieger's insistence on the uniqueness of the various factors in the artistic process ("unique" is a favorite term, recurring frequently through his entire corpus) recalls the embattled and defensive (and counteroffensive) posture of humanists and artists, and particularly of their apologists, vis-à-vis the privileged status enjoyed for about two centuries now by those enemies of the poets whose roll need not be called here. It is probably enough to remember the concept "scientism," and all of its angry metaphorical overtones. If it is not clear to us from the table of contents in *The New Apologists for Poetry* who the enemy is—poetry and science are opposed in every category—it is made clear very early in the book. We learn why theory in the neo-Coleridgean mode has assumed the apologetic stance: "I am especially concerned with those of the 'New Critics' who are trying to answer the need, forced on them by historical pressures, to justify poetry by securing for it a unique function for which modern scientism cannot find a surrogate. . . ."[8] And it is not only the new apologists, Cleanth Brooks and others, but *their* apologist who feels these historical pressures to "secure" a unique function for poetry, to prove even in "these positivist-ridden days,"[9] that the arts, their makers, teachers, and theorists are essential to the community that would be fully human. And so, somewhat sadly, and with his back pressed to the wall by the latest enemies from the camp of ordinary language philosophy, he writes: "It may well be, as some will say, that all these difficulties I have dreamt up are really semantic confusions which would fade with a proper clarification of the terms I use."[10] The problems do not fade, whatever the terms; though, as I shall argue, perhaps Krieger's particular terms, and the mode of approach that his critical presuppositions seem to enforce, make for more difficulties than they resolve. The cultural situation for the New Critics and for Krieger appears not to have changed much from the situation that Yeats and Wilde faced at the turn of the century. And maybe Yeats, who called himself a last romantic, showed the saddest wisdom of all last romantics when, complaining about the spectacular rise and prestige of science in his time, he wrote that there were "people and things we should never have heard of."[11]

One of the most philosophically self-conscious of contemporary critics, Krieger has over the years steadily questioned and qualified his basic commitment to the Kantian point of departure until, in *Theory of Criticism*, he has seemed (by intention) to drain the position of all of its theoretical vigor. He is apparently no longer willing to compartmentalize the aesthetic as an experience cleanly distinct from all other experiences and sufficient unto itself. In fact, he seems no longer to believe in aesthetic experiences, and fears that all talk of them will lead to the reification of what he now believes to be purely verbal and hypothetical in nature. I say "seems" and "apparently" because I believe he has it both ways: his most recent work, while it gingerly distances itself from the philosophical confidence of *The New Apologists for Poetry*, and approaches major philosophical issues with the skepticism and tentativeness demanded by the "critical" attitude, yet manages to save for theory all that his earlier Kantianism had promised:

> At the theoretical level we can ask what would be distinctively poetic about a response that would justify its

being so characterized. . . . we can ask this theoretically
even if we are convinced that all our actual responses to
experiences are hopelessly mixed and confounded, too much
so for us to make a claim about pure "types" of response,
whether cognitive, moral, or aesthetic (to use the Kantian
triad). There are heuristic purposes . . . that require us to
define what a purely poetic response would be, apart from
the muddy psychological facts that surround and invest
the embarrassing, blurred realities of our poetic experiences.
I grant that, in the actual flow of our experiencing, what
we single out as "experiences" differ from one another only
in degree; but I am proposing that we consider defining
an experience that would differ from others in kind.[12]

Having made this anti-Kantian disclaimer (shades of John Dewey),
Krieger feels free to "go on to define the use of language—the poetic—
that would differ from other uses of language in kind, not merely in
degree, even if we actually experience only different degrees of language usage."[13] The stance that can be discerned in this passage is
typical of Krieger's later work and is an excellent measure of continuity and change since his earliest writings on theory. The placing
of aesthetic experience as a heuristic postulate of theory—a convenience
of philosophical gamesmanship which is not to be confused with what
he calls the "actual flow of our experiencing"—pretty much encapsulates Krieger's change; his later criticism, in comparison to the
epistemological robustness of The Tragic Vision and A Window to
Criticism, is a deliberately diminished thing.

Theory of Criticism, like all of his works, reflects both directly, and
in the implications of its rhetoric, his most powerful competitors in the
contemporary critical scene. Lately Krieger's rhetoric has been telling
us that he has come to respect and grant the claims of the poststructuralists in France and America—Barthes, Derrida, de Man, and their
followers—who have made words like "mystify," "mythify," "valorize," and "reify" current in our vocabulary. Such words, important
these days to Krieger, all tell the same story: we are trapped in the
prison-house of language; we have access to no substance beyond
language but only to words in their differential and intrasystemic relations to one another. We have no right, after such assumptions, to
say anything except that all utterances are fictions which never break
out of their fictionality. The only exceptions are the most sophisticated
utterances, which Paul de Man honors with the name "literary." These
kinds of fictions, de Man tells us in the flush of his discovery (ignoring
the fact that Wallace Stevens had been hammering the point home

for a good forty years) achieve their value for the *cognoscenti* of literary theory by recognizing, self-consciously, that they are fictions, that they name nothing but their own fictionality, which is to say their linguistic being—or, from the point of view of traditional ontology, their nothingness. So when Krieger says "aesthetic experience," in his late work, or "unique kind of language," or "organic unity," he intends for us to understand that he is not pretending to name some objective realities but only projecting the desires of the romantic critical imagination— in other words, that "myth of" or "fiction of" or some equivalent is to precede such phrases. And yet, paradoxically, he goes on to write a book on self-consciously mythological assumptions that run counter to the nature of actual human experience, which is said to "flow," to be "muddied" and "blurred"—and these latter are judgments about experience which are not put forth as fictions but as the truth about the way things really are with the "real" world.

One is permitted to ask, thanks to Krieger's candor, why anyone should want to write a book on the theory of criticism whose major theses are grounded on what the writer admits to be intellectual fabrications and not on what he believes to be the truth (the "actual flow of our experiencing")? If it is true that our actual experiences are blurred into one another (note how he cannot bring himself to say "integrated with"), then it is the obligation of the theorist to take into account the mixed quality of experience itself which is said to be real, and not to succumb to the temptation of entertaining us with the elegant illusions of distinction formulated by his critical intelligence. Is it not urgent to grasp what one believes to be the actual interconnections in human experience and refuse to detain oneself by meditating on admittedly fictional entities? Apparently the answer to these questions is "no" when the fictions buttress our isolationist tendencies. For all of its philosophical moderation and caution, for all the distance he has seemed to travel from the Kantian confidences of *The Problems of Aesthetics* and *The New Apologists for Poetry*, Krieger remains in *Theory of Criticism* the romantic isolationist, more embattled (for having to meet the challenges of Derrida et al.), but still the isolationist, who characterizes the continuity of one experience with another as an "embarrassment," with differences between them only a matter of degree.

2

Krieger has always desired that his books be regarded as constituents of a unified corpus; with hindsight we have no difficulty locating principles of coherence that have been steadily emerging for over two decades. The dualistic habits of a romantic mind are in clear evidence from *The New Apologists* onward. In his tactic of establishing double vision (setting the ordinary universe of stock perception in opposition to a rare world that we glimpse through poetry), he makes a fundamental alliance with idealist tradition; Coleridge's two imaginations lurk in the background as a master dualism of postromantic English and American critical history. Each mode of vision is in turn carried and in some ways created by a mode of discourse: either the distinctively poetic kind of language, the organicist ideal of romantic criticism, or "ordinary discourse," a broad term which lumps together everything except the language of poetry. Each mode of vision and discourse reveals a distinct level of reality. Krieger agrees with T. E. Hulme's romantic attribution to the poet of a power of special vision which allows him to break through to the world "as it really is behind the veil that hides it from most of us."[14] The ontological thrust of Krieger's language here and elsewhere must not be ignored: what the poet shows us is not a fiction in the sense that Nietzsche, Stevens, and their recent students have defined that term; the poet makes real discoveries of the hard truth in the here and now—he pierces the veil of stock perception, imposed genera, fraudulent universals. In Krieger's early work it is these latter things which ought to be labeled fictions, since they are cut off from the actualities of being.

So in the sense that the poet's imagination, as our "most significantly cognitive power," is "revelatory of the real,"[15] Krieger's poet is a not-so-distant descendant of Coleridge's poet of secondary imagination, with the important exception that what Krieger's poet reveals, the knowledge he delivers to us, is nothing like what was promised in the transcendentalism of Coleridge's Germanic theorizing. Krieger's poet, like Coleridge's, strips the film of familiarity from our world (his discourse is a "making strange," in the idiom of Russian formalism), not in order to reveal the transcendent universal shining through the particularities of natural fact, but in order to show us the particular in all of its naked and intransigent particularity, freed from the humanly imposed universal invented for the needs of practical life and all action in the world. Along with that of many of his generation, Krieger's existentialism, founded upon the death of God, entails the death of all universals as real structures of being and as principles of cognition. His poet opens up for us the universe of a desolate and forbidding nominalism. The basic claim and motivating force of the earlier work, from *The New Apologists* to the collection *The Play and*

Place of Criticism, is that without poetry we are bound to an inauthentic existence, blind to the fundamental epistemological and ethical situation of life at the existential level, where all binding universals have been forever banished.

All disclaimers in his later books to the contrary notwithstanding, Krieger's early and middle work offers a resolutely cognitive apology for poetry via an existential aestheticism. And more: the special kind of knowledge that poetry is said to bear is not only different from other kinds of knowledge, it is better—by far. Schelling, in his Platonic reversal, thought that it was the poet, not the philosopher, whose mode of perception enabled him to penetrate the transcendent mysteries of being. Likewise Krieger, in a remarkable parallel, asserts that it is the existential vision of the poet, not the discourse of existentialist philosophers, which reveals existence in its pulsing immediacy and *quidditas.*[16] The language of contemporary structuralists is appropriate here: Krieger and the romanticism that he extends confer an elite status upon the alienated, outcast poet. (After such isolation, what recompense!) Whether social and economic factors force an isolation upon the poet that frees him from the grind of worldly activities, and thus allows him the luxury of the purely contemplative life in which his special vision is born, or whether it is the other way around—his visionary burden unsuiting him for the practical life—it all comes to the same thing: the poet alone lives an authentic existence. And, cruelest imperative of all, authenticity for the rest of us may be purchased only if we can somehow participate in the poet's isolated and isolating vision. How quickly romanticism of the isolationist variety drives to self-contradiction; we "join" together in authenticity only by cutting ourselves off from all common modes of vision.

The claim for privileged status will not be inherently repugnant to nonstructuralists and unsentimental social critics. But such claims, especially when they grow out of a romantic isolationism, raise subversive questions about themselves (Krieger is aware of most of them). If the poet is in possession of special vision, how can anyone else share it without detracting from its uniqueness? If the poet's vision will somehow mediate ours, who, since the poet alone has direct vision of the things that he claims to see, can check the authenticity of that vision? How can we be sure that he makes discoveries in being, if no one else can make similar discoveries? Or, to turn the questioning to the linguistic level, where Krieger likes to focus, how, if the poet writes a unique discourse, can the rest of us break into it, so that we, too, can cherish its special meanings? And, finally, what are we to do with

such meanings or visions if we make contact with them, when by definition such meanings and visions are clearly disconnected from common
human experience?

3

Krieger's contextualism, or aesthetic isolationism as I have
called it, represents a consistent (though not always happy and guilt-
free) assault on ancient aesthetic notions of universality and community. It attacks the classical ideal of salient connection among work,
audience, and artist which is casually assumed by philosophers and
critical theorists from Aristotle onward up through (and beyond)
Kant, whose insistence on subjective universals is forgotten by the
celebrants of alienation and autonomy. For Krieger, the traditional,
the normative, the universal, the generic, the conventional, and the
communitarian have value only insofar as they provide a point of
departure for originality, distinctiveness, particularity—for what he
has called, in a revealing redundancy, the "uniquely new."[17] It is
clear from his philosophical assumptions and his rhetoric that what is
unique and what is generic, in language or in persons, cannot embrace
without the former being wholly swallowed up by the latter. The
generic is the enemy, aesthetically and ethically: in language the mark
of the "stock," the "ordinary," and the "merely" conventional; in
human relations, a sign of a "ruthless" and "bloodless" universalism
that would reduce and force individuals into molds, that would treat
the individual as the typical in order to manipulate, use, and dominate
him.[18] By Krieger's reckoning, in matters aesthetic the generic is a sign
of perceptual laziness, of poverty of vision; in matters ethical a sign
of something much worse and very frightening. For Krieger, unlike
Yvor Winters whom he treats on this very issue, the normative does
not provide us with an energizing context within which we choose
to remain, so that we achieve our individual, original variations without
moving beyond the normative's stabilizing and community-preserving
power. His lengthy consideration of such an urge in *The Classic Vision*
betrays an inability to give full respect to it. The normative represents
for him a hostile, death-dealing force which, unless we transcend it
utterly, thereby establishing our pure autonomy and freedom, will
choke us.

The issue of the uniqueness or particularity of (original) expression,
explored at length in the fourth chapter of *The New Apologists*, is
logically dependent on the prior notion of the "uniqueness of poetic
imagination"[19]—on the idea that the consciousness of the poet *as poet*

is severed from all other modes of human consciousness. The poet searches through the givens of ordinary discourse and poetic tradition for a language adequate to carry over into public discourse the uniqueness of his consciousness. But since the public, as the conventional, is inhospitable to the unique individuality of the poetic consciousness, language must be alchemically transmuted, in the creative act, into a discourse which can accommodate uniqueness. Such discourse will need to be discontinuous with all that is generic and conventional in ordinary discourse: it will need to achieve such difference from what Saussure called *langue* that it will become not a linguistic performance sanctioned by a larger system of conventions and rules but a *langue* unto itself. Krieger calls this a contextual, or after Coleridge, an organic discourse, which functions as a network of intrareferential elements, each of which defines and is in turn defined by the linguistic totality (the "context"). Against (and below) such organically functioning discourse is set ordinary language, a system whose elements are said to function (in the teeth of Saussure's thesis) atomistically (rather than interdependently), and whose meanings are paraphrasable or translatable into other terms without significant alteration of meaning (rather than unparaphrasable and untranslatable, as in organic discourse, where meaning is inseparable from the linguistic configuration).

The lineage of these ideas can be traced—to name only the father and one illustrious son—in Coleridge and Croce. In Coleridge's lecture "Shakespeare's Judgment Equal to His Genius," we have the classic differentiation of organically functioning discourse (the *sui generis* language of original genius) from generic expression as the mechanical discourse of the imitative neoclassical mind. In Croce we find the end of the reworking of Coleridgean theory: what is called an "intuition," an aesthetic expression of perfect singularity, is isolated from the integrational (concept-tending) perspectives of generic tradition, from literary history, and from all allegorizing tendencies in the critical mind. Aesthetic expression as intuition eludes any reading that does not merely repeat the words of the work, that would move beyond the aesthetic reality, use it as mere vehicular language which carries us to the imperatives housed in philosophy, politics, and theology.

The kind of linguistic dualism that we find in Krieger's early work is an inevitable consequence of his segregation of poetic consciousness and poetic value and remains a trademark of his criticism to the present. In *The Tragic Vision* the contextual vs. referential dualism is treated as the difference marking off a "monistic" discourse, in which meaning is immanent to the word, from a "dualistic" discourse in which meaning is transcendent.[20] In *A Window to Criticism* the two types of discourse are seen in terms of two kinds of metaphor: the perfectly functional sort (in which the poet forces a transfer of properties between tenor and vehicle, so that tenor and vehicle are miraculously identified) is compared to simile, or mere decorative analogy. His example of miraculism is "The Canonization," where Donne makes us "accept his lovers literally and not just figuratively as saints (totally *as* saints and not just in part like and in part unlike them)"—an experience comparable to what the religious enthusiast undergoes when he sees "the wine *as* blood and not just as a surrogate showing *some* of the properties of blood."[21] Everywhere in his work Krieger speaks of the sign as ordinarily "empty," a mere counter in a dualistic game of relating arbitrarily word and world, and needing transformation into weighty, full, substantive aesthetic symbol.[22] In his latest book his linguistic dualism has been severely qualified and perhaps even neutered by confrontation with the new French critics who owe so much to Saussure's theories. But, even so, Krieger opts for a myth of the aesthetic symbol, as the irreducible minimum, in which meaning is immanent to discourse, unarbitrarily *there* in discourse—even though this semantic immanence must be held as the supremest of fictions.

Coleridge, whether he holds it as real or as myth, set up the original opposition when he distinguished *allegory* in literature—in which the gap between word and thing is sustained and "thing" seems to have an independent reality over and against consciousness—from *symbol*, the sort of discourse in which word and thing appear to intersect, where, in his paradoxical description, word partakes of the reality it represents. In symbol, consciousness alone is real, and all else is its construction. Here is Krieger's reworking of Coleridge in *A Window to Criticism*:

> this [contextualist] literary theory is moved primarily by the need to see poetry as breaking through the seemingly inevitable dualism in our normal sense of language, to make poetry into that magically monistic effigy that is not merely an empty sign through which we are directed to things, but rather both the sign and the substantive thing itself. . . . word and thing—indeed word and world—are made one. Poetry as the word is no longer, like other uses of language, burdened with a simple aboutness, so that it may be more troublesomely burdened with its own expansive embodiment of the substance that is the world.[23]

In the last chapter of *A Window to Criticism*, and in the books that follow, this high romantic optimism about the poet's ability to fashion an unarbitrary, natural discourse, which will give intimate contact with a world that "falls" away from us as it is "deferred" by ordinary discourse, is brought under serious question. Still Krieger remains an important hold-out in the contemporary critical scene against the structuralists who collect all utterances on the level of *écriture*, where the connection between signifier and signified is unmotivated and arbitrary. Krieger holds out for the unarbitrary aesthetic symbol, whether as a reality or a fiction of the romantic critical intelligence, in an attempt to anchor the romantic privileging of the poetic consciousness to the medium of literature itself—an attempt to ground the poet's elite and rare vision, the special knowledge he gives, in a special kind of discourse.

Krieger's difference from Coleridge, a difference between last and first romantics, is clarified by the *ut musica poesis* motif in aesthetic theory of the earlier nineteenth century. Krieger most resembles first romantics when he seeks an aesthetic medium free from representational responsibility. Schopenhauer and Kierkegaard, to cite only two well-known cases, despaired about the medium of language: the word, for them, was too much tied to the things of this world, too visually oriented—and so they turned from the language of literature to the "language" of music because the abstract medium of music was not referential to the world around us. Music, they believed, best facilitated transcendence: in its abstract, aural medium it bypassed the world of the corporeal eye and led us directly into the full presence of the visionary world of the ear. In the gnostic phrasing of Schopenhauer, music is "the metaphysical to everything physical in the world . . . the thing-in-itself to every phenomenon."[24]

> The voice I hear this passing night was heard
> In ancient days by emperor and clown.

Unlike Schopenhauer and Keats, Krieger does not celebrate the "visions" of the ear, nor does he rate music and the auditory over language and the visual. Quite the opposite, as his frequent metaphor of the veil should tell us. In effect he claims that verbal language may achieve music's contextual freedom from mimetic responsibilities, even while he claims that the value of such freedom is to return us to an Eden of lost particularity (not to the mist of the metaphysical), to force a reverse transcendence, as it were, in which we are enabled to pass through the inauthentic universals imposed by our needs to act, so as to possess the earth again and its inhabitants in a primordial freshness of vision.

The claim is that the special discourse of poetry affords us special existential revelation. But does Krieger's linguistic dualism serve or subvert the unique cognitive values which he wishes to assign to the mediating powers of poetry? Does poetry, as he conceives of it, build new bridges to an area of the *out there* that is otherwise beyond reach, or does his theory burn all bridges, and, what's worse, destroy our very capacity to make bridges to the world? Though he tries valiantly to free his theory of all associations with the previous devotees of *l'art pour l'art,* can a contextualist in the end escape the embrace of the aesthete? A helpful statement by Krieger of what it means to believe in the unique cognitive power of poetry occurs early in *A Window to Criticism.* Typically, he is talking about the two functions of language when he writes this: "Negatively, this principle [of contextualism] assumes the incapacity of normal discourse, for all its intentions of functioning transparently, to show more than typical abstractions from the reality it is to window. For this reality is an assemblage of endlessly unique individuals in endlessly unique relations in endlessly unique moments in time, while this discourse is limited in its referential power by the generic semantic character of its language and the generic semantic requirements of its logic."[25] Or, to put it positively, as he did in his essay on Northrop Frye: "the ultimate function of a contextual poetry is to provide existential revelation."[26]

A contemporary model for Krieger's apology (though not for the specific content of his existentialism) and a likely source is an essay by Eliseo Vivas, "The Object of the Poem." In this essay Vivas is preoccupied with a problem that an organicist uncomfortable with his isolationist and sometimes aestheticist sources is bound to confront sooner or later. It is a problem that has consumed Krieger for more than twenty-five years. How, once having so totally isolated poetry and the poetic consciousness, do we get the unique, intrinsic values of poetry in touch with our normal human world? To put it bluntly, why should anyone care about a unique consciousness, a unique language, and unique, existential revelations, all so perfectly severed from our consciousness, our discourse, the world we know and live in day in and day out? For all their isolationist tendencies Krieger and Vivas refuse to go gently into the aestheticist night of irrelevance. It makes sense, Vivas contends, to say that a poem has an "object" (not to be confused with an object of imitation) which in some crucial way is distinct from the poem's mode of linguistic being, even though it may be only through the mediating linguistic whole that we gain access to this object. Vivas would thus avoid the mimetic theory, which would allow us access to the poem's object independently of the poem itself, as well as the formalist theory which declares the question "What is the poem about?"

meaningless since the poem's object is perfectly coincidental with the poem as its wholly immanent god. We see at this point how Krieger, in some of his major statements, takes a radical step beyond his former mentor when, for instance, in *The Tragic Vision* he argues for a monistic poetry, or when in *A Window to Criticism* he declares that in a true poetry the "aboutness" of language is overcome. This radicalization of Vivas's point of view is consistent with his over-all *modus operandi*: to seek, as apologist, the most extreme possible purity for poetry, then, in a brilliant juggling act way up on the high wire, attempt to bring it all back within the largest contexts of our living.

Much of Vivas's argument in "The Object of the Poem" is summed up by his three key ontological terms: "subsistence," "insistence," "existence." "Subsistence" denotes the poem's object when it is situated somewhere out of view, beneath the culture, "knocking at the gate of history." At this level of being the poem's object may be said to be inchoate, "so little grasped at the conscious level by the members of a culture as to be, for them, practically non-existent." "Insistence" refers us to the object as it has been perfectly embodied in the poem's linguistic network—presumably dredged up from the hidden depths of being by the poet. The "insistent object" is no less than the aesthetic realization and revelation in language of the previously hidden, "subsistent object." Finally, there is the "existent object": a set of meanings torn out of the organic whole of the poem, forced into ordinary, referential discourse in order that they might assume a practical function as they are espoused, institutionalized, and given quotidian actuality in men's actions.[27]

The theory of Vivas, though it may seem to preserve what is best in the romantic and classical worlds—insofar as it allows the poet's "creations" to be "discoveries" in being—nevertheless is a full-blown romanticism which exacerbates the problems of romanticism rather than resolves them. By reserving visionary power to the poet alone—only the poet can have a grasp, however difficult and elusive, of subsistent being prior to the writing of the poem—Vivas forces the rest of us to place our full trust on the lonely little poem as our only way back to subsistent being. Without the poem's mediation we are condemned to a certain degree of ontological blindness and to exile from the poem's origin. The poet, then, is possessed of a doubly unique power: first to penetrate the original mysteries of being, then to transform the generic-ridden discourse of reference into a special, insistential language that will carry, as it fully engenders, the poet's vision, which is nothing less than a recovery of an origin that is prior to history.

The theory makes impossible demands on our capacity to believe in the poets. Why should we believe the poet when he tells us, in effect, look what I have dredged up from the heart of things, and entrapped in language for your contemplative delight? Since we have only "ordinary" consciousness, *we* can have no prepoetic intuition of subsistent being; if we could, then we could claim the honorific title of poet for ourselves, and would not need the official poet to bring us to being. Because of the isolationist way of setting up things we have no check on the poet. We have no way of knowing that the poet hasn't simply made it all up, that it is not merely all in his head, his private dream rather than an ontological recovery that he presents to us. And this problematic disjunction between poetic and ordinary vision, which denies us access to the rare subsistent treasures of the poet's intuition, is not resolved by the poet's creation of a "unique" discourse, a "new word" (a phrase of Mallarmé that Krieger is fond of working into his prose).[28] The unique discourse which houses the poet's vision can share no linguistic character with our ordinary discourse, else it were not unique. (As Krieger likes to point out, the concept of the unique is not qualifiable.) We cannot bridge the open space between the insistential and the referential, the poem's discourse and our discourse, because the very making of the bridge would rob the insistential of its distinctive character. No bridge can be made; the space between must never be violated. With the very best intentions, Vivas ends up isolating poetry on what Clive Bell, in his chilling formalism, called the "cold, white peaks of art."[29]

Krieger inherits Vivas's traps and cannot help being caught in them. After the most strenuous efforts to bring poetry back to life from the deep freeze of aesthetic isolation he, like Vivas before him, becomes a victim of the very aestheticist and formalist error for which he has such well-warranted contempt. Krieger has never been unaware of his difficulties. In *The New Apologists* he spoke of the "impossibility" of "consistently maintaining an unqualified organicism"; a chief reason turns out to be that if we maintain an unqualified organicism we are saddled with the manifestly unsound intellectual stance that emerges most clearly in Croce's theory: the poem is "beyond comparison with all other poetic contexts and invulnerable to the commentary of the critic."[30] The first problem (that poems are "beyond comparison" with one another) we owe to the ironic legacy of Coleridge who, in his praise of Shakespeare's genius at working beyond the narrow conceptions of neoclassical genre criticism, went too far and destroyed the normative reach of genre altogether. Genius, Coleridge tells us, is not "lawless": it acts creatively "under laws of its own origination."[31] But laws are not laws that apply to one man only, or to one work. The work of genius is marked, in this celebration of originality, by the fact that it evades all of the generalizing forces of history, literary or otherwise. And even more extremely, if the poem is truly *sui generis*, as Coleridge and Croce say it is (and we should be willing to admit now that the idea of a genre with only one instance is a useless paradox), then even the individual poems within a writer's corpus may share no integrating, over-all identity. Krieger endorses the Coleridgean contradiction when he writes in *The Tragic Vision* that each poem is "a unique system of discourse, obedient only to the laws immanently within itself. . . ."[32] The second impasse that Krieger mentions, the invulnerability of the poem's discourse to the critic's discourse, is only a corollary of the general problem posed by his pervasive linguistic dualism. He puts the critic's problem thus: "he comes to this unique system, to the 'new word,' armed only with old words which can hardly be expected to pierce through to its untranslatable, incomparal·le meaning." We may not open the closed poetic context because, once open, "the poetic context would be prey to an indiscriminate host of arbitrary meanings derived from other contexts. Poetry could no longer hold itself aloof from paraphase; and thus, no longer free of the ordinary demands of reference, it would lose the one characteristic that could set it off from other modes of discourse."[33]

Krieger's willingness to lay the problems of his own position on the line is admirable, rare among contemporary critics, and quite disarming. But such theoretical self-consciousness, though it will save him from arrogant dogmatism, cannot make his position itself any the more acceptable (unless self-consciousness itself is to be our pivotal value). In each of his books after *The New Apologists* he has pushed his work beyond the impasses of the New Criticism by grappling, as the New Critics did not, with the paradox of relating the unrelatable aesthetic enclosure to a larger human context. But the terms of his violent dualisms ensure his defeat. His strategy in *The Tragic Vision* for bringing together the linguistic enclosures he calls poems with existential reality is to invent the critical procedure of "thematics" (not to be confused with "theme," a notion from the old criticism that believed the essential content, the governing idea of a work to be extractable without damage to the work's aesthetic integrity). "Thematics," a critical concept that follows the "organicist aspects of new-critical poetics," is defined as "the study of the experiential tensions which, dramatically entangled in the literary work, become an existential reflection of that work's aesthetic complexity."[34] When, toward the conclusion of *A Window to Criticism*, he asks himself some very tough questions, the notion of thematics is lurking in the background: "Against what, then,

can we check the 'insistent' reality of the poem?" "Through what coincidence is aesthetic complexity somehow the accurate reflection of
existential complexity so that aesthetic soundness automatically, as it
were, involves historic authenticity?"[35]

The questions are especially troublesome for Krieger because he will
not allow himself the extreme neo-Kantian idealism which jettisons all
questions of adequacy and correspondence (questions which always
interest the realist) for the myths created by our symbolic forms. For
Cassirer, Wheelwright, Frye, and their advocates, since all is symbolic
action, the question of a "check," of "accuracy," is a nonquestion which
can, if taken seriously, only promote the naive notion of an external
world. For these neo-Kantians language properly understood can never
be referential (though scientist types may be allowed the myth of the
referential, the myth of a subject-object dualism). For Krieger, as for
Vivas (putting aside for the moment the question of whether they can
justify their theory), the poem in its irreducible realism has an object in
being which it discovers in its veil-piercing language. But if he cannot
take the neo-Kantian way neither can he (again like Vivas) allow himself the mimetic out: "we cannot identify what the work ends by being
an imitation *of,* since it must be the creator as well as the bearer of its
vision so that only it can lead us to its object of imitation."[36] The answer
that he gives to his questions in *A Window to Criticism* remains
"thematics," a notion which he believes will connect the realms of the
aesthetic and the existential because it partakes of both.

Frequently in *A Window to Criticism* he speaks of the poem as a set
of enclosed mirrors, endlessly reflecting one another in internal isolation, yet "somehow" opening out to the world, becoming in this way a
"window" to our historical existence.[37] The word "somehow" tells us
that rational explanation is not forthcoming as to how contrary realms
of vision, being, and discourse are to be joined. The surface solution of
"thematics" is only asserted, not argued. To say that thematics "partakes" of both realms, to say that the aesthetic and the existential are
"entangled," begs the crucial questions. What is the cause of such entanglement? The very definition of thematics is a philosophical sleight-
of-hand which assumes resolved what have proven to be the major
cruxes in Krieger's aesthetic of alienation. "Thematics" assumes that
there can be continuity between contextual discourse and referential discourse, between the insistent reality of the poem and the subsistent and
existent levels of being which lie on either side of the poem. But it is
discontinuity which gives life to Krieger's poetics, which ensures the
distinctive, "unique" character of the values he would ascribe to poetry.
He can make continuities in his system only by destroying the charac-

ter of what he most cherishes as "unique." Though he does not have much patience with the solipsistic idealism of the neo-Kantians, he is subject to a similar charge, since the poem as he imagines it cannot be "checked."

Krieger has no desire to set up house within the "postCrocean *cul de sac*"—"the declaration of the total inaccessibility of the poem to criticism"—but he has no choice and admits it: "The critic . . . alone takes upon himself the futile, self-defeating task of using propositional discourse in order to reveal its limitations, to shame it before the poetic, exposing its utter inadequacy to the experience it claims to talk about." In so many words: "The critic must fail."[38] After such admissions of impotence, there can be no redemption. Krieger's attempts after this to bring together the aesthetic and the existential, poetic language with ordinary language, are efforts to repress the unhappy fact that by his own candor he has become the destroyer of his system. And yet he has gone on, as in the following extended passage from *Theory of Criticism*, to assume the existence of a bridge where there can only be empty space —and no swaying rope affair, either, strung perilously over a deep chasm, but a veritable Oakland Bay structure:

> Each element behind and before the work—a biographical character or incident, a neurotic obsession, a self-conscious urge, a literary source, a philosophical idea or social-political position—is an inadequate measure of its transformed appearance in the work. . . . To the extent that the reader is reading as the poem leads him to read, he will not reduce the element's appearance in the poem to its prepoetic reality. . . . This is often difficult for learned readers, whose research has turned up the several kinds of sources for what is going on in the poem. But if they are critics as well as scholars, they will overcome that difficulty. Indeed, their knowledge will deepen their criticism and render it responsible: in knowing where each prepoetic element leaves off and where the aesthetic entity begins, and in being able to mark the difference between the two, they are well positioned to move in on the aesthetic center of the work.[39]

It must remain a mystery, finally, how we are to bridge the dual realms when the "common materials which enter poetry" are "so transmuted in the creative act that they come out utterly unique."[40] The less romantically inclined among Krieger's readers are likely to note the word "responsible" in the passage above and approve, but will wonder if this critic has earned the theoretical right to anything more than an awful silence.

4

On several occasions in the pages above I have made reference to Krieger's "existentialism" because I believe it (more than the Kantian perspective) to be a foundation of his work. Though qualified considerably in *The Classic Vision* and *Theory of Criticism*, it has continued to play, even in his most recent work, a determining role. It is the fusion, in fact, of existentialism and organicism—a move begun in *The New Apologists* and essentially completed in *The Tragic Vision*—that gives Krieger's contextualist poetic its distinctive character. And we are to understand that what he calls existentialism is validated not by the meditations of Kierkegaard, Nietzsche, Heidegger, and Sartre, but by the perceptions of the poets. Or, to put it in the radical way that he would insist upon: what we call existentialism in philosophy is merely a thinner, generalized version of the unresolvable experiential tensions that are "dramatically entangled" in the linguistic complexities of the organic poem. In Krieger's version of existentialism I find three interwoven themes: the principle of the death of God, which very few thinkers since Nietzsche have successfully ignored; a nominalistic ontology, whose severest consequences he was until recently eager to embrace; and, following from the latter, a savaging of rational man—a debunking of all of the generalizing habits in human thought and expression, and at moments an outright rejection of those habits as the basis of inauthenticity.

Given the Continental backgrounds of existentialism, it comes as a mild shock to remember that the intellectual origins of Krieger's thought are solidly Anglo-American, and are to be in part located in the psychologism of I. A. Richards and the transformation of Richards into literary-critical terms in the New Criticism of Cleanth Brooks. The first step is Richards's view of the poet as a supreme juggler, whose vastly inclusive consciousness can contain and balance a welter of opposed attitudes and impulses, with none subordinated or sacrificed to another for purposes of coherent action. The complex consciousness, the suppression of action in the contemplative (Vivas's "intransitive") mode of awareness, is sustained primarily by the ironic attitude; in Richards and his New-Critical inheritors, what is meant by irony is not an indirect way of saying something but a tactic which apparently allows one to escape all saying, all stance-taking. Irony, after Richards, becomes a synonym for complex awareness. The transition from Richards to Brooks, then, is a transition from subjectivist and psychologistic concern with complexly balanced impulses within the poet, to objectivist and realistic concern with the complex texture of the existential world which we all would see if only we could suppress our needs to act (for in acting we reduce complexities by classifying them as neat generic screens: the "veil" of Hulme and Bergson). The transition from Richards to Brooks is the elevation of irony from its place in the private psyche of the poet to the key to human experience at large. Since we cannot help but act (and thereby deliberately blind ourselves to the way it is), we turn to the isolated, "impractical" poet who with his techniques of irony, ambiguity, and paradox is able to express his vision within a medium, and thereby (though very problematically, as we have seen) make his knowledge of the real state of sublunary nature available to the nonpoets of the world. This complex vision of the poets is valorized as "mature" by T. S. Eliot, Brooks, Krieger, and the New Critics because it is a discovery of the true nature of things behind the veil of sleepy, quotidian living.[41]

The concept of complexity is hardly enough, as the following passage will demonstrate, where Krieger is ostensibly speaking about Brooks, but is actually pressing Brooks's position to the radical edge:

> . . . Brooks considers our actual experience in the world to be infinitely complex. No single abstract moral or scientific system can do justice to all the data. . . . Only the poet is able to handle this complexity, the complete texture of reality, with any real fairness. . . . The poet may begin by expressing one viewpoint, but by various devices like irony he should imply the equal tenability of conflicting viewpoints (and, as with Richards, one must assume the more viewpoints and the more conflicting they are, the better). The poet must not choose among these positions but rather must continue to see all around the problem without sacrificing the total view to a partial insight. Only the poet's "unity of sensibility," given him by his tradition, can struggle with all these recalcitrant elements and lose none of them in the organism which is the created poem.[42]

If it is not apparent where Krieger is heading (and that Brooks explicitly turned his theory away from such consequences), then it is unquestionable what he intends for organicism in this passage from *The Tragic Vision*:

> . . . I must insist, on behalf of recent criticism in its consistently organic moments, that every self is to be confronted with the anti-self, every claim with its antithesis, with no possibility of an all-reconciling synthesis—unless it is one that is accompanied by a newly disruptive anti-synthesis. At least I must insist on all this in the good work, by which I

must mean the work that demands the more delicate prob-
ings of the literary discipline of thematics since in its complexity it remains disdainfully inaccessible to the vain
attempt to empty it by crudely tearing at it here and there to
come up with some philosophical generalizations. And again,
I suppose, I am allowing a single conception of the phenomenology of our moral life to support a single aesthetic
methodology in that I acknowledge that, in support of this
view of thematics, I must deny that the existential world . . .
can be anything less than a bewildering complex of seeming
contradictions.[43]

When Krieger speaks of our experience in the world as "infinitely
complex," when he insists that in literature every self must be confronted with the antiself, "every claim with its antithesis, with no possibility of an all-reconciling synthesis," he is doing much more than
insisting on complexity in the vision of literature: "complexity" does
not require the outright pattern of unresolvable oppositions that
Krieger embraces under the concept of Manichaeism. "Mature" awareness of the difficult, the problematic, and the subtly shaded difference
gives way to the unbridled nominalist vision of chaos; "reality is" (as
he phrased it in a passage from *A Window to Criticism* which I have
already quoted) "an assemblage of endlessly unique individuals in endlessly unique relations in endlessly unique moments in time." Here,
then, is the reality behind the veil: a raging chaos of particulars which
cannot be authentically synthesized in our discourse because there is no
unifying ground in being for such synthesis. The kind of generalizing
discourse that brings particulars together is the discourse, generically
bound for action, which places the veil—as a fiction of connectedness—
between us and the "complete texture of reality."

The only kind of discourse which can be adequate to the Manichaean
texture of reality is the discourse which subverts its own generalizing
and referential nature, the discourse which Krieger calls organic. We
now recognize this discourse not so much by its nonreferential quality,
its self-sustaining character—since it is clear that organic discourse *is*
referential, as a totality, to the world behind the veil—but by the
quality of its astonishing self-consciousness, its unwillingness to assert,
to make a point, to take a stance (in the sense that taking one stance
means not taking any others, and means even denying the value of
others). The denial that the universal can be authentically (ontologically) grounded leads to the epistemological denial that universals
within thought and discourse can have any authentic power to open
the way for us to the real nature of human experience. Normal dis-

course only succeeds in encasing us comfortably in the false (though safe and sane) world demanded by our needs to act and required by our collective psyches which refuse to bear as a daily burden the chaos of the world behind the veil. The aesthetic mode of discourse alone is "adequate to" the existential because the aesthetic alone can "entangle" in its ironic labyrinth of verbal textures the existential level of our experience. It is not his desire to take *a* position that marks a writer as unsophisticated, immature, and unrealistic, but his taking of an "immature" position. The writer becomes honest, mature, and right, "adequate to" existential reality, by counterposing against every thrust a counterthrust.

This view wipes out much traditional literature, and Krieger does not shrink from the conclusion: "It goes without saying that the contextualist approach carries with it—and quite explicitly—the downgrading of many poems in the accepted canon, especially the allegorical, the satirical, the didactic."[44] Though he does not add this, it also goes without saying that the literary modes which he mentions must be discredited as dishonest, as untrue to experience insofar as they are willing to offer, after all qualifications are made, a governing perspective on human affairs. Since any system of moral norms must be grounded ontologically (for Krieger) in order to be "authentic," and since the very notion of the normative is denied in thunder by the disorder of our experience (the normative can only be a therapeutic fiction, in Stevens's sense), we are required to find in literature as the ultimate in sophistication the antiposition that all positions are false, the antidoctrine that no doctrine may be affirmed. Failing to find in a work that all views are denied, or, which is the same thing, that all views are permissible, we must deny those works admission into the privileged realm of imaginative literature. To put it positively: we may admit into the canon what is traditionally known as satire as long as we can find in it (impose upon it?) places where the satiric voice recognizes that its norms are only "self-righteous," and in such self-consciousness satirizes the moral force of its norms out of existence in self-subverting irony. All position-taking is "shabbily pragmatic," Krieger tells us, an uncourageous self-blinding to "the nightmare reality out of the underground depths in us all."[45] All position-taking, that is, except existentialist position-taking.

Of course if the real state of sublunary nature is as Krieger says it is, and if we in fact want literature to tell us the truth about ourselves— not an unreasonable demand to make upon the poets—then what Krieger says about the way words in poems behave, or ought to behave, and about what we truly experience, or ought to experience—his rationale, in other words, for conferring value, or denying it—all of it becomes powerfully persuasive. If we grant the first "if" the rest follows, whether we like it or not, and we must accept his judgments about allegory, satire, and other apparently noncontextualist modes of expression. But ought we to grant the first "if," which is recognizable by now as another modernist shibboleth, the conventional view that "tough-minded" post-Nietzscheans have been articulating (sometimes in a self-congratulatory way)? Krieger grants, disarmingly, the superciliousness of the existentialist posture,[46] but cannot help assuming it himself as, for instance, when he declares that "the ethical once shattered, there is no higher return to community—although, of course, for the less daring there may always be retreat."[47] That remark pretty much throws down the gauntlet for those who do not agree with his assumptions, so I will pick it up by asking on what grounds it is being claimed that the ethical has been shattered? On what grounds is it being claimed that behind the veil of our quotidian existence lies a frightening, nominalistic reality? How can one know what is behind the veil?

I want to raise, in other words, the question of authority, both the poet's and the critic's, as conceived by this theorist. I believe that one cannot know the things that Krieger claims to know without claiming for himself the privilege of the traditional metaphysician. And for reasons that he has himself suggested, I believe that one cannot urge such claims upon the rest of us without involving the severest of contradictions. We need to remember that the point of transforming I. A. Richards through Cleanth Brooks was to move to an objectivism of some sort: to read Richardian neural complexity as the landscape of human affairs, the way it is for our most mature and courageous observers of the human world. But from where, in fact, do those courageous people who are not poets derive their knowledge? From the poets, who alone have the visionary power to engage the deepest strata of so-called objective reality, and to manage minimal intuitions of subsistent being prior to their making of poems. Leaving aside again the difficulty of checking the poet's vision, that whole matter of bridging the unbridgeable, we note that Krieger has not offered compelling evidence for his existentialism—beyond his reading of the poets. By the logic of his position, and from his own admission, Krieger must gather his evidence *wholly* from his readings of the poets.

Perhaps we should let it go at that—say that those readings, and there are many of them, are generally persuasive and that they illuminate a broad range of literary forms, spanning several centuries. And isn't that enough? It is never enough for theorists, and perhaps it

cannot be enough for most of us since we are all likely to be confronted
by the uninhibited student with questions like, Why do I read literature and what can it tell me about my life and the lives of others?
Answers to those questions are always theoretical. It certainly has not
been enough for Krieger just to do close readings. Despite a series
of modest withdrawals and qualifications, he has continued to press
his claims for literature as universally binding. The withdrawals and
qualifications have, however, blurred the essential point of his claims
and have insulated his position from the critique that it deserves. Thus,
he has reminded us in several places that it is the Manichaean *face* of
reality to which he refers, the way things appear to him—in so
many words, the "phenomenology of the moral life,"[48] not its ontology:

> there is really no *metaphysical* commitment to Manichaeism
> in the position. It derives from literary works and a critical
> method adequate to them, not from a philosophic analysis
> of the nature of reality. Inasmuch as it is concerned with
> fictions, which deal only with the dramatic—the phenom-
> enological—level of existence, this critical approach, in its
> persistent concern with tensions, can suggest no more
> than an *apparent* Manichaeism, a Manichaean *face* of
> reality. This suggestion would not speak at all to the
> ontological question about the ultimate nature of reality.[49]

Such disavowals of metaphysical privilege and the concomitant avowal
of the "critical" attitude blunt the force of his earlier claims about
"the complete texture of reality" and appear to succeed in placing
him beyond the range of those who would charge him with urging
claims that are undemonstrable, beyond inspection, because they are
metaphysical. But the "face" of the Manichaean and the so-called
"phenomenology" of the moral life are not said to be contingent
upon Krieger's private awareness as an "endlessly unique individual"—
which given his nominalism is all that he can in theory say. The nightmare reality is in us all, he tells us, but how, in theory, can he claim
to know that unless he is claiming his perspective, his experience with
literature as normative? But where are the norms in a posited existential
chaos?

The Manichaean, again, is only a "face"—meaning that what is
behind the face he is not prepared to say; but his rhetoric tells a different story. For at every turn the Manichaean is said to be "behind"
the veil; the Manichaean is said to be "ultimate"; the Manichaean is
said to be "universal"; the Manichaean is said to characterize "the
extra-propositional nature of reality"; the Manichaean is declared a
"brawling chaos" "actually out there."[50] All of this is the talk of an

ontologist who believes that what *he* sees is not a projection of his private psyche but is grounded in the nature of things "behind" the illusions of everyday life. That little preposition "behind," which Krieger uses so much, carries tremendous force in his writing, and in the writing of all realists. Along with most post-Kantians he believes that classic philosophical realism is "naive," but his is the rhetoric of the existential realist, a point which he obfuscates by appealing, as a last resort, to skepticism with a phrase like "phenomenological full-ness" behind the "veil."[51] Traditionally speaking, what is behind the veil is real; the veil itself is a phenomenological construct. To say, as he does, that what is behind the veil is also a construction not only makes nonsense out of the concept of the phenomenological but also drains his position of its realist urgency (you'd better attend to litera-ture because it shows what is actually there for us all): it is to say that the poet's vision is not a veil-piercer at all, not a deep diver into the subsistent depths of our moral experience, but just another personal myth, a veil itself which we may or may not find interesting but which cannot, as construction, make universal claims upon us. As a creation of one of those "endlessly unique individuals" the poem cannot be taken as "existential revelation";[52] at best it is a demonic fiction. To speak of phenomenological fullness behind the veil, then, is also to destroy the force of the metaphor of the veil, the ancient opposition of illusion and reality which has been the vehicle all along for Krieger's moral and epistemological polemic on behalf of poetry. So his un-compromising nominalism—which ought to condemn him to silence—is compromised by one universal, which he believes phenomenologi-cally grounded: "the universal principle of ceaseless and absolute opposition of contradictory claims, both maintained at full and equal strength, as it characterizes the Manichaean vision."[53] The qualifica-tion lent by phenomenology does not make much difference in the practical force of Krieger's position; existential ontology (we might recall a similar notion in the subtitle of Sartre's *Being and Nothingness*) does not remove the bite of ontology plain and pure.

But let us put aside the question of authority and credit, for pur-poses of argument, the unbearable vision offered by Krieger's exist-entialism, either as he credits it, as existential revelation, or as Northrop Frye would read it, as myth, the demonic projection of despairing, ironic man. This vision is said to be entangled in the labyrinth of the nonreferring poem which undercuts itself in every way at every point. The final irony of Krieger's aesthetic existentialism, like Stevens's, is that it seems more aestheticist in its thrust than existential. For the lesson of the tragic literature of our time, as Krieger reads it, is that "all moral action authentically undertaken—from the worst to the best intended, undertaken in pride and in humility alike—is for these authors doomed not only to destroy the agent but to damn him as well."[54] The tragic hero will learn bitterly that the universal he believed grounded in being was in fact only a private perspective, not ethical at all, and so doomed to produce moral evil. This shocking awareness is the awakening to the Manichaean or morally unsponsored universe. The "tragic existent" then moves, as Krieger sees it, to the single-minded demoniac worship of evil. But the tragic author, the "tragic visionary," maintains the multivision of nominalism; refuses to reduce all to a single embracing principle; allows the tragic work to speak as a dramatic polyphony of discrete and autonomous voices.[55] The theme that emerges from all of this is a theme that isolated romantics have been working out for years: "All action, then, is impossible. . . . Action presupposes adequacy of ethical belief and personal guiltlessness, while in its extremity it reveals the bankruptcy of system and the inherent vice as well as the folly of him who believed in the perfection of system and the purity of personal motive. . . . existential ambiguity makes every act an act of self-damnation."[56] Since it is impossible, in this view, to be moral men, we had better retreat to our ivory towers.

5

Since the publication of *A Window to Criticism* in 1964, Krieger's has been the criticism of the ever-diminishing claim. Literature's "existential revelations" remain in his later work as straw men to be undercut by an expanding self-consciousness situated somewhere beyond good and evil. In recent years the symbolic fatherhood of Eliseo Vivas has been cast off and replaced by that of Wallace Stevens, the champion of nonstatement and corrosive self-meditation. And the ultimate feat these days, as we have seen, is to believe in a "fiction" which, from the very start, you do not believe in. In Stevens's perilous, schizoid phrasing of the idea: "The final belief is to believe in a fiction, which you know to be a fiction, there being nothing else, the exquisite truth is to know that it is a fiction and that you believe in it willingly."[57] So last romanticism comes into existence when it becomes fully realized that the grandiose claim of first romanticism, that the poetic imagination is the most significant thing the world has ever known, crashes on the rocks of skepticism *and yet survives*. When the much-wished-for drowning and wondrous sea change do not come, what is left is the desire of the first romantic trapped within the impotent body of despairing, ironic man. Poets like Stevens become obsessed with telling us in poem after poem how impotent poetry is, while the connoisseurs of metapoetics and *mise en abyme*—Krieger has now joined them—write reports on this situation in literary history proclaiming it as the final sophistication. Krieger does not move blithely into this poetics, but move he does as his career-long tactic of swallowing his opposition fails him, and he is swallowed up by the theoreticians of deliberate triviality.

Krieger's claim, in *A Window to Criticism*, that the poetic word appeared to overcome (like Coleridgean symbol) the quality of "aboutness" which afflicts normal language,[58] runs head-on into Saussure's principle of linguistic difference, accepted by all contemporary structuralists and poststructuralists, that signifier and signified are connected in an arbitrary or unmotivated way. We do not need to read very far into *A Window to Criticism* before we understand that the claim for a natural fitness between word and meaning is a response to the challenge to New Criticism offered by Ernst Cassirer, Philip Wheelwright, and Northrop Frye, the major twentieth-century apologists for the mythic consciousness. In the distinction he draws between the common-sense positivism of Frazer in *The Golden Bough* and the magical perspective of Wheelwright in *The Burning Fountain*, Krieger gets quickly to the heart of the myth position. Frazer is

> not ready, as Wheelwright is, to view his own common-sense notion of language and reality critically, to be open to the magical view that sees in existence a "fluidity" that "involves a flowing-into-one-another and disappearing-into-one-another of distinctions that to our way of looking at the matter are clear and definite." This possibility stems from "an indefinable coalescence" between entities that allows the Navaho to sense the clouds, and with them the rain, literally within the puff of his tobacco-pipe smoke. Our capacity to entertain this vision allows us to enlarge our awareness of what poetry as this special kind of language can do. . . .[59]

In the mythic consciousness of the universe as "flow," where the spatial discreteness of things is broken down and all things move into one another in a "single plane of being," the ontological gap between subject and object is closed, the object as object (in Coleridge's terms) disappears, and the "mere sign," as Cassirer shrewdly puts it, "which suggests something distant and absent," is transformed into a language of presence: "for the mythical consciousness there is no such thing as *mere* mimesis, *mere* signification."[60] Krieger brings his language this close to the discourse of Cassirer, Wheelwright, and Frye, and their vision of an "unbroken continuous whole,"[61] in an effort to co-opt their theories, in considerable vogue in the late 1950s and early 1960s.

But then he begins to make his distance in ways that are predictable from his isolationist habits. The mythic vision of the poet, as the neo-Kantians formulated the idea, seems to Krieger to be a property of a certain moment in consciousness, rather than a property of a certain kind of language, and, more problematically, it is not a moment of consciousness owned strictly by the poet, but a visionary possibility for human consciousness in general. As a consequence, with no proper distinguishing and isolating of the poetic from ordinary consciousness, there can be no proper distinguishing and isolating of the poetic function of language: "symbolic" discourse may occur anywhere, even as Coleridge could find "poetry" in some writings in the Bible and in some historians, because the creative power that energizes language is a possibility for any consciousness, not just the poet's. And, though a similar charge can be leveled against him, Krieger is disturbed—at least the realist in him is disturbed—by the neo-Kantian impulse to consider the idea of a real world and of reference in language as mere "fictions" of the scientific intellect. Wanting to incorporate the neo-Kantian poetic within the confines of his contextualism, he must first qualify and tame the theorists of myth in ways which will predict his later self-consciousness. He must deny himself the "primeval mythico-religious" basis of the neo-Kantians, and claim that the vision of myth has but a phenomenological validity, is mediated and controlled by the poet's self-conscious manipulation of language—a process that springs not from the poet's (and our) capacity to sustain, in an essentially atheistic high culture, the primitive's faith of animism, but from the poet's ability to work certain "miracles" of language and our capacity, within the aesthetic mode, to partake of those miracles.[62]

In his review of *Anatomy of Criticism*, Meyer Abrams pointed out that the book was meant to allay the monistic thirst of the human spirit;[63] *A Window to Criticism*, with all of the qualifications noted, has at its core an identical urge:

> How can a sophisticated culture manage the monistic way
> of language that was lost to it in its early days? If we
> assume our continuing need for the totally substantive,
> fully empowered effigy, our need to feel an immediacy in
> the word that can match the immediacy of our experience,
> in short our need to transcend the empty character of
> words as pointing tools, how can our Platonized language

> in its fallen duality permit the need to be satisfied? Obviously I am trying to say that poetry can still be this effigy for a culture that has lost all its self-conscious ways of achieving it.[64]

The emphasis in this passage is typical of the book as a whole in its concern with the "monistic experience of the symbol."[65] It focuses on the subject's "side" of the aesthetic experience, on how we come to feel ourselves intimately reintegrated with our world through aesthetic meditation, rather than, as in *The Tragic Vision*, on what the symbol unveils of our existential reality. The "need" which must be satisfied is identical with the "need" felt by our primitive ancestors, and satisfied for them (lucky folk) by the accident of their " 'pre-logical' psychology and 'pre-logical' sense of language":

> The authentication of his naive language was thus self-induced and sustained by his animistic faith. However, any possibility of this kind of symbolic experience must be externally and objectively authenticated once our sophisticated sense of language and the epistemology it sanctions have taken hold. In our late language only the [aesthetic] object can force this experience upon us, closing its context to enclose its god and make us respond to a monistic sense of "presence" in the symbol.[66]

Sophisticated ironic man, unable to get over the primitive, monistic nostalgia of his "aboriginal self"[67]—despite his conventional assumption of the death of God—finds sanction for his nostalgia in the aesthetic experience (as Matthew Arnold predicted he would). Ironic man finds his best hope, in Krieger's words, in the "unified symbolic experience"[68] which is triggered in us by the poet's unarbitrary discourse —a kind of writing which will undo the damage of the fall from presence as it recovers presence for us in its language. Krieger cites Shakespeare's sonnets as chief examples of poems which do not "stand as mere assertions based on the fiat of faith." Shakespeare, he argues, makes his poetry "force a response that has the immediacy and the symbolic union of the religious response . . . not just by proclaiming equations between the unions asserted in dogma and those he asserts for love, but by using these analogous unions as the materials for a poetry that *earns* its way to its own union within the self-enclosed walls of meaning that poetic devices have tightly constructed."[69] Our humanity, he believes, demands these restorations of the primitive experience, but all restoration is owed—here is his difference with the myth critics—to a distinctively poetic language which is uniquely capable of performing this feat of psychic redemption.[70]

In the last dozen or so pages of *A Window to Criticism* Krieger becomes uncomfortable with his "miracle" of poetic language and its
many echoes of the Eucharistic mysteries. (For ironic man could it have
been otherwise?)

> As Shakespeare so often shows, there can be no miracle
> that does not insist on being had both ways, at once assert-
> ing itself as miracle and asserting its own impossibility
> (which proves it as nothing less than miracle) by showing
> our common sense its denial, at once demonstrating its
> substantive union and the unyielding matter of its
> separateness.[71]

The entire argument of *A Window to Criticism* is inaugurated and
concluded with a meditation on the nature and function of metaphor,
which Krieger believes to be the aesthetic ground of the miraculism
of poetic discourse. The astonishing identity forged between tenor
and vehicle (always the key to what he calls "incarnating"[72] or "re-
ductive" metaphor: Donne's lovers are not *like* saints, they *are* saints)
is countered within metaphor itself, somehow, by an "unmetaphoring"
movement—the skeptical voice of self-consciousness, that very feeling
of embarrassment that high-cultured man has for things monistic and
mythic.[73] Incarnating metaphor shows our "common sense its denial"
of metaphor's own monistic nature by insisting on the separateness of
tenor and vehicle, though as it does this ("even as" it acknowledges
"its absurdity and impossibility") it simultaneously "maintain[s] the
need to assert it," to show us the "word made body."[74] The "even as"
construction in Krieger's sentences, as his critics and the author himself have acknowledged,[75] is the grammatical sign of his attempt to
keep contradictions together in the movement of a coherent argument—to say one thing and in the same breath to take it back.
(Krieger's view is that his own prose at such points reflects the more-
than-rational way of imaginative discourse—but it may be, simply,
that his prose is moving beyond rational limits.) The "incarnating
metaphor," he tells us, "polarizes the very elements it identifies, and
in the same act."[76]

But does "incarnating metaphor" essentially deny, or does it assert
that for the duration of the "symbolic experience" we see identity
as a phenomenological datum? As elsewhere in his theory, there is
here no bald ontological claim for identity; but again I would urge
that the word "phenomenological" and its various cognates ought not
to obscure the ontological resonances of Krieger's rhetoric. The claim
that "presence"—a weighty theological term carried by the metaphor

of incarnation—is symbolically mediated may be countered with a fact: that presence is always presence-for-someone, is always the relationship of an object to a subject, or, more accurately for this context, the relationship of an ultimate Subject to a human subject. (Thus Wordsworth: "I have felt a presence. . . .") "Presence," whatever we denote by the term, is never an "in-itself"; the Incarnation guarantees immanence as well as transcendence. Krieger's attempt to mute (by aestheticizing) the ontological implications of the concept of "presence" points us to his discomfort with his own concept of "incarnating metaphor" and all of the theological tones we hear when the word "incarnation" is put into play. When he says of "miracle" that "unless reason itself was there to proclaim it—proclaiming with it, of course, its downright impossibility," there would be no miracle, he leaves a delicate issue clouded.[77] Is the "reason" that is "there," that denies miracle, the reason of the self that reads the poem? If it is only the reading self that makes the denial, then the *poem's* miraculous claim is untouched. Even, however, if we read Krieger's difficult prose as saying that the reasonable voice is *in* the poem, situated alongside the mythic voice which proclaims miracle, we may yet see the miracle as unqualified since, as he notes, it is in the nature of miracle to resist rational explanation or denial. To say that reason, whether in or out of the poem, denies miracle is only to assert the definition of miracle.

The issue is broached again in *The Classic Vision*, a work which may be read in its theoretical sections as a clarification and resolution of the issue of skepticism and belief that was raised in *A Window to Criticism*. Assent to the incarnating moment of metaphor becomes assent to illusion—to an alteration of vision close to Cassirer's description of the world of mythic consciousness. To experience incarnating metaphor is to experience the "destruction of discrete entities, the blurring of the bounds, the limits, that create the property and propriety of entity-hood."[78] But, now, with unmistakable meaning, Krieger declares that the moment of incarnation "must bear within itself the rational denial of its absolute nature." The "magic" of metaphor is but "seeming," "discourse remains only discourse": "Our more rational selves find hidden within the poem, for all that would make it a new word, the comforting assurances that our prosaic sense of distinction . . . may yet be preserved."[79] And, if that is not clear enough, then the following drives it home:

> Even as the enclosing metaphor captures the motley
> variety of experience's soft center with the hard edge of
> its extremity, thereby reading all of life within its own
> closed visionary system, there is a counter-metaphorical

motion at work as well: in the skeptical denial that restores
distinction (that restores our sense of duality where there
are two entities), there is an opening outward beyond the
miracle (beyond the metaphor, the work, and the world of its
words) to the world that we know and what that world
refuses to permit.[80]

Krieger appears to have given up on the notion of a uniquely poetic
kind of discourse and, with it, on the miracles it was said to have
wrought. The miracle of the unarbitrary, natural, "full," and "unfallen" word is a trick of language which, however astonishing, we
recognize as trick. The ironic disclaimers in the poem do not merely
(because of their rational basis) affirm the miraculous, but actually
discredit the miracle of incarnating metaphor. If what is now openly
called "illusion" sounds suspiciously related to the "veil" for which
Krieger has so much epistemological contempt, we must keep in
mind his effort, in the definition of the classic vision, to distinguish
between the "canopy" and the "veil."[81] The "canopy" is his metaphor
for an aesthetic illusion which we knowingly duck under in order to
keep ourselves protected from an existential horror we have already
experienced, while the "veil" signifies mere blindness, the condition
of not knowing the score about a world we have not authentically
experienced and may never experience. The metaphor of the canopy
is a perfect introduction to Krieger's latest book, Theory of Criticism,
and what appears to be the elegant and last-ditch hedonism in his
newest apologies for poetry.

The guiding genius of Theory of Criticism is Wallace Stevens, who
anticipated Krieger's latest opus with his incessant talk about the
necessity of projecting improving fictions upon an unbearable world,
with his characterization of the imagination, in a well-known and
essential passage, as canopylike, and with his openly hedonic apology
for poetry. Theory of Criticism is in some ways the apotheosis of
Stevens's poetics. Its reading of the poetics of supreme fictions attempts to convince us not only that that position is central to post-
Nietzschean intellectual history—not a startling argument—but (and
Krieger does this openly) that theoretical history from Plato and
Aristotle onward was at its most sophisticated and illuminating (if
inconsistent) moments moving with Hegelian inevitability toward
Stevens's (and his) perspectives: even that literature itself was moving toward this ecstasy of agonized self-consciousness. About half
of the book is an analysis of the history of criticism from this Stevens-
like point of view, and a defense of what he calls—in response to
the avowed antihumanism of recent French criticism—the unity of the

humanist theoretical tradition and the "traditional Western poetic."[82]

The basic message of the book—that the miracles of poetic language, whether we call them existential revelations of the Manichaean face of reality or monistic effigies, are to be deconstructed as illusions self-consciously imposed upon our impoverished world—is put forward reluctantly as the last and irreducible truth of critical theory. There is here both a sense of nostalgia and the gesture of the theorist making his last stand. Poetry and criticism used to entertain grand visions, but having passed through our existential nightmares, having learned how hard it is, we now know the truth, and can hope only for momentary relief from our troubles. Literature helps us to perform a heroic weight-lifting act, as it pushes off the "weight of the world" (for a while); Krieger asks: "how can man's formal impulse lighten the weight of the unformed world?"[83] Existential reality "threatens," it is "chaos," an "oppressive burden"; the role of literature is to help us "sustain" and "bear" the "weight of the world."[84] Given that sort of language (and there are many instances of it in *Theory of Criticism*), it is difficult to understand his rejection of the hedonism of the pleasure principle which he correctly attributes to Stevens. Perhaps we best understand that rejection by recalling that his earlier work always made more philosophically respectable claims, and that in *The New Apologists* he was very hard on the hedonism of the aesthetes. But at the theoretical bottom of *Theory of Criticism* we have to find hedonism because he has eliminated everything else, except as fiction.

There is a sense in which everything in the early work remains as "fictional play." In both *The Classic Vision* and *Theory of Criticism* the claim is made (in the mode of Vivas) that literature may constitute culture, but the subversive and trivializing qualification is quickly added: "only for a moment." The qualification is understandable because Krieger has rigorously excluded (or almost) the realist option which would allow the poet to dredge up into the light meanings and values from subsistent being. In another approach to value, literature is seen, in its fictionality, as unveiling the consciousness of the maker of the fiction. But how can language, which can give us knowledge about nothing external to itself ("it contains no more than itself"), how can it "contain" or "refer" us to the Cartesian nonlinguistic realm of the *cogito*? In still another approach, Krieger wants to claim that fictions can provide us (he echoes the neo-Kantian philosophy of symbolic forms) the "perceptual norms" for our vision; but once again one wants to ask what the word "norm" can mean for a nominalist? Krieger wants us to understand that he locates these various claims for literature in the double thrust of incarnating metaphor affirming its miraculous transformations and denying itself in a countermetaphorical move—but to do this, to locate value in such a radically problematic linguistic maneuver, makes the matter of value more elusive than the fabled *ignis fatuus*.[85]

Theory of Criticism, with its cultivation of contradiction, may yield us, as the product of Krieger's style and thought, the fruits of paralysis. As he traces the history of theory from the naive times of ontology (when we thought we could know and speak referentially of being) to the sophisticated times of the fiction (when we "know" that we can know nothing but the projections of our minds), Krieger tells us that our exile from being forever denies us the privilege of the realist's stance. He tells us, in the critical mood of Kant, that reality is unknowable *ding an sich*; yet he often contradicts himself by claiming the realist's privilege for himself when he suggests that he knows exactly what reality is in itself: chaotic, oppressive, burdensome. These are held as perceptions of truth, not as fictions, and they come no doubt out of his existentialism. So there is really only one way to read the soothing, sanity-inducing pleasures of the well-ordered, harmonized world of the fiction: as escapist. We must add the usual provision of this new son of Stevens: that we be aware of the antifictive, illusion-destroying movement within the poem itself which insures that we will never forget where and who we are, and which will confer the old New-Critical honorific judgment of "maturity" upon the poem, the poet who made it, and the reader who is able to maintain this schizoid balance.

In *Theory of Criticism* Krieger appears to have granted too much to his enemies. To say against Derrida, as he has said, that poetic language gives us the "illusion of identity," of the unarbitrary, is to grant Derrida's Saussurean point that in language there are only differences; Krieger's fiction of identity, his fiction of the unarbitrary, refers us to the reality of difference and the reality of the arbitrary.[86] Similarly, to say that poetic language gives us an "illusion of presence"[87] is to grant with Derrida that in fact presence is always deferred and fissured. Krieger's response to Coleridge, in other words, is that the word "arbitrary" is not a misnomer, and that the destruction of the antithesis of word and thing (in a moment of presencing or incarnation) is an illusion of poetic language that we can know as illusion because it is undermined by a counter-metaphorical move within the poem itself.

Even in his latest work, then, we can detect Krieger's alliance with what I described earlier (through Kant, Nietzsche, Vaihinger, Sartre, and Stevens) as the tradition of conservative fictionalism. It is the existentialism of that tradition which governs his repetition of the most common misreading of Derrida—that he is an existentialist. As

Krieger puts it, "Derrida seems at times to use linguistic absence as a cover for the metaphysical disappearance of God."[88] Derrida in fact never indulges the mystification of an absent signified standing at some untraversable distance from a "present" signifier. The so-called "absent" center, Derrida writes, must be determined *"otherwise than as loss of the center."*[89] In Krieger's reconstruction, however, Derrida serves a Stevens-like proposal: in a last effort to establish the privilege of the literary sign, Krieger says that good literature generates a self-conscious fiction of an absent presence. Proceeding on the basis of what he calls the "existential theme of absence," he weds existentialism with deconstruction: "literature itself is no enemy to the deconstructive impulse. Far from it. Indeed, one might well argue that in its reflexivity and self-consciousness literature not only deconstructs itself but is the very model for our use in the deconstruction of other discourse."[90] To hold to the things that Krieger wants to hold to *as fictions only* makes only self-subverting sense.

It seems just to criticize his latest work with a quotation from *The Tragic Vision* which says all that needs to be said about the avatars of Wallace Stevens:

> One may prefer to say that it represents a supreme act of human courage to create meaningful communal structures of value on a substructure of acknowledged nothingness. Perhaps, as humanists say, man's creating God *is* a more sublime act than God's creating man. Perhaps. But the honest existentialist—anxious to confront his ontological status—would see the naturalist's structure in the void as an evasive act of bravado, not a closing act of bravery. . . . [the tragic visionary] does not, like the naturalist, try to play both sides of the street to earn the prize of an ungrounded something: a world philosophically negated which is somehow made to yield the existential ease that would come if there were a meaning and purpose to be grasped.[91]

6

Alongside Krieger's romantic isolationism and the instinctive nominalism we find everywhere in his mode of arguing, and functioning as a lonely but powerful counterimpulse to the debilitating self-consciousness of his work after *The Tragic Vision*, is a moral emphasis that is cautiously classical in its dependence on guarded versions of the ideals of objectivity, realism in epistemology, the universal, and community. What seems to be underneath this emphasis is the traditionalist's contempt for those ideals which stress the private and the personal, a contempt for the theories of recent vintage which celebrate the pleasures of deliberate misreading (originality first, now, and forever). The Krieger that I am about to describe has no use for the idea that the critic is a poet in the same sense that Milton or Wordsworth were poets. He believes that literature has an educative role to play in our lives and that the best way to avoid the educative impact of literature is to assume, as readers, that the text exists in order to call forth the imaginative play of the critical mind.

Krieger's early formulation of the question of value in *The Problems of Aesthetics* takes us into the heart of the matter:

> If the object of aesthetic experience is an object of value,
> we must discover the locus or the seat of this value. Is it in
> the mind of the spectator, in the object, or in the relation
> between the two? Does the spectator create or project the
> value himself, does he share with the object in creating it,
> does he share with other spectators in its creation, or
> does he merely discover the value, which was there before
> his arrival and remains unchanged after his departure?[92]

When the same issues are raised in *The New Apologists*, Krieger takes what in the contemporary scene would be termed the antistructuralist hard-line. I. A. Richards is attacked for his subjectivism and what I would call his Rorschach literary theory which turns the text into an inkblot ("Tell me what *this* one reminds you of. . . ."). The inkblot, whatever else it may do, clearly cannot function as a coercive, objective, or "normative structure," designed to elicit normative responses. Leaning heavily on Vivas's essay, "The Objective Basis of Criticism," Krieger sets up an alternative to the position he finds in Richards:

> The work has within it a "discriminable structure" or a
> "system of norms" which is open to inspection. The quali-
> ties *of* the work and *in* the work are phenomenally
> "anchored" to this structure or these norms. But the
> reader *discovers* these qualities (which exist prior to his
> interest); he does not *create* them. They are in the object
> because he can talk about the structure which contains
> them. . . . While no critic may be correct, yet every evalua-
> tion is corrigible by an appeal to the structure. The give
> and take of critical discussion seeks to eliminate what is
> idiosyncratic in order to establish more and more success-
> fully what is in the object.[93]

What is essential philosophically to this passage never leaves Krieger:

the insistent objectivism (note what he italicizes); a sophisticated as opposed to a naive realism (he speaks of the phenomenal object, not the naked *ding an sich*; yet realism it is); and, as the basis of epistemological optimism, the appeal to community ("the give and take of critical discussion"). We can know, he is saying (if only we will not indulge ourselves), a transpersonal structure, and we get to it by being willing to burn off the idiosyncratic, personal subjectivity which we lay over the poem. We open the possibility of objectivity in reading by entering into the community of scholars. These ideals never leave Krieger, but somewhere in the mid-1960s he becomes wistful about them as he begins to adopt (and finally does adopt in his last book) an epistemology which would block them out of intellectual play.

In *The New Apologists* Krieger's argument for the "resident" capacity of an aesthetic structure to "house" value is placed on a middle ground between the embarrassments of the absolutist and relativistic extremes.[94] His thinking here is morally urgent, and survives even the epistemological assault that he himself mounts in *Theory of Criticism*:

> objectivism alone can, with logical consistency, at least give its proponent the knowledge that he may be wrong with respect to other judgments and not merely different from them: he is enabled to debate the issue. It can free him from the feeling of incorrigibility and, consequently, from the spiritual pride which underlies absolutism as well as relativism, and can return him to the humility which is both proper and profitable for an imperfect humanity. . . .[95]

But with an essay delivered at the MLA convention in 1967, Krieger begins to grow more and more fascinated with the idiosyncratic in our perceptual acts, less and less sanguine about the possibilities of intersubjectivity—which is to say less and less sanguine about the possibilities of genuine communication, genuine community. By an easy and fatal step, Kant's notion that perception is under the control of interior *but universal* categories is converted into the notion (joyfully put forth by Nietzsche in *Beyond Good and Evil* and other works, and enthusiastically supported by a number of Krieger's contemporaries) that the idiosyncratic is in control; that no perception is "privileged" because all perceptions are about equally subjective, in the private sense of that term. Inaccessibly enclosed as we are in our private cells of the self, it becomes very difficult to see how we can really engage in the give-and-take demanded by community existence; difficult to understand what the concept of the normative—a privileged concept if there ever was one—can mean; difficult to see how the text can be anything but an ink-blot which will support any overlay that we would project upon it. The door is open to all-out relativism and all-out trivialization of literature and the critical effort. Yet, though he subscribes to such epistemological despair, he refuses to yield to the consequences. The text, he tells us, does not "with equal adequacy, sustain all comers"; the "experienced reader" (here is the structuralist appeal to a professional community) knows better. Like Shelley before him, Krieger grants the "little world of self" and then urges us—like Shelley again—to break out of it; to "open ourselves" to the "beckoning" power of the imaginative work whose impact upon us, if only we will forego our arrogant isolation, will "change our ways of seeing and of living," will be "the force that helps define who . . . [we] are to become."[96]

Krieger's most recent and fullest development of these issues is his third chapter in *Theory of Criticism*; his habit of pushing his thinking to unresolvable contradictions is brought to stark perfection in this chapter, as we learn on one page that "all experience, as experience, remains internal and even arbitrary, idiosyncratic," and, then, on the next, that the "responsible critic is always tempted to posit 'out there' an object that, formally sovereign, draws him to it, resisting his tendency to draw it to the contours of his own personality."[97] In another passage we learn that, because of the privacy of our experience, all claims of the organic critic that poems possess totality of form, perfect intrinsic pattern, must be treated as critical fictions. As we attribute a total pattern we, not the poet, fill in all the blank spaces (another structuralist echo) and we create, in effect, what is called a text. The elaborate development of this issue in *Theory of Criticism* sets Krieger apart from the earlier New Critics (and from his earlier books); reading is no longer an innocent activity of naive mimesis.[98] Yet a few sentences later, with some desperation, Krieger contradicts himself when he writes: "We must try to know when the filling-in follows the lead of indication plotted in the poem and when it is only our own arbitrary act serving our willful adherence to the myth of wholeness." Then he makes the point which dramatizes the futility of his plea; he has, after all, come out epistemologically for a flat-out subjectivism: "We must try to know this, but theoretically, of course, we cannot."[99]

The epistemology is decidedly pessimistic in the later Krieger, but the ethics remains as optimistic as ever. In these pages on the act of reading he tells us repeatedly that the work is "beckoningly" out there; that we must try to guard "whatever normative and sharable element may yet be saved out of the critical procedure"; that we must not "inflate" ourselves "arrogantly" in order to play freely with the work. We need to preserve "dialogue," the "collective" endeavor, the "corrigibility of the individual judgment," and so the basis of community itself.[100] In a moment of some impatience he says: "as readers of literature and its criticism, we never, in our own persons, turn away from the fact that the work *is* beckoningly out there; and it's the same work that all those other fellows are talking about, some more faithfully than others, though none altogether faithfully. At some level, in spite of persuasive epistemological skepticism, all of us share Dr. Johnson's hard-headed, rock-kicking impatience with the unbridgeable private worlds of solipsism." We ought, with "humility," he says, let the poem "educate us and enlarge us."[101] The ethical surge of Krieger's rhetoric in these and other places is moving and, these days, even courageous. With Georges Poulet and E. D. Hirsch he would stand against the free-play of the self-cultivating misreaders. But he cannot earn his ethical spurs: too much in his work gives aid and comfort to his enemies.

In a recent response to some of the reviewers of *Theory of Criticism* Krieger summarizes with sterling candor his method and intention:

> In the book I have tried to hold fully and press simultaneously both halves of the following oppositions: both the poem as object *and* the poem as *intentional* object; both the concept of a discrete aesthetic experience *and* a notion of *all* experience as indivisible and unbroken; both the discontinuity of the poem's language system *and* the continuity of all discourse as *a* system; both spatiality *and* temporality, mystification *and* demystification in the work's workings upon us; both the poem as self-willed monster *and* the poet as a present agent subduing a compliant poem to his will; both fiction as reality *and* fiction as a delusive evasion of reality; or, put another way, both a closed, totalized, metaphoric reduction seen as our autonomous world *and* an open fullness of reality that resists all reduction and gives the poem the lie. Finally, then, both the verbal miracle of metaphorical identity *and* the awareness that the miracle depends on our sense of its impossibility, leading to our knowledge that it's only our *illusion* of identity held with an awareness that language cannot reach beyond the Structuralist principle of difference.[102]

That statement is prefaced by this one: "Somewhere in my argument I have anticipated most objections by trying to include them too within my paradoxical contours in advance—if one can accept my tactic just at the outer edge of what may be permitted to argument."[103] To accept the tactic is to grant Krieger's later works the status of nondiscursive symbolist poem; or, alternatively, to grant him Whitman's intentionality (I am large, I contain multitudes). It is to grant, as I have not, that, in more than one sense, he is beyond criticism.

Seven

You, boast, indeed, of being obliged to no other Creature, but of drawing, and spinning out all from your self; That is to say, if we may judge of the Liquor in the Vessel by what issues out, You possess a good plentiful Store of Dirt and Poison in your Breast. . . . the Question comes all to this; Whether is the nobler Being of the two, That which by a lazy Contemplation of four Inches round; by an over-weening Pride, which feeding and engendering on it self, turns all in to Excrement and Venom; producing nothing at last, but Fly-bane and a Cobweb: Or That, which, by an universal Range, with long Search, much Study, true Judgment, and Distinction of Things, brings home Honey and Wax.

Jonathan Swift, *The Battel of the Books*

Before Schleiermacher introduced the discipline of general hermeneutics, the term "hermeneutics" was used almost exclusively by biblical interpreters, and indeed the name itself suggests a sacred origin, being cognate with Hermes, the messenger of the gods. According to Boeckh, the Greek *Ermenia* is derived from an older, uncertain root that antedates both the messenger-god and the process of interpreting. It is uncertain, then, whether the god or hermeneutics came first.

E. D. Hirsch, *The Aims of Interpretation*

E. D. Hirsch: The Hermeneutics of Innocence

As a theorist who speaks unapologetically for rational values, E. D. Hirsch stands pretty much by himself in the landscape of contemporary critical theory. The rhetorical force of his position, in fact, rests on the disarming candor and clarity with which he rejects everything (from the New Criticism to poststructuralism) that has been *au courant* in the last thirty years of critical theorizing. By warning us again and again of the dangers of subjectivism and relativism, his theoretical writings suggest an effort to teach those of us under the tutelary spirit of the modernist and postmodernist spider how to bring home the honey. The mentality of Swift's allegorical spider is equated implicitly by Hirsch with romanticism, or at least with that part of romanticism which, as revolt on behalf of concreteness, contingency, organic process, and radical notions of the value of originality in personal perspective and in expression, is said to look forward to twentieth-century developments in existential phenomenology in the thought of Heidegger, Sartre, and Merleau-Ponty. What energizes the spider, according to Hirsch, is the organic fallacy (my term, not Hirsch's): "the metaphorical doctrine that a text leads a life of its own."[1] Presumably, avoidance of the fallacy would make it possible to implement his desire that literary study be conducted "as a corporate enterprise and a progressive discipline."[2]

This utopian hope for the study of literature appears to be based on conservative theoretical ideals which, minus the wit and drama of Swift, resemble calcified versions of neoclassical aesthetics that are grounded on distaste for the individuality of things. Hirsch is not really the anti-romantic that he so often appears to be, but a romantic himself—much like the Wordsworth of the "Preface"—who is intent on preserving the viability of Enlightenment norms of typicality by making them account-able to the interior life. Wordsworth tells us that we may avoid the "trivial" and the "mean"—for an expressive poet these words translate as the "personal" and the "private"—by imitating the "great and uni-versal passions of men."[3] In his first book, *Wordsworth and Schelling: A Typological Study*, Hirsch assents to the Wordsworthian perspective when he takes as his controlling critical norm what he calls a "cultural selfhood"—a concept that can be linked to the thought of Wilhelm Dilthey—which preserves for romanticism the classical value of "gen-eral nature" (the "unstreaked tulip") by turning it inward so that it may be read as a "general subject" released from the overly particularized determinants of time, place, and the personal will.[4] Wordsworth, Shel-ley, and Emerson, among others, endorse a socially directed ideal of the poetic character which celebrates its capaciousness and comprehensive-ness. The poet, in Emerson's phrase, is the "representative man," whose selfhood escapes the utterly temporalized human being which emerges from Martin Heidegger's *Being and Time*, a treatise that appears to be Hirsch's philosophical *bête noire*.

1

Hirsch's war on the organicist principle is total and cannot be overly dramatized. Not only does he attack its mildly irrationalist im-plications in romantics like Coleridge (who tells us that organic form "shapes, as it develops itself from within"), but he is unrelenting in locating and rooting out more recent versions of the fallacy. Heidegger's meditation on language in *On the Way to Language*, for example, is seen by Hirsch as an especially extreme and virulent form of the romantic sickness. "Language speaks" is the way that Heidegger puts it else-where, not man. "Man acts as though he were the shaper and master of language, while in fact language remains the master of man."[5] Some-thing very like organic self-sufficiency—once celebrated by romantics as the linguistic identity of a form of discourse ontologically segregated from allegorical writing, whose hallmark was the arbitrary relationship

of signifier and signified—becomes in Heidegger the ontological principle of all discourse. No longer is it the poets alone who find their conscious, willing selves absorbed into the mastering forces of discourse.
Human being, for Heidegger, "dwells" in language because language
"has appropriated us to itself."[6]

Against the Coleridgean romanticism of the New-Critical tradition in
Anglo-American criticism, which rests on the dualism between the organic discourse of poetry and the referential form of all other modes,
Hirsch asserts the essential ontological homogeneity of all forms of
writing: "The literary text (in spite of semimystical claims for its
uniqueness) does not have a special ontological status which somehow
absolves the reader from the demands universally imposed by all
linguistic texts of every description."[7] If this traditional romantic claim
(the unique ontological status of the literary text) is grounded on thin
air, then it follows that the hoary Kantian claim for the uniqueness of
the "aesthetic experience" is likewise grounded (because all texts, as
Hirsch argues, impose a single, universal demand upon us as readers).
He can rule these theories out of critical discussion because he does not
believe in the double-faced epistemology which has supported them.
There is not one way of knowing peculiar to science and "ordinary consciousness," and another (i.e., "imaginative") and better way of knowing peculiar to art and the humanistic disciplines (whatever critics in the
romantic mode have been stressing for the last two hundred years or
so). In Hirsch's words: "the much-touted cleavage between thinking in
the sciences and the humanities does not exist."[8]

Against Heidegger Hirsch asserts a distinction that he takes from
Saussure:[9] a text—any text—because it is an actualization from an ideal
linguistic system of possibilities and conventions, owes its particular
formal and semantic identity to a conscious, selecting will that interacts
with the system, and in so doing realizes a linguistic possibility. Hirsch
believes Heidegger to be making a claim for all texts which the New
Critics and other romantics claimed for the poetic text alone: "The text,
being independent of any particular consciousness, takes on the autonomous being of language [i.e., *langue*] itself."[10] Coleridge's modest organicist attack on the subject and the undisguisedly antihumanist
thought of the later Heidegger, the structuralists, and Jacques Derrida:
all are seen in Hirsch's perspective as constituting a single, unbroken
line of irrationalist denigration of the traditional subject, a heavy and
largely successful siege against the "author" and his "authority." The
authorizing power of what Hirsch calls "will" or "intention," or what
less organically committed romantics like Wordsworth and Shelley located as an interior realm of feeling or vision, or what that recent ro-

mantic Georges Poulet called the point of departure, are all banished in structuralist thought as illusory nonlinguistic metaphysical centers of determination.

The effort, then, is not only to do away with the romantic privileging of "literary language" (the title of Hirsch's major theoretical work is not *Validity in Literary Interpretation*) but also to reinstate the authorial will as a source for determinate linguistic meaning. As source, or governing center, authorial will stands outside the realm of language. In the idiom of contemporary French criticism, Hirsch wishes to reinstate as the ontological ground of meaning a finite human subject which is itself not reducible to the pronoun "I," a subject, in other words, which cannot be brought under the mastering forces of the grammatical and syntactical regulations of a given discourse. A text, literary or otherwise, is a determinate entity, a *parole* whose meaning is posited and frozen for all time by an act of the author's will: "The author's or speaker's subjective act is formally necessary to verbal meaning,"[11] as Hirsch puts it. So a text does not have an independent life of its own—a meaning which, because it is vital and dynamic, is independent of an "author" and finally indeterminate since it forever changes in the endless processes of time.

For all their differences, then, Hirsch is willing to lump together the Coleridgeans and the Heideggerians because he sees both mounting an attack on the expressive theory of human utterance and the traditional ontology of the subject-object model which supports that theory. Heidegger's three objections to the view that speech is the "audible expression and communication of human feelings" lead us directly into the heart of Hirsch's concerns:

> First and foremost, speaking is expression. The idea of speech as an utterance is the most common. It already presupposes the idea of something internal that utters or externalizes itself. . . .
> Secondly, speech is regarded as an activity of man. Accordingly we have to say that man speaks, and that he always speaks some language. Hence we cannot say, "Language speaks." For this would be to say: "It is language that first brings man about, brings him into existence." Understood in this way, man would be bespoken by language.
> Finally, human expression is always a presentation and representation of the real and the unreal.[12]

With none of Swift's or Hirsch's fear of the spider and its works, and coming from a philosophical tradition which has no use for the subject-object model which generates spidery and beelike values, Heidegger boldly reverses the cause and effect relationship of the speaker and his speaking: he appears to welcome the spider when he tells us that language is a "web" of relations—he extends the metaphor to some length—a web which "has woven us into the speaking."[13]

One consequence of this exposure and avoidance of the organic fallacy which is thought to enervate Continental as well as Anglo-American critical theory is the exposure and avoidance of the two errors that lead to the intellectually unacceptable dead ends of anarchic subjectivism and vicious relativism. Hirsch calls these two errors—really two sides of the same coin—"radical historicism" and "psychologism."[14] Both the psychologistic and the historicist errors are based, he thinks, on the incontestable fact of the "multiplicity of persons."[15] Upon this fact of the infinite multiplicity of human reality, Hirsch offers a reconstruction of Heidegger's philosophical intention. His first point is that if human being is saturated by temporality, then it is constituted by its temporal location and givens, and must be unique, *sui generis*, in each of its countless manifestations across history. Distinctive time and place yield a distinctive person who "experiences" the meaning of the text before him in a distinctive way, because the text is constituted (forestructured) by a unique consciousness each time it is "read." Heidegger's presumed view that a person in one cultural era can have no "authentic" access to a text created in another cultural era would appear to follow from his radical temporalizing of human being; but, as Hirsch demonstrates with great force and persuasiveness, given this sort of presupposition, Heidegger's conclusion is tame and sentimental. If human being is inescapably temporal, then not only can there be no communication between eras, but there can be no "understanding"—whatever that term can mean in such a perspective—between members of the same cultural context, from moment to moment, since no one person has been temporalized in precisely the same way as another. "The 'life theory' of a text," Hirsch concludes, is a notion that belongs in the same family with Heidegger's radical historicism, for the theory "implicitly places the principle of change squarely where it belongs, that is, not in textual meaning as such, but in changing generations of readers."[16] If Heideggerians like Hans-Georg Gadamer are correct about the historicity of understanding, then all readings of texts become, as Hirsch argues, fictive expressions whose value lies in what they might tell us about the reader, and not in anything about the text to which the readings are presumably directed.

Though not as openly as he might, Hirsch consistently offers alternatives to the ways of Coleridgean organicism and Heideggerian historicism. Texts are fixed sequences of signs, not organic beings; they do not mysteriously bring themselves into existence; they do not shape their own semantic identities; they do not, in themselves, change in the course of time. The meaning and linguistic way of being of a text are separable not only for purposes of analysis: they are ontologically distinguishable. The meaning of a text can be translated out of its particular linguistic configuration, because, as Hirsch stresses time and again, meaning (if it *is* meaning) is "reproducible."[17] In *The Aims of Interpretation* Hirsch offers us his doctrine of synonymity as a counter-force to the organicist doctrine that form compels meaning: "synonymity is in fact possible, and . . . on this possibility depends the determinacy of meaning, the emancipation of thought from the prison-house of a particular linguistic form, and the possibility of fields of knowledge generally."[18] "Reproducibility," or "synonymity" of meaning, is somehow grounded on the theory of the arbitrary relationship of signifier and signified, a Saussurean principle that Hirsch sees in dramatic relief against the nonarbitrariness of romantic "symbol."

I have taken some caution to surround my phrasing of Hirsch's criticisms of Heidegger and Gadamer with skeptical qualifiers, because Hirsch appears to me to have misunderstood Heidegger and Gadamer about as badly as it is possible to misunderstand them, and I believe that there are interesting reasons for this misunderstanding. The basic charge, that Heidegger and his followers are solipsistic relativists, stems from a traditional conception of the subject-object model which relegates the subject *qua* subject to the privacy of its perspectives. According to Hirsch, Heidegger's solipsism (his "cognitive atheism") is rooted in an idea of the purely temporal status of human reality which is rigorously insisted upon in *Being and Time*. From this temporalizing of human reality it appears to follow that we are all locked in the prison-houses of our unique consciousnesses. Access to the past is impossible, but no less impossible is access to our own cultural context. But Heidegger never accepted the epistemological model upon which such a devastating critique of his work is mounted, and never showed any interest in the subject *qua* subject. For one thing, his notion of human reality as *Dasein* is an integrated one which does not permit an inner-outer distinction; for another, *Dasein* is in no way to be understood as the unique possession of a personal, individuated being: the purpose of the analysis of *Dasein* is to disclose its transpersonal and transcultural existential modes. I have indicated in chapter 3 that there may be grave problems with this kind of analysis, but they are not of the sort that Hirsch imposes upon Heidegger's text. The rejection of Descartes might lead to difficulties, but solipsistic relativism is patently not, in *Being and Time*, one of them.

Hirsch has not only mistaken the meaning of *Dasein*; he has ignored the analysis in the penultimate chapter of *Being and Time*, in which *Dasein*'s historicity is established, not as a self-destructive solipsism, but as a storehouse of universal potentials or temporal possibilities of human being which becomes the basis for historical knowledge. Gadamer's theory of tradition is an extension of this Heideggerian point: knowledge of the past is real because the arbitrary (local) prejudices of consciousness can be sloughed off as we acquire certain unarbitrary forestructurings of the past which permit us authentic historical contact. To use Hirsch's favorite terms: the "relevance" of our historicized being is always "meaningful." Tradition is the basic temporal continuity which links our *Dasein* with the *Dasein* that is past, but it is only through the *Dasein*-that-we-are that traditional consciousness can be achieved. There is, in so many words, no unmediated historical knowledge. That is reserved for God, or for theorists like Hirsch who believe that objective knowledge can be acquired in a massive act of dispossessing ourselves of the only route to knowledge that we have: the historicized self. What Hirsch's readings of Heidegger and Gadamer may ultimately indicate is the traditional Anglo-American fear and manhandling of any sort of thought which does not work from Cartesian premises.

Beneath his assumptions lies the view of human nature that we find in rigid rationalistic humanisms, a view which, though it leans heavily on Husserl's theory of intentionality, attempts assiduously to avoid contact with any theory of consciousness associated with existential phenomenology. Though consciousness and meaning, in Hirsch's system, are not free of the "history" that may be typologically reconstructed, what is essential to hermeneutical consciousness and the meaning it intends can be separated from the historical being of the interpreter. If there is to be "objective interpretation," then the act of severance—the characteristic act of Hirsch's thinking—must be performed: "meaning" must be severed from "significance," understanding from evaluation, interpretation from criticism, and fact from value. Underneath it all, the severe Cartesian division of object from subject is preserved by Hirsch as he transposes it into the more acceptable dualism of Husserlian phenomenology, where "intentional object" is cleanly cut off from the realities of actual human consciousness. These various acts of severance, which serve the heuristic needs of his hermeneutics, are reflections of a fundamental dualism that is the basis of his thought.

2

Hirsch contends that in order to avoid confusing "meaning" (which is determinate and grounded in authorial will) with "significance," "value," or "criticism" (the relationship of meaning to just about anything else, but mostly to the imperatives of another culture, another time), it is necessary to recognize, first, that "meaning is an affair of consciousness not of words. Almost any word sequence can, under the conventions of language, legitimately represent more than one complex of meaning."[19] Second, we are asked to reinstate the original author as "the determiner of meaning" because his controlling consciousness alone (though banished from hermeneutical theory by romantic organicism, symbolist ideas of impersonality, New-Critical anti-intentionalism, and Saussurean and Heideggerian attacks on the very notion of the human subject as a prelinguistic, ontological center) represents the ground of the "only compelling normative principle that could lend validity to an interpretation."[20] With admirable bluntness Hirsch says that if a "theorist wants to save the ideal of validity he has to save the author as well. . . ."[21] But Hirsch's bluntness and nononsense manner invite responses in kind: What *is* an author? What is the character of consciousness? How is it possible to separate so cleanly "meaning" and "words"? What are the consequences of that division?

For Hirsch the question is not, What is consciousness?, but, What is the most important function that consciousness can perform? His answer, put forth in the last appendix to *Validity in Interpretation*, is clear and unqualified: the function of consciousness, which is the *sine qua non* of a civilized cognitive life, is the activity of formulating the "type idea" (in traditional epistemology, the "concept"). In what he sees as its ability to "subsume more than one experience and therefore to represent more than one experience," Hirsch situates the type idea as the mental structure most "essential and fundamental to language."[22] It is a measure of his commitment to a type-making—and, as we shall see shortly, type-seeing—consciousness that he can speak of this most anciently recognized of mental functions as a "miraculous feat"[23] (a phrase that we generally associate with literary theorists of romantic inclination and their talk of the "imagination," the special function of which is to do something like the opposite of what Hirsch describes in his "Excursus on Types"). His expression of wonder also indicates his inability to explain how it is that the mind does this sort of thing: "No doubt this kind of process can and does occur, but the theory does not explain how two traits (from two different entities) are *judged* to be the same."[24]

Hirsch does not move complacently into an extreme rationalism. There are moments when he wants to come to terms with particularity and originality: "type concepts are indispensable in all attempts to understand an individual entity in its particularity."[25] He appears to be saying that type concepts are only heuristic tools that enable us to approach and open up individual entities in their particularity. In the next breath, however, he accepts as "inescapable" Dilthey's motto, *Individuum est ineffabile,* and by so doing makes nonsense of the idea of understanding "an individual entity in its particularity."[26] All of the evidence suggests that Hirsch *intends* to make nonsense of the particular, to put it out of the reach of consciousness and humane discourse. Thus: "Types are constitutive of all meaningful experiences. . . ."[27] And this is so because the type appears to have an origin in a certain *a priori* capacity of consciousness. At the end of his excursus on types Hirsch makes an appeal to Kant's epistemology, an ultimate philosophy of types, in which mental categories determine our cognitive experience; what we know as the phenomenal world is a world whose origin is the structure of consciousness. The particular, for Kant, though it may seem to be available as a fiction of aesthetic experience, is, strictly speaking, unknowable because there is no innate capacity in consciousness to experience things in that way. And yet even with this explicit Kantianism on the table, Hirsch does not want to let go of particularity and is forced into a rare moment of internal contradiction when he says "our idea of a particular thing is always a type idea."[28] When he speaks of the "inescapable constitutive function"[29] of types he, too, like Kant, must relegate particulars to cognitive darkness. The type-making function of consciousness turns out, in his hermeneutical system, to have an unconscious, *a priori*-like base which insures that types are all that we can see: "types" are the irremovable Kantian lenses which focus our hermeneutical experience. The major difference between the type categories of Kant and those of Hirsch is that Kant's are the basis of an eternal geometry of consciousness: they are universal and therefore transcend culture and history; while Hirsch's (and here he follows Dilthey quite strictly) are culturally bound. This difference between Hirsch's Dilthey-mediated Kantianism and Kant himself may, however, be overstated and misleading. Not only do both show their instinctual rationalism in ruling out of bounds the particular, but Hirsch's "type" functions transcendentally within a cultural frame *as a universal for the culture.* The cultural type emerges as a static, spatialized entity (a "structure") which rises over the temporal flow it would enclose. Hirsch's typological assumptions keep him clear of organicist excesses and the epistemologically slippery "particular" of intuitionist theories such as those of

Croce and Bergson. But it may be that his responses to organicism and the spidery mentality are themselves excessive. It is possible to imagine things worse than spiders.

The purpose of the first chapter of *Validity in Interpretation*, to defend and reinstate the author as the ground of determinate and sharable meaning, is best understood against this background of Hirsch's meditation on types. The task of the interpreter who seeks "validity" is "to reproduce in himself the author's 'logic,' his attitudes, his cultural givens, in short, his world." Even though the process of verification is highly complex and difficult, the ultimate veridical principle is very simple—"the imaginative reconstruction of the speaking subject."[30] Though Hirsch's allusion to Saussure's *le sujet parlant*—a diachronic fact—and to the whole scholarly process of retrieving the cultural forms of another time would appear to involve his method deeply in history and the historical person, and even to recall the feared Heidegger and his existential phenomenological tradition, his actual intention is almost the opposite: "The speaking subject is not, however, identical with the subjectivity of the author as an actual historical person; it corresponds, rather, to a very limited and special aspect of the author's total subjectivity: it is, so to speak, that 'part' of the author which specifies or determines verbal meaning."[31] The "actual historical person" is not the author that Hirsch would reinstate, because the "actual historical person," saturated as he is in process and particularity, is inaccessible to a hermeneutical system in which types are constitutive, and in which types alone are what may be retrieved by the historically minded critic. Hirsch's conception of person, then, is severely dualistic in its recollection of the opposition of body and soul: a person is not a unified whole composed of fused elements of typicality and singularity, but a mechanical entity with separable "parts": the "part" that can be known via typological reconstruction (traditional metaphysics calls it the soul) is the "cultural subject," the detached subjectivity of the historical person shared by other persons of his "times." The concepts of "cultural subject," "cultural givens," author's "world," and the "part" of the author "which specifies or determines verbal meaning" are in the end interchangeable.

In its antagonism to the historicism of post-Heideggerian thought, Hirsch's hermeneutics retreats to the methodology of the *Zeitgeist*-seeking deterministic historicism of the nineteenth century. The "cultural subject" is nothing but its "cultural givens," and both are by Hirsch's admission deliberate reconstructions from a matrix of contingency and process which, or so it is claimed, lie on the other side of human knowledge. Though with the aid of the pre-Heideggerian German hermeneutical tradition (Schleiermacher, August Boeckh, and Dilthey) he has made old-line historicism considerably more sophisticated in its epistemological instruments, it is difficult to see how Hirsch's basic theoretical principles represent a serious and significant advance over those of Hippolyte Taine, or how they avoid falling into similar philosophical pits.

Hirsch's refinement of the old historicism is implicitly summed up by his adjudication of the Brooks vs. F. W. Bateson disagreement over Wordsworth's "A Slumber Did My Spirit Seal."[32] It seems that we are to decide what Wordsworth really meant not by appealing to the crude notion of the "spirit of the romantic age," but by reconstructing Wordsworth as cultural subject in the year that he wrote the poem—the spirit of '99, so to speak. In his preference for Bateson's exclusive pantheistic reading of Wordsworth, an unintended irony in Hirsch's historicism comes to the surface. Wanting to pay reverence to a past that is not ourselves, by reconstructing a pantheistic-tending cultural selfhood which *must* have constituted Wordsworth's individuated subjectivity, and which is discontinuous with the hedonistic cultural selfhood imposed upon Wordsworth by Brooks from *his* cultural situation, Hirsch trivializes Wordsworth's time for us by cutting it cleanly away from our human concerns. The cultural subject that is ourselves, in this argument, is not traced or marked by the history that was; the meaning of the past, in other words, has no meaning for us. If we could have access to the past—the logic of Hirsch's theory will not permit it—it is not clear why we would be interested to have contact, since such a past is irrelevant. The sort of solipsism that Hirsch charges Heidegger with is a theoretical consequence, rather, of his own position.

Hirsch is epistemologically more lugubrious even than Samuel Johnson, who preferred "just representations of general nature" not because he believed "general nature" was all that could be experienced, but because such representations, unlike those of an overly particularized kind, would, he thought, please many and please long. In the terms of Saussure's distinction between *langue* and *parole*, which Hirsch has applied with precision, we cannot know the *parole* as *parole* but only as the manifestation of a system of norms, only in the light of *langue*. The proper object of Hirsch's hermeneutics is the speaking subject, not in itself, but as a manifestation of the cultural *langue* which dictates all that a "cultural subject" may speak. To push the subject-in-culture to the level of *langue* is in a sense to externalize history and the self, to transform them into objects of typological meditation by draining them of process and particularity, of everything, in other words, that is inimical to typological reconstruction. What Hirsch decides about particularity of meaning—that it must always remain a "meaning of a particular type"[33]—applies equally to his conceptions of consciousness and the self. It is entirely unsatisfactory to have to conclude from his premises (as from those of recent structuralists) that our literary-interpretive experiences are limited to the recognition and articulation of the typological features of a text and the typological self which brought that text into being. But we have no choice. All that is *valid* to say about a text is determined by what Hirsch calls the "second decisive characteristic of a type [which] is that it can always be represented by more than one instance."[34] What this means, practically speaking, is that after we have recognized the "Ode to a Nightingale" as an instance, in its structure and theme, of what Meyer Abrams has located and defined as the "greater romantic lyric," we have come to the end of the interpretive line—because we have run up against the limits of cognition.

Some sort of Crocean or Bergsonian extreme cherishing of concreteness and particularity is not a satisfactory alternative to Hirsch's rationalist faith in types. It has been the embarrassment of the romantic tradition in critical theory ever since Kant—and especially the embarrassment of New Critics who follow Hulme and Ransom—that, once having isolated the aesthetic experience as *sui generis* and cut it away from everything dear to Hirsch's concerns, they have been conspicuously incapable of putting things back together in an integrated human context. The New-Critical problem, as we have seen it in Krieger's texts, is just the reverse of Hirsch's. For Hirsch, particularity is the great dark beast who would turn all into violent anarchy and silence if it should ever get its claws into universals—hence the particular and the type are kept at safe distance from one another so that communication and community may be preserved. For Croceans and Bergsonians it is the type that is the beast who destroys humaneness, as it seizes the other, whether aesthetic phenomenon or person, for an object of will to be manipulated in cold blood. For this kind of New Critic the way to the poem and the way to the person are identical: in an act of Schopenhaurian humility, we repress our personal, willing selves, and in so doing preserve our humaneness and the humaneness of others. And it is the poem above all, in Ransom's or Krieger's poetics, which properly prized will carry us into this human world of autonomous selves, the recognition of whose sacred individuality is the guarantee of our dignity as well as theirs. The critic of this sort tends, at best, to see the type, or universal, as the veil of maya; at worst, as the instrument of a murderous fascistic impulse. Like Hirsch, but for the opposite reason, this kind of critic will want to keep his unique particular at a distance from the type, lest mere proximity cause fatal contamination.

Both the partisans of the type and the partisans of the particular lead us to unacceptable extremes. One calls up the specter of the Orwellian nightmare, while the other points the way to the anarchist's paradise. A more useful theory of self and poem based on Foucault's historicism would not simply occupy a safe middle ground, taking the best of two worlds: it would be a theory different in kind because its primary assumption would be that concreteness and universality are not distinct realms of being, but integrated modes of discourse. In Foucault the "universal" is what is enforced in expression by discursive formations, disciplines, the historical *a priori*; "concreteness" or individuality, on the other hand, is the force which, when successfully articulated in texts (and this is rare), resists dynastic repression and cultural determinates, but only within their restraining contexts. The act of separating the universal from the concrete, whether it is performed in the service of typology by E. D. Hirsch, or in the service of existential uniqueness by Murray Krieger, is an act which, by Foucault's lights, violates historical reality. At certain high critical altitudes, Falstaff may be seen as an instance of the type *miles gloriosus*; the "Ode to a Nightingale" as an instance of the literary universal, "greater romantic lyric" (both being productions of universal models). But there is only one Falstaff, and one "Ode to a Nightingale," and a theory which cannot come to terms with that obvious fact of our critical experience is open to the critique that arid structuralisms have been subjected to. Equally in trouble, though, is the theory which is so sentimentally attached to the idea of free existential uniqueness that it finds itself in chaos, in possession of no normative principle with which to discriminate between identity and difference, the type and the unique, and therefore finds, ironically, that it has shut itself out of its promised land of perception.

With the understanding that for Hirsch meaning is always a typological affair, it follows rigorously that meaning is always "reproducible" and "sharable" (two important words in his vocabulary). The familiar dualisms in his terminology (understanding vs. evaluation, meaning vs. significance, interpretation vs. criticism) are clarified further if we read "understanding" as "understanding of type," "meaning" as "instance of type," and "interpretation" as the reconstruction of the particular type (the "intrinsic genre") that constituted the author's willful positing of meaning. Larger than the individual text, but not as large as the vague traditional concepts of genre like lyric or tragedy, the intrinsic genre is not really a genre in the old sense, nor is it "intrinsic" in the New-Critical sense of the term.[35] Close to an oxymoron as a critical concept, the intrinsic genre might be best understood via the Husserlian terminology of Hirsch's essay of 1960, "Objective Interpretation," which became the protoessay for *Validity in Interpretation*. The intrinsic genre is there the sort of structure called a text's "horizon"—an idea which Hirsch defines with the help of Husserl as a disembodied species (a *type*, again) of intentional act, which would explain the kind of intending that might emerge from the consciousness of a cultural selfhood. The act of interpretation becomes valid when the critic, sloughing off all that is personal and historical in himself, first lifts himself into the author's horizon, and then reproduces it in his own discourse. This is not Martin Buber's leap of empathy, by virtue of which we mystically inhabit the world of another person, but the act of rational reconstruction by virtue of which we contact a cultural subject of the past. The intrinsic genre of Wordsworth's disputed Lucy poem would be Wordsworth's "horizon"—or what we could reconstruct of it—around the time he wrote the poem.

Since Hirsch rejects the more integrated vision of person offered in the tradition of existential phenomenology, he means, when he speaks of "intentionality," to refer us only to Husserl and his especially central notions of the "phenomenological reduction," or *epochē*, and the eidetic reduction, both of which seem to be behind the search for "types" in meaning and selfhood that are free of the "accidental" accretions of person and all worldly involvement. To borrow a distinction from Sartre that is anathema to Husserl's epistemology, and which Hirsch cannot afford to take into account, Hirsch's hermeneutics is based upon a vigorous theoretical debunking of our prereflective experience of the world and an equally vigorous insistence that all acts of verbal meaning are posited from the standpoint of a "reflective consciousness" which has been purged of the personal and the contingent. Verbal meaning does not issue from the temporalized and embodied prereflective consciousness—the question as to *who* is doing the intending is irrelevant to Husserl and Hirsch, and is not really answered by "cultural subject," since the cultural subject is but a retrospective reconstruction, not an existential fact. Any aspect of meaning which is a residue of the prereflective consciousness is only a "symptom" (Hirsch believes) of the person who intends the meaning, not an essential part of meaning itself. As symptom, it is not open to typological analysis. Symptomatic features of the text become semantic parallels to the "real historical person" —and both are out of play in Hirsch's system.[36]

Husserl's effort to bypass the highly specified perspective of the prereflective consciousness was grasped effectively by Hirsch and translated faithfully in this way: "All events of consciousness, not simply those involving visual perception and memory, are characterized by the mind's ability to make modally and temporally different acts of awareness refer to the same *object* of awareness. An object for the mind remains the same even though what 'is going on in the mind' is not the same. The mind's object therefore may not be equated with psychic processes as such. . . ."[37] "The remarkable fact of consciousness," as he put it another place, "is that the objects of its awareness are not the same as the subjective 'perceptions,' 'processes,' or 'acts' which are directed toward those objects."[38] In an effort (like Kant's) to establish an intersubjective ground for cognition, it was necessary for Husserl to rule out the personally contingent tones and dispositions of the individual consciousness, and all the differences of time, so that the object of consciousness could emerge in the clarity of its essence (as *eidos*). And it is altogether necessary for Hirsch, given the purpose of his hermeneutics, to establish scientific agreement in interpretation, that he subscribe to Husserlian intentionality, and insist that interpreters interested in "corporate" goals do likewise. But the question of *who* is doing the intending, under what conditions, where and when, though irrelevant for the goals of this sort of epistemology, is powerfully relevant in any critical theory which is founded upon reinstating a historically constituted author.

Much of the strength and weakness (and ambiguity) of Hirsch's hermeneutics rests, then, on his employment of Husserl's austere intentional theory of human consciousness. A particular object like a table, and a particular text like Wordsworth's "A Slumber Did My Spirit Seal," are what Husserl would call "intentional objects"; they remain unchanging, or self-identical, through the variety of culturally and temporally located "intentional acts" which grasp them. The power of Hirsch's argument for validity in interpretation depends, as we have seen, on the cogency of his dismissal of those psychologistic and radically historicist theories that would ask us to believe that intentional objects—like texts—can never be stripped of the subjective accretions laid on them by the time-ridden interpreter. What he asks us to do is to suppress "significance" (or "relevance")—our individual experiences of the meaning of a text—for the sake of a valid interpretation, because "significance" or "relevance" are products of, and indexes to, our values and our cultural contexts, not reflections of the text's original meaning. As we dissolve our specified historicity, we enter the reassuring world of authorial intention. Verbal meaning is a construction of the interpreter of texts, but (and this is the ambiguity) properly achieved, it is a perfect mimesis of authorial meaning which (Hirsch permits the implication) was similarly constructed in an abstention from prereflective consciousness.

3

Consistently held through *Validity in Interpretation* in its version of persons, Hirsch's blend of phenomenology and rationalism is also the foundation of his account of the coming-to-be of verbal meaning, and of his putatively Saussurean stress on the arbitrary nature of the linguistic sign. Though he rejects the romantic view that the poet's medium has an organic vitality which shapes itself into an integrated formal and semantic identity that cannot be broken down, he is willing to grant that "considerations of style, genre, and local texture may play a larger part in . . . [the author's] final meaning than that played by his original intention." He concludes, however, that "these interesting observations have hardly any theoretical significance. . . ."[39] There is something deliberately arch in that last remark which may help us to grasp Hirsch's polemical and philosophical purposes. What he calls mildly interesting (but supposedly lacking in theoretical significance) is simply a central preoccupation of literary theory, since the days of Coleridge and Schelling, with the formative role in the creative process played by the technical and traditional resources of the artist's medium. Hirsch ignores the attempt of Coleridge and other moderate romantics to strike a balance between the respective roles of the self-conscious, willful (intentional) craftsman and what appears to be (by the common testimony of the poets) a kind of possession induced by the aesthetic medium. He fears, without sufficient reason, that all organicist theories of poetic creation inevitably turn the poet into a somnambulist and the poem into a science-fiction monster, a formless beast that changes its identity as it "grows" through the processes of history.

But Hirsch leaps to another extreme. Though somewhat obscured by the concession to matters of style, local textures, and genre, his ultimate point comes clear in his refusal to assign any *theoretical* meaning to those concessions. Though he appears to grant organicists full due, in actuality Hirsch grants them nothing of philosophical substance, because however great the modification performed upon intention by the linguistic medium and literary tradition, verbal intention itself, fully conscious, fully possessed, remains the prelinguistic origin or place of residence in the subject of a type meaning. "Original" verbal intention is the interior side of a process (at bottom quite mechanical) of making external a skeletal structure of meaning which may be fleshed out (or decorated) in the final "larger" meaning represented by the finished text, but which cannot be altered in its basic typological form by matters of style or local texture. This process of expression, as Hirsch explains it, however we may choose to grasp it metaphorically, must never be understood teleologically as an organic process in which mere potential slowly unfolds into the fullness of being.

As Derrida has demonstrated in his critique of Husserl's favorite principle, the phenomenological voice, verbal intention (*vouloir dire*) is never itself verbal—so Hirsch's response to a number of contemporary philosophers, critics, and linguists who claim that meaning is compelled by linguistic form would appear to be predictable. Can there be doubt toward whom the doctrine of synonymity, just recently announced, is directed? Yet Hirsch used to take a cagier stance which apparently eschewed absolutism on these matters. Early in *Validity* he says that the "rejection of absolute, a priori generalizations with regard to linguistic effects that are variable and local is one of the main points of this book." Thus: "Sometimes a use of language is uniquely constitutive of meaning; sometimes, apparently, a particular choice of words merely imposes limitations and is not uniquely required for the meaning that is actually willed."[40] But by the end of the paragraph it appears that what Hirsch actually wants to do is to reject the idealistic absolute of the Whorfians in order to assert an absolute more congenial to his own method: "It seems to follow that the language-bound quality of utterances, that is, the degree to which language is constitutive of meaning, can vary from null to somewhere in the vicinity of 100 percent."[41] This is to say that since meaning is *never* 100 percent language-bound, it is *always* to some important degree independent of any particular linguistic configuration. For Hirsch to grant that meaning can in certain instances be fully language-bound would require that he subvert his epistemology of the constitutive type. Since all texts are instances of types, all texts are translatable, because types, to be types, must subsume many instances.

Another perspective is yielded by his strategic misuse of Saussure's cardinal principle of the arbitrary relationship of the signifier and signified. This notion, to Hirsch, becomes the confirmation in linguistics of a typological epistemology and of a principle of discursive synonymity. The father of structuralism is turned against structuralism. Saussure's principle of the arbitrary relationship of signifier and signified is made to say that "*different* linguistic forms can mean exactly the same thing, that perfect translation is theoretically possible, as is perfect synonymity."[42] The doctrine of Saussure tells Hirsch that meaning preexists language, but Saussure explicitly says that this is not the case because words do not stand for "pre-existing concepts." "Instead of pre-existing ideas, then, we find . . . *values* emanating from the system. When they are said to correspond to concepts, it is understood that the concepts are purely differential and defined not by their positive content but negatively by their relations with the other terms of the system. Their most precise characteristic is in being what the others are not."[43] The signifier is arbitrarily related to the signified in the sense that the nature of things does not enforce the connection; with respect to culture the connection is necessary. In the example that Hirsch gives,[44] and contrary to his contention, "bachelors" and "unmarried men" do not "objectively" mean the same thing; rather they are *made* to shed their distinctive signifiers by the operations of a highly special linguistic context which forces them into sameness. Hirsch's example proves, in other words, not that meaning is independent of context and convention, but the opposite. In our usual cultural context, as a matter of fact, "bachelor" tends to signify a positive (or at least a neutral) state of being, while "unmarried man" signifies an excluded, negative, sometimes even unnatural state of being (i.e., "bachelor" and "unmarried man" are differentially grasped values "emanating from the system"). Such oppositions are generated by different linguistic forms—they are not synonymous. But this misreading serves Hirsch's purpose well, for he wants to use Saussure's widely established authority to deny the natural connection between word and thing claimed by a variety of neo-Coleridgean theorists of "symbol," and to affirm that all discourse functions to represent preexistent concepts.

So by denying the claim for a distinctive literary ontology, he affirms the ontological singularity of all discourse. The very language of his concessions to writers like Joyce makes it clear that he believes that even *Ulysses* and *Finnegans Wake* are to a degree translatable: "Many poems are less language-bound and thus more fully translatable than Joyce's two novels. . . ."[45] Hirsch casts the widest of nets; in two sweeping statements he embraces all texts from those of Keats to—and this will grate hard on certain sensibilities—the text of one R. B. Braithewaite, the author of *Scientific Explanation*: "I have no doubt that most of the texts which we call literary are to some degree language-bound, but it is a mistake to believe that they are all equally so. Is it not possible that on this criterion something like a continuous series stretches from Keats to Braithewaite, a series that certainly does not depend on normal genre classifications like poetry and prose, lyric poem and novel?"[46] And not only does Hirsch argue at the theoretical level against the possibility of *knowing* a unique, language-bound text, but he is willing to say that all texts are typological in their linguistic being: "verbal meanings, i.e., shared meanings, are always types and can never be limited to a unique, concrete content."[47]

In the following remarks Hirsch summarizes the major theoretical emphases I have explored to this point, and looks ahead to the last cluster of issues in his hermeneutic that I wish to investigate:

> verbal meaning can be defined more particularly as a *willed type* which an author expresses by linguistic symbols and which can be understood by another through those symbols.[48]

> In what sense is meaning genre-bound? First of all, it is obvious that not only understanding but also speaking must be governed and constituted by a sense of the whole utterance. How does a speaker manage to put one word after another unless his choices and usages are governed by a controlling conception? There must be some kind of overarching notion which controls the temporal sequence of speech, and this controlling notion of the speaker, like that of the interpreter, must embrace a system of expectations.[49]

> the intrinsic genre is as necessary to the speaker as it is to the interpreter. The speaker is able to begin expressing determinate meanings before he finishes his utterance because those meanings (carried by a particular sequence of words) are determined by the kind of meaning he is going to complete in words that have not yet been chosen.[50]

> The genre purpose must be in some sense an *idea*, a notion of the type of meaning to be communicated; otherwise there would be nothing to guide the author's will. On the other hand, there must also exist the motive force of will, since without its goal-seeking the idea could not be realized through the temporal activity of speaking. The author has an idea of what he wants to convey . . . an idea equivalent to what we called an intrinsic genre. In the course of realizing this idea, he wills the meanings which subserve it.[51]

In a note on this last passage Hirsch qualifies himself: "My description departs from that of Aristotle and the neo-Aristoteleans by its insistence on the entirely metaphorical character of an entelechy when that concept is applied to a form of speech."[52]

The issues raised by all these passages are classic in aesthetic and literary theorizing since Kant: Does the process of expression have a point of origin as well as a terminus? What, if anything, "exists" at the point of origin? Is "something" purely "interior" made "exterior" in the process of writing? Who, or what, is in control of this process? There is an origin of expression, for Hirsch, and that origin (the Derridean notion of "center" is appropriate here) is the culturally typified and type-making authorial consciousness. This consciousness, though it is the residence of meaning, Hirsch carefully (as Husserl before him) keeps clean of language, because any sequence of signs, he believes, "under the conventions of language," can "legitimately represent more than one complex of meaning." Writing in itself is radically indeterminate and must be excluded from the house of authorial intention if "meaning" is to be determinate, sharable, and reproducible. So by closing off the author's pure inner space of intention from writing, Hirsch valorizes a generic voice over the text; the meaning carried by this generic voice is wordless, determinate, and constitutive of a text's meaning; it is the intrinsic genre, the author's "inner horizon," which, as it guides all speaking as well as all interpretation, functions as a metaphysical entity (and not just as the invention of hermeneutic necessity). This intrinsic genre, of which the author is in full and self-conscious possession ("how does a speaker manage to put one word after another unless his choices and usages are governed by a controlling conception?"), directs the process of expression not teleologically, as in an organic process where there is a slow unfolding of a *telos* that is not reached until the end, but willfully, as in a mechanical process where an intention is transposed (but never transformed) from its nonlinguistic inner space into a sequence of signs, an intentional object which can be understood only by way of the maker's purpose.

Though this process of writing is inevitably temporal, as Hirsch notes, it is a curious temporality in the service of a regimenting and static activity: what "controls the temporal sequence of speech" is "some kind of over*arching* notion." It is a fundamentally spatial metaphor, then, which guarantees the all-important determinate quality of the cultural selfhood and its verbal intention—a spatial metaphor which frees selves and meanings from the dynamism of time. In the course of externalizing this "arched" intentional structure ("realizing this idea," in Hirsch's words), the author wills, often unconsciously, the many nuances and implications "which *subserve*" his intrinsic genre; these unconscious meanings sit under and within the arch, and therefore exist in a purely determinate way as subtle productions of the particular type which is the origin of the text, and which controls the process of making a text. Because these nuances, implications, and ambiguities exist as part of the type (distant members of the family, so to speak), they must never be conceived as the radically indeterminate fringe

which licenses the radical historicism that Hirsch fears will make a bad
joke of all genuine hermeneutical effort. Properly understood, the
finished text is a transparency through which we gain a clear and unambiguous view of the intrinsic genre and the cultural voice which wills
a sequence of signs into existence.

Hirsch practices his theory conscientiously in his books on Wordsworth and Blake, and in *Validity*, itself, at one point, in a courageous
illustration of what he has been arguing for, not only *says* that texts are
instances of types but goes on to dramatize his point in an astonishing
way: by trying to show that a passage from *Paradise Lost* maintains its
"meaning" even when he tampers with the diction. He can do so, he
argues, because the conception of the intrinsic genre "has a degree of
tolerance by virtue of which the later words of the utterance could be
varied within limits without altering the determinate meaning of the
earlier words."[53] I offer as the *coup de grâce* this quotation which appears to imply, among other things, that given certain generic clues we
might "generate" the characteristics of texts:

> Since a type is something that can be embodied in more than
> one instance, it is something whose determining character-
> istics are common to all instances of the type. Further-
> more, since the type can be represented in more than one
> instance, it can be shared or known by more than one
> person. When another person has learned the characteristics
> of the type, he can "generate" those characteristics without
> their being given to him explicitly. It is sufficient merely
> to give him a decisive clue as to the particular type that
> is meant.[54]

If the activity of writing "originally" means—note here the awk-
wardness of Hirsch's conception—the evolving of a "new literary
genre,"[55] then the activity of reading astutely would entail the predic-
tion of generic meaning even before encountering the full text in its
linguistic actuality. Now, if all Hirsch means to say is that those of us
with knowledge of the family to which a given text may belong have
certain advantages over those who do not, then his ideas are useful
(especially in the classroom), but it must be said that they are of no
theoretical interest. But if he means, as he seems to mean, that the type,
in its interior, prelinguistic identity, is constitutive both of the making
of meaning and of its understanding, then his ideas are theoretically
questionable at best. Unless Hirsch is willing to take adequate measure
of Saussure's linguistics, and the work that Derrida has done in recent
years, he will continue to be unconvincing.

4

In *The Aims of Interpretation*, the collection of theoretical essays written and published after *Validity in Interpretation*, Hirsch vigorously restates his position while bringing his rhetoric closer to all those thinkers in contemporary theory (he calls them "cognitive atheists") against whom he writes.[56] The idea that the text in itself is radically indeterminate is somewhat refined in readerly (structuralist) perspective:

> the nature of a text is to mean whatever we construe it to mean. I am aware that theory should try to provide normative criteria for discriminating good from bad, legitimate from illegitimate constructions of a text, but mere theory cannot change the nature of interpretation. Indeed, we need a norm precisely because the nature of a text is to have no meaning except that which an interpreter wills into existence. We, not our texts, are the makers of the meaning we understand, a text being only an occasion for meaning, in itself an ambiguous form devoid of the consciousness where meaning abides.[57]

In itself an ambiguous form, the text is made determinate and un-equivocal by the deployment "of a single, privileged, precritical approach" which will locate an "original meaning" that is synonymous with the "author's intention."[58] (Hirsch's readerly structuralism is only a veneer: the "consciousness where meaning abides" is finally the author's, not the interpreter's.) In other words, the so-called "pre-critical approach" is not really an "approach," since its aim is to make itself a pure diaphaneity, a self-dissolving and self-dispossessing medium through which intention, or what Hirsch in a telling metaphor calls the "soul"[59] of speech, is perfectly discernible. Though his own research into the roots of the word "hermeneutics" makes it problematic whether there is a sacred origin which is the object of interpretation ("whether the god or hermeneutics came first"),[60] in his redeemed (secular) theory there can be no doubt. While all others are condemned to a fallen lot (the indeterminate text which triggers many approaches, many doomed quests for the hidden god of meaning), Hirsch's approach (nonapproach) claims, in its ability to achieve an Edenic transparency of self, to recover the inaugurating god or soul of discourse. That, at any rate, is the presumed value and pleasure of a hermeneutics of innocence.

But this would-be hermeneutic innocence is undercut by the terms of Hirsch's own argument. The recovery of an "object of knowledge" (meaning) outside of every "context in which it is known" (significance) —since Hirsch explicitly rejects the possibility of mystical communion with an author—must be at every point linguistically mediated.[61] Intentionality (or what he calls a cultural selfhood) is itself a text and must be subject to the fundamental condition of textuality that he has announced: radical ambiguity. It is clear that he wishes to free intention from the contaminations of writing, but how this is to be done he never tells us. Hirsch's most rhetorically tricky argument, that in disagreeing with him all cognitive atheists, and anyone else who doesn't subscribe to his views, affirm his main point (texts are controlled by a determinate intention; hence there is a ground for calling him "wrong"), can be turned on Hirsch himself.[62] So-called cognitive atheists may agree with him because he is himself a cognitive atheist. And as for those who are not cognitive atheists—I know of no major contemporary thinker who is one—perhaps Hirsch will permit himself the generosity to admit that when they disagree with him they are not *actually* agreeing, for his version of textual determinacy, as the works of Jacques Derrida and Michel Foucault amply and variously demonstrate, is not the only one available.

One of the thinkers Hirsch labels a cognitive atheist, Derrida, in fact provides us, in his analysis of the convergence of structuralism and phenomenology, with just the sort of knowledge that we require to define the contemporaneity that Hirsch is so anxious to avoid (he believes himself a throwback to Schleiermacher). Though the terms "genesis" and "structure" are presumably the signposts of a violent opposition in contemporary theory (one thinks of Benveniste's remark that no one is interested in the search for origins after their critique in structural linguistics),[63] Derrida shows in one of the key essays in *Writing and Difference* that genesis and structure are reinforcing conceptions of a single metaphysical disposition. His analysis of this illusory opposition which has animated the debate between phenomenologists and structuralists helps to focus what we have already seen in evidence in Hirsch. What Derrida says about Husserl ("In Husserl's mind . . . there was never a 'structure-genesis' problem but only a privilege of one or the other of these two operative concepts, according to the space of description")[64] applies with equal force to Hirsch. Like Husserl, Hirsch does not disqualify genetic description in general, but only those genetic (and relativist) philosophies (psychologism, historicism) that are produced by causalist perspectives. Authorial intention is an absolute (not a relative) genetic ground for Hirsch's hermeneutics. But if intention is fundamentally genetic, it is also necessarily structural (a typological force very close to Husserl's discussion of consciousness in his *Encyclopaedia Britannica* article).[65] As genesis, intention guarantees original meaning; as structure, it guarantees that all meanings of a given text are governed by an internal legality of rules. The interpreter is therefore left to his innocence—merely to see, merely to "discover" the productive mechanism. I refer again to Hirsch's spatialized, structural metaphor of the "overarching notion" which renders the production of every nuance of meaning subservient to the overarching type, and which functions at the same time as an internal genesis that is situated, as intention, just the other (subjective) side of writing (deferral of origin, presence, intention, etc.). Hirsch's search for an origin (soul, original meaning) which will provide determinacy is at the same time a search for a *telos* which, as enclosing structure, will not only contain the origin (as its proper home or body) but somehow also will delineate its full character. Despite his many attacks on contemporary theorists from Heidegger to Derrida, Hirsch is an exemplary representative of the contemporary scene and as interesting an illustration as we are likely to find that the much-touted shift from traditional to contemporary critical theory conceals significant common investments.

Eight

The whole of literature would respond in a similar
fashion, although the techniques and the patterns would
have to vary considerably, of course, from author to
author. But there is absolutely no reason why analyses
of the kind here suggested for Proust would not be applicable, with proper modifications of technique, to
Milton or to Dante or to Hölderlin. This will in fact
be the task of literary criticism in the coming years.

Paul de Man, "Semiology and Rhetoric"

Paul de Man: The Rhetoric of Authority

Recently in the *Hudson Review* William Pritchard playfully dubbed Yale's four best-known literary critics the "Hermeneutical Mafia."[1] Who could have imagined that the term "Mafia" would degenerate into a metaphor for avant-garde literary theorists? But perhaps there may be some value in extending a much-assaulted figure to the fearsome Yale group. Assuming there is a Yale Mafia, then surely there must be a resident Godfather. One is forced to finger Paul de Man, who exhibits qualities that may earn him the role of Don Paolo, *capo di tutti capi*. Reading the prefaces and acknowledgments of Harold Bloom, Geoffrey Hartman, and J. Hillis Miller, one is struck by the tone of respect, even reverence, with which the name of Paul de Man is mentioned. It is not difficult to locate reasons. Bloom's latest thesis about literary history was announced by de Man three years before the appearance of *The Anxiety of Influence*; Hartman's thesis in his book on Wordsworth was anticipated by de Man in an obscure essay; Miller's turn from Poulet to Derrida in an essay on Poulet was not much more than a repetition of de Man's earlier essay on Poulet. The question is, why should Bloom, Hartman, and Miller—potential dons in their own right—appear to be executing the orders of Godfather de Man?

In the manner of a don whose power is assured and unquestioned, de Man has found it necessary to speak only sparingly; in comparison to his prolific lieutenants he is almost invisible. We know that according to certain dark traditions the don need not speak often, nor elaborately, because when the don speaks he speaks with total authority, and it is de Man's "rhetoric of authority," as I'll call it, which has distinguished his criticism since its earliest days. This is a critic who has always given the impression of having a grip on truth. Even while, in *Blindness and Insight*, he was telling us that there was no truth, or if there was, that it could never be known, he spoke transcendentally of the "foreknowl- edge we possess of the true nature of literature."[2] Unlike Hartman, whose prose, in its pursuit of the labyrinthine ramifications of a point, is the very model of the scholar's descent into the inferno of self-con- sciousness; and unlike Bloom, whose emotionally pressured and strident style gives away a critic not altogether confident of how what he pro- poses will be received, de Man has not had to speak in anything but a cool and straightforward manner.

The epigraph that I've chosen from one of his latest pieces is repre- sentative of the de Man style at its most intimidating.[3] He speaks openly of the "whole of literature" responding to his thesis. But how does he know? Is he making the claim from a transcendental ground, having discovered the *a priori* form of all literary discourse? In two subordinate clauses, we observe him granting a qualification: he tells us that tech- niques of analysis will have to be modified from author to author. But the tone of his qualification is set with that tired little scholarly aside— "of course"—which in this instance projects the tone of the critic's voice, condescending to an elaboration, but telling us, as he does so, that such practical matters are for others to worry about. The final sen- tence clarifies his stance: "This will in fact be the task of literary criti- cism in the coming years." If we had any doubts, we know now that de Man is making not an empirical but an idealistic claim. He presumes to tell us not only what literature has been but also what it must be. And, somewhat chillingly (perhaps it is best to drop the metaphor of the Godfather at this point), he tells us not what literary critics ought to be doing but what "in fact" they shall be doing. In one way or an- other, whether in the philosophical garb of the Sartrean existentialist, or in the guise of the Derridean poststructuralist, de Man has been speaking that way about literature and criticism for many years.

1

In his earlier essays—I single out for analysis three major representative statements: "Intentional Structure of the Romantic

Image" (1960), "Symbolic Landscape in Wordsworth and Yeats" (1962), and "The Rhetoric of Temporality" (1969)—de Man's critical perspective is dominated by existentialist concepts. These are derived largely from Sartre's early work, *Being and Nothingness* and *The Psychology of Imagination*, in some smaller part from Heidegger's *Being and Time*, and, ultimately, from the major sources of Heidegger and Sartre: the phenomenology and aesthetics of Hegel. From *Being and Nothingness* de Man picks up and accommodates to romantic literary contexts *pour soi* and *en soi*, the key terms of Sartre's phenomenological ontology, and the relations of these terms to both good and bad faith, authentic and inauthentic existence. From *The Psychology of Imagination* he appears to use another (and parallel) Sartrean dualism, that of imagination and perception, once again for the purpose of exploring the problems of romanticism.

It is difficult to be confident about de Man's existentialist backgrounds because he almost never quotes (or even alludes) to the primary philosophical texts. Nevertheless, it is almost impossible to imagine a sophisticated European intellectual coming into maturity just after World War II who would not be moved profoundly by existentialist thought. But we need not rely on speculation about the postwar *Zeitgeist*. There are solid conceptual clues in de Man's writing which point us directly to Sartre. In the essay "Intentional Structure of the Romantic Image" he is preoccupied by a few lines from Friedrich Hölderlin's "Brot und Wein" in which the poet meditates on the relations—or disrelations, more accurately—of words and natural objects, and their respective origins.

> By calling them [flowers] *natural* objects we mean that their origin is determined by nothing but their own being. Their becoming coincides at all times with the mode of their origination: it is as flowers that their history is what it is, totally defined by their identity. There is no wavering in the status of their existence: existence and essence coincide in them at all times. Unlike words, which originate like something else ("like flowers"), flowers originate like themselves: they are literally what they are, definable without the assistance of metaphor. It would follow, then, since the intent of the poetic word is to originate like the flower, that it strives to banish all metaphor, to become entirely literal.[4]

What Sartre designates as *en soi*, or being in-itself, is simply all non-human being, and corresponds to what de Man is restricting in the passage to the natural object. The flower is the sort of being whose existence and essence coincide, whose identity is never in question, and whose temporal existence is in a sense atemporal—a flower cannot be said to have a history. Since its identity in flowerhood cannot be subverted or changed by the possibilities of temporal life, the flower is sustained as a sure teleological unfolding from an original entity which is transcendental in the sense that it contains "an infinity of manifestations of a common essence, in an infinity of places and at an infinity of moments."[5] Thus free of all temporal contingency, flowerhood represents permanence itself, a perfect stability of being. What Sartre designates as *pour soi*, human reality, consciousness (de Man extends the term to include language, since it is "engendered by consciousness"),[6] is clearly echoed in de Man's manipulations of terms which recall the Sartrean slogan that in human being "existence precedes essence." As Heidegger had earlier contended, human being, because it is lacking in timeless identity, not only "has" a history but in some sense "is" history. Human being is a hole in being trying to fill itself, in order to achieve a fullness and stability of identity that can only belong to the in-itself, and which if achieved would wipe out the humanness of its being. Sartre's point is that the *pour soi* achieves the stability and permanence of the *en soi* only in bad faith, a condition of willed ignorance or self-delusion. In order for human being to exist "authentically" it must never exchange the reality of its purely temporal mode of existence, its eternal condition of about-to-be, for the illusory comforts and certitudes of a spatialized condition which in our anthropomorphizing sentimentality we bestow upon the *en soi*.

De Man's contribution to a reading of romanticism, in this earlier phase of his career, lies in his (implied) insistence that Sartre's dualism, with its predisposition to view with contempt all transcendental urges to bypass the claims of unredeemed time, is fully adequate to the drama enacted in poetry from Hölderlin, Keats, and Wordsworth, to Mallarmé, Yeats, and Rilke. The direction of de Man's existentialist argument should remind us (by way of its negation) of the central claim for poetic language that we find in numerous romantic theorists: that the poetic word attempts to originate as flowers originate ("*wie Blumen entstehn*"). The poetic word or "symbol" (the term is dictated by literary history—an idea against which in "The Rhetoric of Temporality" de Man will mount a vigorous attack) "strives to banish all metaphor"— i.e., banish all similitude—and "to become entirely literal." De Man's argument against traditionalist theories of romantic symbol is that the symbol, in its striving to link itself (to recall Coleridge's description) with the reality which it would represent, in its effort to jump the gap between word and thing, in its very *laboring* to generate a monistic situation (a natural bond between sign and object) necessarily signifies that its true or authentic condition is as arbitrary sign that affirms the distance between word and thing, and between subject and object. The essence paradoxically attributed to the poetic word—it can somehow name being as unmediated presence without at the same time, in the naming process, deferring presence, thereby making it absent—not only should recall the romantic notion of symbol, but also the story that Heidegger tells in *An Introduction to Metaphysics* of the primal union of word and thing understood as *logos* and *physis*. Sartre's attempt to evade his intellectual progenitor lies in his insistence that what Heidegger thought primally integrated was, in actuality, primally divorced; hence the antithesis of the for-itself and the in-itself. In his revision of romantic poetic de Man follows Sartre; the Coleridgean or Heideggerian effort to recover through poetic discourse the presence and union at the origin is in de Man's perspective no more than a self-delusive effort to impose union upon original division.

The point is worth emphasizing, because readings out of context from de Man's collection of essays, *Blindness and Insight*, and from his recent Derrideanized work on Nietzsche tend to project the false image that, as the American counterpart to Derrida, he refuses all metaphysics. Reading later de Man into his essays on romanticism of the 1960s will give one the misleading view that he had passed beyond metaphysics before it became fashionable to do so. My argument at this point is that de Man used to be thoroughly metaphysical in the existential mode. His attacks on the interpretations of romanticism authored by Abrams, Earl Wasserman, and Wimsatt, and on the so-called mystified moments of the earlier romantics themselves, are not fueled by the poststructuralist belief that all talk of origin is deluded, but by the notion that a certain kind of talk (transcendental, theological, monistic, untragic) is wrong: origins are acceptable, in other words, as long as we have the proper (existentialist, secular, dualistic, tragic, fearful, and agonized) view of them.

So there is a metaphysical complacency in the earlier work of de Man—never fully expurgated in the later essays, but only disguised with different philosophical content—and it surfaces in his pride of historical place. De Man's claim to truth about the nature of things is coupled with another claim, that the hard-nosed, unclouded confronting of such truth is an event of recent philosophical vintage—a courageous discovery made by his intellectual times after centuries of weak-kneed issue-dodging and self-mystification. In its most generous form de Man's existentialism generates a myth of historical progress. As he puts it in his essay on the romantic image, the works of the early romantics are "at most" "*underway*" toward "renewed insights"; the

"self-contradictory" passages that he examines from Rousseau, Hölderlin, and Wordsworth presumably point forward, from their place in
semidarkness, to the brilliant illumination that he finds in Yeats.[7] In its
least generous form de Man's existentialism suggests that there is no
contradiction in those early romantics, but simply unrelieved mystification, pure error: an unreflective yearning for the image to be "reborn
in the manner of a natural creation,"[8] a nostalgia for unmediated contact with the natural object—in Saussure's terms, a yearning for a signified without a signifier.

De Man explains romantic nostalgia by arguing that the romantic
image or symbol in its mystified, unself-conscious form grants the "intrinsic ontological primacy of the natural object."[9] In Sartre's terms,
the *pour soi* in an act of bad faith attempts to flee its condition as human
being by, first, giving primacy to the *en soi* and then desiring to be
en soi. But, again, since the act of bad faith in Sartre can never be successfully self-deluded—in a nagging corner of consciousness we are
reminded of what we are doing to ourselves, forced to remember that
we are condemned to the freedom of our temporal mode of existence—
so in de Man the poetic image achieves its effects "only by a deliberate
forgetting of the transcendental nature of the source" of the natural
object. The nostalgic mode of existence of the poetic image is "itself a
sign of divine absence," and the "conscious use of poetic imagery an
admission of this absence." In a perfect echo of Sartre's discussion of
the *pour soi* de Man tells us that the poetic image can never achieve "the
absolute identity with itself that exists in the natural object."[10] For
nineteenth-century poetry as a whole, including the apparently anti-
natural poetry of Mallarmé, and for most of the inheritors of romanticism in the twentieth century, the ontological priority of the natural object is not challenged. Either poets experience time and again the failure
to achieve "unmediated vision" in the merging of consciousness with
the object; or, like Mallarmé, they fail to free consciousness altogether
from nature and the natural standpoint in an effort to achieve a poetic
counterpart to Husserl's phenomenological absention from natural
being; or (this would appear to be the majority report) the romantic
writer experiences an "alternating feeling of attraction and repulsion"
toward nature that may become in poets of ultimate sophistication "the
conscious dialectic of a reflective poetic consciousness."[11]

In the conclusion of his essay on the romantic image de Man implies,
however, that the achievement of such dialectic is not quite the promised
land. For the tragic adventure of the nineteenth-century poet can only
be brought to a satisfactory resolution by a fully Husserlian imagination
that does not yearn nostalgically for union with the natural object; by

an imagination that looks with contempt upon nature as "blank abyss"; by an imagination that comes into play when the light of sense is extinguished. This "possibility for consciousness to exist entirely by and for itself, independently of all relationship with the outside world, without being moved by an intent aimed at part of this world," was prefigured by Wordsworth at the end of *The Prelude* where he spoke of imagination as an "unfathered vapour."[12] It is this latter possibility— of an imagination without ground, its own origin, the desire for which Harold Bloom calls the anxiety of influence—toward which, in de Man's words, the early romantics are "underway." It is this autonomous imagination which is the *telos* of the long journey of nineteenth- and twentieth-century inheritors of romanticism. His apparent caution in speaking of this *telos* is undercut by his optative projection of the autonomous imagination as the virtual fulfillment of all of his critical desires: "We know very little about the kind of images that such an imagination would produce, except that they would have little in common with what we have come to expect from familiar metaphorical figures."[13]

De Man's position in the essay on the romantic image encapsulates existential modernism, and more specifically a Sartrean humanism which places at the beginnings a primal divorce of consciousness and nature, sees as naive and sentimental any urge toward reconciliation, and congratulates itself for its courageous discovery that language, since it cannot recapture an integrated and unmediated origin, may therefore properly fulfill its being by passionately realizing its purely human project with no regrets, no looking back, and no self-doubt. Though he has no use for the theological kind of position that Heidegger found in the pre-Socratics—and locates his theory after the fall of the *logos* from ontological presence—de Man's humanism has force only within a context in which the Edenic view of discourse is posited as a forbidden ideal which is very nearly impossible to resist.

2

The articulated purpose of another early essay, "Symbolic Landscape in Wordsworth and Yeats," is to clarify the "fundamental discrepancy" between "two poets both labeled as 'romantic'."[14] Less forthrightly articulated is a second purpose, underlying and giving point to the first, to set forth a thesis about historical change between Wordsworth and Yeats—a change that not only establishes difference, but (as in the "Intentional Structure of the Romantic Image") a *telos* of progress as well: a movement from mystification and partial mystification to full awareness. Sartre's sharp distinction between "perception" (a mimetic sort of faculty which keeps us in contact with the real as it is) and "imagination" (a creative faculty of fundamentally gnostic disposition, *contra natura*) is taken over by de Man and somewhat modified, so that perception and imagination may enter into an agonistic relationship with each other.[15] De Man's submerged thesis may be sensed in these two statements from his opening paragraphs:

> The delicate interplay between perception and imagination could nowhere be more intricate than in the representation of a natural scene, transmuted and recollected in the ordering form of Wordsworth's poetic language. . . . Wide as the scope of Wordsworth's vision extends, it would never encompass Yeats' occasional claim of rejecting natural reality altogether, to ". . . scorn aloud / In glory of changeless metal / Common bird or petal." A considerable distance separates Wordsworth's involved but persistently reverent "look[ing] at the subject" from Yeats' intermittent contempt for "natural things."[16]

The point of view is initially formulated with caution: Yeats's rejection of nature is "intermittent," "occasional"; Wordsworth's reverence is "involved," complicated by a gnostic tendency to bypass nature altogether. But in the working out of the thesis through the sonnet "Composed by the Side of Grasmere Lake" and Yeats's "Coole Park and Ballylee, 1931," de Man tends to elide nuances and qualifications as he moves toward a historical generalization which elevates Yeats over a Wordsworth whose sentiments seem, upon retrospect, increasingly primitive. By the end of the essay we are given not a Yeats occasionally scornful of nature, but a poet who rejects the primacy of the natural landscape, a poet wholly devoted to occultist traditions who considers the "incarnate state of the soul a relative degradation," and whose greatest effects are achieved through what are called "non-natural or even anti-natural uses of language."[17]

Though de Man will continue to express his pride of historical place in later essays, never again, as in these two earlier pieces, will he allow it to emerge in a generalization about historical progress away from the dark night of that mystification which grants ontological primacy to the natural object. More and more de Man will be saying—his essay on Derrida's reading of Rousseau is the chief example of this—that the best of writers have always demystified themselves, and in pressing that thesis he will move more and more toward a position, as he does in "The Rhetoric of Temporality," in which history, at least in its conventional senses, is denied altogether.

Published in 1969, but with origins that likely date from late 1967 and early 1968, "The Rhetoric of Temporality" is roughly contemporary with several essays collected in his book of 1971, *Blindness and Insight*. Though he gives no reason for not including in that collection what is probably his best-known essay, it is not difficult to construct the likely rationale: "The Rhetoric of Temporality" represents a culmination of the existentialist position that de Man turns away from, in order to pick up Derridean perspectives, in the late 1960s and early 1970s. In the manipulation of key terms in "The Rhetoric of Temporality"—"symbol," "allegory," "temporality," and "irony"—may be discerned an effort to explore more fully, and in more traditional literary categories, the Sartrean oppositions that had covertly exerted control in the essay on the "intent" of the romantic image.

De Man's major purpose is to reexamine and reverse the "valorization" in romantic and neoromantic thought "of symbol at the expense of allegory."[18] Following Coleridge, and echoing his own discussion of a "poetic language of origination" in an earlier essay, he describes symbol as a kind of discourse not yet fallen from the presence of being that it names. Symbol would be the aesthetic equivalent of the connection between *logos* and *physis*, and romanticism the literary and philosophical movement that would recapture the pre-Socratic unity between thought and being that was presumably dissolved by the history of Western thought beginning with Plato. In the Sartrean terms which de Man favors, symbol is simply the language of bad faith, a discourse that would transform *pour soi* into *en soi*, time into space, and contingency, process, and the nonidentity of human being with itself into a condition of certitude, fixity, and the illusion of the self-identity of human being as essence that both precedes and is coincidental with its existence. Traditionally "dismissed as non-poetic,"[19] allegory becomes for de Man the truthful discourse of the *pour soi*, a language of good faith that would grant the ontological independence of nature without at the same time granting its privilege, without at the same time being ruled by the desire to transpose categories of human being into categories of natural being. By disavowing the natural connection between word and thing, allegory affirms the arbitrary nature of the linguistic sign. But for de Man the arbitrariness of the sign, here and in later essays, does not carry the message of Saussure which has animated structuralist thought—that the sign, as arbitrary, is necessarily produced culturally and historically. Rather, the arbitrariness of the sign is made to carry an existentialist theme illuminating the tragic separation of human and natural being, the inescapable temporality of discourse (with temporality understood in a culturally empty way), and the absence of God whose presence alone could underwrite the unmediated discourse of symbol. De Man's message to traditionalist scholars of romanticism is that allegory, not symbol, is authentic discourse and that the romantics themselves at their most honest were aware of this truth and of their mystification in the metaphysical dream of a symbolic language.

"The Rhetoric of Temporality" is de Man's most openly metaphysical essay. His position emerges clearly in his debates with the chief American interpreters of romanticism, Wimsatt, Abrams, and Wasserman, who claim for major romantic poets a "working monism," a "radical idealism" in which the priority of the subject is asserted over that of objective nature.[20] De Man thinks that the assertion of the subject's priority is a confusion of the critics, generated by periodic confusions of the romantics themselves; it is a view, in any case, not compatible with the overall poetic practice of the romantic poets whom he finds giving a "great deal of importance to the presence of nature" and to an "analogical imagination that is founded on the priority of natural substances over the consciousness of the self." "It could well be argued," he writes, "that Coleridge's own concept of organic unity as a dynamic principle is derived from the movements of nature, not from those of the self."[21] As evidence for a thesis he had broached in "Intentional Structure of the Romantic Image," he quotes a passage from *The Prelude* (the same passage had been put into evidence in the earlier essay) on the "woods decaying, never to be decayed/The stationary blast of waterfalls. . . ." His commentary brings back his Sartrean presuppositions: "Such paradoxical assertions of eternity in motion can be applied to nature but not to a self caught up entirely within mutability. The temptation exists, then, for the self to borrow, so to speak, the temporal stability it lacks from nature, and to devise strategies by means of which nature is brought down to a human level while still escaping from 'the unimaginable touch of time.' "[22] In another passage de Man tells us bluntly that the priority of the subject in romanticism is "illusionary" and that such a notion can only arise when the subject "in fact" borrows from the outside a temporal stability which it lacks within itself and to which "in truth" it bears no resemblance.[23] The belief in the organic interdependence of subject and object "represents a temptation that has to be overcome" in order for the "authentic voice" of romanticism to become "audible," and in order that we may experience "the most original and profound moments" in romantic poetry.[24] If symbol, which de Man says must be rejected because it is "regressive," "postulates the possibility of an identity or identification," then allegory, by renouncing "the nos-

talgia and the desire to coincide," keeps "the self from an illusory identification with the non-self, which is now fully, though painfully, recognized as a non-self." When romantic literature articulates this painful
knowledge of a self caught in the "void" of "temporal difference," at a
"distance" from itself—when, in so many words, romantic literature is
functioning not symbolically but allegorically—it "finds its true voice,"
it speaks with an "entirely good poetic conscience."[25] Allegory is the
discourse of good faith because it generates a rhetoric of temporality
that, in effect, functions as a mimesis of the condition of the for-itself
(a self that *is* at a distance from itself), while symbol, as a rhetoric of
spatiality, is a discourse of a self hiding from the knowledge of human
reality, a discourse in which image and substance coincide in a simultaneity that is permitted by the illusion that image and substance "do
not differ in their being but only in their extension." In the world of
allegory "time is the originary constitutive category" because it is the
essence of the allegorical sign to refer us to a previous sign which, by
definition, is "pure anteriority."[26]

The question as to whether or not Paul de Man's interpretation of
romanticism is the correct one, and its corollary, whether or not
Abrams, Wasserman, and Wimsatt are mystified about the true dimensions of their subject, is a matter for another kind of study. What concerns me here is the epistemological status of his interpretation and the
confidence with which it is set forth. Perhaps the first thing to be noted
—and maybe the last thing as well—is that de Man does not argue in
any formal sense for the logic and truth of his position. One has the
impression of a critic who comes bearing from existentialist quarters
certain prepackaged conclusions, not arguments, and who intends to
put across his interpretation mainly by crafty rhetorical maneuvers.
De Man's primary rhetorical technique is no less shrewdly effective for
being almost as old as the proverbial hills. He assumes the privileged
position of a writer in possession of truth and then proceeds to pump up
the ego of his readers, lifting them to his own level of awareness by assuming their acceptance, as revealed truth, of existentialist ideology. He
tells us, in effect, that we all know that thus and such is the case and,
therefore, wise reader, I shall not bore you by belaboring the obvious:
"Such paradoxical assertions of eternity in motion can be applied to
nature but not to a self caught up entirely within mutability."

But where has it been established that (1) the self is in fact "entirely
caught up in mutability" and (2) that the romantics believed that to be
the case? It is not that the romantics didn't recognize the Sartrean issue;
rather they confronted it with a painful honesty that denies de Man's
retrospective superciliousness. Man, Emerson tells us in "Self-Reliance,"

is "ashamed before the blade of grass or the blowing rose. These roses under my window make no reference to former roses or to better ones; they are for what they are; . . . There is no time to them. . . . [Man] cannot be happy and strong until he too lives with nature in the present, above time."[27] The degree to which the self is felt to be caught up in mutability is a real question for a romantic consciousness. It may be that de Man and his existentialist readers will never succumb to the "regressive" temptations of the symbol, but the critique of Wordsworth assumes the Sartrean type of perspective which Wordsworth himself never assumed. Wordsworth worried that the self might be entirely caught up within mutability, hoped against hope that that was not the case; because he was in doubt, because such fears about the self rattled against another—and in his view more desirable, not mystified—idea of the self, we have (among several reasons that might be adduced) the troubled, tortured, and dramatic ruminations that unfold in the best poems. These are the ruminations of a writer for whom there are real questions, real conflicts, a writer for whom, at enormous psychic cost, nothing is "entirely" this way or that way. One could argue that it was lucky for poetic history that Wordsworth was not as sure as de Man is about the nature of selfhood.

The judgment that the substitution of symbol for allegory is "in fact" an act of "ontological bad faith" can only issue from a mind which has settled ontological doubts and has no metaphysical problems.[28] And likewise, the authoritative assertion that Coleridge was borrowing the organic principle from nature and then imposing it upon an alien realm of being, human reality, makes sense only if one has already come confidently to the conclusion that human reality and natural reality have no ontological connection. It is one thing to argue that the romantics stared the specter of ontological dualism squarely in the face; quite another to assert that dualism of the existential variety is truth, that the romantics in their hearts knew it to be truth and spent much time hiding from the fact. Time and again de Man's rhetoric projects the image of the philosophical realist, in full possession of the knowledge of being, ruthlessly bringing to epistemological trial those who have deliberately ensconced themselves in illusion. Little phrases like "in truth," "of course," and "in fact," crucially placed and repeated, tell a story that is filled out by the charge of "regression"; by the existentialist weight of frequently used terms like "authenticity," "bad faith," and "good conscience"; by traditional realist rhetoric (we have seen this in Krieger) which distinguishes freely and easily between the real and the illusionary, the true voice and the false voice; and by the claim—the best guide to de Man's presumption of unproblematic, objective knowledge—to know the most "original" and "profound" moments of romantic literature. And we note the metaphors of depth and ground.[29]

In the last section of "The Rhetoric of Temporality" de Man attempts to link his idea of allegory to a concept of irony, and to bring the broad existentialist theme carried by allegory into contact with a literary strategy which he believes the allegorist must inevitably turn to in order to elaborate his vision. In the end de Man can find no difference between allegory and irony since both designate an activity of consciousness "by which a man differentiates himself from the non-human world": "the two modes, for all their profound distinctions in mood and structure, are the two faces of the same fundamental experience of time. . . . The knowledge derived from both modes is essentially the same. . . . Both modes are fully demystified. . . ."[30] If we have had difficulty hitherto coming to terms with de Man's definition of allegory, given what we have conventionally understood the term to mean, then at this point we perhaps begin to feel ourselves back on familiar territory. However much he might wish to revise the theory of allegory, in the end it appears that he does not so much wish to displace the traditional idea as to add to it. For in the end authentic literature, in his perspective, looks a great deal like traditional allegory, a didactic mode of discourse in which metaphor, image, and other aesthetic strategies all serve a system of meanings independent of an aesthetic "surface." In the traditional conception, as we recall, aesthetic surface is not constitutive of depth; variations in technique need not disturb a theme or message which has an existence independent of the aesthetic mode. Distinctions "in mood and structure" are unimportant when it is the task of literature to carry the Christian burdens imposed upon it by Spenser and Bunyan, and they remain unimportant when other philosophical burdens are imposed by Sartre and de Man. In either case the presumed authority of a particular metaphysical perspective demands that literature, whatever its aesthetic mode, or its context in history and society, project endlessly a small number of mythoi and their variants. It "remains necessary," de Man writes, "if there is to be allegory, that the allegorical sign refer to another sign that precedes it. The meaning constituted by the allegorical sign can then consist only in the *repetition* (in the Kierkegaardian sense of the term) of a previous sign with which it can never coincide, since it is the essence of the previous sign to be pure anteriority."[31] Without broaching the subject of temporality, or alluding to Kierkegaard, the authors of a well-known handbook of literary terminology imply a similar point about allegory and its necessary investment in a strategy of repetition when they define allegory as "a form of extended metaphor in which objects, persons, and actions in a narrative, either in prose or verse, are equated with meanings that lie outside the narrative itself,"[32] and that must be in some sense repeated inside the narrative in order for the equation to be completed, in order for allegory to be allegory.

More specifically, by irony de Man, with the aid of a text by Baudelaire (De l'essence du rire), means a reflective and reflexive activity of consciousness which uncovers a "division of the subject into a multiple consciousness"[33] (this is a rare unveiling: it happens only for poets and philosophers). Irony is essentially a kind of consciousness that gets born inside lyric, assenting, and unfallen modes of consciousness within the romantic and neoromantic mind. Ironic consciousness is not a fixed point but a process of moving away from the lyricism of symbol (and its identifying, monistic urges) toward the detached, alienated, and dualistic posture of consciousness which de Man attaches to the allegorical. This process is described as a "progression" in which "self-knowledge is certainly implicit"—but it is an empty kind of knowledge which looks suspiciously like cognitive impotence:

> the man who has fallen is somewhat wiser than the fool who walks around oblivious of the crack in the pavement about to trip him up. And the fallen philosopher reflecting on the discrepancy between the two successive stages is wiser still, but this does not in the least prevent him from stumbling in his turn. It seems instead that his wisdom can be gained only at the cost of such a fall. . . . The ironic, twofold self that the writer or philosopher constitutes by his language seems able to come into being only at the expense of his empirical self, falling (or rising) from a stage of mystified adjustment into the knowledge of his mystification. The ironic language splits the subject into an empirical self that exists in a state of inauthenticity and a self that exists only in the form of a language that asserts the knowledge of this inauthenticity. This does not, however, make it into an authentic language, for to know inauthenticity is not the same as to be authentic.[34]

The passage is a model for much of de Man's later work because it represents a modest change in tone from his existentialist confidence. The mystified, inauthentic, empirical self that understands itself, in effect, through the categories of Sartre's en soi becomes unavoidable; all we can hope for is a self-consciousness, carried by ironic language, which will lift us into the "knowledge of inauthenticity," a state not to be confused with a positive knowledge of authenticity, a doing and being of authenticity. Neither is there a possibility of an authentic voice, contrary to what de Man believed earlier, nor can the *telos* of historical progression any longer be taken seriously. Even to call, as he does, the knowledge of "inauthenticity" a "progression in self-knowledge" is inaccurate, since the ironic self will inevitably fall back into mystification, only to rise again, then fall, and then rise in an endless oscillation between mystification and a self-consciousness impotent to evade its future mystification. Nothing is left for the self except to "ironize its own predicament," to observe with detachment the "temptation to which it is about to succumb," and to engage in an irony of irony by "reasserting the purely fictional nature of its own universe and by carefully maintaining the radical difference that separates fiction from the world of empirical reality."[35]

The metaphysical dualism which structures de Man's thought in his early essays is converted in the final pages of "The Rhetoric of Temporality" into the more familiar—and very crippling—aesthetic dualism of contemporary critical theory that will preoccupy him in the lead essay of *Blindness and Insight*. Like bad faith, "fiction" designates an apparently unavoidable tendency to reconstitute the self in more comfortable categories, while "reality" refers to the state of things as they really are. The latter is a state about which presumably nothing can be known, but a state about which everything that needs to be known is smuggled in through the back door of implication; the categories of reality in itself are unfolded as the antithesis of fiction, just as the *en soi* in Sartre is unfolded as the antithesis of the *pour soi*. The resolution of the antithesis between a *fiction* of bad faith and *reality* (that is putatively inaccessible) is *irony*, the knowledge of the fictiveness of fictions, of the "essential negativity of the fiction"[36]—a telling (because nostalgic) phrase of de Man's which is apparently to be understood in opposition to the "positivity of reality." The ironic attitude, in this account of it, would be the aesthete's haven, since poetry under its supervision could have no contact with the world. But de Man wavers: the same fiction vs. reality dualism that would isolate poetry is used to give poetry the highest philosophical role. Irony "engenders a temporal sequence of acts of consciousness which is endless" because it divides the "flow of temporal experience into a past that is pure mystification and a future that remains harassed forever by a relapse into the inauthentic." This temporality is not organic; it is, rather, a temporality that is the "common discovery" of allegory and irony, in their "common de-mystification of an organic world postulated in the symbolic mode . . . in which fiction and reality . . . coincide."[37]

De Man's turn to the presumably guarded language of fictions represents a change in tone, but no change from the substance of his existential position. He may assert that the ironic writer makes no metaphysical claims, but proceeds to conclude that irony "discovers" and "reveals"—his words—the "temporal void," our "truly temporal predicament."[38] So far from being incapable of rendering authentic knowledge, de Man's ironic poet-philosopher would appear to be its sole repository. Thus de Man's choice of the fiction vs. reality model to explain the disrelation of language and world, though it may appear to be a refusal of metaphysics, is itself a model of metaphysical thinking because it guarantees him the privileged position of unproblematic, unmystified, and objective knowledge of the fictiveness of fictions and, by implication, of the reality of reality. The so-called temporal reality discovered by irony and allegory is peculiarly static and innocent of social and historical change. Temporality is called a "sequence of acts which is endless,"[39] but the sequence is closed at both ends and perfectly predictable as it moves incessantly from mystification to demystification and back again. All writers of ironic consciousness are trapped in the same way. Irony gives us a static view of the human condition because its perspectives are essentially mandarin, as de Man admits in all but words when he tells us that the ironic writer "remains endlessly caught in the impossibility of making [his] knowledge applicable to the empirical world."[40]

3

In his collection of 1971, *Blindness and Insight: Essays in the Rhetoric of Contemporary Criticism*, de Man makes a substantial effort to move beyond the impasse that we see developing in the final pages of "The Rhetoric of Temporality." Despite disclaimers in his foreword to the effect that the book is unsystematic, that because the various essays were written occasionally any pattern that emerges from them is at best a retrospective discovery, *Blindness and Insight* is yet offered (and in almost the same breath) as a unified totality. The first piece, "Criticism and Crisis," plays (without being specifically presented as such) the role of introduction; the five essays that follow are spoken of as a single section illustrating a "paradoxical discrepancy"— the theme of "blindness and insight"; the seventh essay on Jacques Derrida is offered as a "somewhat more systematic" (and certainly it is a fuller) version of the problem he finds recurring in essays two through six; the final two essays are said to illustrate how the theory explored in the first seven "influences our conception of literary history."[41] So in speaking of the structure of a book that is presumably without structure, de Man gives us a traditional conception of literary unity—a book with a rather clearly demarcated beginning, middle, and end.

But the unity of *Blindness and Insight*, with all of its poststructuralist theoretical support and atmospherics, is repeatedly threatened by the metaphysical hangover of his existentialist days; the impasse reached at the end of "The Rhetoric of Temporality" is not overcome in this book. The notion of fictionality, introduced expressly for the purpose of situating literature this side of metaphysical assertion, and of removing the critic from the privileged position of keeper of metaphysical truth, only reinforces, in the end, the Sartrean perspectives that de Man had felt so comfortable with in the early phases of his career. Though he acknowledges that *Blindness and Insight* has its own pattern of blindness[42] which he, since he is its author, is incompetent (in one of his favorite phrases) "to put into question," I believe that de Man's candor is only *pro forma* and that his various analyses, and especially the tone of those analyses, are marred at every point by the suggestion that he is in undisputed, authoritative, and truthful possession of the texts he reads.

The clearest statement of the theme of blindness and insight is presented in the foreword, when de Man claims that in all of the critics he examines "a paradoxical discrepancy appears between the general statements they make about the nature of literature (statements on which they base their critical methods) and the actual results of their interpretations. Their findings about the structure of texts contradict the general conception that they use as their model. Not only do they remain unaware of this discrepancy, but they seem to thrive on it and owe their best insights to the assumptions these insights disprove." This pattern of discrepancy, he concludes, "is a constitutive characteristic of literary discourse in general."[43] The thesis is broached again, and somewhat fleshed out, in the introductory pages of the essay on Derrida when de Man speaks figuratively of the relationship of insight to blindness as one always lying "hidden within the other as the sun lies hidden within a shadow, or truth within error."[44] And if by slim chance we miss the figure the first time, he repeats it a few paragraphs later when he describes a writer's movement toward insight as a movement "toward the light"—a movement permitted "only because" the method of these critics "remained oblivious to the perception of this insight."[45] In his translation of *blindness* as all rational and logical procedures, reflective habits of thought, programmatic intention; in his relegation of rational consciousness itself to darkness, falsehood, illusion; in his concomitant elevation and exaltation of *insight* (intuition, imagination, spontaneity, the unconscious) as the way to the sun-light of truth and reality—and in the insistence that the rational and and the intuitive are closed off from each other—de Man reinstates a romantic epistemology in extreme form. The theme of blindness and insight is metaphysical through and through.

It is the pattern of the discrepancy of blindness and insight—with, by definition, no writer able to account for his own blindness: could he do so he would not be blind—it is this pattern itself which is pre-sumably constitutive of literary language. But as he works his way through a number of essays on the New Critics, Ludwig Binswanger, Lukács, Maurice Blanchot, and Poulet, it is clear that de Man does not prize the whole pattern of discrepancy, but only one of its constituents. What he calls "insight" is at every turn privileged as truth and litera-ture. What, for example, in the essay on Lukács, is described as pro-grammatic intention is judged "entirely wrong," a veiling of an "insight of major magnitude."[46] Likewise the conscious methodological reliance of the New Critics (and of a number of other modern critics not identified as such) on a natural model is described as an "error" of reification, an error grounded on the unexamined premise that the human process of making literature, or any other artifact, is coinciden-tal with nature's organic way. This error causes the critic to bypass, by "deliberate rejection," a principle of human intentionality that (in de Man's exposition) owes much to a well-known distinction made by Hegel in his aesthetics and by Heidegger in *Being and Time*, where, as we saw, in the analysis of tool, he distinguished between being *at* hand and being *for* the hand.[47] And, one last example, Poulet's overt search for the *cogito*, an original and constitutive self-consciousness whose location is thought to be the other side of discourse, is presum-ably in Poulet's actual practice contradicted by his "hidden"[48] criti-cism of language, a criticism of language that looks suspiciously like a decentered discourse, heralded by Derrida, "situating" the subject for-ever in language. The insight-content privileged in the essay on the New Critics, and which the New Critics are said unwittingly to articulate, is distinctly phenomenological. But when de Man exchanges his phil-osophical heroes, when Derrida enters the scene and Heidegger exits, then the privileged philosophical content of the insight undergoes a corresponding change.

The theme of blindness and insight, then, is a mask for a thematic criticism which alters with alterations in contemporary philosophical preference. What never alters, however, is de Man's Olympian stance. For whether he speaks as existentialist or poststructuralist, he speaks from unwavering belief in the enduring truth of his metaphysical perspective. Where else but out of such belief do statements come about a critic who is "entirely wrong," or about another critic, Maurice Blanchot, whose studies of Mallarmé are said to "miss the mark."[49] If de Man is as sure as he appears to be that no critic can raise a question about his own blindness, then that view ought to have made him at least wary, somewhat more tentative and cautious, and perhaps even more generous in his evaluations of other critics. Ought he not to be chastened by his acknowledgment that his own judgments must in some sense be blinded? Though he conveniently claims for himself the status of a reader "in the privileged position of being able to ob- serve the blindness as a phenomenon in its own right," his announced position ("there are no longer any standpoints than can a priori be considered privileged. . . . All structures are, in a sense, equally falla- cious") denies him the right to know anything "in its own right."[50] What we witness in all of this is a strange discrepancy between a frightfully sobering theory of literary discourse and the actual practice of a critic whose judgments, authoritative in tone and style, betray the theory.

In the opening essay, "Criticism and Crisis," an even more serious contradiction is starkly on display. In his description of crisis de Man everywhere aligns himself with those Continental critics who bring the bad news that a "literary or poetic consciousness is [not] in any way a privileged consciousness, whose use of language can pretend to escape . . . from the duplicity, the confusion, the untruth that we take for granted in the everyday use of language. . . . unmediated expression is a philosophical impossibility."[51] Though he is mentioned only twice in *Blindness and Insight*, and though his definition of the sign is never articulated with precision, the authority behind de Man's statement is supposed to be Saussure. At times de Man, like Hirsch, will speak incorrectly (in the name of structuralism and "post-Saussurian linguis- tics") about a "discrepancy between sign and meaning," between expression and what has to be expressed (as if meaning had a disem- bodied existence independent of the sign).[52] The intent of Saussure's description of the sign, however, is not to drive a wedge between sign and meaning by telling us, as de Man does, that sign and meaning can never coincide. As we have seen, Saussure tells us that signifier and signified have a connection which from the point of view of culture is indissoluable and necessary, though "arbitrary" from the point of view of nature. He also tells us (indirectly, as Emile Benveniste has shown) that the relationship of the whole sign (signifier plus signified) and "reality" is, as well, arbitrary, unnatural, and culturally enforced.

But Saussure, misread, is strategically useful to de Man because he gives him powerful support in linguistic theory for his own long-standing attack on the privilege of so-called poetic discourse. Working out of a post-Saussurean perspective, de Man can say with some confidence that the notion of a privileged, unmediated mode of discourse is a mystification. But his structural linguistics is mixed with more than a little of his existentialism. The idea that there is no privileged discourse, an idea which implies that there can be no privileged standpoints, is taken beyond structural linguistics into metaphysics when he writes "All structures are . . . equally fallacious and are therefore called myths." The inconsistency in Saussure discovered by Benveniste—Saussure allows "reality," a third, ontological, culturally empty term, to enter his analysis alongside signifier and signified—is dramatically repeated by de Man: all structures are equally fallacious with respect to what, if not with respect to "reality"? But how can this critic affirm *that* without courting the most crippling of all contradictions? De Man's discourse alone, apparently, escapes duplicity and mediation because de Man alone occupies a perspective in which it is possible to separate fiction and reality, to judge fiction fallacious for not meeting the real in a relationship of adequacy, and to know the real unfallaciously—for itself. What de Man calls an "important truth"—"the fact that philosophical knowledge can only come into being when it is turned back upon itself,"[53] when it recognizes the mediated character which cuts it off from contact with reality—is the antistructuralist truth of the fiction vs. reality model that preoccupied him in "The Rhetoric of Temporality."

Despite his charge to critics that they follow the lead of structuralism and demonstrate that the problematics of the sign "prevails in literature in the same manner as in everyday language"[54]—which is to say that critics will have to demystify all claims of the privilege of poetic discourse—de Man proceeds (implicitly) to privilege his own discourse as free of the problematics of mediation, and then also to reprivilege literary discourse "as the only form of language free from the fallacy of unmediated expression." Literary discourse achieves the effect of the "self-reflecting mirror": by pointing to its own fictional nature it separates itself from "empirical reality." This art of self-reflection, this unique self-deconstructive ability of literature to speak of its own fictionality or mediating character de Man believes "characterizes the work of literature in its essence."[55] When, in an echo of a distinction that Frank Kermode would make in the same year in *The Sense of an Ending*, he isolates fiction from myth by saying that fiction "knows and names itself as fiction," he does not intend to propose an aestheticism of nonreferential discourse, even though that is what it appears he is proposing. By pointing to its tortured self-conscious maneuvering de Man means to tell us that literature does refer, does issue in metaphysical statement: "Poetic language names this void"—this "presence of nothingness"—"with ever-renewed understanding. . . . This persistent naming is what we call literature."[56] Or more clearly yet: "Here the human self has experienced the void within itself and the invented fiction, far from filling the void, asserts itself as pure nothingness, *our* nothingness stated and restated by a subject that is the agent of its own instability."[57] Nowhere in *The Psychology of Imagination*, in which he explores the aesthetic ramifications of *Being and Nothingness*, does Sartre better describe a mode of discourse that would earn the honorific title of the "authentic" by being a perfect simulacrum of what he conceived to be human reality. Alongside the theme of blindness and insight, which keeps the writer in the dark about his own truths (and thus in need of the kind of critic that Paul de Man calls for and is), and which may or may not, depending where we look, carry the weight of existentialist metaphysics, we need to place the theme of fiction and reality—which always bears existentialist weight, and which never puts the writer in the position of being unaware of his deepest perceptions.

In contradiction to his announced theme, the poetics of fully self-conscious, self-deconstructive writing is elaborately developed (though not along the lines of the model of the fiction vs. reality opposition) in the essay on Derrida, the two essays on literary history, and in several essays published since *Blindness and Insight*. The one fixed point in this theoretical maze is de Man's unassailable confidence in the truth of his perspective on things. Thus he tells us, "Rousseau is one of a group of writers who are always being systematically misread."[58] The usual implication is intended: de Man can tell an accurate reading (in this instance, his own) from a misreading (Derrida's and all others who have written on Rousseau). The difficulty with Derrida's interpretation, in this view of it, is that it indulges the very myth of historical progress (and the arrogance of the critic who believes himself to exist in the era of final revelation) that de Man himself indulged in earlier essays. More specifically, Derrida commits the error of thinking about Rousseau what de Man had once thought: that Rousseau, in the manner of Wordsworth and Hölderlin, is a partially mystified writer, who, because his literary landscapes are immersed in contradiction, is in need of deconstruction. In Rousseau's case, de Man writes, "the misreading is almost always accompanied by an overtone of intellectual and moral superiority, as if the commentators, in the most favorable of cases, had to apologize or to offer a cure for something that went astray in their author"[59]—perhaps an accurate description of Derrida's commentary and the history of commentary on Rousseau, but unquestionably a fair account of de Man's own attitudes toward the romantics in "Intentional Structure of the Romantic Image" and "The Rhetoric of Temporality."

Derrida's main theme in his treatment of Rousseau is the theme of logocentrism that we encounter in all of his writings: "the recurrent repression," as de Man phrases it, "in Western thought, of all written forms of language, their degradation to a mere adjunct or supplement to the live presence of the spoken word. . . ."[60] Classically (and naively) in evidence in Lévi-Strauss, Derrida finds in Rousseau the same assumptions, though in more devious and ambivalent form. De Man's disagreement with Derrida is that though Rousseau "defines voice as the origin of written language," his "description of oral speech or of music can be shown to possess, from the start, all the elements of distance and negation that prevent written language from ever achieving a condition of unmediated presence."[61] Derrida is willing to allow that Rousseau's text provides powerful refutation of the doctrine of presence, but not willing to allow that Rousseau is fully conscious of a pattern of duplicity which de Man claims was the same pattern that he found in literary critics examined in early chapters of the book.[62] At best, de Man says, Derrida is ambivalent about his willingness to allow Rousseau that sort of unmystified, self-deconstructing consciousness which has a grasp of its inclinations toward inauthenticity; at worst he assumes a posture of moral and intellectual superiority for knowing what Rousseau presumably does not know.

The justice of his critique of Derrida aside, in his own claims for Rousseau as a self-deconstructor de Man is not only contradicting his earlier views—it would be ungenerous to disallow him a revision in 1971 of an essay published in 1960—but, more seriously, is contradicting what between the covers of *Blindness and Insight* he has said about his central theme. Once more: Lukács, Poulet, Blanchot, and the others were not allowed consciousness of the duplicitous directions of their writing. The very meaning of "blindness and insight," after all, depended upon such unawareness; de Man's conception of the critical function of his discourse rested there as well. Now what is being called the essence of the literary is a text that "has no blind spots," a text that "implicitly or explicitly signifies its own rhetorical mode and prefigures its own misunderstanding as the correlative of its rhetorical nature; that is, of its 'rhetoricity.' "[63] Since in de Man's opinion Rousseau's text does just this sort of thing, it is literature in exemplary form. De Man is keenly aware of Rousseau's textual strategies—he is no misreader. But Derrida's reading, for all its refinements, is ultimately fooled by Rousseau's rhetorical mode and therefore qualifies as a classic example of a misreading prefigured by the text in question, just as (de Man will argue) *The Birth of Tragedy* has engendered its misreading as a text of existentialism by a long line of critics who are unable to see existentialism as merely a voice among voices, all fully under the playful control of a master narrator in the deconstructive style.

Particularly at this point, I think, in the essay on Derrida, de Man's work raises in acute form the question of the relationship between literature and criticism. With respect to the critics he had treated earlier de Man writes: "Their blindness . . . consisted in the affirmation of a methodology that could be 'deconstructed' in terms of their own findings . . . in all cases the methodological dogma is being played off against the literary insight, and this interplay between methodology and literature develops in turn the highly literary rhetoric of what could be called systematic criticism."[64] The use of the passive voice in the passage ought not to blind us to the fact that it is de Man, not Lukács or Poulet, who is doing the deconstructive act; that it is de Man who is playing off methodological dogma against literary insight; that it is again de Man who is developing a "highly literary rhetoric" into something that "could be called systematic criticism" (a term which at this point means a union of the literary and the critical). What also cannot be ignored is an initial, blatant identification of literature with a particular thematic content or insight (i.e., "the literary insight," the "interplay between methodology and literature"), and then the development of a submerged second meaning for the term. So there is, at a lower and purer level, the "literature" that is insight and that de Man identifies with thematic content (for example, Poulet's self which is actually language), and at a higher, mixed, and more sophisticated level "literature" as a discourse which unifies the first type with the highly self-conscious activity that plays insight against method in a *literary rhetoric* described as systematic *criticism*—the self-canceling text of Rousseau, clearly, but also the text of de Man himself.

The potential ambiguity of the two literatures is addressed forthrightly in de Man's final paragraph where we learn, among other things, that there is no ambiguity, that he intends a hierarchic ranking with great privilege (though not quite the greatest) bestowed upon his own writing:

> Lukács, Blanchot, Poulet, and Derrida can be called "literary," in the full sense of the term, because of their blindness, not in spite of it. In the more complicated case of the non-blinded author—as we have claimed Rousseau to

be—the system has to be triadic: the blindness is transferred
from the writer to his first readers, the "traditional" disciples or commentators. These blinded first readers—they
could be replaced for the sake of exposition, by the fiction
of a naive reader, though the tradition is likely to provide
ample material—then need, in turn, a critical reader who
reverses the tradition and momentarily takes us closer
to the original insight. The existence of a particularly rich
aberrant tradition in the case of the writers who can
legitimately be called the most enlightened, is therefore no
accident, but a constitutive part of all literature, the basis,
in fact, of literary history. And since interpretation is
nothing but the possibility of error, by claiming that a
certain degree of blindness is part of the specificity of all
literature we also reaffirm the absolute dependence of the
interpretation on the text and of the text on the
interpretation.[65]

This passage, from the last paragraph of the essay on Derrida, leads
directly to the last two essays in the volume on literary history and
to some essays de Man has published since the appearance of *Blindness
and Insight,* and recalls Harold Bloom's thesis about literary history.
Though the lines of demarcation are not clearly drawn, de Man seems
to use the term "literature" here in four different senses: (1) the
blinded kind of Lukács, Blanchot, Poulet, and Derrida; (2) the non-
blinded kind (superior because "more complicated") represented by
the self-deconstructing text of Rousseau; (3) the combination of the
"enlightened" second type with the "rich aberrant tradition" of naive
misreaders that its rhetorical mode has engendered ("a constitutive
part of all literature, the basis, in fact, of literary history"); and (4) the
kind, midway between the first two types, represented by de Man's
text on Derrida and Rousseau, a kind certainly superior to the first
type since it is not blinded, but not superior to the second type since
it can have only a parasitic relation to it. De Man's text, in his words,
"takes us closer to the original insight," and, as it clears away the
detritus of a tradition of misreaders, set things right with literary
history (if only momentarily). For all of its rich poststructuralist texture, de Man's characterization of the best criticism is familiarly traditional, based as it is on what he would call a mystified mimetic principle
of represencing, which he knows is mystified. That is why his text remains distanced from the original, can only get us "closer" to the
original but not quite there. Though de Man is too far into poststructuralist thought at this point to allow himself the naive mirror metaphor
of much conventional criticism, he asserts for his text the function of

a simulacrum, and he remains indebted to the traditional privileging of the notion of a primary literary text as full plenitude and presence which the critic can only hope to approach.

4

The conception of literary history that begins to emerge at the conclusion of the essay on Derrida, and then becomes the main topic of "Literary History and Literary Modernity" and "Lyric and Modernity," does not have the radical implication for the critical act that it will have in the hands of Harold Bloom. As a rather conservatively intended term characterizing the activity of critical interpretation, "misreading" means for de Man in important part what it has always meant for traditional critics. However inevitable, misreading is undesirable—it is reading that is in error and that does not (to recall his phrasing) get close enough to the primary text. The fresh meaning that de Man adds to this old notion of misreading—and it is a contribution that cannot be too highly praised—is that when misreading goes on in the work of a critic like Derrida, who has trained himself at the highest levels, it is most likely attributable not to the critic's professional limitations but to his having been deceived by a rhetorical feature of the text that is not recognized as such. The good reader (this is a more problematic claim) is one who is sensitive to the ways, the cunning, unblinded modes of narration found in the highest literature, in which the text puts its own rhetoricity in question. In these essays on literary history there is no intention of placing the good critic within the poet's territory of intrapsychic warfare: the critic is always outside, and, however exalted a function he may enjoy in de Man's theory, is not quite a poet himself. The statement in the foreword—that his interest in criticism is "subordinate" to his interest in "primary literary texts"—deserves to be taken at face value as an accurate description of the role of the critic sketched in the collection as a whole, though in his most recent work it would seem no longer in operation.[66]

In "Literary History and Literary Modernity" de Man spins out his major claims in a meditation on a text of Nietzsche (*Vom Nutzen und Nachteil der Historie für das Leben*) in which Nietzsche's familiar theme of life as will to power is developed as the need of human being to reject by violently suppressing, in acts of symbolic murder, the past, the father principle, all generative process—all the tyrannies of "it was." "Life," as de Man glosses Nietzsche, consists in "the ability to *forget* whatever precedes a present situation"—an idea specified to mean that our health and happiness are moments "at which all anteriority vanishes, annihilated by the power of an absolute forgetting."[67] All knowledge and conscience, then, insofar as they imply retrospection and anteriority, are to be scrapped in an act of "ruthless forgetting" which turns human being into pure *homo faber*, whose action, "lightened of all previous experience, captures the authentic spirit of modernity."[68] This spirit of modernity, which is no merely "descriptive synonym for the contemporaneous or for a passing fashion," is linked to authentic human being, since both stand in opposition to the historical sense, and both equally well define the essence of the literary: "literature has always been essentially modern."[69] Modernity, life as will to power, and the literary are conflated "as a form of desire to wipe out whatever came earlier, in the hope of reaching at last a point that could be called a true present, a point of origin that marks a new departure." Yet, as de Man shrewdly notes in a statement that will mean much to Harold Bloom, Nietzsche's "shrill grandiloquence . . . may make one suspect that the issue is not as simple as it may at first appear."[70] And it isn't.

De Man's own investment in this most romantic of romantic ideals—the ideal of originality—needs underscoring. For what he calls the principle of literary history and the essence of literature never relinquish the privileging of origin and the dream of an existence, unpatterned and unhedged by exteriorities, which, whether located in transcendental never-never land or in de Man's modernist equivalent of an autonomous fiction severed from social, political, and economic forces, remains fundamentally a desire for an unqualified freedom of being, doing, and writing. "The human figures that epitomize modernity," he candidly admits, "are defined by experiences such as childhood or convalescence, a freshness of perception that results from a slate wiped clear, from the absence of a past that has not yet had time"—and de Man's choice of verb tells us what we need to know—"to tarnish the immediacy of perception. . . ."[71]

After further consideration of the issue in Nietzsche, mainly through a reading of what is implied by his grandiloquent shrillness of tone, de Man's celebration of origin becomes deeply sobered by the nostalgic reflection that the "claim to being a new beginning turns out to be the repetition of a claim that has always already been made." "The distinctive character of literature thus becomes manifest as an inability to escape from a condition that is felt to be"—we note the adjectival choice—"unbearable."[72] Anteriority is both inescapable and unbearable because the paradox inherent in modernity is that, as soon as it "becomes conscious of its strategies" (and it cannot fail to do so because modernism in its denial of anteriority is necessarily "a concern for the future"),

> it discovers itself to be a generative power that not only engenders history, but is part of a generative scheme that extends far back into the past. . . . Considered as a principle of life, modernity becomes a principle of origination and turns at once into a generative power that is itself historical. It becomes impossible to overcome history in the name of life or to forget the past in the name of modernity, because both are linked by a temporal chain that gives them a common destiny.[73]

In a specific application in "Lyric and Modernity" that foretells Bloom's fleshing out of the general thesis, modern poetry is said to proceed from a deliberate misreading of Baudelaire that concentrates on his "superficial themes and devices," and thereby makes the earlier poet over into a weak and easily destroyed father-figure.[74] Literary history is a process of anxiety, a nightmare of family romance, and the desire for origins and autonomy is doomed to what will be called "intertextuality." So romanticism is the essence of all literature and literary history and there are only two kinds of writers: those who privilege the origin and live in the self-delusion that they achieve it, and those higher, unblinded romantics who privilege originality with the courageous and tragic awareness that the desire for a new departure is bound to frustration. In the idea of intertextuality, and its support, the conception of the self as interpsychic phenomenon, what we see proposed as the essence of literature and literary history in de Man (and Bloom) is, first, one more brand of formalism, another attempt (reminiscent of Frye's efforts) to defend literature as a whole and literary study as an autonomous institution. Second, it is a grudging acknowledgment that autonomy of the symbolist–New-Critical variety is sadly untenable—would that we could occupy the isolate self, would that we could create the aesthetic monad, de Man's argument implies. And third, if we take intertextuality and its psychological counterpart as ramifications of the social dimension of human being (and such translation seems warranted given the substance and tone of de Man's argument), then what we have is a backhanded and bitter admission that social being is both fundamental and inescapable.

Despite common sources in Nietzsche's meditations on history and genealogy, de Man's would-be historicism needs to be differentiated from Michel Foucault's. While the general outlines of Foucault's essay on Nietzsche correspond to de Man's "Literary History and Literary Modernity," in de Man the emphasis is fundamentally negative: on the frustration of would-be romantic innocence and aboriginal freshness of perception, on the awareness that the claim for originality has "always already been made." Foucault's emphasis, on the other hand, though it takes full account of the impulse to escape lineage and dynastic repression, falls squarely on the traces of the genealogical forces that mark the text and that are *always already there*. De Man's nostalgic definition of literature ("The distinctive character of literature thus becomes manifest as an inability to escape from a condition that is felt to be unbearable") points us away from history as an undesirable condition. Foucault's positive genealogical view of discourse encourages us to focus on actual historical formations; his genealogical method "permits the discovery, under the unique aspect of a trait or a concept, of the myriad events through which—thanks to which, against which" discourse is produced.[75] De Man and (as we shall see) Bloom have great trouble crediting the "thanks to which" because the romantic spirit prefers not to say "thinks to which."

5

The nonauthoritative secondary statement that results from the reading will have to be a statement about the limitations of textual authority.

Paul de Man, "Genesis and Genealogy in Nietzsche's *The Birth of Tragedy*"

Several essays published since the appearance of *Blindness and Insight* give us the strongest evidence yet available of a formalism in de Man's thought severe enough, pure enough, to recall *fin-de-siècle* aestheticism. These latest essays reveal a critical intention to place literary discourse in a realm where it can have no responsibility to historical life. As an autonomous, closed, fortresslike world, literary discourse will countenance no conditioning by, no investment in, other kinds of discourses, unless those discourses can be robbed of their own determinative force as they are taken in by the self-deconstructing dynamics of what is called literary language. The issue here, as Foucault has argued, is not one of allowing history, as something "outside" discourse, "inside." The issue is one of allowing the myriad discourses that *are* history to have some power. The difficulty is that de Man and too many poststructuralists unnecessarily grant power only to the self-deconstructing move of the literary, a move which succeeds in emptying literary discourse of everything but the *aporia*, the undecidable. This is the error (if it can be called that) of isolationism, which has repeatedly emasculated formalist thought. At the level at which de Man explores it, literary discourse is itself beyond change. The clearest example of this full turn toward transcendentalism is the essay of 1972, "Genesis and Genealogy in Nietzsche's *The Birth of Tragedy*," at once a dazzling reading of the rhetorical features of a text long considered to be one of the foundational documents of existentialism, and another farewell (this time perhaps final) to the existentialist themes that de Man has had trouble escaping.

De Man mounts his argument against conventional existentialist readings of *The Birth of Tragedy* not by attacking the older scholarship on Nietzsche (represented, say, by Walter Kaufman and A. C. Danto) but by boldly challenging the readings emanating from France in recent years that proclaim a new Nietzsche. While granting that Gilles Deleuze and Sarah Kofman manage exceptionally sensitive readings of the textual dynamics of Nietzsche's book, de Man undercuts his compliment by claiming that both only end up reinforcing the traditional view. In the Derridean vocabulary that has increasingly taken over his rhetoric, de Man argues that Deleuze and Kofman place truth, presence, and being on the side of Dionysus by citing metaphors of depth, parenthood, and origin that (he admits) Nietzsche himself associates with Dionysus. In this perspective, *The Birth of Tragedy* is a melocentric text which valorizes voice over writing, Dionysus over Apollo, the diachronic over the synchronic. But the arguments of Deleuze and Kofman are based on illusion, for Nietzsche only apparently valorizes Dionysian voice as presence. "The most recent readings of *The Birth of Tragedy*," de Man concludes, do not question "its logocentric ontology."[76] So when Kofman saddles Nietzsche's early text with her genetic interpretation of the relationship of Dionysus and Apollo, she is setting up in miniature a model for the interpretation of Nietzsche's career as a whole—with metaphor, in the early work, part of a binary system that opposes metaphorical to literal meaning and that "reasserts, willy nilly, the authority of meaning," and metaphor in the late work as interpretation, unanchored by the norms of the literal.[77] And more: the stubborn authority of Kofman's model in Nietzsche scholarship de Man sees as a sign of a much larger investment:

> The same pattern is always repeated: within Nietzsche's complete works, in the history of romanticism, in the relationship between Rousseau and Nietzsche, in the relationship between romanticism and modernity etc. We now begin to see what is at stake in the reading of *The Birth of Tragedy*, what problem stands behind the *a priori* assertion

> of the genetic structure: the relationship between language
> and music, between literal and metaphorical diction, be-
> tween narrative (diegesis) as representation and narrative
> as temporality.[78]

With the assistance of some unpublished fragments contemporaneous with *The Birth of Tragedy* de Man moves from a thematic to what
he calls a "more rhetorical" reading of the text. "It is time," he says,
"to start questioning the explicit declarative statement of the text in
terms of its own theatricality." The system of valorization that has
fooled Deleuze and Kofman by privileging "Dionysus as the truth
of the Apollonian appearance, music as the truth of painting, as the
actual meaning of the metaphorical appearance, reaches us through
the medium of a strongly dramatized and individualized voice."[79]
With his keen awareness of the text's theatricality, de Man resists
being taken in by Nietzsche's existentialist rhetoric and delivers a
reading whose brilliant command of hitherto unnoticed or misunderstood detail is powerfully persuasive, and which for purposes of argument I want to assume is faithful to the text's interdependent range
of voices. But it must be noted that de Man's grounding of his method
on a dramatic metaphor is not particularly original with him and recent
poststructuralist method; in the 1940s Cleanth Brooks appealed to the
dramatic metaphor in order to explain how the New-Critical approach
to lyric avoids committing the "heresy of paraphrase." Though working from many different philosophical assumptions, Brooks and de
Man appeal to a dramatic principle out of the same desire to free literary texts (a broader umbrella for de Man) from declarative statement.
This is how Brooks approaches the slippery last two lines of Keats's
"Ode on a Grecian Urn": "any proposition asserted in a poem is not to
be taken in abstraction but is justified, in terms of the poem, if it is
justified at all, not by virtue of its scientific or historical or philosophical truth, but is justified in terms of a principle analogous to that of
dramatic propriety. Thus the proposition that 'Beauty is truth, truth
beauty' is given precise meaning and significance by its relation to the
total context of the poem."[80] By turning, in so many words, to the
theatricality of the poem's inner dynamics, Brooks avoids imputing
Platonic idealism to Keats; the famous line is spoken as by a character
in a play, not delivered *ex cathedra*. By the same strategy de Man avoids
making Nietzsche into an existentialist. His major conclusion about *The
Birth of Tragedy*, that it is "curiously ambivalent with regard to the
main features of its own discourse,"[81] not at all ambivalently recalls an
earlier critical tradition's insistence that poetry is fundamentally ambivalent and self-ironic.

The comparison can be pursued a step further. Both Brooks and de Man turn toward an aestheticist conception of the literary as non-referential discourse in order to make, on behalf of the literary, ultimately referential claims: Brooks in order to make the claim that literature's privilege is to yield us a perception of the complex, nonlinguistic textures of human experience as viewed through the eyes of what Eliot called the "mature" writer; de Man, from a more cautious post-Saussurean point of view, in order to make something like the opposite claim, that language cannot speak with authority about anything, much less about reality—about anything, that is, except about the nature of language itself. Yet since there is nothing but language, "wall-to-wall discourse" as Edward Said put it,[82] then in the ability of literary discourse to tell us about the essence of discourse in general we are given about as large a philosophical claim as can be permitted within poststructuralist assumptions. And it is a claim, as de Man rightly suggests in his essay on Derrida, which Derrida himself would deny categorically can be made for any discourse. Literary language makes a *statement* which, though not an ontological statement in any conventional sense (since it is in the nature of the sign to defer presence endlessly, forever put it out of reach), is yet a statement about all the being we are permitted to know in our poststructuralist days: linguistic being. "An intra-textual structure within the larger structure of the complete text undermines the authority of the voice that asserts the reliability of the representational pattern on which the text is based."[83] From that judgment about *The Birth of Tragedy* de Man moves to this generalization:

> The outcome of this interplay is not mere negation. *The Birth of Tragedy* does more than just retract its own assertions about the genetic structure of literary history. It leaves a residue of meaning that can, in its turn, be translated into statement, although the authority of this second statement can no longer be like that of the voice in the text when it is read naively. The non-authoritative secondary statement that results from the reading will have to be a statement about the limitations of textual authority.[84]

De Man's courting of contradiction in this passage must not obscure the traditional nature of his claim for literature as discourse that yields us the deepest truths about the human condition. When he says that *The Birth of Tragedy* is an "extended rhetorical fiction devoid of authority,"[85] all he means to say is that it is devoid of traditional authority to speak about the truth of being. He does not mean that literary language is wholly devoid of authority: fictions in poststructuralist perspective speak with all the authority that can be imagined about their impotence to speak with traditional authority. And since literary language alone understands this universal condition of linguistic impotence (the *aporia*), de Man gathers for his version of poststructuralism all of the elitist advantages of the romantic position without apparently having to be saddled with any of its metaphysical embarrassments. Or is the poststructuralist position in de Man's hands still metaphysics in all but words?

In "Semiology and Rhetoric" (1973) and "Action and Identity in Nietzsche" (1975), de Man has pressed his poststructuralism into theoretical impasses from which critical theory will have a hard time escaping. Here, at last, may be the critic's final crisis. Just as the self-deconstructing text puts itself into question by distancing itself from its own rhetorical mode and not from some putative reality (as de Man had maintained earlier), so the critic now finds himself closed off from the last refuge of the metaphysician, the fiction vs. reality antithesis. Because the critic can no longer occupy the space somewhere between fiction and reality, he can no longer measure the distance between them, can no longer assert the Sartrean claim that fictions name ontological nothingness, and can now no longer refrain from asking tough questions about his own discourse as metaphoric interpretation.

De Man begins "Semiology and Rhetoric" by criticizing recent semiological critics (Barthes, Gérard Genette, Tzvetan Todorov, A. J. Greimas) for reducing rhetoric to eloquence and persuasion and then subsuming it to an unproblematic grammatical structure that governs an "infinity of versions"—including transformation and derivations—"from a single model."[86] Discourse viewed as fundamentally a grammatical system tends toward universality and the univocal voice. Calling on a tradition that distinguishes grammar and rhetoric and defines rhetoric as intralinguistic figure and trope, and with the indispensable assistance of C. S. Peirce, de Man argues that rhetoric may subvert grammar and logic, and that when it does so what we have is literature. In this equation of the figural potentiality of language with literature, literary discourse becomes fundamentally problematic because it cannot, as is the semiological critics' wont, be decoded into grammatical system. Not only cannot the reader (or "interpretant," after Peirce) situate himself between the sign and its object, but the sign itself, after Derrida's meditation on difference, cannot relate to its object as "univocal origin": "The interpretation of the sign is not, for Peirce, a meaning but another sign; it is a reading, not a decodage, and this reading has, in its turn, to be interpreted into another sign, and so on *ad infinitum*."[87] After modestly denying that he can manage a "concise theoretical exposition" of the problem, and after citing examples from the television program "All in the Family," Yeats, and Proust, de Man proceeds to a concise statement of his conclusions against a complacent structuralist semiotics: "The grammatical model . . . becomes rhetorical not when we have, on the one hand, a literal meaning and on the other hand a figural meaning, but when it is impossible to decide by grammatical or other linguistic devices which of the two meanings (that can be entirely contradictory) prevails. Rhetoric radically suspends logic and opens up vertiginous possibilities of referential aberration."[88]

But de Man fudges. His own definition of the rhetorical issue would seem not to allow him the right to decide that the text is "undecidable"; would not allow him to canonize the concept of "undecidability" as he does in one of my epigraphs, as the key to the "whole of literature."[89] Radical indeterminacy—and that is what is being proposed for literary discourse (shades of the New-Critical insistence on "ambiguity")— cannot be spoken of with such confident determinacy unless the critic believes that his discourse is not itself literary; and de Man's rhetorical perspective will not allow him the position. At the end of the essay he denies the difference between criticism and literature, as he must, but why, then, does he again allow himself the conventional metaphor (we saw it before in the essay on Derrida), of the good critic in his discourse "trying to come closer" to the text under analysis?[90] Why does he allow himself to arrogate truth to a critical discourse that would imitate, at a lower level of intensity, a primary text called literary? After granting Peirce's semiotics, one cannot allow oneself the epistemological complacency that one can get closer to a text; one cannot decide that the condition of undecidability is the universal condition of literature. One can only "read," which is to say, "interpret," which is to say, create metaphors, which is to say create one's own "literature."

The consequences of such cognitive impotence and irrelevance are admirably confronted in "Action and Identity in Nietzsche," an essay which appears to expurgate, once and for all, all of de Man's conservative urges to save the critical function. The argument proceeds by way of exploration of two passages from The Will to Power. In one passage (section 516 in the Kaufman translation) Nietzsche takes apart the axioms of logic, and, in particular, the law of contradiction, by showing that the law of contradiction cannot be claimed to be adequate to the truth of things, for such claims must presuppose a "previous knowledge of entities" in which such entities are comprehended outside of verbal processes. The law of contradiction is a way of creating reality as we should like it to be, a mode of assertion in the imperative mood, not a mimesis of the way things are. Nietzsche attempts to show that the so-called prime law of reality probably springs from the nature of sense experience; from the fact that we cannot experience simulta-

neously opposite sensory qualities, we make an unwarranted leap to
the truth of entities in themselves and assert that opposite qualities
cannot be ascribed to the same entity at the same time. The general
point is a common theme in Nietzsche's later work: that all being is
linguistically posited. The specific application in this section is that
conceptualization is itself a verbal process, which de Man reads as a
form of metonymic substitution:

> The convincing power of the identity principle is due to
> an analogical, metaphorical substitution of the sensation of
> things for the knowledge of entities. A contingent property
> of entities (the fact that, as a "thing," they can be acces-
> sible to the senses) is, as Nietzsche's early treatise on
> rhetoric puts it, "torn away from its support . . ." and
> falsely identified with the entity as a whole. . . . concep-
> tualization is primarily . . . a trope based on the substitu-
> tion of a semiotic for a substantial mode of reference. . . .[91]

Nietzsche shakes up our ontological confidence "forever," de Man
believes, not by affirming irrationalism, the favorite romantic ontological alternative to traditional ontology, but by denying affirmation
of anything.[92] Through the deconstruction of logic we enter the
nonaffirming, intratextual world of tropology. That is de Man's first
point.

His second point, made via section 477 of *The Will to Power* and
some passages in *The Genealogy of Morals*, is that the idea of language as speech act, so prized by J. L. Austin, John Searle, and Stanley
Fish, and which seems to follow upon the deconstruction of the principles of logic, is yet another aberration resting upon the illusions of
metaphysics: "now that we know that there is no longer such an illusion as that of knowledge but only feigned truths, can we replace
knowledge by performance?"[93] The "act" of speech, which is made to
rest upon an after-the-fact constitution of a subject-substratum for the
act, is itself a metaphoric movement, a type of synecdoche. There is no
ontological authority for speech act theory:

> the text on the principle of identity established the uni-
> versality of the linguistic model as speech act. . . . But the
> later text, in its turn, voids even this dubious assurance, for
> it puts in question, not only that language can act rightly
> but that it can be said to act at all. The first passage . . .
> on identity showed that constative language is in fact
> performative, but the second passage . . . asserts that the
> possibility for language to perform is just as fictional as
> the possibility for language to assert. . . . in Nietzsche, the

> critique of metaphysics can be described as the decon-
> struction of the illusion that the language of truth *(epistémè)*
> could be replaced by a language of persuasion *(doxa).*[94]

The conclusion that de Man draws from Nietzsche's assault upon our most cherished assumptions is honest and devastating. Speech act theory depends upon the metaphysical notion of the subject as coherent center from which acts are directed. But if it turns out that the mind which thinks it acts coherently, with a full awareness of the "misleading power of tropes," does not even "know whether it is doing or not doing something, then there are considerable grounds for suspicion that it does not know *what* it is doing."[95] Any discourse, critical, literary in the conventional sense, or philosophical, can be brought under the newly broadened umbrella of the literary, now defined as the kind of language which, unlike naive metaphysical or empirical discoursing, presses itself into the *aporia*, a realm so undecidable, so self-confused that there is no legitimate way of taking its measure: "Rhetoric is a *text* in that it allows for two incompatible, mutually self-destructive points of view and therefore puts an insurmountable obstacle in the way of any reading or understanding."[96]

Where has de Man left things? Even should we agree that in the world of wall-to-wall discourse the *aporia* is inevitable—and I believe it is necessary to agree to this and to the poststructuralist problematic upon which the idea rests—we must resist being pushed there, unless we wish to find ourselves with de Man and other avant-garde critics in the realm of the thoroughly predictable linguistic transcendental, where all literature speaks synchronically and endlessly the same tale. In the rarefied region of the undecidable, what is called literature is emptied of all linguistic force except the force of its own duplicitous self-consciousness. In this realm the discourse of literature would suppress the powerfully situating and coercive discourses of politics, economics, and other languages of social manipulation. The undecidable, with its roots in the Derridean nonconcept of "differance," and as it is manipulated by de Man, looks like the ultimate idealistic ploy to complete the search for a mode of discourse that would successfully resist the temptation to privilege the natural object. It may be that, as it is practiced these days, the criticism of differance is only the authority for a new allegorization of literary texts; for de Man the criticism of differance reveals the true intention of the romantic image. And for de Man the undecidable, or the moment of *aporia*, which he would not hesitate to equate "with literature itself,"[97] looks very much like freedom itself, the formalist's final response to a repressed and alienated social existence.

Nine

We dwell with satisfaction upon the poet's difference
from his predecessors, especially his immediate predecessors; we endeavor to find something that can be isolated
in order to be enjoyed. Whereas if we approach a poet
without this prejudice we shall often find that not only
the best, but the most individual parts of his work may
be those in which the dead poets, his ancestors, assert
their immortality most vigorously. And I do not mean the
impressionable period of adolescence, but the period of
full maturity.

T. S. Eliot, "Tradition and the Individual Talent"

. . . we still need to clear our minds of Eliotic cant on
this subject.

Harold Bloom, "The Internalization of Quest-Romance"

Would I had phrases that are not known, utterances that
are strange, in new language that has not been used, free
from repetition, not an utterance which has grown stale,
which men of old have spoken.

Khakheperresenb, an Egyptian scribe (circa 2000 B.C.)

Harold Bloom: The Spirit of Revenge

Ever since the publication in 1959 of his first book, Harold Bloom has been preoccupied with the task of defining a revisionist poetics against the New-Critical position associated with some of the most illustrious of his former graduate teachers at Yale. In the neo-Freudian language of his recent tetralogy on the theory of literary history, W. K. Wimsatt, Cleanth Brooks, and Robert Penn Warren are Bloom's dangerous precursors, the impossibly demanding father-figures who must be symbolically slain in an act of "misprision," or willful misreading. Such an act will presumably clear imaginative space for the young apprentice whom Bloom calls (after Wallace Stevens) the ephebe. Within this unoccupied space the strong poet-to-be (or young critic: Bloom's system will allow no distinction) believes himself free to make his own unique identity, to create himself out of nothing.

After numerous books, introductions, and essays, Bloom can hardly be termed an ephebe, not even by his most unsympathetic readers. Yet he has persisted over the years—like an ephebe anxiously unsure of himself—in a variety of attacks on his New-Critical forebearers. With much irritation, in an essay on Yeats published in 1968, he tells us that though he desires to be a "pure critic," a positionless critic who plainly propounds a poet, he is forced into polemics because "so many extra-critical cultural preferences have become critical principles among the followers of Eliot, and their students, and now, *their* student's students[;] . . . one is compelled to affirm again the continuity of the best modern poetry with nineteenth-century poetic tradition."[1] In *The Anxiety of Influence* Bloom alludes to the New-Critical program as such as if it were fully operative, and not out of fashion as it has been for the past two decades or more: "Let us give up the failed enterprise of seeking to 'understand' any single poem as an entity in itself."[2] And in one of his latest books, *Poetry and Repression*, he says with some weariness: "Few notions are more difficult to dispel than the 'common-sensical' one that a poetic text is self-contained. . . ."[3] On occasion Bloom has hinted darkly at a conspiracy inspired by the New Critics. He claims in a new preface for a new edition of *The Visionary Company* that the romantic tradition—he stretches it from Spenser to Stevens—"has been deliberately obscured by most modern criticism."[4] (These conspirators are elsewhere alluded to wittily as that "multitude of churchwardenly critics"[5] who make it difficult for us to appreciate one of his favorites, Percy Shelley.) But he takes perhaps his most characteristic stance against the New Critics in the essay "The Central Man: Emerson, Whitman, Wallace Stevens" (1963). Writing with self-revealing pique and considerable polemical force, he says this: "We need to thrust aside utterly, once and for all, the critical absurdities of the Age of Eliot, before we can see again how complex the Romantics were in their passionate ironies, and see fully how overwhelmingly Stevens and Crane are their inheritors and continuators, as they are of Emerson and Whitman as well."[6]

By saying that the New Critics, and especially their Yale wing, are a major source of Bloom's critical anxiety, I have made a claim that is not quite consistent with the theory of influence. The observable, programmatic father, after all, is Northrop Frye; the archetypalism set forth in the *Anatomy of Criticism* dominates Bloom's apprentice books and—just as the Freudian program stipulates—is unceremoniously and ungratefully dismissed (but not quite evaded) in the tetralogy on influence. In those early books Frye is being used by Bloom—as he was used by many in the late 1950s and early and middle 1960s—to get beyond the narrowing and entrapping fascination of the New Critics with the single work. The conception of the poem as "aesthetic monad," as Frank Kermode has shown, reflected the deeply alienated way in which central modernist poets and critics regarded themselves. On the other hand, in the archetypalist and mythical dimensions of literature the writer sloughs off his self-consciousness, his morbid con-

cern with personal expression and isolating originality; he becomes a
kind of "mid-wife" and his work, as one of the "techniques of civiliza-
ation" and a projection of a global consciousness which is the origin
of the total dream of man, becomes a "focus of community," and for
us, as readers, the basis of a liberal education as it liberates us from the
claustrophobic world of the aesthetic monad.[7] Hence *The Visionary
Company*. Bloom's career, then, with its multiple fathers, is itself a
complicated example of the theory of influence—more complicated,
in fact, and more historically resonant than his programmatic statements of the theory might permit us to understand.

1

If Bloom has been preoccupied with "thrusting aside" the
New Critics from the beginning of his critical career, he has also from
the very beginning been making formative intellectual decisions on
the basis of that hostility—decisions which often do not evade but
rather reinstate their influence. One of the leitmotifs of his first book,
Shelley's Mythmaking, is an attack on the New Critics for their uninformed denigration of Shelley and the major romantics (with the
exception, as always, of Keats). One feels that Bloom speaks truly
when he writes that "critics as eminent as Eliot, Leavis, Tate, Brooks,
and Ransom, among others, have assured us that the bulk of [Shelley's
poetry] is not good poetry, without evidencing that they knew it well
enough to judge dispassionately."[8] And yet at crucial turns in his
plea for Shelley, he appeals to familiar New-Critical norms. We are
told at one point that the lyrics of *Prometheus Unbound* are built on
"ironic foundations that can withstand contemporary criticism"; in
another place he quotes Brooks and Warren out of *Understanding
Poetry* in order to buttress his point about "prophetic irony";[9] and
most tellingly, in his analysis of "Hymn to. Intellectual Beauty," he
cleverly and convincingly dispenses with the very dispensable New-
Critical notion that poems need sensuous imagery in order to be successful, only to have recourse, in the next breath, to the much deeper
and definitive New-Critical principle of the organic autonomy of the
discrete poem. After complaining that it is "popular these days to
accuse Shelley of a profusion of metaphors, of an inability or refusal
to employ continuous and 'organic' metaphor in an extended fashion,"
Bloom proceeds to demonstrate that the particular extended "chain"
of metaphors employed in the "Hymn" is inevitable—that the "imagery
surely deserves to be characterized as uniquely successful, for imagery
and theme are unusually unified here."[10]

Bloom's first book contains his last attempts to write what the New Critics and their followers liked to call, with not a little smugness, "close analysis of the poem itself." Yet Bloom does not so much abandon the New Criticism as relocate its idea of autonomy from the single poetic text to the psychology of the poet's imagination. The controlling philosophical principle of *Shelley's Mythmaking*, and of the work immediately following that book (notably *The Visionary Company* and *Blake's Apocalypse*), is not the Kantian autotelism generally associated with the New Critics, but a visionary theory of imagination that Bloom could have derived from a number of sources. The benevolent theoretical fathers in the early books are Martin Buber and Northrop Frye. It is clear, however, that what Bloom chooses to quote and emphasize in Buber and Frye are twentieth-century restatements, *contra* New Criticism, of what he most admires in the romantics: not the idea of the autonomy of the linguistic construct itself—the early romantics were always dubious and qualified spokesmen for that notion—but the idea of the autonomy of the human imagination as that transformative and redemptive power of desire working within consciousness, independent of any artistic medium. In its radical acts of recreating the givens of phenomenal experience, the redemptive imagination yields to us, beyond all subject-object dualisms, a universe humanly continuous and radiant with presence.

The anti-Kantian corollary of this theory of visionary imagination is drawn out in the essay "The Internalization of Quest-Romance," where Bloom says that poems are "scaffoldings for a more imaginative vision, and not ends in themselves."[11] He moves easily from Buber's key contention—"When *Thou* is spoken, the speaker has no thing for his object"—to this linkage: "We have here [in Buber] a mode of imaginative perception which leapfrogs over Coleridge's Primary Imagination directly into his Secondary. . . ."[12] Bloom identifies this mythopoeic or visionary imagination as the "center" of romantic poetic theory: "a metaphysic, a theory of history, and much more than either of these . . . a vision, a way of seeing, and of living. . . ." The visionary imagination shared by the major romantics (Bloom's "visionary company") is the ground of our renovation, of "apocalyptic hope."[13] In his earlier criticism, Bloom's personal commitment to the visionary strain in romantic aesthetic was never in doubt; he liked to take it upon himself, then, to press with missionary zeal the general human urgency of his reading of romanticism: "When Thou has altogether become It, irredeemably, and the poet, like the scientist, dwells in the world of experience alone, we shall suffer more of the lovelessness and overanxiousness of Coleridge's crowd than we do even at present."[14] Only, I think, with some such statement in mind can we hope to understand what is behind the portentous (and nostalgic) first sentence of *The Visionary Company*: "Blake died in the evening of Sunday, August 12, 1827, and the firm belief in the autonomy of a poet's imagination died with him."[15]

One of the ambiguities in the work preceding his tetralogy on influence lies in Bloom's occasional (but telling) inability to decide exactly what makes for the continuity he sees in the romantic line that "runs from aspects of Spenser and of Milton, through Blake and Wordsworth, Coleridge, Shelley and Keats on to Tennyson, Browning, Swinburne and William Morris, Yeats, . . . D. H. Lawrence, . . . Wallace Stevens and Hart Crane. . . ."[16] In the book on Shelley the force of continuity is an unqualified commitment, on the part of Bloom and his poet, to an unproblematic "center," the redemptive imagination, or what he calls in the important 1968 essay on Yeats "the saving transformation that attends some form of humanism."[17] Yet in his second book, *The Visionary Company* (1961), and only a few sentences after speaking of Blake's "firm belief in the autonomy of a poet's imagination," he writes of skepticism and discontinuity: "What separates us from the Romantics is our loss of their faithless faith, which few among them could sustain even in their own lives and poems."[18] Bloom's vacillation on this important historical question of continuity is an index to a crucial issue in contemporary accounts of the literary history of the past two centuries, but more importantly, it illustrates the amazing force of the New-Critical habit of mind upon an anti-New Critic as strenuous as Bloom. His extended romantic tradition is offered self-consciously as an alternative to Cleanth Brooks's establishment of the main line of ironist English poetry in *Modern Poetry and the Tradition* (1939). As he puts it in *The Visionary Company*, what distinguishes his poets from Brooks's group "are not only aesthetic considerations but conscious differences in religion and politics."[19] It is in this vein that he goes on to define the romantic faithless faith as a "metaphysic, a theory of history . . . a vision, a way of seeing and of living."

Bloom's vacillations aside, what is essential to his romantic line is a full commitment to the mythopoeic imagination. It is a commitment earned (Blake's "firm belief") only because it takes irony into account and transcends it; a commitment with large extrapoetic sources and implications; a commitment that no self-respecting member of Brooks's metaphysical company would make without a countering thrust of the sort of irony that New Critics think subverts belief and makes the poem invulnerable to all didactic reductions—including reduction to visionary propositions about metaphysics, history, and poetry. For Brooks and the New Critics, a poem is a special mode of discourse whose statement-denying dynamic tends to keep the reader's consciousness trapped within an enclosed aesthetic space. For Bloom, the great hope is for a secular substitute for the God who can no longer be assented to, and for a discourse that will release consciousness from the entrapments of a fallen world (including the constrictions of a pure and isolated aesthetic space). Such a discourse will make possible a visionary displacement of things as they are by an utterly human universe, where relations are forever I-Thou because all relations are founded upon sufficient imagination, a communal possession of a human (and humane) company.

Still, the notion of "firm belief" is a redundant phrase which may, and in this instance does, betray subversive perceptions. The view of the high romantic as a skeptical visionary is a link to Bloom's work on influence, where, when he speaks of the romantic line, he speaks no longer (with Frye) of the "saving transformation that attends some form of humanism," but of an "honest acceptance of an actual dualism as opposed to the fierce desire to overcome all dualisms."[20] The mythopoeic Bloom, in search of a redemption authorized by poetic tradition—a redemption which he saw correctly would be blocked by New-Critical revisions of literary history—found his romantics in opposition to the metaphysical poets on religious grounds: the early Bloom's romantics not only desire to defeat dualism but actually achieve victory over dualism in visionary consciousness. With reference to modernist readings of Stevens, he once wrote that only a "forcing ironist, determined to confront an unqualified hopelessness," would read Stevens's "qualified assertions" as "asserted qualifications."[21] But the later Bloom of the tetralogy on literary influence appears to have become a forcing ironist himself who stands in despairing contradiction to his mythopoeic interests of the early 1960s, when an acceptance of ineradicable dualism would have constituted a sell-out to that loveless, anxious crowd who confront the world as It, not Thou.

Bloom's early theory of poetic tradition breaks down, and precisely at the point that more conventional readings of the history of English poetry would locate the beginnings of romanticism: in the later eighteenth century. The much-documented shift from classic to romantic is massively summed up for us in M. H. Abrams's *The Mirror and the Lamp*, a book whose title metaphors signal a loss of all external spiritual authority as sanction of redemption, and the concomitant rise of the self—respectively, God and Satan of romantic humanism—as the naked and apparently unsupported human source of the autonomous imagination which Bloom celebrates in Blake: all in all a dubious, because inevitably ironic, authority for redemption. It may be that the conflict in Bloom's writing between a basically confident mythopoeic impulse, initially formulated in opposition to New-Critical norms, and a skeptically grounded imagination (which owes much to New-Critical concepts of irony and complexity) is resolved by noting that the humanist's ground of celebration, the self, is itself ungrounded, is itself at the mercy of treacherously shifting moods. The uncentered self can hardly be the anchor of anything but continuing drama and conflict. But we are left by Bloom with alternative theses about romantic tradition: either it is held together by a faith in a saving, transformative humanism—the "High Romantic insistence that the power of the poet's mind [can] triumph over the universe of death . . . the estranged object world"; or it is unified by a commonly held, tough-minded dualism that we have trouble seeing in earlier romantics because (here comes the recent Bloom) later romantic poets like Stevens, and modernist critics like Brooks, willfully misread them as noumenally naive believers in the healing powers of the imagination in order to establish the distinctive sophistication of their own intellectual identities.[22]

2

The debate in the earlier criticism of Harold Bloom over alternative ways of totalizing poetic tradition, his struggles to escape New-Critical norms of irony and autonomy, his impassioned defenses of the visionary, religious values of poetry—all of this appears in recent years to have been cast aside for a new principle of totality in a theory of "misprision." Literary influence is seen as willful misreading; poetry as willful misreading; critical interpretation as willful misreading; even (and this after Freud) life is seen as internecine warfare, one huge and demonic "family romance." Basically worked out before Bloom by Nietzsche and Paul de Man (and by Walter Jackson Bate in a book that deserves more recognition, The Burden of the Past and the English Poet, 1970), the thesis is most provocatively and clearly put forth in the first volume of his tetralogy, The Anxiety of Influence (1973). The last three volumes—A Map of Misreading (1975), Kabbalah and Criticism (1975), Poetry and Repression (1976)—are increasingly saturated by a terminology drawn from the periphery of rhetoric and from the religious periphery of occultist tradition. With the help of de Man's reading of Nietzsche, Bloom has put forth bold and important ideas which threaten to make the moribund subject of influence the pivot of the most satisfying historicism to appear in modern criticism. But I would guess that the ultimate impact of his four books will be to take the subject of influence away from source-hunters and echo-recorders, either to relegate it to the radical relativists at the fringe, or to reinforce our most traditional of approaches to literary study.

Bloom's warfare with his New-Critical father-figures is not so much given up in his later books as it is augmented by sibling rivalry, another well-known cause of family disaster. The threatening siblings turn out to be no other than the new French critics, the structuralists, and particularly poststructuralist figures like Jacques Lacan and (most troublesome of Bloom's siblings) Jacques Derrida. Against the New-Critical precursors in America and the new rivals from the Continent, Bloom continues, with unfortunately misleading emphasis, to attempt to clear space for himself in order to create his critical identity out of nothing. Despite his strenuous efforts, he remains a captive of the positions he opposes, a perfect illustration of his theory.

Reductiveness, a sometimes debilitating quality of the earlier criticism, becomes in the later work self-consciously violent. The history of poetry, he tells us, is indistinguishable from poetic influence. In his refusal to recognize any longer the constitutive role of extraliterary forces ("differences in religion and politics") upon identity, Bloom turns himself into a remarkably odd scholarly creature: the historian as aesthete. (The first citation in *The Anxiety of Influence*, by the way, is to Oscar Wilde.) Bloom recognizes the extremity of this stance, and can be charmingly self-ironic about it: "That even the strongest poets are subject to influences not poetical is obvious even to me, but again my concern is only with *the poet in a poet* or the aboriginal poetic self."[23] That is shrewd, disarming, and also question-begging and evasive. What about those "influences not poetical"? And what is the poet in a poet? Something isolate and impregnable to all externally originating influences except those literary in character? The unspoken assumption is that poetic identity is somehow a wholly intraliterary process in no contact with the larger extraliterary processes that shape human identity. As an idea, "the poet in a poet" sounds suspiciously like nineteenth-century faculty psychology, appealed to by romantics (and their defenders) for the purpose of establishing the self-sufficiency of poetry. A poem is something very different from scientific and other modes of discourse, romantics like to argue, because it is created by an isolated and distinctive activity within consciousness (the poetic faculty) which is not to be confused with, or collapsed into, two other distinctive modes of consciousness, the cognitive and the moral. I allude to the Kantian triad, and its isolationist and formalistic tendencies, to suggest that Bloom must rely on the sort of aesthetic doctrine which reaches its fulfillment in the hermetic and alienated view of the poetic character that we find in Mallarmé (never a man speaking to men, always a high priest speaking to privileged initiates). The more integrative tendency in romanticism, expressed by Coleridge's notion that the imagination brings the whole soul of man into activity, is foreign to Bloom's recent poetics. The New Criticism, along with a number of other modernisms, is a descendant of this isolationist side of romanticism which is expressed in the familiar division of the world into two camps, with poetry over here, and everything else lumped somewhere over there, into one great repulsive pile. When Bloom speaks of the poet in a poet, when in *Poetry and Repression*, the last volume of the tetralogy, he speaks of "literary language,"[24] he links himself to this aestheticist tendency in romantic and New-Critical literary theory. The contrast here with the mythopoeic Bloom of the earlier books, who joined all realms in the fiery synthesis of visionary consciousness, could not be more stark.

The drift of Bloom's theory of influence can be observed in his wiping out of Geoffrey Hartman's distinction between "authority" (a concept drawn from the spiritual order) and "priority" (a concept drawn from the natural order). Hartman's distinction has the virtue of preserving a difference between the realm of persons and the realm of nature—a difference, ideally, between virtue and power—and the practical wisdom of encouraging us not to compete in an arena where we cannot win. Bloom seems to recognize all of this, yet feels forced to write: "The argument of this book is that strong poets are condemned to just this unwisdom . . . [they must fight] nature on nature's ground. . . ."[25] Whether or not poets are in fact condemned to such suicidal competition with one another, it is clear that Bloom's books on influence would lose their force if he respected the distinction between authority and priority: "for the commodity in which poets deal, their authority, their property, turns upon priority."[26] Within the tradition of mimesis, where priority per se is rarely a value—where concepts of originality, spontaneity, and novelty, though not rejected out of hand, are looked upon with considerable distrust, and getting there first counts almost for nothing—in this tradition "influence," as Bloom notes, is "health." He goes on to caricature and to condescend to the mimetic tradition's supposedly last, unproblematic representative: "Ben Jonson has no anxiety as to imitation for to him (refreshingly) art is *hard work*. But the shadow fell, and with the post-Enlightment passion for Genius and the Sublime, there came anxiety too, for art was beyond hard work."[27] This view of how it was to be a poet in those pre-Enlightenment days is not credible (Bloom himself does not really believe it) but no matter: he needs to take that view in order to make his claim about the coincidence of authority and priority. And he is forced to claim such coincidence because of his commitment to a demonic version of the ideal of originality. In the end, he manages to draw out every bit of malevolent potential from the late Enlightment and romantic fascination with originality: anarchism, radical relativism, solipsistic subjectivism, morbid and paralyzing self-consciousness, gnosticism and Manichaeism—all are consequences of Bloom's celebration of the ideal of originality: which brings us around to the Arch-Fiend.

Of course, in his tradition, Bloom's view of Satan as the hero of *Paradise Lost* is the conventional one. His contribution to the deliberate romantic inversion of *Paradise Lost* is his reading of the epic "as an allegory of the dilemma of the modern poet, at his strongest. Satan is that modern poet, while God is his dead but still embarrassingly potent and present ancestor, or rather, ancestral poet." Satan, whom Bloom terms mysteriously "a stronger poet even than Milton," becomes, in this misreading, the "type of the post-Enlightenment ephebe"; God is an allegory for everything outside the self—nature, society, "cultural history, the dead poets, the embarrassments of a tradition grown too wealthy to need anything more"; and the God-Satan relationship is seen as the sole model for reading all father-son relationships. The alternative to this reading, which Bloom tells us uneasily is only "apparently frivolous," is (banish the antiromantic thought) to "accept a God altogether other than the self."[28] In Satan's envy of God's originating power, in his ensuing lust for origins and original action, he is led, as Milton shows in the allegory of sin and death, to a creative (read: onanistic) act of self-fornication and incestuous repetitions. We may locate here both the literary beginnings of Bloom's romantic ideal of originality and an exceedingly grotesque structural model for his reading of Freudian "family romance." (One need not be a member of C. S. Lewis's "angelic school,"[29] as Bloom thinks, in order to grasp the force of Milton's language at the end of the second book of *Paradise Lost*.) In the history of philosophy he finds a parallel to Satanic self-abuse in the consequences of Descartes's epistemology: "Cut mind as *intensiveness* off from the outer world as *extensiveness*, and mind will learn—as never before—its own solitude. The solitary brooder moves to deny his sonship and his brotherhood. . . ."[30] The rhetoric of this passage on Descartes may suggest that Bloom himself does not like what he describes. But not so: for out of all "this bad" (he's alluding to Stevens again), we find our postromantic "good."

Out of the agonies of the most profound kind of alienation, where the self, in the typically modernist phrasing of Walter Pater, is forever hidden, imprisoned behind the impenetrably "thick walls of personality," we find a pure good: "Discontinuity is freedom." Satanic originality, however, is an illusion, and so is freedom conceived as discontinuity: "The poet confronting his Great Original must find the fault that is not there. . . ." Like Satan, the romantic poet engages in acts of "self-saving caricature, of distortion, of perverse, willful revisionism" in order to experience the freedom of the "unique self."[31]

As "pure or absolute consciousness of self,"[32] enforced upon the Satanic modern poet by that astral disease called influence (*influenza*), self-consciousness becomes—here Bloom follows Hartman—the constitutive psychic posture of all poets after Milton. But again, he has trouble making up his mind. Self-consciousness, an indelible psychic scar that is the effect of poetic *influenza,* is fitting punishment for misprision, a "sin against continuity."[33] In view of his consistent ascription of deep ungenerosity to the modern poet, we can add to the cardinal sin against continuity the sin against community. But Bloom's apparent moral relegation of the Satanic consciousness (the rhetoric recalls Swift's lamentation for classical values), in many ways reminiscent of Milton's own relegation, is yet not to be taken for what it says. Unlike Milton, who is accused of being "mean" to Satan, Bloom is permissive: in his translation of Milton's moral and theological perspectives into the history of intrapoetic relations he appears to have swallowed whole Satan's rhetoric of victimization consistently put forth in the early books of Milton's epic. "The strong poet . . . is both hero of poetic history and victim of it. This victimization has increased as history proceeds because the anxiety of influence is strongest where poetry is most lyrical, most subjective, and stemming directly from the personality."[34] Unlike Hartman, who sees in the modern poet a profound need to break out of self-consciousness, Bloom establishes an esoteric terminology to describe a willful drive deeper into the self, toward solipsistic discontinuity—a drive away from community and toward increasing lyric inwardness that will purchase the romantic's *sine qua non,* the unique self: "a poet's stance, his Word, his imaginative identity, his whole being, *must* be unique to him, and remain unique, or he will perish as a poet."[35]

It is difficult to say what, outside of the testimony of the devil himself, would sanction this view of romanticism as the search for the unique and irreplaceable self which wants to articulate a uniquely original language. The preponderance of testimony of romantic poets and theorists since Wordsworth has claimed rather the opposite. Wordsworth overtly rejects the idea of the private self because he wishes to speak the natural language of natural men, and by so doing reach through to interior universals, "general passions." Schopenhauer celebrates a pure subject freed of all distinguishing, personalizing determinations. Emerson wishes to make himself representative so that the young men will find *him* more *themselves* than *they* are. And Eliot wants to escape private personality in order to associate his mind and feelings with the general mind and feelings of Europe. The problem here is decidedly ethical and, as Bloom knows before anyone else, its solution is to be found in Shelley (in the "Defense"), who says that poetry is the "great instrument of moral good,"[36] not because the poet teaches delightfully the precepts of moral philosophy, but because he, above all others, is possessed by the power of empathy, is wonderfully capable of making his self capacious and comprehensive—un-unique and un-particular. (Or is it that Bloom is slaying Frye at this point, whose conception of poetic relations stresses communitarian sharing within the literary universe?) Freed from morbid introspection, the romantic would be released into the community of interiority where he could explore the general structures of subjective existence. But Bloom's recent version of romantic aesthetic in *The Anxiety of Influence* is so far from touching on the principles of the ethical life that one might suppose that he had deliberately emptied romantic poetics of all ethical implication. If awareness of, and respect for, the other's sanctity is minimal to ethical life, then Bloom's poets move in the ethically barbarous world of the child. To the infantile statement that he finds in Thomas Mann's diary—"To be reminded that one is not alone in the world [is] always unpleasant"—Bloom adds an approving judgment: "profound."[37]

Bloom's final point about his allegory of Satanic consciousness and the dilemma of the modern poet facing the embarrassments of tradition is ironically a Miltonic one: Satanic creative imagination, though it desires invulnerability from the external determinations of time and place, must fail. We do not create ourselves *ex nihilo*: the history of poetry since Milton is not a history of achieved autonomy, perfect isolation, in which "tradition" is really a chimera, a misnomer for a series of discontinuous originating acts which never touch each other; it is rather the history of failed efforts to achieve autonomy. Poets, in this reading, are condemned to dialogue with their ancestors, condemned to intertextual continuity, condemned, in the end, to a community of embittered, would-be originators. So there is tradition after all.

In terms of Bloom's career as a whole the theory of influence is the most elaborate and contorted attempt yet to establish the continuity of a romantic tradition. In place of Buber, Frye, and the mythopoeic imagination, we now have Satan, Freud, and the horrors of "family romance." Continuity lies precisely in the ephebe's attempt to make himself discontinuous with his precursors—Bloom's revisionary ratios (clinamen, tessera, kenosis, daemonization, askesis, apophrades) are merely six strange names for the six strategies of evasion which cannot succeed. In the end we achieve not priority but only "illusion of a fresh priority."[38] At our best, in the sixth revisionary ratio, apophrades, we so express ourselves as to make it appear that our precursors are imitating us, as we outdo them at what they tried most characteristically to do at their best. This all appears to add up to a triumph for Bloom over the New Criticism and historicism old-style. "All criticisms," he concludes, "vacillate between tautology—in which the poem is and means itself—and reduction—in which the poem means something that is not itself a poem." His kind of criticism "must begin by denying both tautology and reduction, a denial best delivered by the assertion that the meaning of a poem can only be a poem, but another poem—a poem not itself." A poem is, in a neat formulation which he will crucially revise in Kabbalah and Criticism, a "dyad."[39]

Bloom appears pretty well to have evaded old-line historicism, though he would need to admit that his appeal to Descartes's epistemology and its effects draws in the history of ideas, and somewhat qualifies his aestheticism. But he has not evaded what he believes to be the central error of New-Critical doctrine. The principle of continuity in the tetralogy is precisely an aestheticist impulse. Poems are created by the poetic faculty; the poetic identity is somehow ontologically severed from human identity. And so all those forces outside of poetic history, as Bloom narrowly conceives it, have no bearing upon the discourse of poetry. The psychic and social life of the poet as a man in the world count for nothing; history in a big, inclusive sense cannot touch the sacred being of intrapoetic relations, those dyads which taken together constitute an elite and inviolably autonomous body of discourse. Have we reached here Bloom's apophrades? Have both the New Critics and Frye, in misprisioned version, returned from the dead in order weakly to imitate this latest phase of Harold Bloom?

3

In the second volume of his tetralogy, A Map of Misreading, Bloom is preoccupied by the challenge of recent Continental criticism—"the anti-humanistic plain dreariness of all those developments in European criticism," as he glancingly refers to it in *The Anxiety of Influence*.[40] The new cause of anxiety is the most imposing of the post-structuralist figures in France, Jacques Derrida, whose threat to the tradition of humanism, classical and romantic, has, as we have seen, been worrisome to a number of commentators on the recent critical scene. But before he gets down to his quarrel with Derrida, Bloom reviews several of the important themes that we have seen in his work to this point.

As of 1975 he is still smarting from New-Critical attacks on the romantics which (he thinks) created the malicious myth of modernism —a myth that helped to foster the belief that romanticism was a historically isolated movement discontinuous with the best thought and writing of the seventeenth and twentieth centuries. But with high disdain Bloom tells us that modernism was never a real historical phenomenon, only the illusion of one: "Modernism in literature has not passed; rather it has been exposed as never having been there."[41] The idea that modernist literature is discontinuous with romanticism— a staple of New-Critical literary history—is simply a *kenosis*, the revisionary ratio that, by insisting on discontinuity, imposes naiveté on our precursors in order to affirm our originality and (a heavy New-Critical value) our "maturity." From this incisive insight into the historical situation of the New Critics, Bloom leaps into a brand of historicism which might conceivably have been the invention of the wit of Oscar Wilde, but which is offered with straight-man solemnity. Poets do not stand in some sort of symbiotic relationship to history, in the usual sense of that word, but are shaped by, and in their expressive responses shape in turn, only other poets: "Influence, as I conceive it, means that there are *no* texts, but only relationships *between* texts."[42] (This latest formula—with the new code word "text"— is the French version of the Freudianism at work in *Anxiety*.) Or more emphatically still, while making a distinction as chilling as any in contemporary criticism: "A poet . . . is not so much a man speaking to men as a man rebelling against being spoken to by a dead man (the precursor) outrageously more alive than himself. . . . the poet-in-a-poet *cannot marry*, whatever the person-in-a-poet chooses to have done."[43] Again, in ironic illustration of his own theory, Bloom commits himself to the aestheticist position: the imputation of mean egotism to the poet (he cannot be "generous"); the claim for clean disjunction between poetic self and the total person; the explicit (and questionable) elitism in the idea that poets only speak to other poets—these are the assumptions of a historian-turned-aesthete.

The theoretical point of *A Map of Misreading* is not, however, mere repetition of *The Anxiety of Influence*, but a desperate humanist effort to establish, in the face of Derrida's massive critique, the priority of voice over discourse, a primal Scene of Instruction over what Derrida called, in his analysis of Freud, the Scene of Writing. The notion of a Scene of Instruction is intended to rescue romantic humanism from its recent enemies, and to

> remind us of the humanistic loss we sustain if we yield
> up the authority of oral tradition to the partisans of
> *writing*, to those like Derrida and Foucault who imply for
> all language what Goethe erroneously asserted for Homer's
> language, that language by itself writes the poems and
> thinks. The human writes, the human thinks, and always
> following after and defending against another human,
> however fantasized that human becomes in the strong
> imaginings of those who arrive later upon the scene.[44]

What Bloom finds most disturbing (and this is dubious at best) in the thought of Derrida and Foucault is a theory of linguistic determinism and monism which is the hidden principle of recent deconstructors. This theory derives from late Heidegger and, behind him, from the linguistic thought of Ferdinand de Saussure—and particularly from Saussure's double-faced principle of the arbitrary and differential character of language, a principle which would banish from human experience all nonlinguistic realms of value, meaning, and order, including the realm most prized by romantics and phenomenologists, that of consciousness. In response to the charge that he had destroyed the subject, Derrida replied that it was not true, that he found the subject "absolutely indispensable. I don't destroy the subject; I situate it."[45] But to "situate" the subject, in Derrida's thought, means to subvert the traditional Western humanist perspective on the theme of free subjectivity, to place the subject as a function within a system of writing. There is no prelinguistic ontological subject; no meaning-authorizing inner space of the self; no ground for expression outside of an expressive medium itself. What we find "inside"—and at this point in Derrida's argument we are forced to put "inside" in quotation marks—is not a spirituality, or presence that evades the flood of textuality, but a sort of protowriting which he calls the "trace": the subject is seen as essentially text, caught and engulfed by the truly authoritative forces of *écriture*.

A critic with Bloom's personal investment in romantic tradition, however defined, is likely to find recent structuralist thinking about the subject repugnant. And Bloom does. In a thinly veiled and savage allusion he says, "if we are human, then we depend upon a Scene of Instruction, which is necessarily also a scene of authority and of priority." At this Scene of Instruction, which is a scene of persons, not of writing, "speech is more primal" than writing, and poems carry the authoritative voice of a titanic father-figure.[46] Poems are to be fundamentally understood as *davhar*, the Hebrew word for "word" which means "at once word, thing, and act, and its root meaning involves the notion of driving forward something that initially is held back. . . . *Davhar*, in thrusting forward what is concealed in the self is concerned with oral expression, with getting a word, a thing, a deed out into the light."[47] Bloom's philological exercise serves him well: *davhar* is an encapsulated summary of the thrust of romantic expressivism, and (for him) an ancient authority against the deconstructive mood of Continental theory. So "influence remains subject-centered, a person-to-person relationship, not to be reduced to the problematic of language."[48] Toward the end of *A Map of Misreading* he returns to his dialogue with Derrida, this time poising against him Emerson's romantic authority. In Emerson's concept of "eloquence," which he reads as "personal energy" and "personal property," Bloom finds the support he needs to claim ontological priority for a subject which cannot be situated within discourse as a grammatical function, and he finds just the sort of subject he needs—so personal, so acquisitive—to support his neo-Satanic thesis about influence.[49]

The structuralists and the poststructuralists appear to represent for Bloom a more serious (because more fundamental) threat to the romantic tradition than the New Critics represented in his earlier career. Seeing clearly the Saussurean and Derridean attempt to destroy the Cartesian self—a concept without which programmatic romanticism becomes meaningless—Bloom closes his chapter on Emerson by comparing Emerson and Derrida on play, game, and the missing center. As an answer to Derrida's subject-situating statement ("anxiety is invariably the result of a certain mode of being implicated in the game, of being caught by the game, of being as it were from the very beginning at stake in the game"), Bloom quotes this from Emerson's essay "Nominalist and Realist": "For though gamesters say that cards best all the players, though they were never so skilful, yet in the contest we are now considering, the players are also the game, and share the power of the cards."[50] Emerson, he concludes, came to prophesy

> a peculiarly American *re-centering*, and with it an American mode of interpretation, one that we have begun—but only begun—to develop, from Whitman and Peirce down to Stevens and Kenneth Burke; a mode that *is* intra-textual, but that stubbornly remains logocentric, and that still

follows Emerson in valorizing eloquence, the inspired voice, *over* the scene of writing.[51]

Bloom's interest in Emersonian "eloquence" (the "inspired voice") is an extension of his long-standing bias for literature in the prophetic mode, and a sign of a deep-seated nostalgia, that would move him beyond New-Critical irony and Derridean textuality as *mise en abyme*, for the pure voice of the prophet whose presence and prophecy shine through poetic transparencies of language as sun through a sparkling clean window. But Emerson himself—his transcendentalist enthusiasm to the contrary—is often a problematic representative of romantic aesthetics who seems to have worried about the disjunction of voice and writing more than Bloom. No one ought to accuse Emerson of being a proto-Derrida, a partisan of the scene of writing. Yet though clearly on the side of "eloquence" and a transcendental spirituality, he had occasion to doubt the availability of such presence to consciousness and language:

> poetry was all written before time was, and whenever we are so finely organized that we can penetrate into that region where the air is music, we hear those primal warblings and attempt to write them down, but we lose ever and anon a word or a verse and substitute something of our own, and thus miswrite the poem. The men of more delicate ear write down these cadences more faithfully, and these transcripts, though imperfect, become the songs of the nations.[52]

The poem must be "miswritten," since what the poet does is to try to bring down into time what is in essence atemporal (that which was "before time was"); the "transcripts" are always imperfect because music (a conventional romantic metaphor of vision and transcendence) cannot be situated in a linguistic medium. The imperfect authority of an imperfect transcript necessarily puts out of reach the music of transcendent being, and necessarily subverts the priority of the primal voice, the "eloquence" of which would presumably carry into time the news from above. Language is but the "tomb of the muses."

Those not yet convinced by the new French criticism may find attractive Bloom's intended alternative to Derrida. But he cannot earn his alternative. It is easy to predict what Derrida's response would be to this new celebration of logocentrism; also easy to predict what he would say about the idea that "the players are also the game," for that is what he means by "situating" the subject. In the end Bloom's critique of Derrida becomes anxiety-ridden rhetoric, not argument; assertion, not analysis. For one thing, no important romantic regarded voice, self, or vision as "personal property": no important romantic ever regarded them so unproblematically. For another, Bloom's phenomenological concept of interiority as *davhar* fails to meet head-on the various challenges offered in Derrida's critique of Husserl, or in Murray Krieger's critique of Poulet and the entire expressive position, or in Samuel Alexander's analysis of a similar problem in Croce.[53] Any case for the self must take the criticisms of these theorists into account, but Bloom has not. And, finally, though he may find that the reduction of the subject and of influence to language trivializes the human condition, he has offered no convincing argument that "influence is subject-centered, a person-to-person relationship," nor has he earned the further claim that poetry "is written by the same natural man or woman who suffers daily all the inescapable anxieties of competition."[54] The aestheticist impulse in his criticism severs the natural man from the poet, and the Freudianism in his theory dissolves the conscious human subject and so robs Bloom of any genuine claim to humanism. Derrida brings the self into the problematic of language; Bloom's version of the self denies freedom and individuality, as it dooms the subject to one activity—the endless and endlessly evasive expression of father-figure anxieties over which it has no control and which it finally cannot evade. In Bloom there is no such thing as a subject—only relations between subjects: this is the lesson of the family romance. There are important differences, but both Bloom and Derrida present, the former unintentionally but as formidably, antihumanist theories of the self.

4

It is not only that Bloom cannot earn the wished-for alternative to Derrida—he appears at times to want to join him. To his theory of poetic influence as misreading he adds a theory of critical interpretation as misreading. All readings, now, become misreadings; all interpretations, misinterpretations—and all misinterpretations, errors necessary to life, errors made in the service of the will to power which Bloom understands after Nietzsche and Nietzsche's new partisans as the willful misinterpretation of reality. Bloom's subject-centered texts give way to Derrida's decentered texts, texts that are fundamentally open without either *telos* or the control traditionally supplied by meaning-governing origins. The generalization of the theme of misreading, only a very minor motif in *The Anxiety of Influence*, is strong in *A Map of Misreading* ("reading is . . . a miswriting just as writing is a misreading. . . . all poetry necessarily becomes verse criticism, just as all criticism becomes prose-poetry")[55] and dominates in *Kabbalah and Criticism*. As a consequence of his theory of misreading, Bloom is able to establish rather boldly the academic elitism of his aesthetic historicism. The critic as poet joins the poet as critic: not simply by inhabiting, as they do these days, the same English department, but by making a spiritual pact.

The justice of his claim that Kabbalism is the "classic paradigm upon which Western revisionism in all areas was to model itself"[56] has been sufficiently called into doubt. So I shall turn directly to the implications for the critical theory of misreading that Bloom manages to draw out of the Kabbalah. He is candid in his presentation, never once eluding us with rhetorical slipperiness, even when it means that he must revise, in public, his ideas about monads and dyads. What I quote now comes in the middle of a difficult discussion of Charles Peirce and advances us to Bloom's *ultima*, the triad:

> When he comes to Thirdness, I confess that I do not understand what Peirce is saying, in his own terms, but find him supremely useful if I interpret him as talking about poems (which are not in his mind at all). That is, he helps me to see that poems are truly triads, ideas of Thirdness, rather than monads, as the New Critics regarded them, or dyads, as I called them in *The Anxiety of Influence*. . . . Let us, by misprision, translate Peirce into the realm of poetry. A poem is an idea of Thirdness, or a triadic relation, because the sign is the new poem, its object is the precursor text (however composite, or imaginary), and the interpreting thought is the reading of the poem, but this reading is itself a sign.[57]

The implications of all this are stated a few pages later:

> when you *know* both precursor and ephebe, you know poetic history, but your knowing is as critical an event in that history as was the ephebe's knowing of the precursor. The remedy for literary history then is to convert its concepts from the category of being into the category of happening. To see the history of poetry as an endless, defensive civil war, indeed a family war, is to see that every idea of history relevant to the history of poetry must be a *concept of happening*. That is, when you *know* the influence relation between two poets, your knowing is a conceptualization, and your conceptualization (or misreading) is itself an event in the literary history you are writing. Indeed your *knowledge* of the later poet's misprision of his precursor is exactly as crucial a concept of happening or historical event as the

poetic misprision was. Your work as an event is no more or less privileged than the later poet's event of misprision in regard to the earlier poet. Therefore the relation of the earlier poet to the later poet is exactly analogous to the relation of the later poet to yourself.[58]

Much that is characteristic of the Yale way of deconstruction is embedded in those passages. First of all there is the method of the joyful misprisionist: "I don't understand Peirce, and it doesn't matter anyway. For my purposes I'll make him say. . . ." As well, there is the redefinition of the poem in the crucial conversion of dyad to triad. Earlier a dialectical event between ephebe and precursor, the "poem" is now understood as a process which sweeps up ephebe, precursor, and critic. The idea of the triad, I believe, is to drive home a point that scholars mightily resist: that their writing is part of the unfolding of literary history and not an ideologically innocent report on its true meaning. Critics and poets, in other words, are partners in a common process of interpretation. But Bloom's appropriation of Peirce would make the critic a creative competitor who knowingly distorts, one who might "read" in an ideologically innocent way, but one who prefers to "misread" in order to pump up the value of his own writing. This reversal of traditionalism does not escape the traditionalist epistemological model; it merely affirms the model in nightmarish perspective. The confusing deployment of the honorific term "poetry" is a rhetorically empty solution to a genuine semiotic problem. To say that the critical event of interpretation is a sign directed toward another, anterior sign (the poem) is not the same thing as saying that the poetic sign is obliterated by an egocentric act of competition. (Bloom's repeated capitalistic implication aside, discourse is no one's "personal property.") It is only to say that the poetic sign is always engaged linguistically, that two systems of interpretation and the respective values emanating from these systems are necessarily entangled in any reading, and that such entanglement makes possible the process of literary history. This process is given life by human differences which need not signify egocentric competition or the will to symbolically murder our fathers.

By calling a poem something that is composed of what the precursor writes, the ephebe's deliberate misreading of this, and the critic's deliberate misreading of the ephebe-precursor relationship, Bloom would grab for criticism a piece of the creative action. The puny New-Critical monad and Bloom's dyad of *The Anxiety of Influence*—a critical concept of potential power—are both obliterated in a cacophony of selfish Satanic voices. The statement that the critic's "work as an event is no more or less privileged than the later poet's event of misprision in regard to the earlier poet" is false modesty: no significant critic has ever claimed that criticism was "more privileged" than the imaginative literature upon which it comments. Bloom seems to be saying something like this: "In the days when people were burdened by the formalist delusion that there was a difference in kind between poetry and criticism, you poets condescended to us critics because you believed that what you were doing was much more valuable than what we were doing. Now that we know better, we critics promise you poets that we won't do to you what you did to us. We won't pretend that our creativity is any more significant than yours." Bloom's idea that criticism is poetry invites an interpretive anarchy: a programmatic subjectivism that can only lead to the purest of relativisms. Bloom's theory provides us with a rationale for judging trivial all talk about poetry. "Some of the consequences of what I am saying dismay even me," he writes.[59]

Poetry and Repression: Revisionism from Blake to Stevens, the last book of the tetralogy, is largely occupied with misreadings of Bloom's favorite post-Blakean romantics. All of the terminology of "revisionary ratios," "psychic defenses," and "rhetorical tropes" is employed without mercy. The following passage from the chapter on Wordsworth is extreme, but on the whole it is representative of the murkiness of Bloom's demonstrations in the tetralogy:

> Let us map *Tintern Abbey* together. The poem consists of
> five verse-paragraphs, of which the first three (lines 1–57)
> form a single movement that alternates the ratios of
> *clinamen* and *tessera*. The fourth verse-paragraph is the
> second movement (lines 58–111) and goes from the ratio of
> *kenosis* to a *daemonization* that brings in the Sublime. The
> fifth and final verse-paragraph is the third and last move-
> ment (lines 112–159), and alternates the ratios of *askesis*
> and *apophrades*.[60]

When his analyses are not obscured by his own special terminology, they tend to flatten poetic texts into allegories of his critical system. Thus, of Yeats's "The Second Coming" he says, with unintended comic effect: "In the opening figuration, the center is man, unable as falconer to maintain a control over a 'turning and turning' movement that he has trained. But a falconer is also every poet, and the falcon is his trope, and we can translate 'turning and turning' as 'troping and troping,' so that the discipline of falconry represents not only a mastery of nature but a mastery of language."[61]

What is added to Bloom's theory by *Poetry and Repression* is the theme of gnosticism. Though casually in evidence here and there in the earlier books, and broached seriously in *Kabbalah and Criticism,* gnosticism does not become an integral part of the system until this final volume, where Bloom quickly and easily translates it into a *clinamen,* or revisionist swerve. In seeking unmediated knowledge of an alien, wholly transcendent God, the true gnostic heretic veers dangerously toward another heresy—that of the Manichaean variety. He sets up a "doubly radical dualism"—man-nature, nature-God—and therefore the necessity of vaulting over both the body and nature.[62] This bypassing of physical reality is the route to a deep transcendence into divine essences which turn out to be located within the self's spiritual core. The gnostic (this is the connection with his earlier books on influence) finds salvation and freedom, "which pragmatically seems to be freedom from the anxiety of being influenced by the Jewish God, or Biblical Law, or nature."[63] This provocative reading of the psychological impulse behind gnosticism is then transposed into poetry and seen as a major tendency in post-Enlightenment poetic traditions, and specifically as a major dimension of the romantic imagination. Bloom believes that it could be argued that a form of gnosticism is "endemic in Romantic tradition without, however, dominating that tradition, or even that Gnosticism is the implicit, inevitable religion that frequently informs aspects of post-Enlightenment poetry. . . ."[64] Not only could it be argued, but it has been so argued (though not with the same terms) by one of Bloom's colleagues, Geoffrey Hartman, whose work on Wordsworth is echoed strongly in this discussion of Yeats: "The place of the gnostic alien or transmundane God in Yeats is taken, alternately, by death, or by the imagination. . . . [the imagination] 'is not the essence or the cause of the sensible world, but rather the negation and cancellation' of nature."[65]

In any comparison of the two meditators on the gnostic tendency of romantic imagination, Hartman can be usefully distinguished from Bloom. By arguing that the negation of nature is the authentic act of the romantic imagination, Bloom remakes romantic tradition in the image of Edgar Allan Poe and those of his French symbolist inheritors (like Mallarmé) who desire to make language "immaculate," free from all reference to empirical impurities. Hartman, while seeing this impulse in romanticism, seeing it powerfully expressed in Wordsworth, nevertheless claims (correctly, I believe) that the primary movement within a romantic consciousness is toward linkage and mooring of the self in the natural world; that the great dread, in other words, is just this gnostic severance from things, a severance which leads to the apocalyptic casting out of nature. I would argue (on the side of Hartman) that gnosticism is the inevitable fear of romantics, not their inevitable religion. Bloom's misunderstanding of the central intention of romantic poetics makes historical sense only if we recall the gnostic claims for music made by Schopenhauer and Kierkegaard, among others, and substitute the apocalyptic promise that German romantic theorists saw in music for the main direction of romantic theories of poetry. In Schopenhauer's words: "Music is distinguished from all the other arts by the fact that it is not a copy of the phenomenon . . . but is the direct copy of the will itself, and therefore exhibits itself as the metaphysical to everything physical in the world, and as the thing-in-itself to every phenomenon. . . . music . . . could to a certain extent exist if there was no world at all, which cannot be said of the other arts."[66] Gnosticism is the fulfillment of Bloom's search for a mode of poetic experience and for a critical stance discontinuous with all that we know as father-haunted and community-bound. Gnosticism makes most sense, perhaps, when we see it as the conclusion of this recent phase of Bloom's intellectual biography. The four books on influence, all without notes, all without indexes, represent his attempt to free himself from the anxiety of various influences, and by creating his critical self out of nothing to stand alone as the most fearsome Titan in the landscape of contemporary poetics.

5

By the word "unhistorical" I mean the power, the art of *forgetting* and of drawing a limited horizon round oneself. I call power "superhistorical" which turns the eyes from the process of becoming to that which gives existence an eternal and stable character—to art and religion.

Friedrich Nietzsche, *The Use and Abuse of History*

The peculiar difficulty of dialectical writing lies . . . in its holistic, "totalizing" character: as though you could not say one thing until you had first said everything; as though with each new idea you were bound to recapitulate the entire system.

Fredric Jameson, *Marxism and Form*

Much of what I have written about Bloom to this point is unsympathetic. I have been in part responding (it is hard not to) to those tonal and rhetorical emphases in his writing that have provoked a number of his readers (Hilton Kramer is a notorious example) to savage and, in some ways, uninformed commentary. It would be easy to convict Kramer of misreading Bloom in the conventional sense of that word, but such exoneration of Bloom ought not to soft-pedal a serious issue: that it is Harold Bloom's presentation that has diverted attention from the real worth of his ideas. If his ideas are important, if they deserve a cool, unemotional consideration (and I believe that they do), then it is Bloom's responsibility to take care that his rhetoric does not lead readers astray.

I believe that there are serious theoretical problems in the books on influence, but those problems (most of them stem from his heritage in aestheticism) are hardly special to Bloom, for one thing, and, for another, the theoretical gains registered by his recent work may outweigh the losses. No theorist writing in the United States today has succeeded, as Bloom has, in returning poetry to history; he has managed better than most to move beyond both the New-Critical concern with the isolated, autonomous monad and the poststructuralist tendency to dissolve literary history into a repetitious synchronic rhetoric of the *aporia.* Despite the implications of the misleading (and misled) debate he has carried on with Derrida, his work on influence escapes the formalism of the single aesthetic enclosure and almost escapes the more residual formalism of the enclosed *cogito,* that free and imperial subject that has moved various criticisms of consciousness. Poems and poets, he has argued convincingly, are "relational events or dialectical entities, rather than free-standing units"; his theory of influence "does away not only with the idea that there are poems-in-themselves, but also with the more stubborn idea that there are poets-in-themselves. If there are no texts, then there are no authors—to be a poet is to be an inter-poet. . . ."[67] The theory has been put to work in a highly successful study of Wallace Stevens which fully situates Stevens in poetic history since Blake and Wordsworth by showing us in massive detail how Stevens's discourse is produced by a romantic genealogy that traverses his poems' figurations and from which (in futility) his eloquence would free itself as distinctive voice. (The Stevens book is the best proof of Bloom's theory, but since there is very little overt theorizing in it, its import is likely to be missed by theorists; the book is not likely to be read by those with most to gain from it.) Stevens's poems and Stevens's poetic identity are shaped not substantially—Bloom's theory and practice evade spatial perspectives—but differentially, that is, temporally, not as entities making reference to other (distant) entities ("Wordsworth," "Shelley"), but as processes, or as *"diachronic rhetoric,"* as Bloom would have it.[68] Their being can be measured only by taking account of the being that "was" and continues to be within a discourse that is "now," a discourse within which the dead poets speak and continue to be present, as outrageously alive as the living poet. In Bloom's recent work Santayana's famous maxim about history becomes superfluous because forgetting is impossible. The intention of the historicist programs that I find in some of Barthes, Derrida, and Foucault is very nearly brought to fruition in the newest literary historicism.

The problems with the theory are not so much problems of principle as they are of tone, rhetoric, and scope. For reasons that are unclear to me, Bloom has chosen to articulate his position in ways that tend to guarantee hostile rejoinder. He has drawn more attention to himself than to his ideas: the imitations of the Blakean prophetic mode in *The Anxiety of Influence*; the proliferation and deployment of a difficult and undomesticated terminology; the gleeful investment in Satanism; the dubious scholarship of *Kabbalah and Criticism*; the refusal to sufficiently acknowledge philosophical debts—these are some of the things that have focused not unwarranted attention on the critic Bloom. A friendly response to these problems might note that the esoteric subject of *Kabbalah and Criticism* has scared off some readers who do not hesitate to plunge into Hegel; and the scholarly inadequacy of its treatment has diverted theorists from seeing that the book contains Bloom's most luminous and persuasive statements of the theory of influence. The irritation caused by his Blakean indulgences may in the end cause more embarrassment to his hostile reviewers than to Bloom himself: what is worse, the tired formalist piety of bowing down to the poets, or the act of flaunting that piety? It is of course an interesting game to track down Bloom's debts to Nietzsche, de Man, and Bate, but it is a game in which Bloom will emerge the winner. To demonstrate his debts and anxious attacks on his predecessors is only to reinforce the point that he has been pushing all along. To say that he is unoriginal is to indulge a myth that much of contemporary theory has laid to rest. Clearly Nietzsche implied it all; just as clearly, Bloom has made the Nietzschean insights count as no one before him has.

Bloom's touting of Milton's Satan and the Satanic stance is harder to apologize for and it leads us into a substantial issue. The onanistic selfishness that Bloom attributes to the strong poet is probably accurate. The problem, however, is not the ethics of the poets. The problem is that Bloom's exclusive concentration on the titanic willfulness of strong poets has succeeded in reinstating, against every theoretical point he has made, the principle of the author—if not in splendid isolation, then in splendidly isolated dialogue with his strong ancestors. So despite the fact that he has been received as a radical destroyer of traditional methodology, there is a conservative impulse in Bloom's theory which succeeds in shoring up the institution of literary studies as we have always known it. His concentration on the *poet* in a poet, and on strong poets rather than weak ones, are confirmations of the way that most literary scholars in America teach and have been taught (great books; major—i.e., "strong"—writers of England and America; the Olympian perspective of the typical sophomore survey which tends to enforce exclusive comparison between strong writers, there being nothing else to compare; etc., etc.). The difference—that Bloom has shown the present repressiveness of the past as older historians could not—can easily be ignored by anyone desiring to appropriate his work for literary study as usual.

Moreover, his misguided debate with Derrida may be used to affirm the freestanding "eloquence" of major writers, even though the preponderance of evidence from his texts demonstrates that "eloquence" is no more than an intertextual phenomenon, a scene of writing, a play of differences, not the product of a primal scene of instruction or of a gigantic imperial will. And his statement that there is no literary history, but only literary biography, in a way reinforces the traditional Cartesian privilege granted to the subject, if only in calling attention to the interbiographies of the traditionally sanctioned great writers. Whether we see romantic writers in Bloom's extended sense as a happy company of visionaries, or as a skeptical company of passionate ironists who knew well the agonies of dualism, or as members of one large, mean-spirited and unhappy Freudian family: in each instance what is ruling Bloom's thought is a need to construct an inclusive and formally self-sufficient totality which would eternalize and isolate literary discourse. Bloom's own principles would ask us to read his latest books as the final revenge of Northrop Frye's literary universe of archetypes and its implications for a liberal literary education. This principle of totalization is reenacted by Bloom's strong poets each time they seek revenge against the father. For such revenge is directed ultimately not against any ancestral poet but against the "it was" of time. Revenge and totalization, therefore, represent respectively the poet's and the critic's metaphysical urges to destroy all becoming in the search for the certitudes of an unmovable, atemporal realm. For reasons not unlike those adduced by Heidegger in his critique of Nietzsche, Bloom may be the last metaphysician among contemporary literary theorists.[69]

Having said that against Bloom's theory, I must also add that there is nothing in the theory of influence that would prevent it from being modified and broadened so as to take into account those criticisms. His historicism is aestheticist because, to this point, he has not cared to see the restrictive family romance of literary language within an encompassing context of a larger cultural family of writing which would draw it into contact with the discourses of other disciplines. He privileges major writers and their dynastic wars only because he has not cared, to this point, to take into account the many sibling minor writers and a whole series of *contemporary* networks of repression from which strong writers must wrest their identities at perilous points in their development. Bloom has shown no interest in Foucault, but Foucault's practice and his fuller account of genealogy would prove useful to any literary historian attempting to break away from the formalisms of older historicisms. Bloom has chosen to see himself in opposition to Derrida, but Derrida's deconstructive procedure would prove useful to a critic who wants to insist that interpretation is a value-making event, not a passive mimesis of the values that are there.

It is on this question of the place and nature of interpretation that Bloom's theory is most vulnerable to the attack mounted by Gerald Graff.[70] Bloom has permitted us to understand that what he means by interpretation is the making of a critical poem that would go into competition with the poetic text supposedly under consideration; he has permitted us to understand that what he desires most is not to engage history but to make his own history in the face of the giants of English poetry; with his flamboyant habits as a writer Bloom has called attention to himself as the bright particular star of our critical heavens. It would be more than self-deluded to fault his ambition, but given the nature of the case we will have to leave to others to decide whether the history he has made is worth studying as an important Western intellectual monument. It need not be left to future historians to say that Bloom has raised the single problem that traditionalists prefer to pretend does not exist, but he has raised it in its most crippling (subjectivist) form. His egocentric negation of reading as transparency (the critical event is as poetically compelling as the poetic event) is an unintended ironic affirmation of the subject-object dualism upon which the theory of transparent reading is based. Within that model, transparency is surely preferable to egocentric privacy and deviation.

If the deconstructive method could speak to the relations of critics and poets, it would not tell us, I think, that criticism is poetry, as Bloom has told us, but that the critic and the poet are both interpreters who can speak to each other because they are mutually constrained by systems of value that transcend the privacy of the personal, "original" consciousness. On Bloom's behalf it needs to be acknowledged that, with the exception of Derrida (but his is a special problem since his hermeneutical presence is mediated and tamed by a definable, universal set of logocentric issues), no one has yet satisfactorily managed, once having brought the issue of the active reader forward, to avoid the extremes represented by Fish and Gadamer. Bloom can be faulted, however, for bringing forward the hermeneutical issue in a manner that makes it an easy target for traditionalists. His use of Freudian family romance is an advance over previous historicisms but it, too, finally succumbs to the subversive temptations of originality, nowhere more conspicuously, perhaps, than in the unspoken premise with which he sets forth his system. The warm compliments he has paid his Yale colleagues seem more than genuine, but they call out for another reading. Bloom represents much that is most valuable in contemporary criticism; he also represents what is most retrograde and anti-intellectual: the desire, articulated frequently in our advanced critical journals and graduate centers of theoretical training, to be an original theorist.

We must . . . conceive of . . . power without the king.

Michel Foucault, *The History of Sexuality*

Afterword

The traditional notion of power that Michel Foucault believes has ruled the history of the West—power as a form of prohibition or exclusion, founded upon a model of a sovereign law; power as a limit set upon freedom—grants a sociopolitical perspective which glosses, puts in context, and offers a critique of the ideas of Murray Krieger, E. D. Hirsch, and Paul de Man, as it illuminates their common desires and fears. Together with Frye's mythicism and elements of phenomenological and American Derridean thought, the formalist theories of Krieger and de Man articulate what Foucault calls, in *The History of Sexuality*, a "soul of revolt," the "pure law of the revolutionary."[1] Accepting as a given of historical reality the traditional (determinist) idea of power as a monolithic, repressive norm that dominates every corner of culture, Krieger and de Man offer a counterforce of autonomous poetic power (Poulet located it in the enclosed space of the Cartesian *cogito*) as a locus of a "great Refusal,"[2] a would-be subversion of the power that is. As self-conscious fictionality or undecidability, poetic power represents, with respect to the basic domination, an underside that is doomed to a perpetual defeat, to perpetually empty gestures of literary freedom. For such gestures of freedom are given definition only as radical ruptures which in the end confirm the basic domination by limiting themselves to a simple negation of what is in force. Formalism, in both its Russian and American varieties,[3] is the literary politics of revolution. On the other hand, in its fear of free-floating ambiguity, Hirsch's affirmation of a cultural selfhood is fundamentally an affirmation of what Krieger and de Man desire to negate: the subjugated subject of established power—or even, with the hindsight provided by *The History of Sexuality*, the structuralism of the *epistēmē* that ruled Foucault's work in *The Order of Things*.

The texts of Harold Bloom represent what is perhaps the most complicated instance of these issues in contemporary theory. His formalism (the desire to totalize literary history) is in evidence even in the later books on influence, especially in his contretemps with Jacques Derrida over the meaning of Freud's theory of repression. Bloom's insistence on a subject-centered model for repression, as a warfare of giant father-psyches, is frequently contradicted by other, and, I think, more fruitful elements in his thought which would disperse both autonomous text and autonomous psyche (the "strong word" produced by a "strict will")[4] in a network of what Foucault calls a "multiplicity of force relations."[5] Power, as a multiplicity of force relations "immanent in the sphere in which they operate," and "not to be sought in the primary existence of a central point"[6] (such central points, say, as Milton or Emerson), is recognized by Bloom in numerous passages in which he tends (implicitly) to affirm rather than to deny an allegiance with Derrida on the question of Freud. What Bloom calls a psyche or a will is, at bottom, nothing more, in Derrida's words, than a "weave of pure traces, differences in which meaning and force are united." The text, then, is not the translation of "some sovereign solitude of the author"; it is a "system of relations," a "*sociality* of writing as *drama*."[7] Bloom's "psychic battlefield" of "authentic forces,"[8] Derrida's social drama of writing, Foucault's multiplicity of force relations which necessarily bears the marks of all "individual" forces within the network—all point to a "complex strategical situation in a particular society."[9] Foucault can speak of a multiplicity of forces, Derrida of a difference of forces, Bloom of a battlefield of forces, because they cannot speak in the singular of a sovereign (kingly) Source of force.

Foucault's revision of the traditional idea of power encourages not only a psychosocial broadening of Bloom's "anxiety of influence" but also a revision of his own earlier investment in the *epistēmē* in the direction of his work on Nietzsche and genealogy. When Foucault writes that "we must not imagine a world of discourse divided between accepted and excluded discourse,"[10] he is indicating a dispersion of power, through a *"polyvalence of discourses,"*[11] which dispenses with the simple contrary of values and discourses implied by the division of historical and aesthetic in traditional critical theory, or, for that matter, by his own division of reason and madness. To describe power as "always already"[12] there in discourse, as a difference or incommensurability of force relations, and to define discourse not as a passive medium of representation but as an act of power, a locus of power, is to take away the option from critical theorists of closing off a literary realm from its practical and diacritical relations with other realms. Literary discourse in the wake of Foucault no longer needs to be forced into contact with political and social discourses, as if these were realms outside of literature which writers must be dragged into by well-meaning critics. For as an act of power marked and engaged by other discursive acts of power, the intertextuality of literary discourse is a sign not only of the necessary historicity of literature but, more importantly, of its fundamental entanglement with all discourses. In its refusal to center power either in a dominant discourse or in a subversive discourse that belongs only to poets and madmen, Foucault's latest work gives us a picture of power-in-discourse that may move critical theory beyond its currently paralyzed debates.

Notes

Preface

1. Fredric Jameson, *The Prison-House of Language: A Critical Account of Structuralism and Russian Formalism* (Princeton, N.J.: Princeton University Press, 1972), p. 187.

2. This is the argument of *Metahistory: The Historical Imagination in Nineteenth-Century Europe* (Baltimore: Johns Hopkins University Press, 1973). Also see *Tropics of Discourse: Essays in Cultural Criticism* (Baltimore: Johns Hopkins University Press, 1978), especially chapter 4.

Chapter 1

1. See Krieger's review, "Critical Dogma and the New Critical Historians," reprinted in *The Play and Place of Criticism* (Baltimore: Johns Hopkins University Press, 1967), pp. 177–93.

2. *Anatomy of Criticism: Four Essays* (New York: Atheneum, 1967), p. 350.

3. Ibid., pp. 4, 29, 72, 115.

4. Geoffrey Hartman, "Ghostlier Demarcations," in *Northrop Frye in Modern Criticism,* ed. Murray Krieger (New York: Columbia University Press, 1966), p. 110. For Frye's response see ibid., pp. 133–46.

5. *Romantic Image* (New York: Random House, 1964), p. 6.

6. Ibid., pp. 127–28.

7. Ibid., pp. 112–13.

8. Ibid., p. 137.

9. Ibid., p. 136.

10. Ibid., p. 161.

11. Clive Bell, *Art* (New York: Capricorn Books, 1958), p. 31.

12. *Anatomy*, p. 96.

13. Ibid., pp. 96–97.

14. Ibid., p. 96.

15. Ibid., p. 97.

16. Ibid., p. 162.

17. Ibid., p. 17.

18. Ibid., p. 341.

19. Ibid., p. 17, among many places.

20. Ibid., p. 17.

21. Ibid., p. 342.

22. Ibid., p. 55.

23. Ibid., p. 73.

24. *The Birth of Tragedy* and *The Genealogy of Morals*, trans. Francis Golffing (Garden City, N.Y.: Doubleday & Co., 1956), p. 39.

25. *Anatomy*, p. 97.

26. Ibid., p. 5.

27. Ibid., pp. 88–89.

28. Ibid., p. 98.

29. Ibid.

30. Ibid.

31. Ernst Cassirer, *An Essay on Man* (New Haven, Conn.: Yale University Press, 1962), p. 161.

32. F. W. J. Schelling, "On the Relation of the Plastic Arts to Nature," in *Critical Theory since Plato,* ed. Hazard Adams (New York: Harcourt Brace Jovanovich, 1971), p. 448.

33. Percy Shelley, "A Defense of Poetry," in *Critical Theory since Plato,* p. 510.

34. William Wordsworth, "Preface to the Second Edition of *Lyrical Ballads*," in *Critical Theory since Plato,* p. 435.

35. *Anatomy*, pp. 97–98.

36. Ibid., p. 132.

37. Jacques Derrida, "Structure, Sign, and Play in the Discourse of the Human Sciences," in *The Structuralist Controversy: The Languages of Criticism and the Sciences of Man,* ed. Richard Macksey and Eugenio Donato (Baltimore: Johns Hopkins University Press, 1972), pp. 247–48.

38. *Anatomy*, pp. 117–18.

39. Ibid., pp. 105–6.

40. Ibid., p. 208.

41. Michel Foucault, *The Archaeology of Knowledge,* trans. A. M. Sheridan Smith (New York: Harper & Row, 1976), p. 21.

42. "Ghostlier Demarcations," pp. 122, 128. For an early effort to place Frye with structuralism see Hartman's "Structuralism: The Anglo-American Adventure," in *Structuralism,* ed. with an introduction by Jacques Ehrmann (Garden City, N.Y.: Doubleday & Co., 1970), pp. 137–58 (the essay appeared first in *Yale French Studies* in 1966). Frye's spatializing impulse

forges another link between his thought and a central element of New-Critical theory. See, for example, Joseph Frank's "Spatial Form in Modern Literature," *Sewanee Review* (Spring and Summer 1945).

43. *Anatomy*, p. 52.
44. Ibid., p. 7.
45. Ibid., p. 72.
46. Ibid., pp. 73, 5–6.
47. Ibid., p. 62.
48. Ibid., pp. 71–74.
49. Ibid., p. 86.
50. For "existential revelation" see Krieger, *Play and Place of Criticism*, p. 227; for "existential projection" see *Anatomy*, pp. 63–65.
51. "Northrop Frye and Contemporary Criticism: Ariel and the Spirit of Gravity," in *Northrop Frye in Modern Criticism*, p. 10.
52. *Anatomy*, p. 74.
53. Ibid., p. 77.
54. Eliseo Vivas, *The Artistic Transaction and Essays on Theory of Literature* (Columbus, O.: Ohio State University Press, 1963), pp. 3–93.
55. Immanuel Kant, *Critique of Judgment*, trans. with an introduction by J. H. Bernard (New York: Hafner Publishing Company, 1966), pp. 51–54.
56. Ibid., pp. 65–68.
57. *Fables of Identity* (New York: Harcourt Brace Jovanovich, 1963), pp. 151–52.
58. Kant, *Critique of Judgment*, p. 44.
59. Friedrich Schiller, *On the Aesthetic Education of Man*, trans. with an introduction by Reginald Small (New York: Frederick Ungar, 1965), p. 77.
60. Ibid., p. 137.
61. Ibid., pp. 125, 128.
62. *Anatomy*, pp. 63–65.
63. Ibid., p. 94.
64. Ibid., p. 34.
65. Ibid., p. 147. Italics mine.
66. Ibid., p. 223.
67. Ibid., p. 33.
68. Ibid., pp. 33–34.
69. Ibid., p. 119.
70. Ibid., p. 122.
71. Ibid.
72. "Criticism as Myth," in *Northrop Frye in Modern Criticism*, p. 101.
73. *Anatomy*, p. 170.
74. Ibid., p. 169.
75. Ibid., p. 184.
76. Ibid., p. 212.
77. *University of Toronto Quarterly* 28 (January 1959): 190–96.
78. *Anatomy*, p. 105.
79. *The Educated Imagination* (Bloomington, Ind.: Indiana University Press, 1964), p. 16.
80. *Anatomy*, p. 350.
81. Ibid., p. 352.
82. Ibid., p. 354.

Chapter 2

1. For these bibliographical facts I am indebted to Robert Denham, *Northrop Frye: An Enumerative Bibliography* (Metuchen, N.J.: Scarecrow Press, 1974).

2. "Criticism as Myth," in *Northrop Frye in Modern Criticism*, ed. Murray Krieger (New York: Columbia University Press, 1966), pp. 75–76.

3. For these bibliographical facts I am indebted to J. M. Edelstein, *Wallace Stevens: A Descriptive Bibliography* (Pittsburgh: University of Pittsburgh Press, 1973).

4. *The Collected Poems of Wallace Stevens* (New York: Alfred A. Knopf, 1974), p. 486.

5. Ibid., p. 406.

6. Ibid., p. 383.

7. Wallace Stevens, *The Necessary Angel: Essays on Reality and the Imagination* (London: Faber and Faber, 1951), p. 36.

8. *Collected Poems of Wallace Stevens*, p. 382.

9. Ibid., p. 215.

10. Frank Kermode, *The Sense of an Ending: Studies in the Theory of Fiction* (New York: Oxford University Press, 1967), p. 4.

11. Ibid., p. 44.

12. Ibid., pp. 18, 36, 54, 58, 179.

13. Ibid., p. 38.

14. Ibid., pp. 6–7.

15. Ibid., p. 24.

16. Ibid., p. 39.

17. Northrop Frye, *Anatomy of Criticism: Four Essays* (New York: Atheneum, 1967), p. 208.

18. For the discussion of *chronos* and *kairos* see Kermode, *Sense of an Ending*, pp. 46–50.

19. Ibid., p. 17.

20. Ibid., pp. 36–37, 62–63.

21. Quoted in ibid., p. 139.

22. Friedrich Nietzsche, *The Birth of Tragedy* and *The Genealogy of Morals*, trans. Francis Golffing (Garden City, N.Y.: Doubleday & Co., 1956), p. 111.

23. Immanuel Kant, *Critique of Judgment*, trans. J. H. Bernard (New York: Hafner Publishing Company, 1966), sec. 49.

24. For the several points from Kant's epistemology in this paragraph see *Critique of Pure Reason*, trans. F. Max Müller (Garden City, N.Y.: Doubleday & Co., 1966), pp. 21–43, 101–2, 121–27, 231–36.

25. *Critique of Judgment*, p. 171.

26. Ibid., p. 157.

27. Ibid.

28. Ibid.

29. Ibid., p. 77.

30. Ibid., p. 172.

31. Paul de Man, "Genesis and Genealogy in Nietzsche's *The Birth of Tragedy*," *Diacritics* 2 (Winter, 1972): 44–53.

32. *Birth of Tragedy*, pp. 21, 27, 28, 29, 31, 32, 34, 46, 53.

33. Kermode, *Sense of an Ending*, p. 64.

34. *Birth of Tragedy,* p. 93.

35. Ibid., p. 33.

36. Ibid., p. 35.

37. Ibid., p. 21.

38. Ibid., p. 33.

39. For two important treatments of Sartre's *Critique* see Fredric Jameson, *Marxism and Form* (Princeton, N.J.: Princeton University Press, 1971), chap. 4, and Mark Poster, *Existential Marxism in Postwar France* (Princeton, N.J.: Princeton University Press, 1975), chap. 7.

40. Jean-Paul Sartre, *Being and Nothingness: An Essay in Phenomenological Ontology,* trans. Hazel E. Barnes (New York: Citadel Press, 1964), p. xlvii.

41. Ibid., pp. xlvii, l, li.

42. Ibid., p. xlv.

43. Ibid., p. xlvii.

44. Ibid., p. l.

45. Ibid., pp. lxii, lxiv.

46. For this discussion of its imagery see *Nausea,* trans. Lloyd Alexander (New York: New Directions, 1964), pp. 33, 134, 136–38, 165, 169, 170, 172, 174, 177, and the entire chestnut tree passage, 170–81. For a discussion to which I am indebted see Fredric Jameson, *Sartre: The Origins of a Style* (New Haven, Conn.: Yale University Press, 1961).

47. *Being and Nothingness,* pp. 147, 27.

48. Ibid., pp. lxvi, lxv.

49. Ibid., p. 65—a classic passage for existentialism.

50. Ibid., pp. 24–25, 54–55, 62–63.

51. Ibid., pp. 33, 5.

52. Ibid., pp. 18, 24.

53. Ibid., p. 50.

54. Ibid.

55. Ibid., p. 25.

56. Ibid., p. 65.

57. Ibid., pp. 77–78, 81, 89–90.

58. Ibid., p. 118.

59. Ibid., p. 78.

60. Ibid., p. 37.

61. Jean-Paul Sartre, *The Psychology of Imagination* (Secaucus, N.J.: Citadel Press, n.d.), p. 8 (the translator's name is not given).

62. Ibid., p. 11.

63. Ibid., pp. 11, 13.

64. Ibid., pp. 16, 17.

65. *Being and Nothingness,* p. 75.

66. *Psychology of Imagination,* pp. 28–33, 120–21, 122, 134.

67. Ibid., p. 138.

68. Ibid., p. 120.

69. Ibid., p. 193.

70. Ibid., p. 177.

71. Ibid., pp. 184, 210.

72. Ibid., pp. 189, 204, 210.

73. Ibid., p. 211.

74. Ibid., p. 208.
75. Ibid., p. 267.
76. Ibid., p. 269.
77. Ibid., pp. 193–94.
78. Ibid., pp. 271–72, 271.
79. Ibid., p. 267.
80. Ibid., p. 281.
81. Hans Vaihinger, *The Philosophy of 'As If'*, trans. C. K. Ogden (London: Routledge & Kegan Paul, 1924), p. 12.
82. Stevens, *Necessary Angel*, p. 36; *The Collected Poems of W. B. Yeats* (New York: Macmillan Co., 1963), p. 233; *Selected Prose of Robert Frost*, ed. Hyde Cox and Edward Connery Lathem (New York: Holt, Rinehart & Winston, 1959), p. 107.
83. For this motif, see Kermode, *Sense of an Ending*, pp. 35, 37, 40, 106, 115, 127, 128.
84. *Selected Prose of Robert Frost*, pp. 106–07.
85. Vaihinger, *Philosophy of 'As If'*, pp. 85–90, 92.
86. Kermode, *Sense of an Ending*, p. 113.
87. Nietzsche, *Birth of Tragedy*, p. 111.
88. Friedrich Nietzsche, *The Will to Power*, trans. Walter Kaufman and R. J. Hollindale (New York: Random House, 1968), p. 269.
89. Paul de Man, "Action and Identity in Nietzsche," *Yale French Studies*, no. 52 (Fall 1975), pp. 16–30.
90. Nietzsche, *Will to Power*, pp. 279, 276, 281.
91. Kermode, *Sense of an Ending*, p. 44.

Chapter 3

1. J. Hillis Miller, *Charles Dickens: The World of His Novels* (Bloomington, Ind.: Indiana University Press, 1969), p. xi; originally published in 1959 by Harvard University Press.
2. Geoffrey H. Hartman, *Beyond Formalism: Literary Essays 1958–1970* (New Haven, Conn.: Yale University Press, 1970), pp. 51–56; Murray Krieger, "Mediation, Language, and Vision in the Reading of Literature," in *Critical Theory since Plato*, ed. Hazard Adams (New York: Harcourt Brace Jovanovich, 1971), passim; Paul de Man, *Blindness and Insight: Essays in the Rhetoric of Contemporary Criticism* (New York: Oxford University Press, 1971), pp. 79–101.
3. Quoted in J. Hillis Miller, "The Geneva School," in *Modern French Criticism: From Proust and Valéry to Structuralism*, ed. John K. Simon (Chicago: University of Chicago Press, 1972), p. 292.
4. Ibid., pp. 291–92.
5. The term is Michel Foucault's; for my treatment of Foucault see chapter 5.
6. Emile Benveniste, *Problems in General Linguistics*, trans. Mary Elizabeth Meek (Coral Gables, Fla.: University of Miami Press, 1971), pp. 3–40.
7. *Selected Letters of Gustave Flaubert*, trans. Francis Steegmuller (New York: Farrar, Straus, and Young, 1954), pp. 127–28.
8. Benedetto Croce, *Aesthetic*, trans. Douglas Ainslie (New York: Noonday Press, 1966), chaps. 1, 15.

9. *Mallarmé: Selected Prose Poems, Essays, and Letters,* trans. Bradford Cook (Baltimore: Johns Hopkins University Press, 1956), pp. 24, 10.

10. W. B. Yeats, "The Autumn of the Body," *Essays and Introductions* (New York: Macmillan Publishing Co., 1961), pp. 189, 191–92.

11. Ibid., p. 193.

12. Ibid., p. 194.

13. Edmund Husserl, *Ideas,* trans. W. R. Boyce-Gibson (New York: Macmillan Publishing Co., 1962), pp. 47–55 for the eidetic reduction and pp. 96–100 for the *epochē*.

14. Ibid., pp. 101, 102.

15. Edmund Husserl, *Paris Lectures,* trans. P. Koestenbaum (The Hague: M. Nijhoff, 1964), p. 10.

16. *Ideas,* p. 47.

17. *Paris Lectures,* p. 8.

18. *Ideas,* p. 100.

19. Yeats, "The Autumn of the Body," pp. 192–93.

20. *Ideas,* p. 100.

21. Edmund Husserl, *Cartesian Meditations,* trans. D. Cairns (The Hague: M. Nijhoff, 1960), p. 35.

22. Georges Poulet, *The Interior Distance,* trans. Elliott Coleman (Ann Arbor, Mich.: University of Michigan Press, 1964), p. vii.

23. Georges Poulet, "Criticism and the Experience of Interiority," in *The Structuralist Controversy,* ed. Richard Macksey and Eugenio Donato (Baltimore: Johns Hopkins University Press, 1970), pp. 66–67.

24. J. Hillis Miller, "Georges Poulet's 'Criticism of Identification'," in *The Quest for Imagination,* ed. O. B. Hardison, Jr. (Cleveland: Press of Case Western Reserve University, 1971), p. 192. The first five sections of this essay appeared in somewhat different form in Miller's first piece on Poulet, "The Literary Criticism of Georges Poulet," *Modern Language Notes* 78, no. 5 (December 1963): 471–88.

25. "The Self and the Other in Critical Consciousness," *Diacritics* 2 (Spring 1972): 46.

26. John Crowe Ransom, "Poetry: A Note in Ontology," *The World's Body* (Port Washington, N.Y.: Kennikat Press, 1964), p. 131.

27. "Criticism and the Experience of Interiority," p. 57.

28. For these sexual metaphors in Poulet see ibid., pp. 57, 59, 62, 63, 68; and "The Self and the Other in Critical Consciousness," pp. 46, 47.

29. *Interior Distance,* p. viii.

30. "The Self and the Other in Critical Consciousness," 46; "Criticism and the Experience of Interiority," p. 72; *Interior Distance,* p. viii.

31. *Interior Distance,* p. vii.

32. Quoted in *Modern French Criticism,* p. 292.

33. Jacques Derrida, *Speech and Phenomena and Other Essays on Husserl's Theory of Signs,* trans. David B. Allison (Evanston, Ill.: Northwestern University Press, 1973), p. 16.

34. Ibid., chap. 1.

35. Ibid., pp. 20, 10.

36. Ibid., p. 20.

37. Ibid., p. 9.

38. Ibid., p. 22.

39. Ibid., p. 15.

40. Ibid.

41. Ibid., p. 22.

42. Ibid.

43. Ibid.

44. "The Self and the Other in Critical Consciousness," 47, 48.

45. "Criticism and the Experience of Interiority," p. 58.

46. Ibid., p. 61.

47. Ibid., p. 72.

48. Ibid.

49. Edward Said, "Abecedarium Culturae: Structuralism, Absence, Writing," in *Modern French Criticism*, pp. 377–79.

50. I am referring to "The Literary Criticism of Georges Poulet," *MLN* 78 (December 1963): 471–488, and to the well-known "The Geneva School."

51. Miller, *Charles Dickens*: "The chapters presented here have as their goal the exploration of the imaginative universe of Dickens, and the revelation of that presiding unity hidden at the center. . ." (p. x).

52. Miller, "George Poulet's 'Criticism of Identification'," pp. 212, 216. The final three sections of this essay reprint "Geneva or Paris? The Recent Work of Georges Poulet," *University of Toronto Quarterly* 39 (April 1970): 212–28.

53. Ibid., p. 217.

54. De Man, *Blindness and Insight*, p. 81.

55. Ibid., p. 101.

56. Ibid., pp. 99, 10.

57. Ibid., pp. 81, 80.

58. Ibid., p. 82.

59. *Structuralist Controversy*, p. 76.

60. "Criticism and the Experience of Interiority," pp. 57–58.

61. William James, *Psychology* (New York: Fawcett Publications, 1963), p. 148.

62. Jean-Paul Sartre, *Being and Nothingness: An Essay in Phenomenological Ontology*, trans. Hazel E. Barnes (New York: Citadel Press, 1964), p. xlv.

63. Ibid., p. xlvi.

64. Ibid.

65. Ibid.

66. Ibid.

67. Ibid., p. xlvii.

68. Ibid.

69. Among the many studies now available on Heidegger, two I have found most useful are: W. B. Macomber, *The Anatomy of Disillusion: Martin Heidegger's Notion of Truth* (Evanston, Ill.: Northwestern University Press, 1967), and Laszlo Versényi, *Heidegger, Being, and Truth* (New Haven, Conn.: Yale University Press, 1965).

70. Though the reading of *das Man* and "being as such" as representations of a typical nineteenth-century aesthetic dualism is my own, I owe a large debt to Stephen Bronner's analysis of *das Man* in his essay "Martin Heidegger: The Consequences of Political Mystification," *Salmagundi*, no. 38–39 (Summer-Fall, 1977), pp. 153–74.

71. Martin Heidegger, *Being and Time,* trans. John Macquarrie and Edward Robinson (New York: Harper & Row, 1962), pp. 23–31.

72. Ibid., p. 41.

73. Martin Heidegger, *An Introduction to Metaphysics,* trans. Ralph Manheim (New Haven, Conn.: Yale University Press, 1959), pp. 14, 100.

74. *Being and Time,* pp. 51–55.

75. Bronner, "Martin Heidegger," 156–57; Heidegger, *Being and Time,* pp. 31–35.

76. Martin Heidegger, *Vom wesen des Grundes* (Frankfurt: Klostermann, 1965), p. 5.

77. F. W. von Schelling, "On the Relation of the Plastic Arts to Nature," in *The German Classics,* vol. 5, ed. Kuno Francke (New York: German Publication Society, 1913), p. 107.

78. Samuel Taylor Coleridge, *Biographia Literaria,* ed. George Watson (New York: E. P. Dutton, 1956), p. 167.

79. *Being and Time,* p. 79.

80. *Ralph Waldo Emerson: Selected Prose and Poetry,* ed. Reginald L. Cook (New York: Holt, Rinehart & Winston, 1969), p. 5.

81. *Being and Time,* pp. 67–68, 98.

82. For the entire discussion of "world" and "tool," see ibid., pp. 91–122.

83. With its numerous metaphoric variants, a major term for Heidegger; see, for example, ibid., p. 36.

84. Martin Heidegger, *Poetry, Language, Thought,* trans. Albert Hofstadter (New York: Harper & Row, 1971), p. 189.

85. *Being and Time,* p. 116.

86. *Introduction to Metaphysics,* p. 62.

87. *Being and Time,* p. 140.

88. *Emerson: Selected Prose and Poetry,* p. 6.

89. *Being and Time,* p. 93.

90. Ibid., p. 97.

91. Ibid., p. 104.

92. Ibid., p. 116.

93. For this information I am indebted to Hofstadter's notes, pp. xxiii–xxv, in *Poetry, Language, Thought.*

94. Ibid., pp. 28–29.

95. Ibid., pp. 33–36.

96. Ibid., p. 36.

97. Ibid.

98. See *Being and Time,* pp. 51–58, for a discussion of "phenomenon" and *logos.*

99. *Introduction to Metaphysics,* pp. 14–15, 100–101, 127–28.

100. *Being and Time,* p. 60.

101. *Poetry, Language, Thought,* p. 192.

102. Martin Heidegger, *On the Way to Language,* trans. Peter D. Hertz (New York: Harper & Row, 1971), pp. 159–60.

103. *Poetry, Language, Thought,* p. 40.

104. Ibid., p. 42.

105. Ibid., pp. 44–45.

106. Ibid., p. 76.

107. Ibid., p. 63.

108. Ibid., p. 69.

109. Ibid., p. 46.

110. Ibid.

111. Ibid., pp. 46, 47.

112. Ibid., p. 47.

113. Ibid., p. 48.

114. Ibid., p. 49.

115. Ibid., p. 63.

116. Ibid., p. 60.

117. Ibid., p. 62.

118. Ibid., p. 63.

119. For these terms see the last two essays in ibid., "Language" and ". . . Poetically Man Dwells . . .".

120. Ibid., p. 207.

121. Ibid., p. 204.

122. Ibid., p. 203. For "bridging" see "Building Dwelling Thinking" ibid.

123. Ibid., p. 221.

124. See Jacques Derrida, "The Ends of Man," *Philosophy and Phenomenological Research* 30 (September 1969): 31–57.

125. *Being and Time*, p. 428.

126. Ibid., p. 433.

127. Bronner, "Martin Heidegger," 169.

128. *Being and Time*, p. 435.

129. Ibid., p. 436.

130. Ibid., pp. 437, 438.

131. Ibid., p. 441.

132. Ibid., p. 442.

133. In "Heidegger's Politics: An Interview," *Graduate Faculty Philosophy Journal* 6 (Winter 1977): 32.

Chapter 4

1. Jonathan Culler, *Structuralist Poetics: Structuralism, Linguistics, and the Study of Literature* (Ithaca, N.Y.: Cornell University Press, 1975), p. 119.

2. Ibid., p. 9.

3. Ibid., p. 29.

4. Roland Barthes, *On Racine,* trans. Richard Howard (New York: Hill & Wang, 1964), p. 162.

5. Culler, *Structuralist Poetics,* pp. 48–49.

6. Ibid., p. 53.

7. Ibid., p. 264.

8. Ibid.

9. Ibid., p. 109.

10. Northrop Frye, *Anatomy of Criticism: Four Essays* (New York: Atheneum, 1967), p. 11.

11. Culler, *Structuralist Poetics,* p. 120.

12. Ibid., p. 113.

13. Ibid.

14. Ibid., p. 126.

15. Ibid., p. 119.

16. Fredric Jameson, *The Prison-House of Language: A Critical Account of Structuralism and Russian Formalism* (Princeton, N.J.: Princeton University Press, 1972), p. 43.

17. Culler, *Structuralist Poetics*, p. 120.

18. Cleanth Brooks, *Modern Poetry and the Tradition* (Chapel Hill, N.C.: University of North Carolina Press, 1939), p. vii.

19. Jameson, *Prison-House*, pp. 52–53.

20. Culler, *Structuralist Poetics*, p. 116.

21. Ibid., p. 117.

22. Ibid., p. 129.

23. Ibid., p. 123.

24. Ibid., pp. 123–24.

25. Ferdinand de Saussure, *Course in General Linguistics*, ed. Charles Bally and Albert Sechehaye, in collaboration with Albert Riedlinger; trans. Wade Baskin (New York: McGraw-Hill, 1966), p. xiv.

26. Jonathan Culler, *Ferdinand de Saussure* (New York: Penguin Books, 1976). In criticizing Saussure's first editors, Culler writes: "their order of presentation is probably not that which Saussure would have chosen and thus does not reflect the potential logical sequence of his argument" (p. 6).

27. Emile Benveniste, *Problems in General Linguistics*, trans. Mary Elizabeth Meek (Coral Gables, Fla.: University of Miami Press, 1971), p. 4.

28. Jameson, *Prison-House*, p. 7.

29. Ibid., p. 8.

30. Ibid., p. 6.

31. Saussure, *Course*, p. 18.

32. Ibid., pp. 22–23, 20.

33. Benveniste, *Problems*, p. 8.

34. Ibid., p. 5; Jameson, *Prison-House*, p. 6.

35. Jameson, *Prison-House*, pp. 10–11.

36. Saussure, *Course*, p. 20.

37. Ibid., p. 19: "Language exists in each individual, yet is common to all. Nor is it affected by the will of the depositories."

38. Benveniste, *Problems*, p. 5.

39. Saussure, *Course*, p. 9.

40. Ibid., p. 14.

41. Ibid., p. 17.

42. Ibid., p. 93.

43. Ibid., pp. 9, 87.

44. Tzvetan Todorov, *Grammaire du Décaméron* (The Hague: Mouton, 1969), p. 15.

45. Jameson, *Prison-House*, p. 22. See Saussure, *Course*, pp. 13–14, where *langue* is defined as a "hoard deposited by the practice of speech in speakers who belong to the same community, a grammatical system which, to all intents and purposes, exists in the mind of each speaker."

46. Jameson, *Prison-House*, p. 18.

47. Edward Said, "Abecedarium Culturae: Structuralism, Absence, Writing," in *Modern French Criticism: From Proust and Valéry to Structuralism*, ed. John K. Simon (Chicago: University of Chicago Press, 1972), p. 378.

48. Saussure, *Course*, p. 8.

49. Ibid., p. 13.
50. Ibid., p. 19.
51. Ibid., p. 66.
52. Ibid., p. 67.
53. Benveniste, *Problems*, p. 45.
54. Saussure, *Course*, pp. 68–69.
55. Jameson, *Prison-House*, p. 30.
56. Saussure, *Course*, pp. 71, 73, 74, 75.
57. Ibid., p. 123.
58. Ibid., p. 124.
59. Ibid., p. 126.
60. Ibid.
61. Jameson, *Prison-House*, p. 39.
62. René Wellek and Austin Warren, *Theory of Literature*, 3d ed. (New York: Harcourt, Brace & World, 1956), pp. 177–78.
63. Jameson, *Prison-House*, p. 187.
64. Saussure, *Course*, pp. 116, 117.
65. Ibid., pp. 118, 118–19, 120.
66. Culler, *Saussure*, p. 30.
67. Claude Lévi-Strauss, *Structural Anthropology*, trans. Claire Jacobson and Brooke Grundfest Schoepf (New York: Basic Books, 1963), p. 210.
68. Claude Lévi-Strauss, *The Raw and the Cooked: Introduction to a Science of Mythology: I*, trans. John and Doreen Weightman (New York: Harper & Row, 1975), p. 18.
69. Ibid., p. 1.
70. Ibid., p. 3. For an explicit statement of his totalizing impulse, see *Myth and Meaning* (New York: Schocken Books, 1978), chap. 5.
71. *Raw and the Cooked*, pp. 5–6.
72. Ibid., p. 11 and n. 3.
73. Ibid., pp. 7–8.
74. Ibid., p. 10.
75. Ibid., p. 11.
76. Ibid., p. 12.
77. Claude Lévi-Strauss, *The Savage Mind* (Chicago: University of Chicago Press, 1966), p. 16.
78. Ibid., p. 17n.
79. Ibid., pp. 16–17.
80. Ibid., p. 17.
81. Ibid., p. 19.
82. Jameson, *Prison-House*, p. 115.
83. Roland Barthes, *Writing Degree Zero* and *Elements of Semiology*, trans. Annette Lavers and Colin Smith (Boston: Beacon Press, 1967), pp. 9, 10–11.
84. Ibid., p. 1.
85. Ibid., pp. 13, 14.
86. Ibid.
87. Ibid., pp. 16–17.
88. Ibid., pp. 42–43, 50–51.
89. *Elements of Semiology*, p. 17.
90. Ibid., p. 21.

91. Ibid.
92. Ibid., pp. 21–22.
93. Ibid., p. 31.
94. Roland Barthes, *Mythologies,* trans. Annette Lavers (New York: Hill & Wang, 1972), p. 11.
95. For Barthes's discussion of *The Family of Man* see ibid., pp. 100–102.
96. Frye, *Anatomy,* p. 105: "The principle of recurrence in the rhythm of art seems to be derived from the repetitions in nature that make time intelligible to us."
97. *Mythologies,* p. 110.
98. Ibid., p. 112.
99. Ibid., p. 124.
100. Ibid., pp. 129–30.
101. Ibid., p. 141.
102. Ibid., p. 146.
103. *On Racine,* p. 172.
104. Ibid., pp. 158, 157n.
105. Ibid., p. 154.
106. Ibid., p. 162.
107. Ibid., pp. 158–59.
108. Ibid., p. 161.
109. Ibid.
110. Roland Barthes, *Critical Essays,* trans. Richard Howard (Evanston, Ill.: Northwestern University Press, 1972), p. 38.
111 Ibid., pp. 38, 74.
112. Ibid., p. 147.
113. Ibid., p. 149.
114. Ibid., p. 152.
115. Ibid., pp. 153, 154.
116. Ibid., p. 151.
117. Ibid., pp. 214, 216, 219.
118. Ibid., p. 164.
119. Ibid.
120. Ibid., p. 165.
121. Ibid., p. 166.
122. Ibid., pp. 166–67.
123. Ibid., pp. 167, 168.
124. Ibid., p. 168.
125. Ibid., p. 251.
126. Ibid., p. 257.
127. Ibid., p. 259.
128. Ibid., pp. 259–60.
129. Ibid., p. 260.
130. Ibid., p. 259.
131. Ibid., p. 260.
132. Roland Barthes, *Critique et vérité* (Paris: Editions du Seuil, 1966), pp. 53–55, 71–73, passim.
133. Roland Barthes, *S/Z,* trans. Richard Howard (New York: Hill & Wang, 1974), p. 3.
134. Ibid.

135. Ibid., p. 5.

136. Ibid.

137. Ibid.

138. Ibid., pp. 7–8, 15.

139. Ibid., p. 12.

140. G. W. F. Hegel, *The Philosophy of History,* trans. J. Sibree (New York: Dover Publications, 1956), p. 17.

141. Roland Barthes, *The Pleasure of the Text,* trans. Richard Miller (New York: Hill & Wang, 1975), pp. 28–29.

142. Ibid., pp. 6–7, 29–30.

143. Ibid., pp. 3–4, 30–31, 43, 44–45.

144. Ibid., pp. 52, 22–23.

145. Ibid., p. 30.

146. Ibid., pp. 34–35.

147. Ibid., p. 32.

148. Ibid., p. 64.

149. Ibid., p. 57.

150. Ibid., p. 53.

151. Ibid., p. 65.

152. Walter Benn Michaels, "Writers Reading: James and Eliot," *MLN* 91 (1976): 848.

153. Stanley Fish, "Interpreting the *Variorium*," *Critical Inquiry* 2 (Spring 1976): 473.

154. Ibid., 468.

155. Ibid., 476.

156. Ibid., 479.

157. Ibid., 476.

158. Ibid., 484.

159. Wolfgang Iser, "The Reading Process: A Phenomenological Approach," *New Literary History* 3 (Winter 1972): 279.

160. Ibid., 281.

161. Ibid., 285.

162. Ibid., 280.

163. Ibid., 299.

164. Ibid., 287.

165. Ibid., 279, 289.

166. Hans-Georg Gadamer, *Truth and Method* (New York: Seabury Press, 1975), p. 164.

167. Ibid., p. 168.

168. Ibid., p. 165.

169. Ibid., p. 207.

170. For the quotations in this paragraph see ibid., pp. 175, 245, 250, 258, 264–65.

171. For the quotations in this paragraph see ibid., pp. 236, 237, 269.

172. Ibid., pp. 246–47.

173. Ibid., p. 248.

174. Ibid., p. 249.

175. Ibid., p. 268.

176. Ibid., p. 271.

Chapter 5

1. *The Structuralist Controversy: The Languages of Criticism and the Sciences of Man,* ed. Richard Macksey and Eugenio Donato (Baltimore: Johns Hopkins University Press, 1972), p. xv.

2. Quoted in J. Hillis Miller, "The Geneva School," in *Modern French Criticism: From Proust and Valéry to Structuralism,* ed. John K. Simon (Chicago: University of Chicago Press, 1972), p. 292.

3. Geoffrey Hartman, "Monsieur Texte: On Jacques Derrida, His *Glas,*" *Georgia Review* 29 (Winter 1975): 783.

4. Eugenio Donato, "The Two Languages of Criticism," in *Structuralist Controversy,* pp. 95, 96.

5. Edward Said, "Abecedarium Culturae: Structuralism, Absence, Writing," in *Modern French Criticism,* pp. 349, 350, 351, 354, 355, 368, 381, 384, 385.

6. Quoted in Jonathan Culler, *Structuralist Poetics: Structuralism, Linguistics, and the Study of Literature* (Ithaca, N.Y.: Cornell University Press, 1975), p. 242.

7. Claude Lévi-Strauss, *The Raw and the Cooked: Introduction to a Science of Mythology: I,* trans. John and Doreen Weightman (New York: Harper & Row, 1975), pp. 5, 6.

8. Quoted ibid., p. 11.

9. Ibid.

10. Jacques Derrida, *Of Grammatology,* trans. Gayatri Chakravorty Spivak (Baltimore: Johns Hopkins University Press, 1976), p. 251.

11. Jacques Derrida, "Structure, Sign, and Play in the Discourse of the Human Sciences," in *Structuralist Controversy,* pp. 247–48.

12. Ibid., p. 248.

13. Quoted in *Philosophies of Art and Beauty: Selected Readings in Aesthetics from Plato to Heidegger,* ed. Albert Hofstadter and Richard Kuhns (Chicago: University of Chicago Press, 1976), pp. 32–33.

14. Northrop Frye, *Anatomy of Criticism: Four Essays* (New York: Atheneum, 1967), pp. 117–18.

15. Georges Poulet, "The Self and the Other in Critical Consciousness," *Diacritics* 2 (Spring 1972): 48.

16. Jacques Derrida, *Speech and Phenomena and other Essays on Husserl's Theory of Signs,* trans. David B. Allison (Evanston, Ill.: Northwestern University Press, 1973), p. 104.

17. *Grammatology,* p. 18.

18. Cleanth Brooks, *The Well Wrought Urn* (New York: Harcourt, Brace & World, 1947), p. 213.

19. *Grammatology,* p. 18.

20. "Structure, Sign, and Play," p. 249.

21. *Grammatology,* p. 50.

22. Immanuel Kant, *Critique of Judgment,* trans. J. H. Bernard (New York: Hafner Publishing Company, 1966), pp. 77, 165, 171, 172.

23. "Structure, Sign, and Play," p. 264.

24. Ibid., pp. 264–65.

25. Wayne Booth, " 'Preserving the Exemplar': Or, How Not to Dig Our Own Graves," *Critical Inquiry* 3 (Spring 1977): 416.

26. "Structure, Sign, and Play," p. 249.

27. *Grammatology*, p. 158.

28. "Differance," in *Speech and Phenomena*, p. 129.

29. Ibid., p. 138.

30. Said, "Abecedarium Culturae," p. 381.

31. "Differance," p. 138.

32. J. Hillis Miller, "Stevens' Rock and Criticism as Cure," *Georgia Review* 30 (Spring 1976): 12; Miller speaks of "the underlying nothingness."

33. Said, "Abecedarium Culturae," p. 385.

34. "Differance," p. 133.

35. Ibid., pp. 134, 141.

36. Ibid., p. 153.

37. Ibid., p. 159.

38. Edward Said, "The Problem of Textuality: Two Exemplary Positions," *Critical Inquiry* 4 (Summer 1978): 693.

39. "Differance," p. 156.

40. *Grammatology*, pp. 158–59.

41. Paul de Man, "Action and Identity in Nietzsche," *Yale French Studies*, no. 52 (Fall 1975), pp. 16–30.

42. "Problem of Textuality," 684.

43. *Grammatology*, p. 61.

44. "Structure, Sign, and Play," p. 267.

45. Ibid., p. 271.

46. Ibid., p. 264.

47. "Differance," pp. 134, 141, 146–47.

48. Ibid., p. 141.

49. See *Grammatology*, pp. 17–18, 20, 30, 34–35, 37, 38. For Saussure's denigration of writing see *Course in General Linguistics*, ed. Charles Bally and Albert Sechehaye, in collaboration with Albert Riedlinger; trans. Wade Baskin (New York: McGraw-Hill, 1966), pp. 23–31 passim.

50. *Grammatology*, p. 33.

51. Rowe's point about intertextuality is made in the introduction to his newly completed manuscript on nineteenth-century American literature.

52. *Grammatology*, p. 19.

53. Jacques Derrida, "White Mythology," *New Literary History* 6 (Autumn 1974): 70.

54. *Grammatology*, p. 46.

55. "The Problem of Textuality," passim.

56. The best example of this that I know in Derrida's texts is his treatment of the Platonic term *pharmakos*. See *La Dissémination* (Paris: Editions du Seuil, 1972), pp. 69–197.

57. Jacques Derrida, *Writing and Difference*, trans. Allan Bass (Chicago: University of Chicago Press, 1978), chap. 1: "Force and Signification"; chap. 5: " 'Genesis and Structure' and Phenomenology."

58. Quoted in J. Hillis Miller, "The Critic as Host," *Critical Inquiry* 3 (Spring 1977): 439–40.

59. M. H. Abrams, "The Deconstructive Angel," *Critical Inquiry* 3 (Spring 1977): 426.

60. Ibid., 429.

61. Booth, " 'Preserving the Exemplar'," 422.

62. Geoffrey Hartman, "Literary Criticism and Its Discontents," *Critical Inquiry* 2 (Winter 1976): 205.

63. Hartman, "Monsieur Texte," 786.

64. Paul de Man, "Political Allegory in Rousseau," *Critical Inquiry* 2 (Summer 1976): 650.

65. Miller, "Stevens' Rock and Criticism as Cure," 10–11.

66. Hartman, "Monsieur Texte," 782.

67. Ibid., 763, 764.

68. Leslie Brisman, "Swinburne's Semiotics," *Georgia Review* 31 (Fall 1977): 596–97.

69. Hartman, "Monsieur Texte," 782.

70. De Man, "Political Allegory in Rousseau," 650.

71. J. Hillis Miller, "Stevens' Rock and Criticism as Cure: II," *Georgia Review* 30 (Summer 1976): 348.

72. J. Hillis Miller, "Tradition and Difference," *Diacritics* 2 (Winter 1972): 9.

73. J. Hillis Miller, "Deconstructing the Deconstructors," *Diacritics* 5 (Summer 1975): 31.

74. J. Hillis Miller, "Georges Poulet's 'Criticism of Identification,' " in *The Quest for Imagination*, ed. O. B. Hardison, Jr. (Cleveland: Press of Case Western Reserve University, 1971), p. 215.

75. J. Hillis Miller, "Stevens' Rock and Criticism as Cure: II," p. 330.

76. Miller, "Stevens' Rock and Criticism as Cure," 23.

77. Hartman, "Monsieur Texte," 760.

78. Paul de Man, "Nietzsche's Theory of Rhetoric," *Symposium* 28 (Spring 1974): 50.

79. Ibid., 51.

80. Stanley Fish, "Interpreting the *Variorum*," *Critical Inquiry* 2 (Spring 1976): 465–485. See Culler, *Structuralist Poetics*, p. 262.

81. Hartman, "Monsieur Texte," 778–79.

82. Walter Benn Michaels, "The Interpreter's Self: Peirce on the Cartesian 'Subject,' " *Georgia Review* 31 (Summer 1977).

83. *Grammatology*, p. 46.

84. Michel Foucault, *The Archaeology of Knowledge*, trans. A.M. Sheridan Smith (New York: Harper & Row, 1976), pp. 4, 5, 6.

85. Ibid., pp. 8, 9.

86. Ibid., pp. 9–10.

87. Ibid., p. 137.

88. Ibid., p. 10.

89. Ibid., p. 12.

90. Ibid.

91. Michel Foucault, *The Order of Things: An Archaeology of the Human Sciences* (New York: Random House, 1973), p. xiv.

92. *Archaeology of Knowledge*, pp. 21–27, passim, and in the appendix, "The Discourse on Language," see pp. 222–24 for comments on the exclusionary power of "disciplines."

93. Ibid., pp. 26–27.

94. Ibid., p. 29.

95. Ibid., p. 32.

96. Ibid., pp. 34–38 passim.

97. *Order of Things*, p. xi.

98. *Archaeology of Knowledge*, p. 38.

99. Ibid., p. 79.

100. Ibid., pp. 73–74.

101. Ibid., pp. 41–42.

102. Ibid., p. 45.

103. Ibid., pp. 47–48.

104. Ibid., p. 224.

105. *Order of Things*, p. xiv.

106. *Archaeology of Knowledge*, p. 224.

107. Michael F. Guyer, *Animal Biology*, rev. ed. (New York: Harper and Brothers, 1937), p. 468.

108. *Archaeology of Knowledge*, p. 216.

109. Michel Foucault, *Madness and Civilization: A History of Insanity in the Age of Reason*, trans. Richard Howard (New York: Random House, 1973), pp. 3, 10.

110. Ibid., pp. 39–46.

111. *Archaeology of Knowledge*, pp. 215–37 ("The Discourse on Language").

112. Ibid., p. 51, 50.

113. Ibid., p. 57.

114. Michel Foucault, "Nietzsche, Genealogy, History," in *Language, Counter-Memory, Practice: Selected Essays and Interviews*, trans. Donald F. Bouchard and Sherry Simon (Ithaca, N.Y.: Cornell University Press, 1977), p. 140.

115. Ibid., pp. 142, 146.

116. See David Carroll, "The Subject of Archaeology or the Sovereignty of the Episteme," *MLN* 93 (1978): 695–722.

117. "Nietzsche, Genealogy, History," pp. 145–46.

118. Ibid., p. 145.

119. Ibid., pp. 146, 148, 147.

120. Ibid., p. 148.

121. Ibid., pp. 149–50.

122. Ibid., pp. 151, 149.

123. Ibid., p. 151.

124. Ibid., p. 154.

125. Bernard Duffey, *Poetry in America: Expression and Its Values in the Times of Bryant, Whitman, and Pound* (Durham, N.C.: Duke University Press, 1978), p. 194.

126. *Archaeology of Knowledge*, p. 126.

127. "Nietzsche, Genealogy, History," p. 156.

128 Ibid., p. 158.

129. Ibid., pp. 156–57, 158, 162.

130. *Archaeology of Knowledge*, p. 130.

131. "Nietzsche, Genealogy, History," p. 162.

132. "Structure, Sign, and Play," p. 249.

133. Antonio Gramsci, *The Prison Notebooks: Selections*, trans. and ed. Quintin Hoare and Geoffrey Nowell Smith (New York: International Publishers, 1971), p. 324.

134. *Writing and Difference*, p. 36.

135. Ibid.

Chapter 6

1. *Ralph Waldo Emerson: Selected Prose and Poetry*, ed. Reginald L. Cook (New York: Holt, Rinehart & Winston, 1969), p. 124.

2. *Mallarmé: Selected Prose Poems, Essays, and Letters*, trans. Bradford Cook (Baltimore: Johns Hopkins University Press, 1956), p. 18.

3. Stephane Mallarmé, "The Evolution of Literature," in *Critical Theory since Plato*, ed. Hazard Adams (New York: Harcourt Brace Jovanovich, 1971), p. 688.

4. Murray Krieger, *Theory of Criticism: A Tradition and Its System* (Baltimore: Johns Hopkins University Press, 1976), p. 24.

5. *The Problems of Aesthetics*, ed. Murray Krieger and Eliseo Vivas (New York: Rinehart and Company, 1953), p. 116.

6. Murray Krieger, *The New Apologists for Poetry* (Minneapolis: University of Minnesota Press, 1956), p. 20.

7. *Problems of Aesthetics*, p. 49.

8. *New Apologists*, p. 6.

9. Ibid., p. 10.

10. Ibid., p. 27.

11. W. B. Yeats, *Essays and Introductions* (New York: Macmillan Co., 1961), p. 145.

12. *Theory of Criticism*, pp. 10–11.

13. Ibid., p. 11.

14. *New Apologists*, p. 34.

15. Ibid., p. 34n.

16. This is a claim made throughout *The Tragic Vision: Variations on a Theme in Literary Interpretation* (Chicago: University of Chicago Press, Phoenix Books, 1966); see for example p. viii.

17. *New Apologists*, p. 70.

18. Murray Krieger, *The Classic Vision: The Retreat from Extremity in Modern Literature* (Baltimore: Johns Hopkins University Press, 1971), p. 18.

19. See *New Apologists*, chap. 6.

20. *Tragic Vision*, p. 234.

21. Murray Krieger, *A Window to Criticism: Shakespeare's Sonnets and Modern Poetics* (Princeton, N.J.: Princeton University Press, 1964), p. 8.

22. Ibid., pp. 4–5, 5–6, 6–7.

23. Ibid., pp. 6–7.

24. Quoted in *The Essence of Opera*, ed. Ulrich Weisstein (New York: W. W. Norton & Co., 1969), p. 183.

25. *Window to Criticism*, pp. 28–29.

26. Murray Krieger, *The Play and Place of Criticism* (Baltimore: Johns Hopkins University Press, 1967), pp. 226–27.

27. Eliseo Vivas, *Creation and Discovery* (Chicago: Henry Regnery, 1965), pp. 212–16.

28. *Window to Criticism*, p. 29.

29. Clive Bell, *Art* (New York: Capricorn Books, 1958), p. 31.

30. *New Apologists*, pp. 135, 136.

31. Samuel Taylor Coleridge, "Shakespeare's Judgment Equal to His Genius," in *Critical Theory since Plato*, p. 462.

32. *Tragic Vision*, pp. 232–33.

33. *New Apologists*, pp. 136, 138.

34. *Tragic Vision*, p. 242.

35. *Window to Criticism,* pp. 206, 208.
36. Ibid., p. 207.
37. Ibid., p. 28.
38. *Play and Place,* p. 10.
39. *Theory of Criticism,* pp. 30–31.
40. Ibid.
41. See *New Apologists,* pp. 119–21.
42. Ibid., p. 126.
43. *Tragic Vision,* p. 242.
44. *Play and Place,* p. 167. For specific remarks on satire see p. 168.
45. *Tragic Vision,* p. 260; *Window to Criticism,* p. 19.
46. *Tragic Vision,* p. 3.
47. Ibid., p. 17.
48. Ibid., p. 242.
49. *Window to Criticism,* p. 19n.
50. *Play and Place,* p. 249; *Tragic Vision,* pp. 246–47; *Window to Criticism,* p. 25n.; *Tragic Vision,* p. 246; *Classic Vision,* p. 9.
51. *Play and Place,* p. 249.
52. Ibid., pp. 226–27.
53. *Window to Criticism,* p. 25n.
54. *Tragic Vision,* p. x.
55. *Classic Vision,* p. 6. Also see *Tragic Vision,* pp. 18–19.
56. *Tragic Vision,* pp. 263–64.
57. Wallace Stevens, *Opus Posthumous,* ed. Samuel French Morse (London: Faber and Faber, 1959), p. 163.
58. *Window to Criticism,* pp. 6–7.
59. Ibid., pp. 26–27.
60. Ernst Cassirer, *The Philosophy of Symbolic Forms,* vol. 2, trans. Ralph Manheim (New Haven, Conn.: Yale University Press, 1955), p. 68.
61. Ernst Cassirer, *An Essay on Man* (New Haven, Conn.: Yale University Press, 1962), p. 81.
62. See *Window to Criticism,* pp. 195, 198, 200–201, 204. For the phrase "primeval mythico-religious" see Ernst Cassirer, *Language and Myth,* trans. Susanne K. Langer (New York: Harper and Brothers, 1946), p. 66.
63. *University of Toronto Quarterly* 28 (January 1959): 190–96.
64. *Window to Criticism,* p. 195.
65. Ibid., p. 198.
66. Ibid., p. 201.
67. Ibid., p. 215.
68. Ibid., p. 204.
69. Ibid., pp. 201–02.
70. Ibid., p. 205.
71. Ibid., p. 213.
72. Ibid., pp. 5–16, passim.
73. Ibid., pp. 210–11.
74. Ibid., p. 214.
75. "Preface" to paperback ed. *Classic Vision* (Baltimore: Johns Hopkins University Press, 1973), p. xiii.
76. *Window to Criticism,* p. 216.
77. Ibid., p. 217.

78. *Classic Vision*, p. 29.

79. Ibid., pp. 29, 30.

80. Ibid., pp. 30–31.

81. Ibid., pp. 48, 47, 49.

82. Murray Krieger, "Theories about Theories about *Theory of Criticism*," *Bulletin of MMLA* 11 (1978): 34.

83. *Theory of Criticism*, pp. 179 (see subtitle of chapter), 98.

84. Ibid.; see for example pp. 162–63, 174, 179, 190, 195.

85. Ibid., p. 192.

86. Ibid., pp. 233, 240–41.

87. Ibid., p. 213.

88. Ibid., p. 226n.

89. Jacques Derrida, "Structure, Sign, and Play in the Discourse of the Human Sciences," in *The Structuralist Controversy: The Languages of Criticism and the Sciences of Man*, ed. Richard Macksey and Eugenio Donato (Baltimore: Johns Hopkins University Press, 1972), p. 264.

90. Murray Krieger, "Literature vs. *Écriture*: Constructions and Deconstructions in Recent Critical Theory," *Studies in the Literary Imagination* 12 (Spring 1979): 5, 12.

91. *Tragic Vision*, pp. 15–16.

92. *Problems of Aesthetics*, p. 413.

93. *New Apologists*, pp. 116–17.

94. Ibid., p. 162.

95. Ibid., pp. 162–63.

96. Murray Krieger, "Literary Analysis and Evaluation—and the Ambidextrous Critic," in *Criticism: Speculative and Analytical Essays*, ed. L. S. Dembo (Madison, Wis.: University of Wisconsin Press, 1968), pp. 35, 36.

97. *Theory of Criticism*, pp. 38, 39.

98. Ibid., chap. 3, passim.

99. Ibid., p. 41.

100. Ibid., pp. 45, 46, 56, 60.

101. Ibid., pp. 61, 63, 64.

102. "Theories about Theories," 36.

103. Ibid., 35.

Chapter 7

1. E. D. Hirsch, Jr., *Validity in Interpretation* (New Haven, Conn.: Yale University Press, 1967), p. 212.

2. Ibid., p. 209.

3. William Wordsworth, "Preface to the Second Edition of *Lyrical Ballads*," in *Critical Theory since Plato*, ed. Hazard Adams (New York: Harcourt Brace Jovanovich, 1971), p. 440.

4. E. D. Hirsch, Jr., *Wordsworth and Schelling: A Typological Study of Romanticism* (New Haven, Conn.: Yale University Press, 1960), pp. 4–5.

5. Martin Heidegger, *Poetry, Language, Thought*, trans. Albert Hofstadter (New York: Harper & Row, 1971), pp. 197, 215.

6. Martin Heidegger, *On the Way to Language*, trans. Peter D. Hertz (New York: Harper & Row, 1971), p. 134.

7. *Validity*, p. 210.

8. Ibid., p. 264.
9. Ibid., p. 232.
10. Ibid., p. 248.
11. Ibid., p. 225.
12. *Poetry, Language, Thought*, p. 192.
13. *On the Way to Language*, pp. 112–13.
14. See *Validity*, pp. 31–44.
15. Ibid., p. 258.
16. Ibid., p. 213.
17. See ibid, pp. 27, 31ff., 224ff.
18. E. D. Hirsch, Jr., *The Aims of Interpretation* (Chicago: University of Chicago Press, 1976), p. 10.
19. *Validity*, p. 4.
20. Ibid., p. 5.
21. Ibid., p. 6.
22. Ibid., p. 265.
23. Ibid., p. 266.
24. Ibid.
25. Ibid., p. 271.
26. Ibid. Also see pp. 176–77.
27. Ibid., p. 269.
28. Ibid., p. 272.
29. Ibid.
30. Ibid., p. 242.
31. Ibid., pp. 242–43.
32. Ibid., pp. 239–40.
33. Ibid., p. 81.
34. Ibid., p. 50.
35. See ibid., pp. 78–89.
36. Ibid., p. 52.
37. Ibid., pp. 217–18.
38. Ibid., p. 37.
39. Ibid., p. 23.
40. Ibid., pp. 29, 28.
41. Ibid., p. 28.
42. *Aims of Interpretation*, pp. 21–22.
43. Ferdinand de Saussure, *Course in General Linguistics*, ed. Charles Bally and Albert Sechehaye in collaboration with Albert Riedlinger; trans. Wade Baskin (New York: McGraw-Hill, 1966), pp. 116, 117.
44. *Aims of Interpretation*, p. 61.
45. *Validity*, p. 121.
46. Ibid.
47. Ibid., p. 50.
48. Ibid., p. 49.
49. Ibid., p. 78.
50. Ibid., p. 86.
51. Ibid., p. 101.
52. Ibid., p. 101n.
53. Ibid., p. 85.
54. Ibid., pp. 65–66.

55. Ibid., p. 106.
56. *Aims of Interpretation,* p. 13.
57. Ibid., pp. 75–76.
58. Ibid., pp. 44, 90, 92.
59. Ibid., p. 90.
60. Ibid., p. 18.
61. Ibid., p. 3.
62. Ibid., p. 6.
63. Emile Benveniste, *Problems in General Linguistics,* trans. Mary Elizabeth Meek (Coral Gables, Fla.: University of Miami Press, 1971), p. 5.
64. Jacques Derrida, *Writing and Difference,* trans. Allan Bass (Chicago: University of Chicago Press, 1978), p. 156.
65. Edmund Husserl, "Phenomenology," reprinted in *Phenomenology and Existentialism,* ed. Richard Zaner and Don Ihde (New York: G. P. Putnam's Sons, 1973), p. 51: "typical forms of intentional processes."

Chapter 8

1. William H. Pritchard, "The Hermeneutical Mafia or, After Strange Gods at Yale," *Hudson Review* 28 (Winter 1975–76): 601–10.
2. Paul de Man, *Blindness and Insight: Essays in the Rhetoric of Contemporary Criticism* (New York: Oxford University Press, 1971), p. 17.
3. Paul de Man, "Semiology and Rhetoric," *Diacritics* 3 (Fall 1973): 32.
4. Paul de Man, "Intentional Structure of the Romantic Image," reprinted in *Romanticism and Consciousness,* ed. Harold Bloom (New York: Norton, 1970), pp. 67–68.
5. Ibid., p. 68.
6. Ibid.
7. Ibid., p. 77.
8. Ibid., p. 69.
9. Ibid., p. 70.
10. Ibid., p. 69.
11. Ibid., p. 71.
12. Ibid., pp. 76–77.
13. Ibid., p. 77.
14. Paul de Man, "Symbolic Landscape in Wordsworth and Yeats," in *In Defense of Reading,* ed. Reuben Brower and Richard Poirier (New York: E. P. Dutton, 1962), p. 23.
15. Ibid., p. 22.
16. Ibid., pp. 22–23.
17. Ibid., pp. 34, 37.
18. Paul de Man, "The Rhetoric of Temporality," in *Interpretation: Theory and Practice,* ed. C. S. Singleton (Baltimore: Johns Hopkins University Press, 1969), p. 174.
19. Ibid., p. 175.
20. Ibid., p. 180.
21. Ibid., pp. 181, 180–81.
22. Ibid., p. 181.
23. Ibid., pp. 184, 190.
24. Ibid., p. 188.

25. Ibid., p. 191.
26. Ibid., p. 190.
27. *Ralph Waldo Emerson: Selected Prose and Poetry,* ed. Reginald L. Cook (New York: Holt, Rinehart & Winston, 1969), pp. 82–83.
28. "Rhetoric of Temporality," p. 194.
29. Ibid., pp. 188, 195.
30. Ibid., p. 207.
31. Ibid., p. 190.
32. C. Hugh Holman, *A Handbook to Literature,* based on the original by William F. Thrall and Addison Hibbard, 3d ed. (New York: Odyssey Press, 1972), p. 13.
33. "Rhetoric of Temporality," p. 196.
34. Ibid., pp. 196–97.
35. Ibid., p. 199.
36. Ibid., p. 200.
37. Ibid., pp. 202, 203, 203–4.
38. Ibid., p. 203.
39. Ibid., p. 202.
40. Ibid., p. 203.
41. *Blindness and Insight,* p. ix.
42. Ibid., p. 106.
43. Ibid., p. ix.
44. Ibid., p. 103.
45. Ibid., p. 106.
46. Ibid., p. 104.
47. Ibid., pp. 26, 27.
48. Ibid., p. 81.
49. Ibid., p. 71.
50. Ibid., pp. 106, 10.
51. Ibid., p. 9.
52. Ibid., pp. 11–12.
53. Ibid., p. 16.
54. Ibid., p. 12.
55. Ibid., p. 17.
56. Ibid., p. 18.
57. Ibid., p. 19.
58. Ibid., p. 111.
59. Ibid., p. 112.
60. Ibid., p. 115.
61. Ibid.
62. Ibid., p. 116.
63. Ibid., pp. 136, 139.
64. Ibid., p. 139.
65. Ibid., p. 141.
66. Ibid., p. viii.
67. Ibid., pp.146, 147.
68. Ibid., p. 147.
69. Ibid., pp. 147, 151.
70. Ibid., p. 148.
71. Ibid., p. 157.

72. Ibid., pp. 161, 162.

73. Ibid., p. 150.

74. Ibid., p. 184.

75. Michel Foucault, *Language, Counter-Memory, Practice,* trans. Donald F. Bouchard and Sherry Simon (Ithaca, N.Y.: Cornell University Press, 1977), p. 146.

76. Paul de Man, "Genesis and Genealogy in Nietzsche's *The Birth of Tragedy,*" *Diacritics* 2 (Winter 1972): 48.

77. Ibid.

78. Ibid.

79. Ibid., 48, 50.

80. Cleanth Brooks, *The Well Wrought Urn* (New York: Harcourt, Brace, & World, 1947), p. 205.

81. "Genesis and Genealogy," p. 50.

82. Edward Said, "Abecedarium Culturae: Structuralism, Absence, Writing," in *Modern French Criticism: From Proust and Valéry to Structuralism,* ed. John K. Simon (Chicago: University of Chicago Press, 1972), p. 361.

83. "Genesis and Genealogy," p. 51.

84. Ibid., p. 52.

85. Ibid., p. 53.

86. "Semiology and Rhetoric," 29.

87. Ibid.

88. Ibid., 29–30.

89. Ibid., 32.

90. Ibid.

91. Paul de Man, "Action and Identity in Nietzsche," *Yale French Studies,* no. 52 (Fall 1975), p. 19.

92. Ibid., p. 108.

93. Ibid., p. 22.

94. Ibid., p. 27.

95. Ibid., p. 29.

96. Ibid.

97. "Semiology and Rhetoric," 30.

Chapter 9

1. Harold Bloom, "Yeats and the Romantics," in *Modern Poetry: Essays in Criticism,* ed. John Hollander (New York: Oxford University Press, 1968), p. 502.

2. Harold Bloom, *The Anxiety of Influence: A Theory of Poetry* (New York: Oxford University Press, 1973), p. 43.

3. Harold Bloom, *Poetry and Repression: Revisionism from Blake to Stevens* (New Haven, Conn.: Yale University Press, 1976), p. 1.

4. Harold Bloom, *The Visionary Company: A Reading of English Romantic Poetry* (Ithaca, N.Y.: Cornell University Press, 1971), p. xvii.

5. Harold Bloom, *The Ringers in the Tower: Studies in Romantic Tradition* (Chicago: University of Chicago Press, 1971), p. 87.

6. Harold Bloom, "The Central Man: Emerson, Whitman, Wallace Stevens," *Massachusetts Review* 7 (Winter 1966): 37.

7. Northrop Frye, *Anatomy of Criticism: Four Essays* (New York: Atheneum, 1967), pp. 98–99.

8. Harold Bloom, *Shelley's Mythmaking* (New Haven, Conn.: Yale University Press, 1959), p. 110.

9. Ibid., pp. 125, 93.

10. Ibid., pp. 37, 39.

11. Harold Bloom, "The Internalization of Quest-Romance," in *Romanticism and Consciousness,* ed. Harold Bloom (New York: W. W. Norton & Co., 1970), p. 3.

12. *Shelley's Mythmaking,* pp. 1, 2.

13. *Visionary Company,* pp. xxii, xxiii, xxii.

14. *Shelley's Mythmaking,* p. 74.

15. *Visionary Company,* p. 1.

16. "Yeats and the Romantics," p. 501.

17. Ibid.

18. *Visionary Company,* p. 1.

19. Ibid., p. xvii.

20. *Anxiety of Influence,* p. 33.

21. "The Central Man," p. 37.

22. *Anxiety of Influence,* pp. 145, 69.

23. Ibid., p. 11.

24. *Poetry and Repression,* p. 3.

25. *Anxiety of Influence,* pp. 9–10.

26. Ibid., p. 64.

27. Ibid., p. 27.

28. Ibid., pp. 20, 21.

29. Ibid., p. 23.

30. Ibid., p. 39.

31. Ibid., pp. 39, 31, 30.

32. Ibid., p. 32.

33. Ibid., p. 78.

34. Ibid., p. 62.

35. Ibid., p. 71.

36. Percy Shelley, "A Defense of Poetry," in *Critical Theory since Plato,* ed. Hazard Adams (New York: Harcourt Brace Jovanovich, 1971), p. 503.

37. *Anxiety of Influence,* p. 53.

38. Ibid., p. 86.

39. Ibid., pp. 70, 71.

40. Ibid., pp. 12–13.

41. Harold Bloom, *A Map of Misreading* (New York: Oxford University Press, 1975), p. 28.

42. Ibid., p. 3.

43. Ibid., p. 19.

44. Ibid., p. 60.

45. Jacques Derrida, "Structure, Sign, and Play in the Discourse of the Human Sciences," in *The Structuralist Controversy: The Languages of Criticism and the Sciences of Man,* ed. Richard Macksey and Eugenio Donato (Baltimore: Johns Hopkins University Press, 1970), p. 271.

46. *Map of Misreading,* pp. 38, 50.

47. Ibid., pp. 42–43.

48. Ibid., p. 77.

49. Ibid., p. 168.

50. Derrida and Emerson quoted, ibid., p. 175.

51. Ibid., p. 176.

52. Ralph Waldo Emerson, "The Poet," in *Critical Theory since Plato,* p. 546. For language as the "tomb of the Muses," see p. 549.

53. Samuel Alexander, "The Creative Process in the Artist's Mind," in *Critical Theory since Plato,* pp. 861–69.

54. *Map of Misreading,* p. 165.

55. Ibid., p. 3.

56. Harold Bloom, *Kabbalah and Criticism* (New York: Seabury Press, 1975), pp. 33–34.

57. Ibid., pp. 56–57.

58. Ibid., p. 63.

59. *Kabbalah and Criticism,* p. 125.

60. *Poetry and Repression,* pp. 65–66.

61. Ibid., p. 217.

62. Ibid., p. 214.

63. Ibid., p. 11.

64. Ibid., p. 212.

65. Ibid., pp. 214–15.

66. Quoted in *The Essence of Opera,* ed. Ulrich Weisstein (New York: W. W. Norton & Co., 1969), pp. 183, 185.

67. *Kabbalah and Criticism,* pp. 109, 114.

68. Harold Bloom, *Wallace Stevens: The Poems of Our Climate* (Ithaca, N.Y.: Cornell University Press, 1977), p. 388.

69. Martin Heidegger, "Who is Nietzsche's Zarathustra?" in *The New Nietzsche* (New York: Dell, 1977), pp. 64–79.

70. Gerald Graff, "Fear and Trembling at Yale," *The American Scholar* 46 (Autumn 1977): 467–78.

Afterword

1. Michel Foucault, *The History of Sexuality,* vol. 1, *An Introduction,* trans. Robert Hurley (New York: Pantheon Books, 1978), p. 96.

2. Ibid.

3. Fredric Jameson, *The Prison-House of Language: A Critical Account of Structuralism and Russian Formalism* (Princeton, N. J.: Princeton University Press, 1972), pp. 50–51.

4. Harold Bloom, *Poetry and Repression: Revisionism from Blake to Stevens* (New Haven, Conn.: Yale University Press, 1976), p. 2.

5. Foucault, *History of Sexuality,* p. 92.

6. Ibid., pp. 92, 93.

7. Jacques Derrida, *Writing and Difference,* trans. Allen Bass (Chicago: University of Chicago Press, 1978), p. 227.

8. Bloom, *Poetry and Repression,* p. 2.

9. Foucault, *History of Sexuality,* p. 93.

10. Ibid., p. 100.

11. Ibid.

12. Ibid., p. 82.

Index